STUDIES IN IMPERIALISM

General editor: Andrew S. Thompson

Founding editor: John M. MacKenzie

When the 'Studies in Imperialism' series was founded by Professor John M. MacKenzie more than thirty years ago, emphasis was laid upon the conviction that 'imperialism as a cultural phenomenon had as significant an effect on the dominant as on the subordinate societies'. With well over a hundred titles now published, this remains the prime concern of the series. Cross-disciplinary work has indeed appeared covering the full spectrum of cultural phenomena, as well as examining aspects of gender and sex, frontiers and law, science and the environment, language and literature, migration and patriotic societies, and much else. Moreover, the series has always wished to present comparative work on European and American imperialism, and particularly welcomes the submission of books in these areas. The fascination with imperialism, in all its aspects, shows no sign of abating, and this series will continue to lead the way in encouraging the widest possible range of studies in the field. 'Studies in Imperialism' is fully organic in its development, always seeking to be at the cutting edge, responding to the latest interests of scholars and the needs of this ever-expanding area of scholarship.

Britain and its internal others, 1750–1800

Manchester University Press

SELECTED TITLES AVAILABLE IN THE SERIES

WRITING IMPERIAL HISTORIES
ed. Andrew S. Thompson

EMPIRE OF SCHOLARS
Tamson Pietsch

HISTORY, HERITAGE AND COLONIALISM
Kynan Gentry

COUNTRY HOUSES AND THE BRITISH EMPIRE
Stephanie Barczewski

THE RELIC STATE
Pamila Gupta

WE ARE NO LONGER IN FRANCE
Allison Drew

THE SUPPRESSION OF THE ATLANTIC SLAVE TRADE
ed. Robert Burroughs and Richard Huzzey

HEROIC IMPERIALISTS IN AFRICA
Berny Sèbe

Britain and its internal others, 1750–1800

UNDER RULE OF LAW

Dana Y. Rabin

MANCHESTER
UNIVERSITY PRESS

Copyright © Dana Y. Rabin 2017

The right of Dana Y. Rabin to be identified as the author of this work has been asserted by her in accordance with the Copyright, Designs and Patents Act 1988. Published by MANCHESTER UNIVERSITY PRESS

Oxford Road, Manchester M13 9PL
www.manchesteruniversitypress.co.uk

British Library Cataloguing-in-Publication Data
A catalogue record for this book is available from the British Library

ISBN 978 1 5261 2040 3 hardback
ISBN 978 1 5261 6495 7 paperback

First published 2017
Paperback published 2022

The publisher has no responsibility for the persistence or accuracy of URLs for any external or third-party internet websites referred to in this book, and does not guarantee that any content on such websites is, or will remain, accurate or appropriate.

Typeset
by Toppan Best-set Premedia Limited

For Craig

CONTENTS

List of figures—ix
Acknowledgements—xi

	Introduction: Empire and law, 'Firmly united by the circle of the British diadem'	1
1	Internal others: Jews, Gypsies, and Jacobites	22
2	'In a country of liberty?': Slavery, villeinage, and the making of whiteness in the Somerset case (1772)	73
3	Imperial disruptions: City, nation, and empire in the Gordon Riots	108
4	'This fleet is not yet republican': Conceptions of law in the mutinies of 1797	145
5	*Wedding and Bedding*: Making the Union with Ireland, 1800	191
	Conclusion	240

Select bibliography—244
Index—254

FIGURES

1.1	'The Dreadful Consequences of a General Naturalization, to the Natives of Great-Britain and Ireland', satirical print, 1751. Image © The Trustees of the British Museum.	*page* 26
1.2	'Scene of Scenes for the Year 1853', satirical print, 1753. Image © The Jewish Museum, London.	27
1.3	Map of Elizabeth Canning's route through London and from London to Enfield. Drawn by Timothy Stiles.	33
1.4	'Elizabeth Canning and Mary Squires', engraving, 1753. Image © The Trustees of the British Museum.	38
1.5	'The Gypsy's instantanious Flight', satirical print, 1753. Courtesy of the Library of Congress Prints and Photographs Division Washington, D.C. 20540 USA.	39
1.6	'The Gypsy's Triumph', satirical print, 1753. Image © The Trustees of the British Museum.	42
1.7	'A Prospect of the New Jerusalem', satirical print, 1753. Image © The Trustees of the British Museum.	56
1.8	'The City Up and Down, or the Candidates Poiz'd', satirical print, 1754. Image © The Trustees of the British Museum.	63
3.1	'The Times', satirical print, 1780. Image © The Trustees of the British Museum.	122
3.2	'Argus', satirical print, 1780. Image © The Trustees of the British Museum.	123
3.3	'Ecclesiastical and Political state of the Nation', satirical print, 1780. Image © The Trustees of the British Museum.	124
3.4	'An exact representation of the Burning, Plundering and Destruction of Newgate', satirical print, 1781. Image © The Trustees of the British Museum.	125
4.1	'The Delegates in Council or Beggars on Horseback', satirical print, 1797. Image © The Trustees of the British Museum.	177
5.1	'An Irish Union!', satirical print, 1799. Image © The Trustees of the British Museum.	193
5.2	'The Mad Music Master', satirical print, 1801. Image © The Trustees of the British Museum.	208

LIST OF FIGURES

5.3	'Carrying the Union', satirical print, 1800. Image © The Trustees of the British Museum.	209
5.4	'John Bull Shewing his Intended Bride the Parliament House', satirical print, 1800. Image © The Trustees of the British Museum.	209
5.5	'Horrors of the Irish-Union', satirical print, 1798. Image © The Trustees of the British Museum	210
5.6	'Union between England and Ireland', satirical print, 1799. Image © The Trustees of the British Museum.	211
5.7	'Party's Not Agreed', satirical print, 1800. Image © The Trustees of the British Museum.	212
5.8	'An English Twig and an Irish Shillelee!!', satirical print, 1800. Image © The Trustees of the British Museum.	213
5.9	'Caricature Shop', satirical print, 1801, courtesy of the Lewis Walpole Library, Yale University.	215
5.10	'Paddy's Escape from the Union Net', satirical print, 1800, courtesy of Trinity's Access to Research Archive (http://www.tara.tcd.ie) CC BY-NC-SA 1.0.	217
5.11	'A Flight Across the Herring Pool', satirical print, 1800. Image © The Trustees of the British Museum.	230

ACKNOWLEDGEMENTS

Finally, an opportunity to thank the people who have helped me to conceptualize, research, and write this book. What a pleasure! The University of Illinois, Urbana-Champaign has supported and nurtured this project in myriad ways. The extraordinary library collection furnished the sources and the staff of helpful librarians were always available to answer questions and help locate an elusive source. The very beginnings of the project were supported with a Mellon Faculty Fellowship and generous travel grants. I had extra time to write with awards of Humanities Release Time from the Research Board and a faculty fellowship from the Illinois Program for Research in the Humanities. The bi-weekly seminar and the engaged conversations pushed me to think about my project from interdisciplinary perspectives.

The Department of History, where I've made my intellectual home since moving to Urbana in 1998, has always provided rigorous and supportive interlocutors. The undergraduate students in my Modern Britain classes and in my classes on gender and crime in the early modern world have helped me to identify the case studies I examine in this book. My thanks especially to the graduate students I've had the privilege of reading and thinking with as they patiently helped me to engage with new historiographies. They made my preoccupations theirs as we conceptualized and problematized law, space, empire, race, and gender in the global eighteenth century. Anna Jacobs, Zach Sell, and Irina Spector-Marks carefully read and commented on the introduction. The Pre-Modern World Reading Group including graduate students and steadfast colleagues including Ikuko Asaka, Clare Crowston, Rana Hogarth, Craig Koslofsky, John Lynn, Bob Morrissey, and Carol Symes, read, commented, suggested, and supported every single chapter. David Roediger and Fred Hoxie read an early chapter and gave quiet and supportive comments hitting on the most important points. Great thanks to Antoinette Burton who stuck with this project in its many iterations reading innumerable drafts, always asking all the right questions, cheering me on, and believing in me. No one could ask for a more supportive scholar as their senior colleague. I'm fortunate that we both landed in east central Illinois in the late 1990s.

A Manuscript Award from the University of Illinois Funding Initiative for Multiracial Democracy Program sponsored a manuscript workshop. The discussion with Andrea McKenzie (History, University of Victoria),

ACKNOWLEDGEMENTS

James Oldham (Law, Georgetown University), Ikuko Asaka, and Craig Koslofsky was wide ranging, engaging, and so very helpful.

Colleagues and friends all over the world have contributed with suggestions and encouragement. Among them Thomas A. Green was always willing to read anything, any time. Isaac Land lent his expertise on all things maritime helping me as I chose to venture into the history of the mutinies of 1797. Brooke Newman encouraged me to probe the category of whiteness. The anonymous reviewers for the press made the book stronger and better with their comments.

Thanks to all of the scholarly communities who heard different chapters and sections of this book as it grew and developed. A special thanks to the Newberry Library where I spent a productive and thought provoking year in 2009–2010. I presented the first chapter to the Fellows seminar in 2010 and returned in 2015 to present the final chapter to the Newberry Library British History Seminar.

Previous versions of chapters 1, 2, and 3 appeared in edited collections and are reprinted with permission. 'The Sorceress, the Servant, and the Stays: Sexuality and Race in Eighteenth-Century Britain', in *Moving Subjects: Gender, Mobility, and Intimacy in an Age of Empire*, edited by Antoinette Burton and Tony Ballantyne (Urbana, IL, University of Illinois Press, 2009), pp. 252–273; 'Empire on Trial: Slavery, Villeinage and Law in Imperial Britain', in *Legal Histories of the British Empire: Laws, Engagements and Legacies*, ed. John McLaren and Shaunnagh Dorsett (New York: Routledge, 2014), pp. 203–217, reproduced by permission of Taylor and Francis Books UK; and 'Imperial Disruptions: City, Nation, and Empire', in *The Gordon Riots: Politics, Culture and Insurrection in Late Eighteenth-Century Britain*, ed. Ian Haywood and John Seed (Cambridge: Cambridge University Press, 2012), pp. 93–114.

My dear and close friend Nancy Abelmann didn't live to see this book published, but her support, and her passion and engagement helped me throughout. During our long walks early in the morning we talked through everything in our lives from kids to work to vacation plans. In her capacity as Associate Vice Chancellor for Research in the Humanities Nancy created the External Grants Faculty Advising program, and with Maria Gillombardo, provided support for the development of the book proposal and several grant applications.Their piercing intellect combined with invaluable care pushed me to think harder and attend to conceptual inconsistencies. Whatever the book's weaknesses, Nancy and Maria only made it better.

My families, the Rabins and the Koslofskys, have been sources of joy and love. My sisters, Roni and Leora along with their families, believed in me and supported me with distraction, fun, and laughter. I'm grateful to my mother, Pauline, for her constant support. I'm sorry

ACKNOWLEDGEMENTS

that my beloved stepfather, Mort, did not live to see the publication of this book.

Over ten years a project goes through many drafts and makes for a lot of conversations with patient friends. Amy Masciola talked with me about these cases even after she had left academia for a fulfilling career in union organizing. Her keen insights and questions strengthened my analysis. Susanne Pohl read my chapter on Ireland and gave me excellent feedback. Maria Mitchell graciously agreed to read the entire manuscript and provided invaluable advice. Trips to Indianapolis with our good friends Karen Petrone and Ken Slepyan, supplied much needed sustenance, laughter, and ziplining. I could never have completed this book without friendship and community: thanks especially to Abby Jahiel, Karen Winter-Nelson, and my book club buddies, Frances Harris, Jo Kibbe, Sharon Irish, Sally McMahan, Bea Nettles, and Carol Spindel.

I always looked forward to my trips to London because they meant visits and long talks with Laurie and Suzi Rabinowitz and their children Samuel, Josephine, and Jacob. I didn't know when I chose to study British history that my visits to the archives would bring the special gift of their friendship. Thank you for your sincere interest in my work and for opening your home to me and my family with generosity and warmth.

To Jonah and Evie my sincere thanks for your patience and for putting up with my distracted states. You are precious to me and you always remind me of what is really important.

The biggest thanks go to Craig Koslofsky to whom I dedicate this book. For his positivity and his generative intellect, his boundless love of research and ideas, his unstoppable belief in me and in this project. I am so lucky to share my work and my life with him.

Introduction: Empire and law, 'Firmly united by the circle of the British diadem'

As Britain's Empire expanded in the second half of the eighteenth century, British law managed interactions among peoples and cultures, linking metropole and colonies in a vast imperial legal web. It was at this time that rule of law – the principles that all are subject to publicly disclosed laws, that all are equal before the law, and that no one is above the law – became Britain's signature ideology, and a central justification for its imperial authority and superiority. Neither at home nor abroad did the rule of law emerge neatly or coherently from abstract principles of English justice.[1] I argue that the new emphasis on equality before the law in an age of imperial expansion was no coincidence. Common English men and women were bestowed – discursively at least – with rights and equality at the very moment that the British appropriated rights and property from colonial subjects. By examining London's women, Jews, 'Gypsies',[2] Scots, Africans, Catholics, working-class men, and Irish, I show that the shifting boundaries between these 'internal others' and those who considered themselves 'true born Englishmen' were increasingly drawn by the law over the course of the eighteenth century in order to clarify the distinction between them. The law reinterpreted religion, nation, and other hierarchies of difference in terms of whiteness, a legal category that emerged through this process that imagined male Anglicans of English heritage and middling status as its normative subjects. This study shows how contact with 'foreign' cultures and communities *at home* – and particularly in London – promoted the ideology of rule of law in the service of empire.

In the cases examined here, from the 'Jew Bill' (Jewish Naturalization Act 1753) to the Acts of Union with Ireland 1800 (39 & 40 Geo. III c. 67 and 40 Geo. III c. 38), Britain's internal others were increasingly framed by their relations to law and to empire. They were both agents and subjects: pulled into the legal system by their quest for the rights and equality promised by the rule of law, but also pushed in by legal mechanisms for defining, defending, and differentiating status and identity. I focus on Britain's internal others as the subjects of litigation, legislation, and popular outcry because for these 'foreign' individuals and communities their status in England now had vital imperial implications. Beyond ideological claims about law, this book traces the interactions between a legal event, its imperial others, and the sources that circulated in the public sphere (in politics, on the streets, and in the press) to show how law was shaped, challenged, and debated, made and remade, as legal authorities and British subjects wrestled with accepting the presence of colonial outsiders and sought to draw a line between colony and metropole.

Each case exemplifies a legal attempt to confront and arbitrate the problem of difference: Jews and Gypsies, slaves and self-emancipated Africans, Catholics, working poor men, and Irish men and women. Each of these events, to quote Pierre Nora, 'testifies not so much to what it represents as to what it reveals, not so much to what it is as to what it unleashes. Its meaning is subsumed in its reverberations'.[3] Together these cases track significant moments in which the legal category of whiteness was produced, and demonstrate how the law worked to supplant and incorporate other kinds of difference to 'hierarchicize, bureaucratize, mediate and channel power'.[4] Once integrated into the sinews of the legal system 'entire populations [were] rendered comprehensible – and thus manageable'.[5] Although legal and governing authorities sought this neat and rational outcome, the reality reveals a much messier, less linear story of integration, resistance, and exclusion. At the heart of this study is the relationship between law and empire for Britain and its internal others.

This cultural history of law in the eighteenth century defines legal events capaciously to include legislative acts of Parliament, criminal trials, riots, and mutinies. My study cuts across legal genres to trace the fates of Britain's 'internal others' as they were framed by their new relationships to law and empire. It moves beyond an imagined contrast between consistent, impartial, and settled law in the metropole and its uneven, erratic application in colonial sites. In doing so it reveals a destabilized metropole: far from a beacon of light or a consistent, predictable standard-bearer. London, wracked with conflict, encompassed, articulated, and legally 'processed' all of the divisions and contested identities of empire. The pronouncements casting the rule of law and equality before the law as stately, universal, and complete obfuscated the reality of the rule of law: an iterative ideological performance – unstable, conflicted, and incomplete.

INTRODUCTION: EMPIRE AND LAW

Race, gender, and the rule of law

Britons often justified their imperial claims in the eighteenth century by citing the benefits of the rule of law, while politicians and press alike celebrated English law's impartiality.[6] Indeed English culture and society embraced the rule of law as a superior and universal value. Yet the ideology of rule of law did not emerge organically or progressively from its abstract claims: it was produced through collision with internal others, among them Jews, Gypsies, Scots, Africans, Catholics, working-class men, and Irish.

What about English women? Did they enjoy the rights of 'true born Englishmen'? A white Englishwoman's legal status was always dictated by the most important man in her life. Until marriage, girls were in the orbit of the most senior male member of their family or guardian, after marriage husbands took charge. According to William Blackstone (1723–1780), 'By marriage, the husband and wife are one person in law: that is, the very being or legal existence of the woman is suspended during the marriage, or at least is incorporated and consolidated into that of the husband: under whose wing, protection, and cover, she performs every thing; and is therefore called in our law-French a *feme-covert*.'[7] The status of England's white women, like that of all of the groups examined here, was situational, contingent, and relational and as such depended on their family's wealth and social status. Single women represented an especially problematic group, whose autonomy contributed to their ambiguous and threatening status as internal others. The legal status of women reveals much about the gendered expectations of the law and how much these expectations could change in an imperial context. As whiteness was produced, we see how class and sexuality inflected race creating a category that was inherently gendered. A white Englishwoman's rights and status, her place of privilege, was specific to her differences from women of color in the colonies and at home.

Despite its rhetoric of equality, the rule of law excluded and brutalized certain colonial subjects, at home and abroad, serving Britain's interests and sustaining its imperial dominance. As the Empire expanded, encompassing ever-greater cultural, religious, ethnic, and racial variation, the law strained to contain and maintain the hierarchies of difference, sometimes plainly contradicting the ideology of equality before the law. I show that in contrast to the professed discourse of rule of law, the English legal process sustained distinctions of race, ethnicity, gender, and class before the law, creating and protecting whiteness as a privileged category. The book follows the struggles between and among legal authorities and subjects as they negotiated the fine line between Anglican English men and the many who called London home but were not considered English. Digging into six cases involving Britain's internal others, I reveal the interrupted and inconsistent application of the rule of law, a fragile metropole, and its tenuous legal authority.

Defining whiteness as both a cultural concept and a legal category was essential to the process of defining difference, setting the limits of equality, and, ultimately, creating empire. London in the eighteenth century is an ideal place to examine how this came to pass, for it was a teeming center of commercial, intellectual, and cultural exchange among diverse groups, what Daniel Statt has called 'the foreigners' mecca' of 'diverse immigrants'.[8] Whiteness emerged as a legal category in the context of a thriving transatlantic slave trade in which freedom and whiteness were equated, not just in Virginia but at home in London, among Africans, South Asians, East Asians, Irish, and Jews.[9] Here, one can see how outmoded hierarchies and boundaries were trumped and trampled in order to assert and accommodate Britain's imperial claims of economic and cultural superiority. Scrutinizing the intersection between law and the developing cultural concept of whiteness in eighteenth-century London helps us to reconstruct the way race defined power.[10]

What constituted the elements, mythical and real, of rule of law in seventeenth- and eighteenth-century England? Blackstone's *Commentaries on the Laws of England* (1765–1769) asserted that 'the first and primary end of human laws is to maintain and regulate these absolute rights of individuals', among them the 'inviolate ... three great and primary rights of personal security, personal liberty, and private property'.[11] Equality before the law was embedded in this ideology, which necessitated 'a general conformity of all orders and degrees to those equitable rules of action, by which the meanest individual is protected from the insults and oppression of the greatest'.[12] England's law comprised both written law, in the form of parliamentary statutes, and unwritten or common law. Bound by precedent, common law, 'contained in the records of the several courts of justice, in books of reports and judicial decisions, and in the treatises of learned sages of the profession', relied on judges who determined, guided, and arbitrated its interpretation and enforcement.[13] England's constitution bestowed Parliament with 'sovereign and uncontrollable authority in making, confirming, enlarging, restraining, abrogating, repealing, reviving, and expounding of laws ... concerning matters of all possible denominations, ecclesiastical, or temporal, civil, military, maritime, or criminal'.[14] Together written and unwritten law made up England's constitution whose 'very end and scope' Blackstone proclaimed was 'political or civil liberty'.[15]

INTRODUCTION: EMPIRE AND LAW

Trial by jury featured prominently as an essential guarantor of those rights. In his letter to William Murray, First Earl of Mansfield (1705–1793) and Chief Justice of King's Bench, published in 1768, John Wilkes (1725–1797), the outspoken journalist and London politician regarded as a champion of liberty, demanded, 'If I am to be tried, I hope it will be by a Jury (and not in the inquisition) by twelve impartial men, sworn to discharge their consciences. This great palladium of English liberty can never be destroyed without subverting the whole constitution.'[16] Wilkes warned against judges who intimidated jurors and he insisted on 'impartiality between plaintiff or defendant, between criminal and accuser' warning against 'unmanly prejudices of either party, country, or religion'. Wilkes reminded the Scottish Mansfield that for 'free Britons' 'no party, no country, no statesman, no judge, no king can oppress for a strict adherence to privilege and justice'.[17] Wilkes fused English liberty, free Britons, and masculinity while denying prejudice of nation or religion. Such an idealized version of British law rested on, and obscured, exclusions based on ethnicity, gender, sexuality, and race.

Blackstone spoke of the rule of law as a responsibility shared among male elites 'called upon to determine questions of right, and distribute justice to [their] fellow-subjects' as jurors, magistrates, or members of Parliament. The stakes were high: order and deference depended on the appearance of 'legal and effectual justice' lest magistrates incur 'contempt from their inferiors' or 'censure' from above.[18] Popular literature expressed concern and apprehension about any miscarriage of justice. *The Cries of Blood, or Juryman's Monitor* (1767) recounted the 'Lives and Melancholy Deaths of several unhappy Persons, who have been Tried, Convicted, and Executed, for Robberies and Murders, of which they were intirely Innocent'. Addressed to 'all lawyers, as well as all of those, who are called upon to serve upon juries' the authors cautioned 'judges and magistrates' that 'it is a maxim generally admitted by all moralists, that it is better that the guilty should escape than the innocent suffer undeservedly'.[19] We see this expectation of consistency and universality in the case studies below. Sir Crisp Gascoyne insisted on investigating the alibi of Mary Squires after her conviction in order to be sure that an innocent woman did not hang; supporters of the Roman Catholic Relief Act 1778 (18 George III c. 60) pointed to the inconsistency between rights afforded Catholics in Quebec and those withheld from Catholics in England; English mariners demanded as theirs the 'rights of a free-born people' during the mutinies at Spithead and the Nore.

Beyond legal commentary and treatises, the discourse of the rule of law and equality before the law resounded in the popular press, especially when a member of the elite was accused of a crime. In January 1760

Laurence Shirley, Fourth Earl Ferrers (1720–1760), shot his steward, John Johnson, at Staunton Harrold, his family's estate in Leicestershire. At his murder trial at Westminster Hall on April 16, 1760, Ferrers conducted his own defense: he denied responsibility for Johnson's murder citing a history of occasional insanity. This defense failed, and he was found guilty and sentenced to death and anatomization. Ferrers hanged at Tyburn on May 2, 1760; the scaffold was hung in black to distinguish him as a nobleman.[20] The *London Evening Post* applauded the fact that he shared the fate of common thieves, highwaymen, and murderers proclaiming: 'the Execution ... does Honour to this Kingdom, in respect to the impartial Administration of its Justice. In many other Countries Murder is too frequently committed with Impunity, especially when the Assassin happens to be rich or ennobled.'[21] In a similar register, *The Northampton Mercury* praised William Dodd's execution for forgery. The Anglican cleric, poet, and theologian, whose hard work never earned enough money to support his extravagant lifestyle, forged a bill of exchange for £4200. Despite his conviction at London's Old Bailey on February 22, 1777, the jury's recommendation of mercy launched a campaign opposing his death sentence, which counted Samuel Johnson among its supporters.[22] Dodd hanged on June 27, 1777, and in recounting the execution the *Mercury* declaimed 'May this fatal Example teach an Obedience to those Laws, which, with undiscriminating Impartiality, consider the Crime only while they forget the Man!'[23]

The ideology of law and the notion of law as organic, negotiated, and created by previous rulings enabled some and compelled others to recognize England's legal institutions and to participate in the legal process. Yet widespread participation did not translate into a monolithic interpretation of what was lawful. The law was a site of struggle in which participants from different social backgrounds actively contested conceptions of right and custom. Devising their own legal formulations, common people, both men and women, went to law to further their own interests and to defend what they considered their rights from encroachment by either their social equals or betters.[24]

Each chapter in this book explores an element of what contemporaries would have recognized as the characteristics of rule of law. The law's claim to impartiality frames chapter 1 on Elizabeth Canning and the Jewish Naturalization Act (26 Geo. II, c. 26) while liberty and freedom are the subjects of Somerset's case of a self-emancipated slave in chapter two. Chapter 3 concerns the debate over Catholic rights and the expectation of equality before the law while chapter 4 reconstructs the claims of sailors in the navy to the rights of freeborn Englishmen. Chapter 5 focuses on the discussion of the constitution and whether or not a Parliament can lawfully disband itself as London's Westminster planned to do in the Acts of Union. Over the course of the half century examined here, we can see how the law was used to construct racial, sexual, and ethnic differences and similarities. The Members of Parliament (MPs) who responded to popular dissent in the summer of 1753 by repealing the Jewish Naturalization Act did not do the same with the Catholic Relief Act 1778, nor did the constitutional arguments made by the Irish Protestants in 1800 result in a reconsideration of Union. Instead governing authorities employed legal mechanisms, drawing and redrawing lines of inclusion and exclusion, to advance imperial priorities.

Historiography

My work speaks directly to tensions and unanswered questions at the intersection of several historiographical trends. The first is the rich and provocative scholarship pioneered by E. P. Thompson, Douglas Hay, and others who problematized the rule of law in eighteenth-century Britain and inspired the rich scholarship on the history of crime.[25] Recent scholarship on crime, law, and empire has certainly substantiated Thompson's claim that 'in a context of gross class inequalities, the equity of the law must always be in some part a sham. Transplanted as it was to even more inequitable contexts, this law could become an instrument of imperialism.'[26] However, legal treatment of outsiders in Britain has not been examined as closely for the eighteenth century. My approach to the way law created difference in the metropole builds on the now twenty-year old 'imperial turn' in British history. Following the work of Catherine Hall and Kathleen Wilson, I have chosen to retell well-known moments in English political history. My perspective, far from stopping at the English Channel, instead discloses the causative impact of empire as embodied in the metropole's others.[27] The blend of cultural and political history exposes the way in which British authorities deployed law to reinscribe key divisions while seeming to transcend them.[28] Most recently the 'legal turn' in Atlantic and imperial history has called attention to the uneven, patchy, and capricious nature of legal regimes established at the frontiers of empires. These literatures have recovered the inconsistent ways by which law spread as empires expanded and interrogate the 'Anglo-American legal tradition' and its assumptions of a seamless migration of England's laws, courts, and legal norms to its colonies. With this project, I join scholars including Lauren Benton, James Epstein, Eliga Gould, and Paul Halliday, who consider the intersection of law and empire using concepts such as the jurisprudence of emergency, legal pluralism, and zones of law.[29] While these studies recover contradictions in the way law functioned in distant imperial sites, this book reconstructs the legal treatment of Britain's internal others in England at the center of the Empire. At the heart of my examination of the law in relation to race, ethnicity, religion, gender, and sexuality is the tension between the stated ideal of equality before the law and its necessarily irregular application in the metropole.[30]

The study of Britain and its Empire has often been defined by the binary of center and periphery, metropole and colony. Despite scholars' insistence since the 'imperial turn' about the co-constituted nature of metropole and colony, and the fruitful and convincing research it has yielded that demonstrates their intertwined nature, the binary persists. Perhaps then it is time to work beyond this binary and deconstruct it by focusing unapologetically on the metropole, which insisted on itself as the legal center of the Empire. In histories of Britain the metropole presents itself as separate from and prior to empire, but this study shows that empire was intrinsic to the unstable, uneven production of law in the metropole as well. If historians are serious about metropole and colony constituting one another, then a history of law in the metropole has as much to tell us about empire as a history of law in the colonies. The two categories are imperial constructs; considered separately they do not hold up analytically.

As the center of news and publication, England's free press, and in particular London's, generated a lively, event-driven public sphere producing written accounts of each of these legal episodes in ballads, pamphlets, songs, newspapers, and novels as well as in records of court cases and legislative procedure. With the tremendous growth in newspapers and their circulation over the course of the eighteenth century scholars credit the press with broadening the discussion of politics and facilitating public debate of policy. Contemporaries valued newspapers as sources of information and they considered England's free press (along with the jury) fundamental to English liberties.[31] The popularity and currency of caricature prints, 'a quintessentially British art form', increased with the expansion of the press, parliamentary reporting, and a growing political awareness. They spread both news and opinion among their consumers.[32] The production and diffusion of print culture shaped perceptions of empire and law by serving as sites of conversation and debate where authors and readers could rehearse different points of view and interpretations of events while enlisting public opinion. The range of published accounts articulated anxieties and opinions: far from static, the very process of distribution made, reflected, and remade popular opinion.

Scholarship on whiteness seeks to trace and analyze 'the ways in which whiteness is brought into being as a normative structure, a discourse of power, and a form of identity'.[33] Its critics have warned of 'ahistoricity, reification, and universalization' that has the potential to 'reinscribe white people at the center of historical narratives'.[34] They have pointed out that some of the most well-known examinations of the topic do so in a white-only context, away from people of color.[35] Although this discussion of whiteness does not engage explicitly with the debates about class and global capital common to the field, examining the history of whiteness as a legal category allows us to see that despite more flexible ideas about racial lines in the eighteenth century, the emergence of racial hierarchies had real, often negative consequences that belied the promise of equality in a cosmopolitan setting.

The noun whiteness was used in the eighteenth century to refer to 'the state or condition of being white conceived in terms of racial or cultural identity'.[36] Ruth Frankenberg has referred to whiteness as 'a location of structural advantage, of race privilege' and 'a standpoint, a place from which white people look at others, and at society'.[37] Discourses of whiteness emerged at the intersection of discourses of class, gender, sexuality, ethnicity, and religion and signaled the extent to which people were thought to be eligible for the rights and privileges of belonging. In *Whiteness of a Different Color*, Matthew Frye Jacobson shows that in the nineteenth- and twentieth-century United States the history of 'races' known as the Celts and Slavs, Hebrews, Iberics, Mediterraneans, Teutons, and Anglo-Saxons operated in 'a system of "difference" by which one might be *both white and racially distinct from other whites*'.[38] In the context of early modern global mobility and Britain's imperial expansion, Jenny Shaw and Cecily Jones have convincingly demonstrated this to be the case for Irish Catholics in the colonies.[39] Building on their work this book focuses on the metropole to trace how 'white', a defined legal status in the colonies, was mapped onto metropolitan exclusions affecting Jews, Gypsies, Africans, Irish, Catholics, working-class men, and women.

In early modern Britain and its Empire, law straddled numerous, often ambiguous, frontiers including formal boundaries of sovereignty and jurisdiction. In the making of empire and imperial formations law defined and maintained a network of relationships between and among these jurisdictions and peoples engaged in possession, dispossession, location, and relocation.[40] In the midst of empire's endemic disruption, mobility, and disorder the law was tasked with fixing, sedimenting, and predicting hierarchies of knowledge and power; reasserting identities and reinscribing regimens of distinction, inclusion, and exclusion.[41] An examination of the interactions between nation, colony, and empire reveals that their impact was never unidirectional: the very contingent flow of ideas and their unpredictable momentum and direction confused normative relationships and unsettled power dynamics, calling into question axiomatic truths about who could make law and on what basis.[42]

The book begins in the tense period between the end of the War of Austrian Succession in 1748 and the Seven Years' War (1756–1763), as Britain gained sovereignty over vast areas as geographically and culturally diverse as Quebec, Bengal, and Senegal.[43] The newly configured Empire had to determine how to incorporate existing legal systems and hierarchies in order to govern these new territories, whether acquired by direct conquest or treaty, and this period resonated with discussions about how to rule the different peoples and places now a part of the Empire.[44]

Each case study in this book reveals how the law simultaneously expanded *and* withheld rights and liberties, and each features a person or group marked as an outsider in London: Mary Squires, a Gypsy accused of abducting Elizabeth Canning; Jewish merchants seeking naturalization without conversion to Christianity; James Somerset, a self-emancipated African seeking freedom; English, Irish, Scottish, and French Catholics who would benefit from religious toleration; Britain's multinational and multiracial sailors at the Empire's front lines; and Irish Protestants fighting to retain their own law-making body in Dublin. During the latter half of the eighteenth century the movement for legal reform did attempt to accommodate internal outsiders by instituting changes that brought the universal promises of the ideology of rule of law to England's diverse population. In the eighteenth century Jews, Scots, Muslim, Hindu, and Chinese witnesses were allowed to swear an oath in accordance with their own customs and religious practices although as Karen Macfarlane has shown, the credibility of non-Christian, non-white witnesses was often impugned by attorneys for the opposing side.[45] When faced with non-English speakers, there is evidence that attempts were made in some cases to provide interpreters and in other cases 'half-foreign' juries were sworn in.[46] Threading this story through the metropole allows us to witness the discrepancies and contradictions inherent in the discussions and debates about how to apply the rule of law to internal others, implicitly excluded from its rhetorical promises. We see that Britain's image as an imperial nation bound by law formed alongside the violence and the restriction of rights in both colonial *and* metropolitan settings.

Equality before the law?

What did equality before the law mean in practice? Medieval law had created a patchwork of jurisdictions, many of which were overlapping, awarding certain privileges to particular groups and allowing certain activities in restricted places. In this sense legal pluralism had always existed in law: different geographical areas, privileges of honor and title, awarded to particular groups of people based on status, belonging, age, and gender, bestowing privileges and setting up hierarchies of access. In the eighteenth century legal categories were consolidated as a part of Enlightenment discourse emphasizing universals. These consolidations were justified under the rubric of rule of law and equality before the law, but equality before the law did not create equality. Instead it mandated the equal treatment of those who inhabited the same category. Fierce rivalry existed between competing legal hierarchies that guarded their hard won privileges. These hierarchies formed the foundations of the rule of law, and they often contradicted each other. The ideology of rule of law nurtured legal pluralism and the inequalities that it generated. This book traces the emergence of the legal category of whiteness in the eighteenth century that imagined male Anglicans of English heritage and middling status as normative subjects.[47] Although created through imperial contact and reinforced by legal process, codification or even explicit mention would have contradicted the universal equality before the law promised by the ideology of rule of law. Women, working-class men, Jews, Catholics, Irish, and people of African descent would come and go through England's courtrooms, their treatment varied, always measured by their proximity to or relationship with normative white subjects.[48]

On the periphery Britain strove to respect local laws and legal traditions while establishing English legal courts and jurisdictions alongside native law-giving bodies.[49] By defining some areas as lawless, the British demonstrated a systematic unevenness in the dispersal of British legal cultures throughout the Empire. Contemporaries divided the known world into zones of law, and Britons were perfectly willing to accept a legal landscape in which there were lawless regions, regions dominated by non-British legal authorities, and those under the jurisdiction of British law. Colonial settlers and British authorities deliberately defined legal lacunae where British law did not apply. The advantages for Britons became obvious when their presence in a zone that fell outside British law empowered behavior and policy unlawful in a metropolitan setting that redounded to their strategic or financial interests. With non-European negotiating partners, the British deployed what Benton calls 'legal pluralism': they defined the Atlantic as a space of 'plural legalities', renamed indigenous custom 'lawless', and designated sites where they could profit from actions forbidden by the law of nations.[50]

When political or economic security seemed imperiled, legal zones in colonial spaces – for example, in British controlled Trinidad during the Napoleonic Wars (1799–1815) – allowed for 'the jurisprudence of emergency' giving Britons latitude to act outside the law based on necessity.[51] Gould argues that Britons believed they carried English law wherever they went, but they envisioned a spatial boundary that marked Britons at home from those in the colonies. Beyond this boundary Britons could engage in forms of violence unacceptable at home. This line allowed colonists to affirm metropolitan norms and customs while they explained and justified the legalities and illegalities in Britain's colonies and their inconsistent and sometimes unlawful nature as emanating from zones of war, chaos, and brutality among people considered savages.[52]

Yet the provision for suspending the rule of law in the case of emergency was by no means restricted to colonial spaces – indeed it was embedded in fundamental legal texts espousing enlightenment universals.[53] As Nassar Hussain demonstrates, John Locke's *Second Treatise* and Montesquieu's *The Spirit of the Laws* both allowed for the state to interrupt the rule of law if its sovereignty or security were at risk.[54] Blackstone echoed these authors when, after praising the liberties guaranteed by habeas corpus and decrying the 'confinement of the person, by secretly hurrying him to jail, where his sufferings are unknown or forgotten', he added the proviso that 'sometimes, when the state is in real danger, even this may be a necessary measure'. Blackstone concluded that 'this experiment ought only to be tried in cases of extreme emergency; and in these the nation parts with its liberty for a while, in order to preserve it for ever'.[55] In each of these examples 'emergency is an elastic category, stretching over political disturbances such as riots, the situation of sovereign war, and even constitutional crises within a state'.[56] Rather than an exceptional interruption, Hussain shows that emergency and rule of law are co-constituted by virtue of the fact that law 'contemplates and provides for its own failure'.[57] Although many of the exceptions to the rule of law happened in colonial sites and are well documented in recent scholarship, our case studies demonstrate the interruption and circumvention of legal process – as well as resistance to these practices – in the metropole.

When the different legal hierarchies clashed in the metropole, actors involved in legal fights could not look away from or ignore their contradictions. This book examines Britain's internal others at home in London who inhabited these different legal hierarchies. The book proceeds from the periphery (inhabited by Jews, Gypsies, highland Scots, slaves, and Catholics) into the center, past the category inhabited by the Empire's multinational mariners and ends with Irish Protestant elites. These internal others, many of whom called London home, found themselves drawn into the lively debates about the rights of Englishmen, often when they went to or were taken to court.

INTRODUCTION: EMPIRE AND LAW

None of these cases is newly discovered. Each has found its way into one or two sentences in a survey of the eighteenth century. But using printed sources such as trial accounts, legislation, pamphlets, newspapers, salacious prints, ballads, and novels, I retell these legal events elaborating the cultural histories of these high political stories, and in the process I expose a different set of significances and their real and material consequences.[58] Together they showcase how empire and the ideology of rule of law shaped each other and demonstrate how Britain's legal apparatus defined and privileged whiteness, how that definition changed over time, and what impact it had on other hierarchies of gender, sexuality, and status.

The abolitionist and reformer Granville Sharp (1735–1813) wrote extensively about the law and the corrupting practices he associated with empire, specifically the limits on liberty embodied by slavery and the slave trade, naval impressment, and the problems with unequal and inconsistent legislative representation in Britain and in the American colonies. But Sharp did not advocate the contraction of the Empire or the discontinuation of Britain's expansive policies: quite the contrary, he offered his writings as correctives, believing that Britain's law and constitution were providentially bestowed and must be dispensed consistently and identically in its colonies. Sharp adamantly refused a system of law in which '*one part* of the empire might determine a question, or enact a law, for the peculiar advantage only of that *one part*, though to the manifest detriment and injury of *another part*'.[59] He made a case for the law as a system and the absolute necessity for consistency among legal institutions and decisions throughout the Empire lest 'the free subjects of *one part* of the empire would be liable to be most materially injured in their *greatest* and most valuable inheritance, *the Law*, by the hasty decisions of men on the *other side of* the empire'.[60] Sharp's treatise is further evidence of the expectation of universality promised by the ideology of rule of law. If taken seriously and applied consistently, the ideology of rule of law and equality before the law on which Sharp insisted had tremendous implications not only for those colonial subjects living across the Empire, but also for foreigners and others perceived as less English living in the metropole. It is precisely these questions and contradictions that preoccupy the analysis in this book.

Chapter 1, 'Internal others: Jews, Gypsies, and Jacobites', examines the fears of British people worried about the infiltration of their nation by 'Hebrew', 'Egyptian', and 'papist' interlopers, identified as threatening because of their religious and ethnic difference. The chapter draws connections between a series of entangled events in 1753–1754: the sensational disappearance and reappearance of Elizabeth Canning; the passage (May 1753) and repeal (November 1753) of the Jewish Naturalization Act; and the execution of Archibald Cameron (June 1753). Cameron, a Scottish highlander, participated in the Elibank Plot, which sought to depose George II and bring Charles Stuart to the throne. The persistent focus on the proximity of religious and ethnic minorities stoked anxieties about who was British, what made Britain a nation, and how nation and empire could coexist while insisting on the normativity of white Anglican Englishness.

In Chapter 2, ' "In a Country of Liberty?": Slavery, villeinage, and the making of whiteness in the Somerset case (1772)', I reframe the arguments made at King's Bench in 1772 for and against the legality of slavery in England in the case of James Somerset, a self-emancipated slave. While some argued it was immoral, no one contested the legality of slavery in the colonies. Defenders of slavery mobilized villeinage as slavery's precedent and analogue while abolitionists insisted on the obsolescence of this practice. A villein, or serf in the medieval manorial system, was a peasant tied to the land and entirely subject to a lord. Somerset's lawyers argued against domestic slavery by claiming that villeinage was no precedent because it was 'a slavery in blood and family, one uninterruptedly transmitted through a long line of ancestors'. Villeins were English by blood, tied to England and their status by lineage and place, and as such decidedly white in eighteenth-century discourse. Through discussions of the precedent of villeinage both proponents and opponents of slavery defined whiteness defensively as the privilege and inheritance of those described by Edward Long, colonial official and historian of Jamaica, as 'genuine and natural-born subjects'.

The Somerset decision acknowledged the existence of multiple jurisdictions in the Empire and the contradictory laws passed and enforced by metropolitan and colonial assemblies. When tensions between Britain and its North American colonies erupted into war in 1776, contemporaries alluded to the jurisdictional challenges in Somerset's case, which had referred to Virginia's laws as specific to 'that Country'. Chapter 3, 'Imperial disruptions: City, nation, and empire in the Gordon Riots', examines the riots that broke out in 1780 as a result of mounting anti-Catholicism and anti-imperialism in Britain, which intensified with the acquisition of Quebec in 1763 and the expansion of the legal rights of Catholics with the passage of the Roman Catholic Relief Act 1778. I argue that those who took to London's streets from June 2–8, 1780 equated the British Empire with the Roman Catholic Church. Only the imposition of martial law enforced by 10,000 troops – an act that contradicted Britain's longstanding aversion to a standing army in the metropole – quelled the burning and looting across the city. The possibility of Catholic toleration threatened the presumption of an exclusively white, Protestant, English birthright.

The French Revolution jolted the British Isles in the 1790s, its rhetoric posing new challenges to the British Empire. To manage growing dissent, the British government overturned the rule of law, banning meetings and publications dedicated to political reform and suspending habeas corpus. Chapter 4, '"This fleet is not yet republican": Conceptions of law in the mutinies of 1797', connects the large-scale mutinies at Spithead and at the Nore with Thomas Paine's publications on natural rights and political expression. The mutineers, a multicultural group of sailors employed by Britain's navy, used the language of liberty, reason, and justice as couched in *The Rights of Man* (1791, 1792) to protest impressment, low wages, and harsh working conditions and to distinguish themselves from African slaves. These dramatic events reverberated in home waters, close to populous English centers, and received considerable media attention. Newspapers, pamphlets, and parliamentary debates conveyed fears of invasion through infiltration and blamed the mutinies on French and Irish republicans. Placing Paine's ideas beside the government's oppressive legal measures to limit the spread of ideas about equality and freedom dramatically demonstrates how the law made difference.

Chapter 5, '*Wedding and Bedding*: Making the Union with Ireland, 1800' examines the Acts that abolished Ireland's Parliament, granting 100 seats to Irish MPs in Westminster's House of Commons and 28 seats to Irish Peers in the House of Lords. The British government imposed the Union with little popular Irish input. Many Protestant elites in Ireland consented to the Union, fearing that it was their only defense against radical Irish nationalists, both Catholic and Protestant, who had led a rebellion in 1798. I argue that the Act of Union, a cornerstone of Britain's oppression of Ireland, was a defensive effort to stave off further economic losses while grappling with the ideological and military implications of the French Revolution. The Irish who opposed the Union defended the existence of an independent Irish Parliament with a claim to superior knowledge and understanding of English law and the British constitution. By alleging a better comprehension of British law than the English had themselves, these pamphleteers, mostly Irish Protestants, claimed the rights of white English Anglicans, briefly reversing the power relationship between metropole and colony with arguments about rule of law.

While the record shows us a diverse England, some contemporaries resisted the incorporation of the colonial experience into the metropole. Britain's imperial expansion and the diversity of its population were not always embraced by all (or any) of London's residents. Some who envisioned a global empire directed, inspired, and led by a cosmopolitan metropole accepted that mixing was integral to the imperial experience, but cosmopolitanism did not necessarily mean equality and often imposed new hierarchies. The relationship between colony and metropole, outsiders and insiders, foreigners and 'good subjects' operated with a boundary defined opportunistically depending on the circumstances. Imperial relationships would be continuously and repeatedly fraught with the tension and arbitrariness of the line drawn and constantly redrawn between those considered English, British, or imperial. While London's economic, political, and cultural influence was felt from the Americas to Asia, these locales made themselves equally felt in London. The multiple interactions served as vehicles of connection and conflict with people from around the world and contributed to a clash and mixture of ideas and cultures. *Britain and its Internal Others* demonstrates how the law promoted and responded to British expansion – creating empire and defining a new category of difference in whiteness that delineated the promise of equality.

Notes

1 I use the term English to refer to aspects of legal culture and process considered by contemporaries to have developed in isolation in England. They do not necessarily predate the Act of Union in 1707.
2 The preferred term today is Roma or Romani. I use the contemporary term Gypsy as it appears in the sources.
3 Pierre Nora, 'The Return of the Event', in *Histories: French Constructions of the Past*, ed. Jacques Revel and Lynn Hunt (New York: New Press, 1995), p. 432. Elsewhere Nora calls events 'a scene of social projections and latent conflicts' (p. 433) 'an encounter of several independent series of causes ... that gathers up scattered meanings' (pp. 434–435).
4 Nassar Hussain, *The Jurisprudence of Emergency: Colonialism and the Rule of Law* (Ann Arbor, MI: University of Michigan Press, 2003), p. 32.
5 Jane Carey, Leigh Boucher, and Katherine Ellinghaus, 'Reorienting Whiteness: A New Agenda for the Field', in *Re-Orienting Whiteness*, ed. Jane Carey, Leigh Boucher, and Katherine Ellinghaus (New York: Palgrave Macmillan, 2009), p. 8.
6 Ian Duncanson, *Historiography, Empire and the Rule of Law: Imagined Constitutions, Remembered Legalities* (New York: Routledge, 2012) and Hussain, *Jurisprudence of Emergency*.
7 William Blackstone, *Commentaries on the Laws of England*, 4 volumes (Chicago, IL: University of Chicago Press, 1979), vol. 1, p. 430. In practice, the status of *feme covert* was largely a legal fiction. Women skirted these restrictions, acting as legal agents with and without the help of their male kin in both criminal and civil courts and in business.
8 Daniel Statt, *Foreigners and Englishmen: The Controversy over Immigration and Population, 1660–1760* (Newark, DE: University of Delaware Press, 1995), p. 31. For more on London's diversity in the early modern period, see Jacob Selwood, *Diversity and Difference in Early Modern London* (Burlington, VT: Ashgate, 2010).
9 The American colonies have been the focus of much historical research on racial formation. For more see Ariela J. Gross, *What Blood Won't Tell: A History of Race on Trial in America* (Cambridge, MA: Harvard University Press, 2008), ch. 1 and the works cited there.

INTRODUCTION: EMPIRE AND LAW

10 Carey, Boucher, and Ellinghaus, 'Reorienting Whiteness'.
11 Blackstone, *Commentaries*, vol. 1, pp. 120, 136.
12 Blackstone, *Commentaries*, vol. 1, p. 6.
13 Blackstone, *Commentaries*, vol. 1, pp. 63–64.
14 Blackstone, *Commentaries*, vol. 1, p. 156.
15 Blackstone, *Commentaries*, vol. 1, p. 6.
16 John Wilkes, *A letter to the Right Honourable William Lord Mansfield, Lord Chief Justice Of England, And One Of His Majesty's Most Honourable Privy Council. upon some late Star Chamber proceedings in the Court of King's Bench. Against the publishers of the Extraordinary North Briton, no. IV* (London: John Wilkes, 1768), p. 5.
17 Wilkes, *Letter to Mansfield*, pp. 7–8.
18 Blackstone, *Commentaries*, vol. 1, p. 8.
19 Anon., *The Cries of Blood, or Juryman's Monitor* (London: J. Cooke, 1767), p. i.
20 Richard Davenport-Hines, 'Shirley, Laurence, fourth Earl Ferrers (1720–1760)', *Oxford Dictionary of National Biography* [ODNB] (Oxford: Oxford University Press, 2004; online edn, January 2008; http://www.oxforddnb.com/view/article/25432, accessed January 31, 2016). For more on the insanity defense in criminal trials, see my book, *Identity, Crime, and Legal Responsibility in Eighteenth-Century England* (New York: Palgrave Macmillan, 2004), esp. ch. 2.
21 *London Evening Post*, May 6, 1760, Issue 5072.
22 Philip Rawlings, 'Dodd, William (1729–1777)', ODNB (http://www.oxforddnb.com/view/article/7744, accessed January 31, 2016).
23 *Northampton Mercury*, June 30, 1777, Issue 15, p. 3.
24 For a discussion of how ordinary people envisioned law, power, and authority, see John Brewer and John Styles, eds., *An Ungovernable People? The English and their Law in the Seventeenth and Eighteenth Centuries* (London: Hutchinson, 1980) and Michael Braddick and John Walter, 'Introduction: Grids of Power: Order, Hierarchy and Subordination in Early Modern Society', in *Negotiating Power in Early Modern Society: Order, Hierarchy and Subordination in Britain and Ireland*, ed. Michael Braddick and John Walter (Cambridge: Cambridge University Press, 2001), pp. 1–42. Garthine Walker has a nuanced response to these earlier works in her discussion of conceptions of authority and agency in *Crime, Gender, and Order in Early Modern England* (Cambridge: Cambridge University Press, 2003), ch. 6, esp. pp. 210–227. For more examples of seventeenth-century participation in the legal system, see Cynthia Herrup, *The Common Peace: Participation and the Criminal Law in Seventeenth-Century England* (Cambridge: Cambridge University Press, 1987) and J. A. Sharpe, 'Enforcing the Law in the Seventeenth-Century English Village', in *Crime and the Law: The Social History of Crime in Western Europe since 1500*, ed. V. A. C. Gatrell, Bruce Lenman, and Geoffrey Parker (London: Europa Publications, 1980), pp. 97–119.
25 The ideology of equality before the law is examined by Douglas Hay in 'Property, Authority, and the Criminal Law', along with the other essays in *Albion's Fatal Tree: Crime and Society in Eighteenth-Century England*, ed. Douglas Hay, Peter Linebaugh, John G. Rule, E. P. Thompson, and Cal Winslow (New York: Pantheon Books, 1975) and E. P. Thompson, *Whigs and Hunters: The Origins of the Black Act* (New York: Pantheon Books, 1975), esp. pp. 258–269. The scholarship on crime in eighteenth-century Britain includes J. M. Beattie, *Crime and the Courts in England, 1660–1800* (Princeton, NJ: Princeton University Press, 1986); Peter King, *Crime, Justice, and Discretion in England, 1740–1820* (Oxford: Oxford University Press, 2000); Peter King, 'Decision-Makers and Decision-Making in English Criminal Law, 1750–1800', *The Historical Journal* 27 (1984), pp. 51–58; John Langbein, *Origins of Adversary Criminal Trial* (Oxford: Oxford University Press, 2005); and David Lemmings, *Law and Government in England during the Long Eighteenth Century: From Consent to Command* (Houndmills: Palgrave Macmillan, 2011).
26 Thompson, *Whigs and Hunters*, p. 266.
27 Catherine Hall, *Civilising Subjects: Colony and Metropole in the English Imagination, 1830–1867* (Chicago, IL: University of Chicago Press, 2002); Catherine Hall, *Macaulay*

and Son: Architects of Imperial Britain (New Haven, CT: Yale University Press, 2012); Catherine Hall and Sonya Rose, eds., At Home with the Empire: Metropolitan Culture and the Imperial World (Cambridge: Cambridge University Press, 2006); Kathleen Wilson, A Sense of the People: Politics, Culture and Imperialism in England, 1715–1785 (Cambridge: Cambridge University Press, 1995); Kathleen Wilson, The Island Race: Englishness, Empire and Gender in the Eighteenth Century (New York: Routledge, 2003); and Wilson, ed., A New Imperial History: Culture, Identity, and Modernity in Britain and the Empire, 1660–1840 (Cambridge: Cambridge University Press, 2004).

28 Scholars of the eighteenth century have taken up the theme of difference. See the special issue on difference in Eighteenth Century Studies 23 (1990) edited by Felicity Nussbaum; Felicity Nussbaum, Torrid Zones: Maternity, Sexuality, and Empire in Eighteenth-Century English Narratives (Baltimore, MD: Johns Hopkins University Press, 1995); Felicity Nussbaum, The Limits of the Human: Fictions of Anomaly, Race, and Gender in the Long Eighteenth Century (Cambridge: Cambridge University Press, 2003); Roxann Wheeler, The Complexion of Race: Categories of Difference in Eighteenth-Century British Culture (Philadelphia, PA: University of Pennsylvania Press, 2000); Dror Wahrman, The Making of the Modern Self: Identity and Culture in Eighteenth-Century England (New Haven, CT: Yale University Press, 2004); Valerie Traub, 'Mapping the Global Body', in Early Modern Visual Culture: Representation, Race, and Empire in Renaissance England, ed. Peter Erickson and Clark Hulse (Philadelphia, PA: University of Pennsylvania Press, 2000): 44–97; and Laura Brown, Ends of Empire: Women and Ideology in Early Eighteenth-Century English Literature (Ithaca, NY: Cornell University Press, 1993). On ethnicity in distinction to race see Colin Kidd, 'Ethnicity in the British Atlantic World, 1688–1830', in New Imperial History, ed. Kathleen Wilson (Cambridge: Cambridge University Press, 2004), pp. 260–277.

29 Lauren Benton, A Search for Sovereignty: Law and Geography in European Empires, 1400–1900 (Cambridge: Cambridge University Press, 2010); Eliga Gould, 'Zones of Law, Zones of Violence: The Legal Geography of the British Atlantic, circa 1772', William and Mary Quarterly 60 (2003), pp. 471–510; James Epstein, Scandal of Colonial Rule: Power and Subversion in the British Atlantic during the Age of Revolution (Cambridge: Cambridge University Press, 2012); Paul Halliday, Habeas Corpus: From England to Empire (Cambridge, MA: Harvard University Press, 2010); P. J. Marshall, 'Britain and the World in the Eighteenth Century: IV, The Turning Outwards of Britain', Transactions of the Royal Historical Society 11 (2001), pp. 1–15. The legal relationship between colony and metropole was pioneered by Jack P. Green, Peripheries and Center: Constitutional Development in the Extended Polities of the British Empire and the United States, 1607–1788 (Athens, GA: University of Georgia Press, 1986); and Mary Sarah Bilder, The Transatlantic Constitution: Colonial Legal Culture and the Empire (Cambridge, MA: Harvard University Press, 2004).

30 Two recent books examine issues of race and integration in nineteenth- and twentieth-century London. Saree Makdisi, Making England Western: Occidentalism, Race and Imperial Culture (Chicago, IL: University of Chicago Press, 2014); and Marc Matera, Black London: the Imperial Metropolis and Decolonization in the Twentieth Century (Oakland, CA: University of California Press, 2015).

31 Donna T. Andrew, Aristocratic Vice: The Attack on Duelling, Suicide, Adultery, and Gambling in Eighteenth-Century England (New Haven, CT: Yale University Press, 2013), pp. 9–10, 37–41.

32 Diana Donald, The Age of Caricature: Satirical Prints in the Reign of George III (New Haven, CT: Yale University Press, 1996), pp. 1–21. For more on caricature, see Amelia Rauser, Caricature Unmasked: Irony, Authenticity, and Individualism in Eighteenth-Century English Prints (Newark, DE: University of Delaware Press, 2008).

33 Vron War and Les Back, Out of Whiteness: Color, Politics, and Culture (Chicago, IL: University of Chicago Press, 2002), p. 13.

34 Carey, Boucher, and Ellinghaus, 'Reorienting Whiteness', in Re-Orienting Whiteness, ed. Carey, Boucher, and Ellinghaus, p. 2.

INTRODUCTION: EMPIRE AND LAW

35 For more on whiteness and its critics, see David Roediger, *The Wages of Whiteness: Race and the Making of the American Working Class* (New York: Verson, 1999); Homi Bhabha, 'The White Stuff', *Artforum International* 36 (1998), pp. 21–24; and Robyn Wiegman, 'Whiteness Studies and the Paradox of Particularity', *Boundary 2* 26 (1998), pp. 115–150. For empire and whiteness, see Radhika Mohanram, *Imperial White: Race, Diaspora, and the British Empire* (Minneapolis, MN: University of Minnesota Press, 2007); Sara Ahmed, 'A Phenomenology of Whiteness', *Feminist Theory* 8 (2007), pp. 149–168. For studies of whiteness in the eighteenth century, see Cecily Jones, *Engendering Whiteness: White Women and Colonialism in Barbados and North Carolina, 1627–1865* (Manchester: Manchester University Press, 2007) and Wilson, *Island Race*, esp. ch. 2.

36 *Oxford English Dictionary* (OED).

37 The third aspect of whiteness is 'a set of cultural practices that are usually unmarked and unnamed'. Ruth Frankenberg, *White Women, Race Matters: The Social Construction of Whiteness* (Minneapolis, MN: University of Minnesota Press, 1993), p. 1.

38 M. Frye Jacobson, *Whiteness of a Different Color: European Immigrants and the Alchemy of Race* (Cambridge, MA: Harvard University Press, 1998), p. 6. See also, Georgia Shiells, 'Immigration History and Whiteness Studies: American and Australian Approaches Compared', *History Compass* 8 (2010), pp. 790–804.

39 Jenny Shaw, *Everyday Life in the Early English Caribbean: Irish, Africans, and the Construction of Difference* (Athens, GA: University of Georgia Press, 2013); Jones, *Engendering Whiteness*; and Michael Monahan, *The Creolizing Subject: Race, Reason, and the Politics of Purity* (New York: Fordham University Press, 2011).

40 Kim Brooks and Robert Leckey, eds. *Queer Theory: Law, Culture, Empire* (London: Routledge, 2010), pp. 4–5.

41 My approach is influenced by queer theory, which begins with the definition of queer: to make strange, to frustrate, to counteract, and applies it as a methodological tool. Although the definition of queer theory remains insistently vague, it seeks to analyze and disturb 'relationships of power and knowledge that shape desires, behaviors, social institutions and social relations'. Nikki Sullivan, *A Critical Introduction to Queer Theory* (Edinburgh: Edinburgh University Press, 2003), p. 51. Deconstructing familiar binaries, such as natural and unnatural, homosexual and heterosexual, queer theory demonstrates the instability and contingency of these categories and the ways they are mutually constituted to uncover how they order ways of knowing and thinking. The law is central to these binaries, and homosexuality, always deemed sterile and barren, threatens bonds of family as well as the possession and inheritance of property. See Sullivan, *Critical Introduction to Queer Theory*, p. 51 and Sue-Ellen Case, 'Tracking the Vampire', *Differences: A Journal of Feminist Cultural Studies* 3 (1991), pp. 1–20. Queer theory situates desire and technologies of containment at the center of its analytical gaze. As Case shows, the desires for freedom, rights, and rule of law often competed with desires for order and hierarchies of ethnicity, religion, race, and gender.

42 Here the insights from queer theory have been especially helpful. Sara Ahmed, *Queer Phenomenology: Orientations, Objects, Others* (Durham, NC: Duke University Press, 2006); Judith Butler, *Gender Trouble: Feminism and the Subversion of Identity* (New York: Routledge, 1999); Michael Warner, *Fear of a Queer Planet: Queer Politics and Social Theory* (Minneapolis, MN: University of Minnesota Press, 1993), pp. vii–xxxi; Cathy Cohen, 'Punks, Bulldaggers, and Welfare Queens: The Radical Potential of Queer Politics?', *GLQ* 3.4 (1997), pp. 437–465; Noreen Giffney, 'Introduction: The "q" word', *Ashgate Companion to Queer Theory*, ed. Noreen Giffney and Michael O'Rourke (Farnham: Ashgate, 2009), pp. 1–13; Leslie Moran, Daniel Monk, and Sara Beresford, eds., *Legal Queeries: Lesbian, Gay and Transgender Legal Studies* (London: Cassell, 1998).

43 Nicholas Rogers in his recent book *Mayhem: Post-War Crime and Violence in Britain 1748–1753* (New Haven, CT: Yale University Press, 2012) analyzes several case studies to highlight the anxieties and preoccupations of Britain in the immediate aftermath of the War of Austrian Succession.

44 For more, see P. J. Marshall, 'Britain and the World'.
45 Karen Macfarlane, '"Does He Know the Danger of an Oath": Oaths, Religion, Ethnicity and the Advent of the Adversarial Criminal Trial in the Eighteenth Century', *Immigrants & Minorities* 31 (2013), pp. 317–345. For more on legal reform, see Leon Radzinowicz, *A History of English Criminal Law and its Administration from 1750*, 4 vols. Volume 1: *The Movement for Reform* (London: Macmillan, 1948).
46 Karan Macfarlane, 'Understanding Justice: Criminal Courtroom Interpretation in Eighteenth-Century London and Twenty-First Century Toronto', *Traduction, Terminologie, Rédaction* 20 (2007), pp. 271–299; Susan Ballyn and Lucy Frost, 'Speaking in Tongues: Non-English Speakers at the Old Bailey', paper read at the conference Tales from the Old Bailey: Writing a New History From Below University of Hertfordshire, July 5–6, 2004; Christopher Stone and Bencie Woll, '"Dumb O Jemmy and Others": Deaf People, Interpreters, and the London Courts in the Eighteenth and Nineteenth Centuries', *Sign Language Studies* 8 (2008), pp. 226–240.
47 In 'Sir Lloyd Kenyon's (1732–1802): Preaching from the Bench' (unpublished paper shared with the author) James Oldham demonstrates the foundational place of Christianity and the Church of England in Kenyon's philosophy and practice of English law.
48 For the treatment of non-white defendants in court, see Peter King, 'Ethnicity, Prejudice, and Justice: The Treatment of the Irish at the Old Bailey, 1750–1825', *The Journal of British Studies* 52 (2013), pp. 390–414 and Peter King, *Ethnicity, Crime and Justice 1700–1830* (forthcoming).
49 The intersection of law and empire pioneered by among others Catherine Hall cited above includes Bridget Brereton, *Law, Justice, and Empire: the Colonial Career of John Gorrie* (Kingston: University of the West Indies Press, 1997); John McLaren, *Dewigged, Bothered, and Bewildered: British Colonial Judges on Trial, 1800–1900* (Toronto: University of Toronto Press, 2011); and Diane Paton, *No Bond but the Law: Punishment, Race, and Gender in Jamaican State Formation, 1780–1870* (Durham, NC: Duke University Press, 2004). The generative conference on Legal Histories of the British Empire resulted in Shaunnagh Dorsett and John McLaren, eds., *Legal Histories of the British Empire: Laws, Engagements and Legacies* (New York: Routledge, 2014).
50 Benton, *A Search for Sovereignty*, pp. 28–33.
51 Hussain, *Jurisprudence of Emergency*.
52 Gould, 'Zones of Law'.
53 Hussain defines emergency as a 'situation of factual danger whereby the existence of the state is threatened, [which] allows for the suspension of the normative universe of a rule of law', *Jurisprudence of Emergency*, p. 16.
54 'The state's sovereignty is unlimited and figured as logically prior to the law that the state submits to and uses to articulate its legitimacy', Hussain, *Jurisprudence of Emergency*, p. 18. According to John Locke in *Second Treatise of Government* (Raleigh, NC: Generic NL Freebook Publisher, n.d.; *eBook Collection [EBSCOhost]*, EBSCO*host* [accessed February 5, 2016]), p. 90:

> This power to act according to discretion for the public good, without the prescription of the law, and sometimes even against it, is that which is called prerogative: for since in some governments the law-making power is not always in being, and is usually too numerous and so too slow, for the dispatch requisite to execution and because also it is impossible to foresee and so to provide for all accidents and necessities that may concern the public, or to make such laws as will do no harm, if they are executed with an inflexible rigour, on all occasions, and upon all persons that may come in their way, therefore there is a latitude left to the executive power to do many things of choice which the laws do not prescribe.

Montesquieu, Charles de Secondat, baron de, 1689–1755. *The Spirit of the Laws* (New York: D. Appleton and Co., 1900), p. 185.

INTRODUCTION: EMPIRE AND LAW

But should the legislature think itself in danger by some secret conspiracy against the state, or by a correspondence with a foreign enemy, it might authorize the executive power for a short and limited time, to imprison suspected persons, who in that case would lose their liberty only for a while, to preserve it forever.

55 Blackstone, *Commentaries*, vol. 1, p. 132.
56 Hussain, *Jurisprudence of Emergency*, p. 17.
57 Hussain, *Jurisprudence of Emergency*, p. 20.
58 Judith Butler, 'Merely Cultural', *New Left Review* 227 (1998), pp. 33–44.
59 Granville Sharp, *A declaration of the people's natural right to a share in the legislature; which is the fundamental principle of the British constitution of state* (London: B. White, 1775), p. 12, emphasis in original.
60 Sharp, *Declaration*, p. 20, emphasis in original.

CHAPTER ONE

Internal others: Jews, Gypsies, and Jacobites

This chapter analyzes a series of legal events involving Britain's internal outsiders that unfolded in 1753: the sensational disappearance and reappearance of Elizabeth Canning (1735–1773); the passage (May 1753) and repeal (November 1753) of the Jewish Naturalization Act (26 Geo II, c. 26) which would have allowed Parliament to naturalize individual Jewish men if they secured the passage of a private Act of Parliament; and the execution of Archibald Cameron (June 1753) a Scottish Jacobite who helped to plan the aborted Elibank Plot. The legal proceedings included: two criminal cases, involving Elizabeth Canning and Mary Squires, a Gypsy, an Act of Parliament, and a Jacobite plan for a failed rebellion. Each involved at least one person or a group defined as other: women, Gypsies, Jews, and Scottish Jacobites. These entangled stories unfolded within days of each other – Cameron's condemnation on May 17 upon an act of attainder passed against him and the others involved in the Jacobite Rebellion of 1745, Mary Squires' pardon on May 21, the passage of the Jew Bill on May 22, and Cameron's execution on June 7 – capturing the imagination of writers, readers, and political cartoonists. But first a little background.

Financial revolution, rule of law, and naturalization

The debates about immigration and naturalization that raged in Britain's parliament, in the press, and on its streets in the late seventeenth and early eighteenth centuries point to the impact of several interrelated developments, particularly Britain's financial revolution and its imperial expansion. Starting in the middle of the seventeenth century Britain expanded dynamically, widening its economic, financial, and commercial networks in the British Isles and across the globe. The financial revolution that unfolded in the late seventeenth century and throughout the eighteenth century created what John Brewer has called the fiscal-military state.[1] The components of this process included the establishment of the Bank of England, the growth of the national debt, commodity markets, colonial possessions, and Britain's involvement in the slave trade. Fiscal innovations expanded the availability of short-term loans that funded new industries like fire insurance, partnership banks, and trading companies, and improved infrastructure with new canals and roads. They created 'a whole range of securities in which mercantile and financial houses could safely invest' or disinvest.[2] Long-term public borrowing created an alternate revenue stream for the government and compensated for the shortfalls of taxes that, though relatively high, did not bring in enough money to pay for the ships and men necessary for the almost constant conduct of war over the long eighteenth-century. The expansion of the government's apparatus, which seemed to contradict long-held English aversions to a standing army and high taxes, was counterbalanced by the discourse of rule of law, an ideology that proclaimed equality before the law and the protection of individual rights.[3]

Indeed E. P. Thompson observed that 'the law was elevated during this century to a role more prominent than any other period of our history'[4] while Douglas Hay has argued that 'the criminal law was critically important in maintaining bonds of obedience and deference, in legitimizing the status quo, in constantly recreating the structure of authority'. Hay concluded that 'the criminal law, more than any other social institution made it possible to govern eighteenth-century England without a police force, and without a large army'.[5] These analyses of the eighteenth century are based on the comments of contemporaries like Reeve Ballard who declaimed in a 1745 assize sermon that 'All Government was design'd for the benefit of the Governed, and the Laws are the Strength and Sinews of it.'[6] Martin Madan (1725–1790) summarized the law's role in legitimating and securing order and good governance: 'the honour and welfare of the kingdom in general, as well as the security and happiness of individuals, must depend on a due administration of the law'.[7] Equality before the law was often expressed though praise for the law's impartiality. At an assize sermon Kent in 1733 James Bate credited 'the due, regular, and impartial Execution of our Laws' to the nation's 'substantial Happiness' while Richard Green averred that 'the most necessary thing for the Welfare of Society is a regular and impartial Administration of Justice'.[8] Green elaborated on the hierarchies fundamental to English society, 'divided into Superiors and Inferiors', but he stipulated that in the eyes of the law all must be considered 'in the Light of Equals, namely, as having all an equal Claim to Justice'.[9] Contemporaries, both elites and ordinary people, touted the rule of law as their English 'birthright' and many exclaimed as Ballard did that 'in no Nation upon Earth, is there such an equal administration of Justice, as in our Nation'.[10] As David Lemmings has written 'a culture of grass-roots participation in legal processes determining issues of life and property was taken for granted and valued explicitly because it betokened freedom, consent, and equity ... given such an inheritance of law, governments and particular laws were expected to conform to notions of substantive justice'.[11]

In the wake of the tremendous growth in the British government and economy, its contact with foreign places and people, and its imperial expansion an intermittent debate unfolded in the English press and in parliament about the place of foreigners seeking to settle in England, their rights, and whether the government ought to pursue policies that encouraged or discouraged immigration. Prior to the Jewish Naturalization Bill and the controversy that ensued in 1753, there had been several initiatives to facilitate the naturalization of immigrants to Britain. Several immigration bills made it to a parliamentary floor debate (1693, 1751), and the two Acts that passed (1709, 1753) were both later repealed.[12]

In the late seventeenth century Josiah Child (1631–1699) advocated more liberal immigration policies, which he argued would promote free trade and decrease the price of labor. Later, 'populationists' like John Toland (1670–1722) and Josiah Tucker (1713–1799) claimed that England's wealth depended on a growing population they believed was depleted by colonial emigration. Although an attempt to pass a naturalization act in 1693 in the wake of the revocation of the Edict of Nantes, in 1685, had failed, Whig efforts to settle Protestants fleeing religious persecution succeeded during the War of Spanish Succession (1701–1714) with passage of the Foreign Protestants Naturalization Act 1709 (7 Ann c. 5). Between May and June 1709 close to 12,000 German refugees – most of them Protestants from the Palatinate – immigrated to England costing the government £130,000. The act was considered a drain on the country's finances and a humiliation to the Whigs: it was repealed when the Tories came to power in 1712.[13]

The opponents of naturalization included anyone who represented or had a stake in monopolies, city corporations, and guilds, foremost among these, the Corporation of London. Each time a new naturalization effort gained momentum in 1747, 1748, and 1751, Tories reprised many of the concerns rehearsed in the debate of the Act of 1709 about the threat that naturalization posed to English men's property rights and employment opportunities. The arguments made against naturalization in parliamentary debates and popular pamphlet literature included elaborate warnings about religious difference: the Act of 1709 aimed at Protestants threw up fears of the increased presence of dissenters in England. This discourse became sharper in 1753 when the subject was Jewish naturalization.[14]

The Empire featured in multifaceted ways in these arguments. John Toland's support for naturalization included a reference to the need to replace English people 'who yearly go to the *Plantations*, and in the service of the *East India* Company; not to speak of our Armies, fleets, or Adventurers'. Advocates of naturalization proposed that new immigrants could move to less settled areas in the British Isles. This internal colonization would serve 'for breaking up and cultivating those desert, yet not barren grounds, of which there is still but too great a quantity in *Scotland* and *Ireland* ... under the name of Heaths, Moors, Bogs, Fens, and Commons'.[15]

The subject of naturalization emerged again in the mid-century after the War of Austrian Succession. Britain faced the realities of the war's expense, which had increased the national debt by more than £30 million. To make matters worse the inconclusive peace did not seem to resolve the imperial disputes and rivalries, particularly with France, that had caused the war in the first place. Social and economic dislocation, the demobilization of 80,000 sailors and soldiers, unemployment, and crime in the post-war period exacerbated panic in the city of London. Extensive analyses of the 'crime wave' appeared in newspapers, pamphlets, and periodicals between 1749 and 1753. Observers noted the frequent and bold nature of crime, the violence that often accompanied it, and the license with which criminals and gangs operated. At stake were the security of property, deference, and the paternalist social order.[16]

Rather than Sir Lewis Namier's characterization of the mid-century as a time of political stability, calm, and confidence, Nick Rogers describes a period 'of deep anxiety, if not panic, about the state of the country and its capacity to continue a war that everyone feared had been abandoned only temporarily'.[17] According to Kathleen Wilson the early 1750s were 'marked by a deepening sense of national malaise, stimulated by xenophobia ... exacerbated by imperial rivalries and tinged by sharpening anti-aristocratic sensibilities'.[18] The unsettled calm of this tense period between the War of Austrian Succession (1748) and the Seven Years' War (1756–1763) threw into relief uncertainty and doubt about Britain's imperial and commercial future.[19]

'The Dreadful Consequences of a General Naturalization, to the Natives of Great-Britain and Ireland' (1751) (Figure 1.1) captured the tenor of the times. The image declared in no uncertain terms that the influx of immigrants into Britain promised Britons a 'dismal Fate'.

Figure 1.1 'The Dreadful Consequences of a General Naturalization, to the Natives of Great-Britain and Ireland'

In the broadside, which included both an image and a poem, Britannia, the ever-generous mother, sheltered and provided for 'vast Swarms of every sort'. Setting her shield and spear aside, she offered an open cornucopia to 'these, of ev'ry Realm the Scum' who beseeched her for 'Relief of all their Wants'. The poem introduced this 'motley Troop' as a Palatine, a Spaniard, a 'Musselman' (Muslim), an Italian, a Jew, a German, a Dutchman, a Blackamoor, and a Frenchman, ragged and barefoot. Counseling against admission of the 'wretched, Ragged, Hungry', the poem advised Britain to provide for its own poor instead. In contrast to more typical representations of British naval power and the Empire's growing strength in the figure of Britannia (usually portrayed standing in the ocean wearing a Corinthian helmet, clad in white robes, and holding Poseidon's three-pronged trident), this print grounded Britannia's throne solidly on British soil.[20]

Decrying the vulnerability of the national body and the limits of the integration and assimilation of non-natives, the print attacked the Naturalization Bill of 1751. With its warning that the 'countless Multitude Must on our Liberties intrude' and its prediction that 'our Artisans/ [are] Hast'ning away to foreign lands', the poem described the anger and fear many eighteenth-century Britons felt about immigration borne of imperial contact. In other words, at home 'Such a base raggamuffian Crew' would constrain Britons' legal rights while encouraging outmigration represented in the far right where a respectable English couple boarded a ship, presumably bound for the colonies.

Populationists proffered a solution to the widespread unemployment and increasingly visible poverty arguing that encouraging immigration would rebuild England's strength after the war and expand commerce. Historians have characterized the Plantation Act 1740 (13 Geo. II c. 7), which allowed for the naturalization of foreigners who had lived in the American colonies for seven years and exempted Quakers and Jews from Christian oaths, as a compromise made to advocates of naturalization. After the defeat of two bills that would have allowed Jewish naturalization in 1746 and 1747, the next big initiative for naturalization in England's Parliament, led by Robert Nugent (1709–1788), MP for Bristol, was a general naturalization bill. Nugent's attempt failed, as did the general naturalization bills proposed in 1748 and 1751.[21]

'A Scene of Scenes'

'A Scene of Scenes for the Year 1853' (Figure 1.2), published in London sometime toward the end of 1753, projected the artist's view of London

Figure 1.2 'Scene of Scenes for the Year 1853'

'one hundred years in the future'. A blindfolded body hanging on a gallows, a crowded mob scene, and a flogging combine to create a jarring array of violent images that interrogate the integrity of legal institutions and the power of the state. Prominently featured at the center of the print is a statue of a well-dressed man, Samson Gideon (1699–1762), a wealthy Jewish Londoner mistakenly credited with initiating the Jewish Naturalization Act, leaning on what appear to be the Ten Commandments. Behind the statue hangs the body of Dr. Archibald Cameron (1707–1753) executed for his participation in the Jacobite uprising of 1745. In front of the gallows Sir William Calvert, a well-known advocate of the Jewish Naturalization Bill of 1753, undergoes a circumcision while others who supported the bill look on, impatiently awaiting the procedure. At the far right a man is being flogged as he leans on the back of a cart labeled 'G[ascoy]ns intire Butt Beer'. This refers to Sir Crisp Gascoyne (1700–1761), the Lord Mayor of London, himself a brewer. A 'Gypsy woman', one Mary Squires, looks on.[22]

The image represents only a few of Britain's 'internal others' in the eighteenth century, the many who called London home who were not considered English. What did rule of law mean for them? How were they treated when they were pulled into a legal setting and what do these interactions reveal about the ideology of rule of law and its promise of equality before the law? The ideology of rule of law and equality before the law allowed for a more rationalized and efficient marking of disparity. The early modern world had marginalized people for religious and ethnic difference, but those markers were increasingly difficult to enforce in a confessionally divided England, Scotland, and Wales, and an ethnically, religiously, and culturally diverse empire at a time when race and skin color entangled to produce yet another category of difference. Law provided a means of integrating those deemed acceptable in a specific time and place and under certain defined circumstances while excluding others.

Britain's claims to equality before the law drew these internal others into the legal and legislative system and their presence and participation in London's courtrooms and streets challenged longstanding notions of English identity. As the Empire expanded and encompassed ever greater cultural, religious, ethnic, and racial variation, London, England, and Britain did too, creating tension between the stated ideal of equality before the law and its necessarily irregular application in the metropole. The following analysis demonstrates the unresolved struggle that took place between those who espoused the ideology of rule of law and the liberal discourse of free trade and cosmopolitanism and those who believed in the distinction between the rights of white, Anglican

Englishmen and the rights and privileges of others. Despite the discourse of rule of law and the growing emphasis on equality before the law and Enlightenment universalism in the eighteenth century, the English legal process maintained and sustained distinctions of class, gender, ethnicity, and religion.

Below we focus on Mary Squires' trial for the kidnapping of Elizabeth Canning and the Jewish Naturalization Act.[23] Both the furor over Canning's case and Jewish naturalization reveal a cultural conflict over empire and its implications – a real split between those who desired the endeavor and those who harbored doubts about it. These two case studies allow us to witness the inconsistencies inherent in the discussions about how to apply the rule of law to internal others, implicitly excluded from its rhetorical promises. The cases reveal alarm about the mix of religious and ethnic minorities living in close proximity and the political challenges the cases evoked over a one-year period, giving rise to anxieties about who was British, what made Britain a nation, and the relationship between nation and empire. They seemed to encapsulate the uncertainties of the mid-eighteenth century, warning of the destabilizing force of 'others', Jews, Scots, and Gypsies, cast as intruders in the metropole. The Canning case, featuring a Gypsy and five single women, showcases the threatening nature of poor single women and their status as outsiders. It serves as a metaphor for the dangers of mobility and commerce in the hands of non-English intruders and signals the much bigger threat posed by Jews and the Jewish Naturalization Act, the subject of the second case study featured here. The two together demonstrate how the legal category of whiteness, which implied a white, male, English, Anglican subject, emerged as a site through which to identify, define, and arbitrate the implications of empire at home.

The sorceress, the servant, and the stays

On New Year's Day 1753 Elizabeth Canning, an eighteen-year-old servant maid, disappeared from her home in London's East End, apparently a victim of kidnapping. When she returned to her mother's home a month later, she explained her disappearance by accusing a woman, later identified as Mary Squires, 'Gypsy', of arranging her abduction, attempting to lure her to a life of prostitution, and keeping her a prisoner on bread and water for 28 days in a house in Enfield. In addition to her allegations against Mary Squires, Canning implicated Susannah Wells, a reputed brothel keeper. At the trial of Squires and Wells held at the Old Bailey in February 1753 a young prostitute, memorably named Virtue Hall, who had been arrested along with them, testified that she was living at Wells' house in January and had witnessed Canning's capture. Based on this evidence, the two older women were arrested and accused of assaulting Elizabeth Canning and stealing her belongings: Squires was sentenced to death and Wells to six months in jail. But contradictory evidence presented at the trial raised doubts about the facts of the case. An investigation by Sir Crisp Gascoyne, Lord Mayor of London, resulted in Virtue Hall recanting her testimony, and on May 21, 1753 Squires was granted a full pardon. Elizabeth Canning was brought to trial for perjury in April 1754; she was found guilty and transported to the American colonies.[24]

As it unfolded, the case became a 'trial of the century', 'the conversation of every alehouse within the bills of mortality', generating an unprecedented amount of published material including broadsides, ballads, pamphlets, and prints.[25] A pamphlet war raged between Canning's supporters, known as the Canningites, and the 'Egyptians', accused of supporting the Gypsy because they raised questions about the young woman's true whereabouts for the first twenty-eight days of January 1753. Although we may never know what really happened, the case points to the relationship between law and outsiders in the mid-eighteenth century.[26]

As in the other cases that unfolded in 1753, the discussion of evidentiary details provided a forum for a debate about the implications of Britain's imperial expansion, specifically the reality of a religiously, racially, and ethnically diverse London populated by Jews, Gypsies, Asians, Africans, Scots, Irish, Catholics, and non-conforming Protestants, for definitions of Englishness as a cultural tradition and England as a nation.[27] Each of the single women who appear in the case could be classified among England's internal others: Elizabeth Canning, a single servant, her mother, also Elizabeth, Suzanne Wells, referred to throughout as a 'bawd', Mary Squires, 'Gypsy', and Virtue Hall, a reputed prostitute. An examination of the nexus of race and sexuality in the narratives of Elizabeth Canning, Mary Squires, and Virtue Hall, reveals the explicit disputes about these women – their whereabouts, their physical integrity, and their moral character. The written record left by the case exposed an unwieldy female autonomy that made a lie of conventions regarding English femininity, domesticity, chastity, and virtue, and collapsed imagined spatial divisions within the metropole. Ultimately discomforts associated with mobility and the mixing endemic of empire propelled the Canning case into the headlines and the alehouses accentuating the moral and social threats believed to lurk in empire's multiplicity of sites and the mobile bodies that moved in its shadows and hidden spaces.[28]

I suggest that although a prurient interest in sex may have spurred initial attention, an examination of the intersection of sexuality and race in the case reveals the story's repercussions for definitions of belonging that gave the scandal its wide appeal. With its exaggerated images of Mary Squires as a Gypsy, defined as 'a member of a wandering race (by themselves called Romany)', who first arrived in England at the beginning of the sixteenth century, 'believed to have come from Egypt', the story foregrounded long-held fears about vagrancy and concerns about insiders, outsiders, and interlopers as it revealed the reality of geographic mobility that shattered early modern notions of continuity, place, and community, considered the most trustworthy means of measuring character and credibility.[29] Each site mentioned in the accounts mapped a specific cultural meaning, each place imagined as distinct and separate. Mention of Aldermanbury Postern confirmed negative associations of London's East End with working-class poverty and crime while Dorchester's proximity to the coast summoned images of smuggling.[30] As the site of Susannah Well's brothel, Enfield Wash contaminated rural respectability, the hospitality offered there immoral, threatening, and criminal. The appearance of all three locations in the same story destabilized a geographical imagination that relied on the strict division of place as an authentic constant and space as a signifier of contact and interrelationships.[31]

Proponents on each side, whether Canningites or Egyptians, read their 'evidence' about who belonged 'to a civilized Nation'[32] and who posed 'the greatest danger to the safety of all his majesty's good subjects'[33] on the bodies of Elizabeth Canning, Mary Squires, and Virtue Hall supporting their case with a set of 'facts' they claimed as authoritative and definitive.[34] Attention to the legal setting must foreground any discussion of the Canning story. Such an examination sheds new light on the intersection of English law and British imperial aspiration in the eighteenth century. Despite Henry Fielding's claim that 'there is nothing more admirable, nor indeed more amiable, in the Law of England, than the extreme Tenderness with which it proceeds against Persons accused of capital Crimes', Squires' conviction and death sentence reflected a cultural consensus about the inherent criminality of Gypsies.[35] Her trial and subsequent pardon along with Canning's perjury trial a year later became a test of the ideology of fairness and equality before the criminal law so often praised as uniquely English and cited as proof of English superiority.[36] The representations of Canning as the virtuous white woman, Hall as the white prostitute, and Squires as a non-white foreign procuress luring Englishwomen into an immoral livelihood determined the definition of the crime and the credibility assigned to each witness. The adversarial process created evidence to validate Canning's accusations and to substantiate her story despite its myriad inconsistencies.

The first story

On Wednesday January 31, three days after Canning's reappearance, the *London Daily Advertiser* reported her return to her mother's house in Aldermanbury Postern. In the 'extraordinary account' attributed to Elizabeth herself, Canning described her visit with her aunt and uncle, Alice and Thomas Colley, on New Year's Day at Saltpetre Bank. After dinner, Mr. and Mrs. Colley walked her half of the way home, leaving her at Houndsditch (Figure 1.3). She continued to Moorfields by Bethlehem-wall where she said 'two fellows ... pulled off her hat and gown, cut off her apron, then gagged her, and threatened her with bitter imprecations if she cried out to cut her throat'.[37]

They carried Elizabeth to the house of 'one mother Wells' in Enfield where they arrived at four in the morning. According to Elizabeth the two men left her at the house, and 'the woman of the house immediately cut off her stays ... and with horridest execrations forced her into a room, where she was kept upon bread and water'.[38] The story of the crime abruptly shifted to Elizabeth's escape four weeks later when she 'broke her way through a window almost naked, and in that wretched condition came home' leaving 'several unhappy young women in the house, whose misfortune she has providentially escaped'.[39] The threat of sexual transgression shapes this account. Mary Squires, the Gypsy, did not appear in this version of the story; instead, the article implied that the owner of the house, Susannah Wells, had cut off Elizabeth's stays.

The first pamphlet about the case appeared following the arrests of Squires and Wells on February 1. It still referred to the women in the house as 'an old woman and two young ones', adding an alleged promise from the old woman that Elizabeth would 'want for nothing' 'if she would do as they did (which was whoring and thieving)'.[40] The pamphlet ascribed ownership of the house to 'that notorious woman ... mother Wells' and later referred to her as 'that monster of a woman'. It appealed to 'public-spirited people, and every one who has any regard for the safety of their own children and relations' for 'compassion and charitable contributions' and called for immediate action to detect and prevent 'the same inhuman and cruel usage' from 'such a nest of villains ... the greatest danger to the safety of all his majesty's good subjects'.[41] A moral panic spread concerns about young Englishwomen, their safety and virtue.

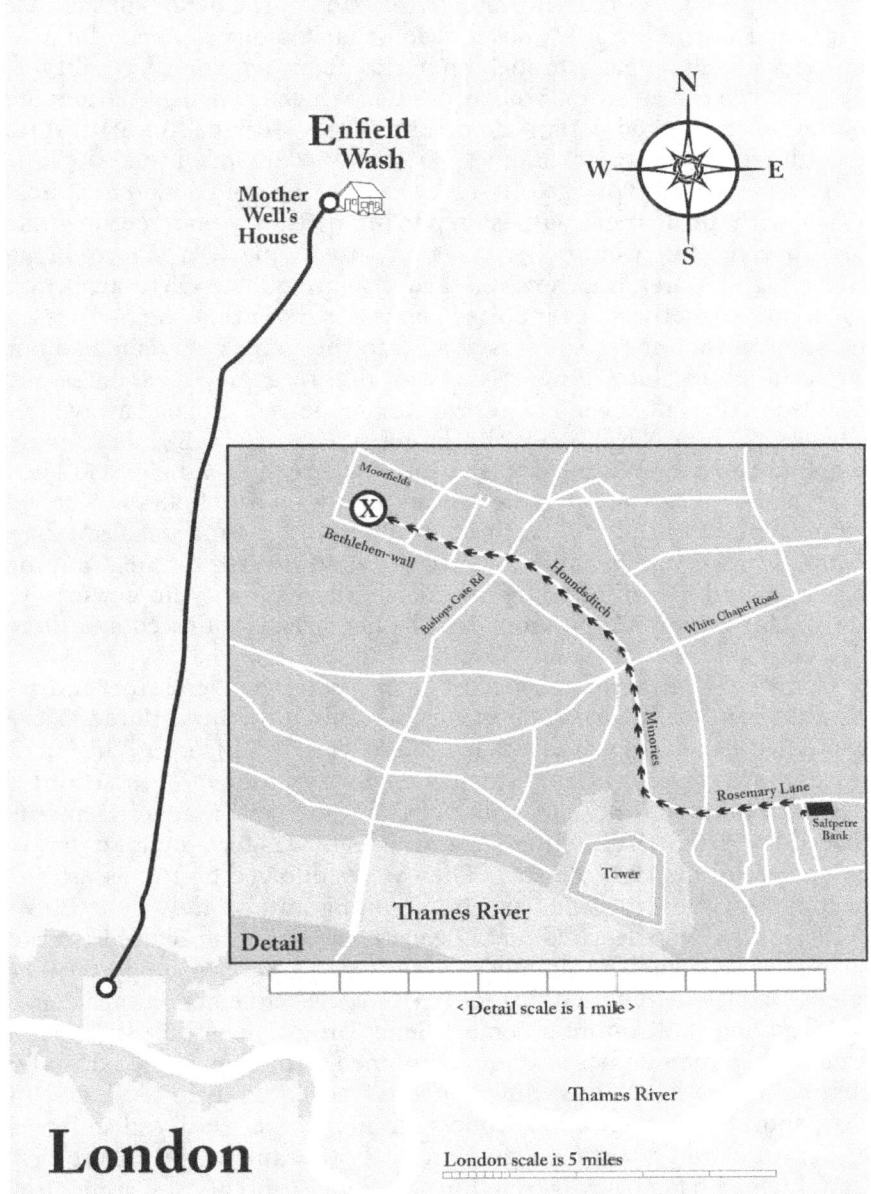

Figure 1.3 Elizabeth Canning's route through London and from London to Enfield

The obsessive speculation and (re)iteration of the details of the case confirm Kristina Straub's observation that 'anxieties about English identity are channeled through anxieties about women's sexuality ... [which] both threatens and constitutes that which is English'.[42] Alternate narratives expressed doubts about Elizabeth's story calling it 'absurd, incredible, and most ridiculous'.[43] Detractors demanded to know how she could have been dragged 10–12 miles from central London to Enfield Wash without a single witness reporting it, they wondered how she had survived for twenty-eight days on only a 'quartern loaf' of bread and a jug of water, and how she had disciplined herself to apportion the food so exactly. They inquired about her claim that she had passed no stool in the month she was gone, and they asked why she had not come home earlier seeing as she was able to escape as soon as she decided to do so.[44] Several of her earliest supporters dropped away after she was taken to Susannah Wells' home on February 1. Elizabeth could not find the stairs that led to the room where she said she had been kept, and her description of the attic as dark with bare floors was belied by two windows and a 'Quantity of Hay'.[45] Most glaring was Canning's dramatic change to her story: during the visit to Wells' home, Canning first saw and identified Mary Squires as the woman who cut off her stays. Until then only Susannah Wells had been implicated and there had been no mention of any Gypsy.

Canning's detractors accused her of sexual transgression and its results: venereal disease, abortion, childbirth, or infanticide. They explained her disappearance with references to a lover, a lying in, a miscarriage, or a salivation (treatment for syphilis).[46] These counter narratives may have originated in the missing person advertisements placed by Elizabeth's mother suggesting 'she was forcibly taken away by some evil-disposed Person'. They were followed by the assertions of the midwife, summoned by Mrs. Canning immediately upon Elizabeth's return, who declared that Elizabeth had not borne a child.[47] More suspicion of sexual misconduct came from Canning's supporter, Dr. James Dodd, who revealed that for five months before her disappearance she 'had had the Common Female Benefit totally obstructed'.[48] Dodd argued that such an obstruction, combined with Canning's 'naturally costive' nature, explained how she survived on so little food. Daniel Cox, another of Canning's defenders, discussed the relative cleanliness of her shift and concluded that the lack of stains on it meant that Canning had had no sexual relations during her absence.[49] Canningites and Egyptians alike showed no inhibitions about discussing the most intimate physical details of Canning's bodily functions and fluids. We see in this case the relational nature of Englishness, its ephemeral and constantly changing definition made visible in the women involved.

INTERNAL OTHERS: JEWS, GYPSIES, AND JACOBITES

The Gypsy becomes a witch

In light of the 'absurdities, inconsistencies and improbabilities' that riddled Canning's story, the definition of the crime and its investigation magnified markers of race, ethnicity, and nation. The first version of the story made no mention of the Gypsy; instead the story's tellers dichotomized familiar representations of Canning, the virtuous servant, chaste and domesticated, and Wells, the lewd, fallen woman, scolding and promiscuous, to construct a coherent narrative – designed for moral panic – out of the conflicting details. By the time of the trial three weeks later, however, the image of Mary Squires – Gypsy, criminal, and procuress – had emerged making the story a shocking, troubling scandal. These narratives relied on portrayals of Gypsies, as 'vagrants, paupers, and nomads' the 'worst face of an uncivilized and unacceptable society'.[50] Movement, mobility, and migration were critical to this representation.

Gypsies first arrived in England in the sixteenth century. Their nomadic lifestyle and association with vagrancy raised suspicion, and they faced prejudice, punishment, and expulsion. The first law against them, 'An Act concerning Egyptians' promulgated under Henry VIII in 1530, referred to 'outlandish People' who traveled from 'Shire to Shire' and used 'great, subtil, and crafty Means to deceive the People'. Accusing them of separating their victims from their money, the statute explicitly mentioned they did so with 'Palmestry' by which they told 'Mens and Womens Fortunes' by 'Craft and Subtilty' or by felony and robbery. The law ordered authorities to confiscate all their 'Goods and Chattels' and to remove Gypsies from the kingdom within fifteen days of their discovery.[51] In 1554 another law made it a felony without benefit of clergy for Gypsies to remain in the realm for more than a month; under Elizabeth the law criminalized associating with Gypsies for one month or 'counterfeiting, transforming or disguising' by adopting their clothing, habits, or lifestyle.[52] Literary sources also emphasized their foreignness and strangeness by stressing their mobility, their dress, and their separateness as a group.[53] Despite these harsh laws and some instances of large group banishment, expulsions ceased by the middle of Elizabeth's reign.[54] Most of those with Romani heritage were now born in England, their births and baptisms recorded in parish records.

Mention of 'an old Gipsey Woman' first appeared in newspapers reporting the arrests of Susannah Wells and Mary Squires on February 3.[55] Canning described Squires as a Gypsy when she was deposed by Henry Fielding on February 7.[56] On February 17 the *London Evening Post* commented that during her examination by Fielding on Thursday February 15, Squires 'behaved as a Person traditionally and hereditarily versed in the antient Egyptian Cunning, making the most religious Protestations of her Innocence; though she was afterwards heard to say, "Damn the young Bitch!"'[57] The story praised the 'Public-Spirited and humane Gentlemen' who had supported the 'poor, injured innocent Girl, and done such singular service to their country, by their Endeavours to eradicate from his Majesty's subjects a Gang of desperate and cruel Villains, of the greatest Danger to a civilized Nation'.[58] The words 'civilized Nation', absent from the earlier account identifying Wells as the perpetrator, appeared for the first time. While the earlier warnings had described threats facing 'his Majesty's subjects', the new wording suggests a focus on national boundaries. The descriptions of Mary Squires, Gypsy, drawing on older legal and literary representations of this group, clearly identified as an outsider, took a prominent place in the narrative with the law as its arbiter. In contrast, Elizabeth Canning, single, servant woman was now included as a white English subject, most certainly a constituent of the 'civilized nation'.

At the February 21 Old Bailey trial of Mary Squires and Susannah Wells, Squires was accused of assaulting Elizabeth Canning, 'putting her in corporal fear and danger of her life' and stealing 'one pair of stays, value 10s the property of the said Elizabeth'.[59] Wells was tried as her accomplice. The trial narrative conspicuously featured Mary Squires, Gypsy, and stereotypes about Gypsies played a central role in the recitation of the crime and its subsidiary details. These descriptions corroborated unflattering, threatening expectations of this ethnic group: an association with criminality, an itinerant lifestyle, a livelihood in sales, distinctive dress, a familiarity with magic, and an association with promiscuous sexuality.[60]

Mary Squires spoke up several times during the recitation of the evidence against her to deny any knowledge of Canning and to declare 'I am as innocent as the child unborn.' Perhaps strategically, she did not speak in her own defense. Instead, several English witnesses appeared on her behalf although many more arrived at the Old Bailey to testify only to be turned away. Their testimony referred to, and at times emphasized, the negative characteristics associated with the group labeled as Gypsies. John Giben said he had known Squires for three years and provided her an alibi. He testified that between the first and the ninth of January 1753 Squires and her children had stayed in his inn, the Old-Ship, in Abbotsbury, six miles from Dorchester and about 130 miles southwest of London. William Clark corroborated this account saying that he had seen Squires at Giben's inn when he went to 'have a pot of liquor' on New Year's Day. Clark explained that the last time he saw Squires was on January 10, 1753: 'I met with them on the road, we went some way together, we parted at Crudeway-foot, four miles from Abbotsbury and three from Dorchester.' Thomas Grevil testified that he had seen Squires and her children in Coombe (near Salisbury) on January 14 adding that they 'stopped there but one night'. All three men cited the itinerant nature of Squires' lifestyle to support their contention that she had not been in London on the night of Elizabeth Canning's abduction.[61]

The testimony of her alibi witnesses connected the constant travel associated with Squires and with Gypsies to their engagement in petty trade. When asked how long he had known the defendant, Clark told the court that he had seen Squires and her son and daughter 'three years ago come March, at Abbotsbury, they came with handkerchiefs, lawns, and muslins to sell'.[62] Giben said the same adding that Squires and her children 'offered ... to sell to me, and others, my wife bought two cheque aprons'.[63] This image of Gypsies as rootless, shifty vagrants, engaged in some sort of commerce was reinforced when Clark added that he 'saw them going about the town in the time, to sell things'.[64] Even while providing her an alibi, this testimony fixed the Gypsy as a person of commerce and movement; an outsider made different by her ethnicity and lifestyle.

In their rebuttal of Squires' alibi, the prosecution skillfully inserted a reference to magic, the black arts, and the supernatural so often associated with Gypsies. John Inister said that he had spotted Squires 'several times every day up and down before she was taken'. He implied that he had seen her in Enfield when she claimed to be in Dorchester, and he added that 'she walked into people's houses pretending to tell fortunes. She told mine once.'[65]

In his pamphlet written in June 1753 after Squires' pardon, Allan Ramsay (1713–1784) noted that he 'could not help being surprised to find upon what slight grounds [Fielding] and many other sensible men, had founded their belief in her [Canning's] veracity; and that they should be satisfied with evidence that seems to be in no manner adequate to the nature of the facts meant to be proved by it'.[66] Given Ramsay's observation, and our examination of the trial, I want to suggest that Mary Squires' otherness and foreignness, along with the history of Gypsies in England, were absolutely necessary in order to make Canning's story at all believable. Squires' conviction reflected a belief that Gypsies were inherently dishonest, promiscuous, cunning criminals. Ramsay said as much when he explained that Canning's accomplices remained silent for 'their own preservation' or because 'their friendship for her makes them prefer her safety and character to the life of an old gipsey'.[67] Even the trade conducted by the Gypsies, which might have served as a recognizable trait shared with Englishmen and women, seemed alien, underhanded and corrupt, less systematic and not at all connected to

Figure 1.4 'Elizabeth Canning and Mary Squires'

English trade networks. Ramsay attributed the inaction of those who may have known something about the incident to their perception that their responsibility to testify was nullified by the Gypsy's status as an aged outsider who did not belong to the local or national community. In contrast the pamphlets and newspapers foreground Canning's virtue, whiteness, and Englishness.

The visual representations of the Canning case vividly map the categories of difference onto the bodies of the women involved. Figure 1.4, widely circulated and often reproduced, shows the two protagonists, Canning and Squires, side by side; the sharp distinction between them leaves no doubt as to what the viewer is to think about their respective innocence and guilt.[68] Canning stares at the viewer with a modest but forthright look that captures the incapacity for deceit, the 'Goodness, as well as Childishness and Simplicity of her Character' that Fielding attributed to her when he said she was 'a child in years and yet more so in understanding'.[69] Her face, framed by a bonnet, is completely unobstructed. Although she wears a cape, it is drawn aside to reveal a tightly laced bodice that seems to encase her honor and her virtue. In contrast, Squires looks away from the viewer, her hat and closed cloak suggesting an effort to conceal and obfuscate. The image of Canning is bright, her skin excessively white in comparison to the darkness that enshrouds the portrait of Squires. The young woman epitomizes passivity and docility while the old woman embodies an active agent of threat and deceit.

INTERNAL OTHERS: JEWS, GYPSIES, AND JACOBITES

Figure 1.5 'The Gypsy's instantanious Flight'

Depicted as a crone, a witch, and 'the sovereign of the Lapland race', the prints present Mary Squires as a deceitful interloper, performer of black magic, unwelcome and constantly on the move. By her very presence Squires destabilized English values, institutions, and identities. 'The Gypsy's instantanious Flight from Enfield to Abbotsbury and back again' (Figure 1.5) portrays her menacing mobility and geographical autonomy.[70] As she rides on her broomstick through billows of smoke, Squires shouts to those watching from below 'Fair is foul and foul is fair I fly through fog and filthy air.' The onlookers accuse her of luring 'maids' to prostitution, colluding with the devil, and flying to hell. The references to pollution and 'infected' air convey unease about perceived trespasses and the Gypsy's seemingly limitless ability to move through space unbounded by gravity or the laws of physics let alone convention. Her mastery of the air contrasts strikingly with the earth bound impotence of those gazing at her. From this perspective her pardon on May 21 was a license to elude English law, making her and those influences she represented seem that much more invincible and making Canning a victim for a second time as she faced a felony charge for perjury. While some reasoned that this proved English justice was blind, others feared that the pardon rendered the English criminal legal system, with its ideology of 'equality before the law', powerless to protect 'his Majesty's subjects [from] a Gang of desperate and cruel Villains, of the greatest Danger to a civilized Nation'.[71]

'Virtue coerc'd'

The prosecution's only corroborating witness was Virtue Hall, a young woman who said that she went to the home of Susannah Wells 'as a lodger, but I was forced to do as they would have me', implying that she, unlike Canning, was forced into prostitution.[72] Hall's report that George Squires, 'the gypsie man said, "mother, I have brought you a girl, do you take her?"' echoed stories and warnings about abductions and networks of prostitution run by Gypsies whose reputed lack of moral shame contributed to their supposedly voracious and deviant sexual behavior.[73] Hall said that Mary Squires 'ripped the lace off [Canning's] stays and pulled them off, and hung them on the back of a chair in the kitchen' before pushing Canning up into the room saying 'damn you go up there then, if you please'. Then, according to Hall, George Squires 'took the stays off the chair and went out with them'. This vivid image of Canning's ripped stays captured the violence of the scene and encapsulated for Canning's supporters the loss of innocence, virginity, and purity.[74] Doubts swirled around Hall's testimony and how it came to support Canning's story so exactly.

Fielding had deposed Canning on February 7 and immediately issued a warrant for anyone left at Wells' house. The warrant yielded Hall who appeared before the justice 'in Tears' and 'a trembling Condition'.[75] Fielding promised her that if she told 'the whole Truth of this Affair, I give you my Word and Honour, as far as it is in my Power, to protect you; you shall come to no Manner of Harm'. When she agreed to cooperate, Fielding offered her a chair and began to examine her 'in the softest Language and kindest Manner I was able, for a considerable Time'.[76]

In the face of what he termed 'so many Prevarications and Contradictions', Fielding's 'kindest manner' dissipated. He told Hall he 'would commit her to Prison, and leave her to stand or fall by the Evidence against her'.[77] Fielding framed the stakes for Hall quite explicitly, advising Mr. Salt, Canning's lawyer, within Hall's earshot 'to prosecute her as a Felon together with the Gipsy Woman'.[78] Hall understood the dire consequences of this threat to intertwine her fate with that of Squires and responded accordingly. She 'begged I would hear her once more, and said that she would tell the whole Truth'. With the words attributed to her by Fielding she distinguished herself from the threatening otherness of Squires. Hall situated herself as another white victim of the illicit activity spearheaded by Susanne Wells and Mary Squires at Enfield Wash, and she explained her initial reticence as a result of 'Fears of the Gipsy Woman and Wells.'[79]

With her compliance assured, Fielding 'asked her a few Questions, which she answered with more Appearance of Truth than she had done before'. He then directed Salt 'to go with her and take her Information in Writing; and at her parting from me, I bid her to be a good Girl, and be sure to say neither more nor less than the whole Truth'.[80] Salt and

Hall emerged two hours later with a deposition that corroborated even the smallest details in Canning's story. Hall repeated the same information in front of 'several Noble Lords' a week later.[81]

On February 24, three days after Squires' conviction, Sir Crisp Gascoyne, Lord Mayor and one of the presiding judges at her trial, acted on his doubts about the case and ordered the investigation of the Gypsy's alibi. The corroborating evidence arrived on March 5. The next day, Gascoyne heard from John Hill (1714–1775) that Virtue Hall was in the Gatehouse prison in Westminster where she was supported by Canning's friends who wanted to ensure her presence and cooperation as a witness in case George Squires returned.

According to Hill, Hall showed 'great signs of uneasiness, and a willingness to declare the truth'.[82] When Hall appeared before Gascoyne, she came escorted by Canning's supporters. Although she refused to speak in front of them, 'no sooner had we retired with her, but she instantly burst into a flood of tears, and confessed that all she had sworn was false'.[83] Hall's recantation combined with the affidavits from Abbotsbury led to the collapse of the prosecution's case and Canning's eventual trial for perjury almost a year later in April 1754.

What prompted Gascoyne to act on his doubts? In addition to his personal contempt for Henry Fielding, Gascoyne may have been motivated by the case of Richard Coleman, accused of the brutal murder of Sarah Green in July 1748. Coleman was convicted and executed in 1749 despite 'declaring his Innocence in the most solemn Manner'.[84] In 1751 the real murderers, Thomas Jones and James Welch along with an accomplice James Nicholls, were discovered and prosecuted. In addition to the news stories about their trials and executions in August 1751, reference to this miscarriage of justice appeared in the newspapers when Coleman's defenders petitioned the king for maintenance of his wife and two children and again when his brothers raised money to pay for the prosecution of those who swore false witness against him.[85] This tragic failure of the justice system, 'the second Instance, within these three Years, of the Innocent suffering Death wrongfully in the County of Surrey', could well have impelled Gascoyne, who believed in the rule of law and participated in its administration, to investigate Squires' alibi despite her status as an outsider.[86]

The visual images suggest that the lengths to which Gascoyne went to defend Mary Squires exceeded popular tolerance for the ideology of equality before the law. 'The Gypsy's Triumph' (Figure 1.6) cast Gascoyne as the king of the Gypsies: adorned with a crown, he is credited with saving 'the Sovereign of the Lapland race'.[87] It was not unusual for magistrates in the seventeenth and eighteenth centuries to try to track down distant witnesses and evidence, but the distances involved called

Figure 1.6 'The Gypsy's Triumph'

further attention to far flung networks, real and imagined, and the mobility of those women (and men), internal others who seemed to traverse such large spaces unimpeded.[88] Again we see the struggle between principled support for the ideology of rule of law and the law's impartial, universal administration and fear of its imperial implications at home.

INTERNAL OTHERS: JEWS, GYPSIES, AND JACOBITES

The moral geography of eighteenth-century Britain

The stories surrounding Elizabeth Canning signal apprehensions about sexuality, race, and nation, the geographical mobility of the protagonists insistently drawing attention to a fissured metropole as well as Britain's imperial project. At the local level we have the story of Elizabeth Canning who claimed she was dragged 11 or 12 miles from Moorfields, along the Hertfordshire Road, to the home of Susannah Wells in Enfield. During her trial witnesses placed Mary Squires in Abbotsbury while at her sentencing, Squires claimed that between the end of December 1752 and the tenth of January 1753 she had been at Coombe, Stoptage, Basingstoke, Bagshot-heath, and Old Brentford, traversing at least 140 miles before arriving at the home of Susannah Wells. The attention on sexuality and mobility resurfaced after Canning's trial in 1754 when her supporters feared she would be raped while on board the ship carrying her to the colonies to serve her sentence of transportation.[89]

Mapped onto the individual and collective female body we see England's poor and working, single, white women, previously its internal others, move inside the boundary of the English nation. In an imperial geography, white English women, including wealthy and even poor, single women, were considered civilized and sexually contained, while colonized subjects from warmer climates were represented as prone to excessive carnal desires and unrestrained sexuality. Felicity Nussbaum argued for the mutually constitutive character of these sexual profiles in which the colonized English woman's civility and virtue relied on the invention of the excesses of the 'other' woman. Nussbaum's analysis allows us to see the scandal that was the Canning case: Squires, the 'other' woman, moved seemingly unimpeded between London and Dorchester threatening the chastity of at least two white working-class Englishwomen, Elizabeth Canning and Virtue Hall.

The assumptions reflected in the representations of Canning, Hall, and Squires produced a sharp definition of Englishness in which the poor, single woman emerged as a white, virtuous, and honest victim. This scenario demanded quite a leap of faith in the case of Elizabeth Canning considering the disdain and suspicion with which servants were regarded in the eighteenth century and the slight credibility of Virtue Hall, a prostitute.[90] Certainly the intimate details of Elizabeth's undergarments and bodily functions would never have been discussed publically had she been of elite status. But the Gypsy, described by Fielding as possessing 'scarce even the Appearance of Humanity', and even by Hill, Fielding's detractor, supposedly sympathetic to Squires, as having a face 'like that of no human Creature', was portrayed as lacking all morality, credibility, or assimilability.[91] Even the mobility that exonerated her did not prove her innocence to readers and jurors in eighteenth-century Britain. The presence of Squires in England, a Christian woman, with a quintessentially English last name, the head of her household, was threatening regardless of whether she had committed any crime against Elizabeth Canning. The *London Evening Post* encapsulated this sentiment with the praise they heaped on the 'Public-Spirited and humane Gentlemen' who had supported the 'poor, injured innocent Girl', in 'their Endeavours to eradicate a Gang of desperate and cruel Villains, of the greatest Danger to a civilized Nation'.[92]

In 1753 these portraits of a Gypsy underworld did the cultural work of constituting an ephemerally stable national identity. The disagreement between Fielding and Gascoyne about the Canning evidence demonstrates that national identities are subject to debate and that some versions of Britishness in the eighteenth century were more tolerant of difference than others. The creation or reinvention of difference and foreignness in the courtroom makes this an important site to consider. The legal setting credited circumstantial evidence, rumor, and innuendo with unwarranted authority. With their reputations and their very lives in the balance, the stakes for each woman were tremendously high: the stakes for English law equally so. To retain its efficacy, this instrument of empire, coercion, national integration, and assimilation required the preservation of its reputation for impartiality and equality before the law.[93]

Gascoyne responded to what he perceived as injustice and prejudice when he said of Mary Squires 'surely no poor creature ever before appeared at the Bar, more perfectly deprived of the mercy of the law, which presumes guilt in no one before conviction'.[94] His ostensible belief in the superiority of British law and liberty compelled him to defend the alien Gypsy, Mary Squires, against Canning's allegations. Paired with Squires as the male sovereign of the Lapland race, Gascoyne paid dearly for his campaign, which led to his defeat in the next election for lord mayor and ultimately cost him his political career. His detractors saw his defense of Squires as a corruption of English law by the imperial project.

The Elizabeth Canning case with its focus on mobility and commerce, revolving as it did around five single women, one of whom was a Gypsy, raised doubts about imperial aspiration by disturbing the distinction between colonizer and colonized, citizen and alien, home and away. The case conferred whiteness, 'a location of structural advantage, of race privilege', on the poor, single, servant woman while the Gypsies remained suspicious outsiders despite their commercial prowess.[95] The case backlights the way discourses of whiteness emerged at the intersection of attitudes about class, gender, sexuality, and ethnicity and signals the extent to which people were thought to be eligible for the rights and privileges of belonging. In the context of simultaneous debates over Jewish naturalization where we see the struggles over this quintessentially English attribute articulated even more starkly, the case served as a metaphor and a portentous sign indicating a much more real threat. Again these disputes unfolded in the legal realm over rights and privileges.[96]

The Jew Bill of 1753 and the national body

On April 3, 1753, George Montagu Dunk, Second Earl of Halifax (1716–1771) introduced the Jewish Naturalization Bill in the House of Lords. The bill allowed 'persons professing the Jewish Religion', born outside of England, to 'be naturalized by Parliament, without receiving the Sacrament of the Lord's Supper'.[97] The purpose of this legislation was not the general acceptance of Jews into Britain; naturalization would still require the passage of a private act of Parliament, which would be in the reach of only a few of the wealthiest of England's 8000 Jews.[98] On April 16, 1753, the bill passed the House of Lords, and then made it through the House of Commons on May 22 of the same year. Although it met with little initial dispute inside or outside of Parliament, the Act elicited a tremendous popular furor immediately after its passage: pamphlets and prints, sermons, petitions, and newspaper coverage argued over the significance of the Act throughout the summer and fall of 1753. Jewish peddlers were insulted and harassed in the streets and the murder of Jonas Levi in November of 1753 may have resulted from the passions sparked by the bill's passage.[99] In that month, immediately after Parliament reconvened, the Act was repealed.[100]

The storm over the bill rehearsed disquiets about 'Britain' and its integrity as a nation. In the context of the imperial expansion of the eighteenth century these worries signaled disagreement or at least a heated debate about the place and treatment of those considered strangers, foreigners, or Britain's internal others. Like Canning's cases, the legislation analyzed below often arbitrated whether and how these internal others should be tolerated and to what extent their presence could be accepted and integrated into British society. The repeal of the Act, the 'Jew Bill' as it has come to be known, is attributed directly to popular outcry. While the controversy surrounding the Jew Bill has been studied in the context of Anglo-Jewish history, this incident can also serve to illustrate the broader political and cultural concerns of the eighteenth century traced in this book. Like the other cases that unfolded in 1753, the swift rise and fall of the Jew Bill is a legal event involving internal others, in this case wealthy Jewish men, that became a scandal erupting in the public sphere raising questions about law and empire. The discourse about Jews in the pamphlets and prints highlights contemporary apprehensions about the deep religious and political divisions within the polity. The debates around the Bill underscored the fissured nature of Christian Britain, an echo of rebellion and civil unrest so prominent in the seventeenth century and the Jacobite rebellions in the first half of the eighteenth century. The scandal insistently reminded the English public about the impact of Britain's imperial expansion at home and the disagreements this engendered between those who embraced it, those who rejected it, and those who were unsure.

Analysis of the Jewish Naturalization Act has served as a case study of eighteenth-century parliamentary politics, and Jewish historians have treated it as an important, though atypical, moment in Anglo-Jewish history. Scholars of British politics have claimed that the Whigs retreated from their support of Jewish naturalization because they feared a loss in the coming election of the spring 1754. Jewish historians have minimized the importance of the debate and argued that the controversy had little or no lasting effect after repeal.[101] Certainly the furor over the Bill quieted after the elections of 1754, but is this immediate context the only one in which this event can be understood?

Perhaps the anti-Semitic polemics and the violent imagery loosed against Jewish naturalization have been the source of discomfort that has led to the diminution of the event in most scholarship.[102] Opponents of the Bill deployed the worst defamations of Jews. The prints and pamphlets portrayed Jews as money grubbing, dishonest, cunning interlopers and played on stereotypes of Jews as blasphemous, clannish, ambitious, and traitorous. A sharp focus on the Jew Bill and the attacks on Jewish naturalization would disturb the narrative of integration and assimilation that runs through Anglo-Jewish history and credits Britain with toleration and acceptance of Jews in contrast to other places in Europe.[103] It would also obviously challenge the exceptionalism so typical of more general British narratives that emphasize British liberties.

I argue that the history of the Jew Bill offers a way to understand the British as white Christians, their images of themselves as individuals, and as a community.[104] The discussion of religion that surrounded the bill points again to the disjuncture between the imagined legal subject: Anglican, English, white, and male and the reality of eighteenth-century imperial Britain. At home in London, 'the foreigners' mecca' these 'diverse immigrants'[105] actively sought to join the ranks of English subjects as equals bestowed with all the rights and privileges of 'true-born Englishmen'.

INTERNAL OTHERS: JEWS, GYPSIES, AND JACOBITES

My analysis of the pamphlets and prints that surrounded the Jew Bill builds on the work of Todd Endelman on the role of the Jews as 'foils for the forging of English and British identities'. Endelman argued that 'the agitation sparked by passage of the Jew Bill in 1753 functioned as a lightning rod for the articulation of nationalist sentiments at the time'.[106] In his 1999 dissertation Alan Singer examined the importance of this incident as a catalyst for the formation of a British identity.[107] This examination of the Jew bill, a legal mechanism that failed to integrate difference or to expel it completely, focuses our attention on the role of religion, the relationship between religion and nationality, notions of citizenship and the body politic, definitions of masculinity and femininity, and the line between transparency and secrecy – all of which played out in the context of Britain's imperial expansion.

The place of Jews in Britain's imperial expansion

By the mid-century the financial revolution combined with Britain's imperial expansion made London the center of foreign trade, luxury goods, the insurance industry, and public borrowing: London's Jews were involved in every aspect of its financial and commercial activity. They held stock in the Bank of England, traded in the money market, and advised the government on its financial policies: they owned the national debt, and they actively participated in selling it to the public.[108] Over the course of the eighteenth century as Britain's military expanded, Jews provisioned soldiers with supplies and the government with loans to fund the wars. Jews also imported bullion, fundamental to international trade. Jews traded commodities from all over the world, and they worked as stockbrokers and stock jobbers. Of the 100 licensed stockbrokers allowed by Act of Parliament, twelve positions were allotted to Jews and twelve to aliens.[109]

Jews were active in overseas trade importing and re-exporting commodities and exporting British goods. Their commercial networks made them international brokers around the world. The record of Jewish investment in colonial enterprises is quite dramatic. Between 1691 and 1712, fifty-eight Jewish names show up among the investors in the Royal Africa Company while in the same time period thirty-four Jewish shareholders invested in the South Sea Company. Jewish merchants actively promoted trade in sites all over the Empire including India, the Caribbean, North America, and South America. Jews participated in many different commercial endeavors across the globe, often re-exporting colonial goods that came into London back out to Amsterdam. They were particularly prominent in the diamond trade from India to

Europe and active in the coral trade, importing this luxury good to London from the Mediterranean and re-exporting it to India.[110]

Jewish colonial communities complemented the financial work of their co-religionists in the metropole. The Jewish community in Madras worked exporting diamonds to London throughout the eighteenth century.[111] In the Caribbean taxes earned from the lively sale of commodities by Jewish merchants and shopkeepers filled the coffers of London's Exchequer.[112] As the needs of the colonies changed and sugar reshaped the economy, Jews became involved in many of the financial and commercial endeavors that supported the new cash crop economy including shipping, credit, wholesaling dried goods, manufacturing, and marine insurance.[113]

In England the issue of naturalization applied only to Jewish men born abroad and those most interested in its passage tended to be prominent merchants. Their alien status denied them the legal right to own land or other real property, to own or hold a share in a British sailing vessel, or to engage in the lucrative colonial trade. Those who did engage in foreign trade despite these restrictions were required to pay alien duties including custom rates and special port fees. Although they could afford the expense of naturalization by a private act of Parliament, an option available to foreign-born Protestants, this path was not open to Jewish men because it required receiving the sacrament (that is, the Eucharist in the Anglican service).[114] Although the Plantation Act 1740 allowed for the naturalization of Jews and exempted them from Christian oaths, it applied only to those who had lived in the colonies for seven years – not a practical option for Jews living in London.[115] As an alternative to naturalization, Jews born abroad could purchase letters patent in order to be made 'free denizens'. Denization allowed foreign born Jews to engage in colonial trade, but it did not exempt them from paying alien duties and it did not apply to children born before the purchase of the patent. Even Jews born in England were subject to the legal limits imposed on other non-Anglicans: because of the oaths involved or the sacramental requirement, they could not hold municipal office, be called to the bar, obtain a naval commission, take a degree in one of the universities, vote, or be elected to parliament. The Jew Bill promised no remedy for these limits on the civil rights of Jews. Naturalized Jews would have remained second-class citizens like native-born Jews, Dissenters, and Catholics.

Scholars often cite Jewish support for the Whig government as the reason that the Pelhams and the Church of England supported the bill for Jewish Naturalization. Samson Gideon, the wealthy Jewish stockbroker, featured prominently in the textual and visual sources related to the Jew Bill. Gideon was the biggest of the stock jobbers for the East India Company. He dealt in lottery tickets, guaranteed insurance policies, made loans to the owners and officers of the East Indiamen, and at times dealt in diamonds. In the 1740s he sold between £80,000 and £100,000 annually in East India Company stock.[116] In 1742, at the start of the War of Austrian Succession (1740–1748), Gideon raised a list of Jewish subscribers who arranged a loan for the government of £3 million. He served as a financial advisor to the government, and he sat on the royal exchange as one of its twelve Jewish members. Gideon was especially prominent during the Jacobite Rebellion of 1745 when he led efforts by wealthy Jews to support the government's finances. When government stock collapsed, Jews imported specie, bought up bank notes at par, and subscribed to a new government loan until 'by Degrees, the general Confidence of Mankind was re-established' in the nation's financial institutions.[117] Upon the defeat of the Jacobite Rebellion when the political situation stabilized, Gideon doubled his fortune.[118]

Gideon's grandparents were originally from Portugal, and his father, Rowland Gideon, had lived in Barbados, in Boston, and in Nevis in the West Indies where he had been a merchant. Gideon's mother, Esther, was the daughter of Domingo do Porto, a diamond buyer in Madras. Together this family embodied the imperial history of Jewish life in the eighteenth century, spanning the breadth of Britain's colonial holdings. Like other white colonists, they aspired to take up residence in Britain's metropole. Gideon's father was endenizened in 1679 and in the same year he became a liveryman of the Painter-Stainers' Company. He was endenizened again in 1688 and eventually became a freeman of the City of London. His son, Samson, achieved tremendous financial success, married a Christian woman, and although he never converted, Gideon baptized all of his children.[119]

Gideon was born in England and so would not have benefited directly from naturalization, yet he too reached the limits of acceptance into England's elite circles. He aspired to a baronetcy, but he was refused in 1758. Despite his decades-long loyalty to the English government, especially during the Jacobite Rebellion of 1745 and again during the Seven Years' War, and his acquisition of most of the trappings of a nobleman – he had been granted a coat of arms, had purchased a country estate, and bought land in Lincolnshire and Buckinghamshire – his Jewishness denied him access to this highest social position.[120] Gideon distanced himself from the Jewish community in response to the rumors of his support for the Jewish Naturalization Bill. He wrote to the governing council of the Spanish and Portuguese Synagogue at the height of the controversy over the Act denouncing the effort and resigning from the synagogue and from the Jewish community.[121]

Gideon's biography encapsulated the history of Britain in the eighteenth century, its imperial growth, and London's metropolitan pull for colonial subjects. Despite his economic success and seeming integration into England's elite, Gideon's life also demonstrated the dominance of the Anglican Church. Membership in the Church of England dictated many social and cultural experiences and often excluded those not counted among its members. The same applied to equality before the law. Many opposed the creation of full civil equality for non-Anglicans and believed in limiting access to power (the ability to hold public office) and wealth (freedom to own all types of property) to Anglicans only.

Arguing the Bill

The initiative for the Jew Bill of 1753 came amidst the ongoing debates about naturalization discussed above. Four bills that would have allowed naturalization without the Anglican sacrament prompted by the populationists at the end of the War of Austrian Succession failed in the Irish Parliament between 1743 and 1747. In 1747 and again in 1751 Robert Nugent introduced in the English Parliament the 'General Naturalization Bill', the subject of the image with which we began this chapter. The Bills would have allowed foreign Protestants to be naturalized without the expense of a private act. Both failed. Despite these setbacks, the Spanish and Portuguese Jewish community in London decided to agitate for similar legislation on their behalf. They believed that enough support for Jewish naturalization existed in England and that with their intervention such a measure could pass.[122] Jewish men born abroad sought the rights of Englishmen and they catalyzed the lawful means by which to obtain them.

As a London-born merchant, Joseph Salvador (1716–1786) who became the Act's unofficial spokesman advocated Jewish naturalization for a very personal reason: his brother, Jacob, died in 1749 leaving two sons. Joseph worried that if his nephews died, their land would be forfeit to the crown because the land's owner, Joseph's father, Francis, had been born in the Netherlands. It was Joseph who petitioned the duke of Newcastle on January 14, 1753 for a naturalization act appending seven reasons for the bill. Joseph and his father Francis worked in merchandizing and shipping in the Spanish and Portuguese trade. They may have also engaged in smuggling contraband from Jamaica, and they worked as London factors for English merchants in Cadiz. Later in his life Salvador owned ships, imported both diamonds and bullion, and was a major stockholder in the East India Company. Between 1757 and 1762 he advised Newcastle's administration about public finance, in particular a government loan of which he was a major underwriter. During the Bute administration (1762–1763) he became chief financial advisor to Charles Jenkinson, Bute's under-secretary of state and joint secretary to the treasury. He served as an intermediary between the government and the East India Company, and he supported Robert Clive among the Directors of the East India Company, even marketing diamonds for him. With the money he inherited upon his father's death, Salvador extended his estate in Tooting and bought 100,000 acres of land in South Carolina for £2000. In 1757 he bought a town house in White Hart Court, Bishopsgate. Financial losses in the 1760s eventually led him to sell all of his English property and one-half of his land in South Carolina where he retired in 1784.[123]

Salvador, his life and writings, provide a window into what Jews wanted and how they saw themselves fitting into Britain's national and imperial scene. They established and maintained global connections, but they also aspired to the highest honors bestowed by metropolitan society. Both Joseph Salvador and Samson Gideon were born in England, and they claimed the rights of Englishmen as well as their places in elite social and political circles. They believed they had served the government, and they expected in return its acceptance in the form of full legal recognition. In his pamphlets promoting the passage of the Bill, written under the apt pseudonym of Philo-Patria, Salvador made a direct appeal to law, protesting that withholding naturalization from Jews 'is destroying Men's Rights, on a false supposition; all Subjects have Rights according to the Law and of the Land; they [the Jews] have been many Times acknowledged Subjects, by the Legislature: How then can it be doubted they are Subjects, and that they have the Rights of a Subject'.[124] The *quid pro quo* is clear: having proven their economic utility, Jews were due their well-earned reward, the rights of Englishmen.

Other advocates of the Jew Bill made religious, philosophical, and economic arguments. While some of its religious supporters hoped that naturalization would increase the chances of a widespread conversion of the Jews. other supporters, generally Whigs, who ascribed to emerging liberal values, maintained that Jewish naturalization was the obvious and logical extension of the Toleration Act passed in 1689 and the freedom of conscience espoused by John Locke (1632–1704).[125] According to the anonymous author of *Some Thoughts upon a Bill for General Naturalization* who favored passage of the unsuccessful General Naturalization bill of 1751, 'Whig-Principles are Principles of Reason, of Liberty, or universal Benevolence ... unnarrow'd and unrestrain'd by local Prejudices.' In contrast to a 'meer Animal' to whom 'a stranger is an Enemy because he is a Stranger', men 'cherish him [the stranger] for the Preference, and love him for a Conformity of Affection'. Moreover, 'man propagates those Fruits upon which he feeds, multiplies those Blessings which he partakes, supports and defends those Rights for others which he enjoys in common with them'.[126] Warning that 'narrow Notions in Religion, narrow Notions in Trade, [and] narrow Notions in Policy' will stifle growth, he promised that:

> the same Spirit which Prompts Foreigners to come, will excite Them to struggle with many Disadvantages under which they must labour. Necessity will compel Them to work more or upon harder Terms than the Natives; the same necessity, animated by Emulation, will induce Them to excel, until that Necessity and that Spirit diffusing itself through all Denominations, will from the Endeavours of Individuals to surpass one the other, end in a general Excellence ...[127]

Connecting liberal thought to discussions of free trade, the author argued that the hardships endured by immigrants would encourage hard work and improve Britain's economic prosperity.

Most frequently the proponents of Jewish naturalization emphasized its promise for commercial prosperity. Horace Walpole (1678–1757) wrote that the bill was 'calculated purely for increasing wealth and commerce in the nation',[128] while Josiah Tucker, a proponent of free trade, expounded on the merits of allowing:

> *rich* Foreigners ... to carry on a free and extensive Commerce, by importing all sorts of merchandize and Raw materials, allowed by Law to be imported, for the Employment of our own People, and then Exporting the surplus of the Produce, Labour, and Manufactures of our own Country, upon *cheaper* and *better* terms than is done at present.[129]

Those who favored the bill believed that the strength of any nation depended on a steady growth of its population as well as its access to new markets. They insisted that the naturalization of wealthy Jews would further both of these goals.[130] The expansion of the individuals and groups who might be considered British was motivated by the anticipation of benefits for both parties and implied reciprocal obligations and responsibilities.

Tucker and Walpole echoed earlier rhetoric advocating Jewish naturalization based on superlative commercial traits they attributed to Jews. In *The Spectator* from September 1712 Joseph Addison claimed that:

> They are so disseminated through all the Trading Parts of the World, that they are become the Instruments by which the most distant Nations converse with one another, and by which, Mankind are knit together in a general Correspondence: They are like the Pegs and Nails in a great

Building, which, though they are but little valued in themselves, are absolutely necessary to keep the whole Frame together.[131]

According to Toland's tract written in 1714, the facets of trade were 'shar'd in such a manner, and parcell'd out among the inhabitants of the earth'. Among the jobs were 'Factors', 'Carriers', 'Miners', 'Manufactorers', and 'Store-keepers'. 'Jews may properly be said to be the Brokers of it (the world), who, whithersoever they come, create business as well as manage it'.[132]

Jews themselves proclaimed these qualities as their own. Joseph Salvador expounded on Jewish facility with trade and commerce in two pamphlets he published in 1753 titled *Considerations on the bill to permit persons professing the Jewish religion to be naturalized by Parliament* and *Further considerations on the act to permit persons professing the Jewish religion, to be naturalized by Parliament*.[133] He enumerated the places in Europe where Jews had settled and argued that 'commerce followed them' as did economic prosperity; conversely, he warned that those places that shunned or expelled Jews, like Spain in 1492, suffered economic downturn.[134] In England he asserted 'that the Jews circulate a great Part of our Commerce, and thereby increase the Value of our Estates', and he credited the Jews with 'one-twentieth Part of our [English] foreign Trade' and 'by their Ingress in this Kingdom, increased the Balance of our annual Profits, by one twelfth Part'.[135] He predicted that if they were barred 'this would reduce, the Value of our National Capital very considerably, depreciate, every Part of the National Stock, and raise Interest greatly. What bad Consequences may flow, from thus dismembering our Trade, Time only can show.'[136] His pamphlet surveyed global Jewish commercial endeavors listing diamonds and coral, bullion, shipping, insurance, and trade in manufactured goods in India, Jamaica, England, and the Netherlands. Salvador reiterated in no uncertain terms that 'their Utility has not been deduced, from any particular Ability of theirs, but from their Money, which, if retained in any Shape in our Mass, will equally contribute to our Opulence; that the best Method to keep their Money among us, when they retire from Trade, will be to permit them to realize and live at their Ease'.[137] One of Salvador's strongest arguments for naturalization is the threat that England's Jews will settle elsewhere and take their trade, capital, and connections with them. Salvador concluded ominously that if Jews left England, 'it would strengthen other Nations, and more particularly our Rivals, it would be hurtful to us, and consequently bad Policy'.[138]

Opponents of the Bill argued that Jewish naturalization threatened the British nation in religious, legal, and economic terms. It would, they contended, undermine Christianity, destabilize the English Constitution, and increase poverty. Furthermore, the Jew Bill imperiled the very ownership of land as Jewish merchants would increase their market share at the expense of British merchants and then buy up landed estates.[139] The propaganda images and some of the newspaper articles against the Jew Bill, which were lurid and less 'rational' than the pamphlets, expressed fears that the naturalization of Jews would inaugurate a vast Jewish conspiracy to circumcise British men and to rob them of their masculinity and virility. In a doggerel poem titled 'Advice to the Freeholders', women were counseled, 'that the children of Aaron should mangle and tear one So shocking a Thought is sufficient to scare one. Think well Lady S—n of this Operation And join with good Christians in saving – the nation.'[140] This operation, the circumcision evoked by the Jew Bill's passage, implied a sexual threat made explicit in a vision of the future in the *London Evening Post* titled 'the thirty-fourth chapter of Genesis'. The piece warned that with the Bill's passage 'every male' would be ordered 'to be circumcised: which was accordingly done ... And it came to pass on the third Day, while their Private Parts were sore, that the Jews took their Swords, and slew every male of the Britons'.[141] The Jewish masculinity portrayed here stood armed, aggressive, and dangerous, seeking to appropriate power and threatening the livelihoods, the reproductive capacities, and the very lives of Britain's Christian men.

Genesis chapter 34 recounts the rape of Dinah and the Jewish revenge taken on its perpetrators. When Dinah left Jacob's compound to visit the 'daughters of the land' unguarded by a male chaperone, she was raped by Shechem, son of Hamor the Hivite. Shechem wished to marry her and begged his father to arrange the match.[142] Hamor proposed to Jacob and his sons not a single union, but a more general blending of the two peoples: 'intermarry with us: give your daughters to us, and take our daughters for yourselves. You will dwell among us, and the land will be open before you; settle, move about, and acquire holdings in it.'[143] Jacob's sons agreed on condition that every male among Hamor's people became circumcised. Hamor and Schechem convinced the gentile townsmen with promises that 'their [Jewish] cattle and substance and all their beasts will be ours'.[144] Three days later, following the fulfillment of these conditions, 'when they were in pain', Simeon and Levi, Jacob's sons and Dinah's biological brothers, entered the city and 'slew all the males' and plundered the town.[145]

A search of early eighteenth-century publications reveals countless references to the story of Dinah. Many make only the most cursory allusion to Dinah assuming familiarity with the story and drawing a moral lesson similar to this one from 1709: 'how much we ought to avoid a nice inquisitive Curiosity, and to take heed how we mingle and accompany ourselves with strange Persons'.[146] Some interpretations, especially Thomas Pyle's from 1717 gestured quite explicitly at the naturalization debates of the first half of the eighteenth century and may have even served as a denunciation of the Acts of Union with Scotland. As if with Gideon and Salvador in mind, Pyle interpreted the offer made by Hamor to include a promise 'to incorporate Jacob and his whole Family into their Government, and invest them with all the same Rights and Privileges of the Country, that the Natives themselves enjoyed'.[147] In 1739 Samuel Smith described Dinah's brothers who, 'craftily dissembling the real sentiments of their Hearts' and 'feigning a compliance' with Hamor, 'deluded the unwary Shechemites'.[148] No matter what their particular position on the Bill, this language echoed the tone of the pamphlets against naturalization. Needless to say this position precluded a receptive or expansive posture and instead determined to define difference.

When directed at the national body, these images of Jews suggest concern about the fragility and divisiveness that plagued British society in the mid-eighteenth century. The Jews portrayed in these prints and pamphlets are threatening and aggressive, not at all the emasculated, effeminate images of Jews that also circulated at the same time.[149] When Britannia represents Britain in prints or words, the aggressive sexuality attributed to the Jews is particularly menacing to the young, feminine figure, vulnerable to sexual predation. The violent, militant, and sexually dangerous nature attributed to Jews suggests a physical threat to the nation. Given that the number of Jews in England stood at only 8000 in a population of 5.8 million and that most English Jews in the eighteenth century were poor peddlers, the potential for harm could not have been founded on any real threat to property or politics. The danger seems to have been imagined as a threat to integrity based on uneasiness about difference: a fear of being taken unawares, fear of an infiltration by the Jews as well as a fear that universal circumcision would erase the distinction between different groups and erode their particularity as Christians, as Anglicans, and as Britons.

The written and visual commentary against the Bill blamed the problem of internal division on foreigners residing on British soil and proposed a solution that staked the future of Britishness and of the nation on their exclusion. The pamphlets and prints depicted what are now considered stereotypical, uncontested, and almost innate elements of Britain's culture: law, liberty, and Protestantism, in particular the Church of England, as contingent, contested, and at risk from the Jews who were portrayed as lawless rebels and scheming interlopers. A print entitled 'A Prospect of the New Jerusalem' (Figure 1.7) depicts Jews

Figure 1.7 'A Prospect of the New Jerusalem'

descending on London, renamed 'the new Jerusalem'. Their Semitic features stand out as well as their alliance with the devil holding a bag containing half a million pounds. Like the rewritten story of Dinah, their sly, unannounced arrival is depicted as an invasion akin to a surprise attack, the print a warning to the public of the transformation of Christ's 'enemies the Jews' into 'free and true born English Jews'. The rest of the doggerel warns that these interlopers are in the same category as 'The Devil, Infidels, Hereticks, and Turks!' With this line the print's author points to other unnamed religious groups, specifically non-Anglican Protestants, Dissenters or Nonconformists, who were much more numerous than the English Jews, implying that they threatened the English nation by their very existence made more dangerous by their inclusion in the English political body.[150]

The couplet hints at the unconstitutional nature of the Jew Bill and suggests that its slippery slope would lead to full civil rights for Nonconformists and even Catholic emancipation. Non-Anglican Protestants included Baptists, Congregationalists, Presbyterians, Methodists, and Unitarians as well as independent groups, such as the Quakers and the English Moravians. They certainly posed an even bigger threat to Anglicanism than the tiny minorities of Jews and Catholics. But it was their very proximity to Anglicanism, from a doctrinal point of view, that may have been most disturbing to those who wished to exclude them from certain civil liberties reserved only for those within the Church of England. The vociferous opponents of the Jew Bill wished to retain the constraints on Nonconformist civil liberties and prevent their complete assimilation and integration into the British body politic. While Dissenters were surely targeted by these lines, so were the Whigs, as the government in power and the party responsible for what was considered the disastrous Naturalization Act 1709. As if to drive the point home about religious and political divisions, the last couplet, 'These can't be English, these are Romish works Some Popish Plot to bring in the Pretender', referenced James II and the Jacobite uprisings of 1715, 1719, and 1745.

Opponents of the Bill were caught in a bind. All of the pamphlets were printed and circulated between May and November of 1753 – most were produced after the Bill had passed. Their authors disagreed with the legislation, but they did not want to be associated with the rebelliousness, instability, and unlawfulness of which they accused the Jews. Instead they argued that their opposition to the Bill was a defense of the British polity and its lawful, Christian government. They argued that objecting to the Bill was absolutely necessary in order to save an Anglican Britain from the threats posed by the Act, "which promises *no good* to us ... and may produce *great evils*'.[151]

Jonas Hanway (1712–1786) the philanthropist and social commentator who wrote these lines argued that the very fabric of British life depended on a union of the 'civil polity' with Protestant Christianity, which he described as 'interwoven'. Therefore, he continued, 'I think it would be too dangerous an experiment to try if they would exist [if] any change [were] to happen to either.'[152] Hanway questioned the legitimacy of a law such as the Jewish Naturalization Act, which 'favors an opposition to the acknowledgement of [the] sovereignty' of Christ.[153] The sacrament served, according to Hanway, as a *'badge of honor* as a Christian and a Protestant; and as *a token of fidelity* to the state'.[154] Without the assurance of such a token of fidelity, the state, its security, and integrity, was in jeopardy. Hanway's insistence on the link between the Eucharist and the 'civil polity' was not unrelated to the discussions of circumcision that recurred throughout the debates about the Jew Bill. Both implicated the body as a site on which membership in a community was written, yet one form of membership excluded the other.

In his rebuttal of Joseph Salvador, William Romaine penned *An Answer to a Pamphlet* emphasizing the integrity of the Jewish community and its internal loyalty. He warned of Jewish subversion: by 'admitting them into its Communion' Britain risked 'giving up its fundamental Principles' at the hands of those 'who break those very Bonds of Union, by which the State is cemented'.[155] With this Romaine implied that the Bonds of Union, the strength and force of the state, relied on membership in the Church of England mirroring membership in the nation. The Jews' defiant refusal to accept Jesus Christ as their savior proved their essential rebelliousness. This constant threat of treason coexisted with the Jewish expectation of the messiah, whom they 'look for ... daily, and are always praying for his coming'. The bill's opponents represented this expectation as fraught with the potential for revolt because the Jews would 'raise a rebellion and take up Arms to support his Title'.[156] Again we see active Jewish agents: masculine and armed, dangerous and threatening.

The danger of rebellion born of religious factionalism was not, of course, an abstract one in 1753. England had been torn apart by civil war in 1642, regicide in 1649, instability during the Commonwealth and Protectorate, and the restoration of the monarchy in 1660. The exclusion crisis of 1679–1681 threatened the ascendance to the throne by the king's Catholic brother, James. Although a consensus among ruling elites eventually brought James II to the throne in 1685, a coalition of Whigs and Tories ended his reign just three years later in what became known as the 'Glorious Revolution' of 1688–1689. The reputation of the Glorious Revolution as a peaceful and constitutional transfer of power belies the violence of 1689–1692.

While these political changes and transfers of power were normalized and legalized through the immediate adoption of the Bill of Rights (1689), the Act of Settlement (1701), and the Acts of Union with Scotland (1707), not everyone consented to the new constitutional arrangement. The heirs of James II and their followers, the Jacobites, were by no means content to accept what they considered a traitorous and unlawful arrangement. The public of 1753 lived with the memory of the risings of 1715, 1719, and 1745 as well as rumors that abounded about various schemes, like the Elibank Plot to restore the Stuarts. This very real sense of unease about the religious and political divisions that threatened the nation was summarized by Horace Walpole when he wrote in September 1753 that 'altho' certain circumstances, too long to explain, had spread a face of calm and tranquility over the nation, yet the minds of a certain party are not at all altered; the apparent dead ashes cover sparks, that the least breath will kindle into flame'.[157]

The proponents of the Jewish Naturalization Act contended that the Jews had 'distinguished themselves' in loyal service to the government during the rebellion of 1745 which 'shew'd plainly, how much they interested themselves in the Good of this Country'.[158] In his *Considerations* Salvador described the widespread participation of British Jews: 'their lower People enroll'd their Names in the City Militia ... neglecting their Customs, which lead them never to bear Arms, but on Emergencies'.[159] Wealthy Jews were credited with helping to support the government's finances until 'by Degrees, the general Confidence of Mankind was re-established' in the nation's financial institutions.[160] Perhaps with an implied contrast to Jacobites and Catholics, Salvador concluded *'Are not such subjects worthy of naturalization?'*[161]

Salvador ended his section on the loyalty of the Jews during the Jacobite Rebellion 1745 declaring, 'their Behaviour, in that Year, has merited the Applause of every true Lover of Liberty, and Detester of Popery, Tyranny, and Oppression'.[162] This assertion attempted to redirect contemporary rhetoric that grouped Jews, Catholics, and Nonconformists together by ascribing to Jews the same treasonous, destabilizing nature assigned to non-Anglicans and Jacobites. Emphasizing those groups with a proven record of treason, another pro-bill author asked, 'Can Jews be so bad Subjects as Papists, or Protestant Jacobites, who, if possible, are worse than Papists?'[163] By maintaining the essential difference of Jews from Catholics, Dissenters, and all other foreign elements, by staking his claim on their exceptional loyalty, Salvador presented a counter-argument to those who contended that the admission of the Jews into the body politic would necessitate the inclusion of all other groups defined either as non-English or non-Christian.

Both the advocates and the opponents of the Jew bill shared an underlying assumption: that Jews, whether born in Britain or abroad, were a cohesive group that did not have the attributes of the rest of British society and never could. The supposed self-contained unity and integrity of the Jewish community was expressed by the bill's supporters, among them Jews like Joseph Salvador, who argued that an influx of Jews did not present a potential drain on British resources because 'they maintain their own Poor'[164] and by Josiah Tucker's contention that England would benefit from the group of 'rich Foreigners' who would carry out certain economic functions as a race apart.[165] While the Bill's supporters believed that the advantages of inclusion through naturalization outweighed its disadvantages, neither group argued for the innate Britishness of the Jews. This shared assumption reflects a definition of Britishness produced in the discussion itself. William Romaine expressed this sentiment when he asserted the oxymoronic nature of naturalization as applied to Jews:

> our state can have no natural-born Subjects but Christian, and a natural-born Jew Christian Foreign Englishman, is such a Medley of Contradictions, that all the Rabbies in the World will never be able to reconcile them.[166]

The arguments for and against the Jew Bill signal the deep and painful divisions in the British polity among Protestants, between Catholics and Protestants, supporters of the Hanoverian succession and those who harbored Jacobite loyalties, Tories and Whigs, and probably most important, those who subscribed to an idea of Britain permeable to many different people, groups, religions, and cultures as a part of its imperial project, and those who supported regional autonomy and a more inward looking foreign policy.

The parallel discourses about nation and circumcision worked together to suggest a connection between the integrity of the individual, uncircumcised (male) body and the nation. Circumcision was a ritual of membership and belonging that represented the permanent, irrevocably marked body. It was, in Jonas Hanway's words, a true 'badge of honor' and fidelity that could not be removed. In contrast, Britain's Christian statehood seemed an unstable and contested entity, its members' allegiances fluid and open to persuasion and conversion. The idea that another faith could have legitimacy or authority imperiled the exclusivity of Anglican doctrine as the essence of English identity and superiority and the Anglican, white male as its only legal subject.

The gaze of the prints and pamphlets focused on the integrity of an individual, circumcised body raising worrying questions about the integrity of Britain's social body and its viability as a coherent nation. The Jews imagined in the prints and pamphlets made up a cohesive, united group in precisely the ways that the British were not. The contrast of a divided Britain and the representation of a coherent Jewish nation presented both a threat and an opportunity for galvanizing a broad spectrum of the political culture. In the endless discussion of Jewish disloyalty and Catholic treason what emerges is a similar attribution to Catholics of singularity, coherence, and unity. Although studies of nation and community have pointed to perceived threats from those identities imagined as unfixed and therefore destabilizing, the Jew Bill points in the opposite direction. In this analysis the very integrity of the Jewish community posed a danger to Britain by drawing attention to its confessional divisions.

How do we explain this insistence on a national identity defined by a single faith and practice? England had been confessionally divided since the sixteenth century and the idea that foreigners posed a threat and a source of danger was not new in 1753. However, in the mid-eighteenth century, the resonances of otherness were quite different from earlier connotations. Given Britain's imperial project and its aspirations abroad, the idea of the foreigner and foreignness carried a more ambivalent message. As we have seen in this chapter, the task of empire necessitated some change in these older perceptions of those defined as others. Britain's financial, commercial, and imperial endeavors depended on the networks, both colonial and metropolitan, established and maintained by Jews. The controversy over the Jew Bill suggests disquiet and self-doubt related to Britain's permeability to what Michael Fisher has called 'the counterflows' of outside influences and peoples.[167] The incorporation and assimilation of England's small Jewish population by creating opportunities for naturalization, however circuitous and difficult, would imply the possibility of having to integrate other Christians including Nonconformists and Catholics, and perhaps even 'Infidels, Hereticks, and Turks'.

Conclusion

In the parliamentary elections of 1754 the Tories were determined to use the Jewish Naturalization Bill as an issue to galvanize their base and erode the majority enjoyed by the Whigs. The campaign was vociferous and intense, the Jew Bill featured prominently, and the Whigs suffered losses.[168] The furor caught William Hogarth's attention and inspired him to create the engraving series *An Election Entertainment*

(1754) containing allusions to both the Canning case and the Jew Bill.[169] Polling in London took place between April 29 and May 8 and according to some accounts drew close to 4000 voters.[170] Canning's trial for perjury in April and May 1754 coincided exactly with the parliamentary election campaign: the trial was interrupted by two adjournments to allow several aldermen on the bench to campaign and participate in the elections before finally ending with Canning's conviction and transportation.

Both of these cases served as a forum in which to debate the presence of internal others, Britain's imperial project, and its impact on English culture and society. The results were rarely conclusive. Canning's trial ended with her conviction and transportation to Connecticut, and the lives of the Gypsies in England did not change very much. The prejudice and hostility toward Gypsies is recorded in over 400 pages of testimony of countless witnesses who appeared at the trial. And despite the repeal of the Jewish Naturalization Act in November 1753, London's Jews continued to pursue their livelihoods in England although denied the rights bestowed by naturalization.

That this debate unfolded through legal events and the circulation of cheap pamphlets and prints is no coincidence. Each of the cases concerned the application of the rule of law and equality before the law and how far and to whom legal authorities and English subjects would apply its principles. The legal setting arbitrated Britain's reception and treatment of its internal others. While some found acceptance and prosperity, the legal process under the cover of equality before the law and rule of law drew and redrew lines of difference depending on the specifics of the case, excluding those perceived as threatening, powerless, or unable to contribute something deemed worthwhile. As pictured in the print, titled 'The City Up and Down, or the Candidates Poiz'd' (Figure 1.8) Sir John Barnard (c.1685–1764) an MP for London summarized the legal heart of the matter when he said 'I am strictly speaking neither a Friend to the Jews nor their Enemy; excepting when they aim at having equal Rights and Privileges with my Fellow Citizens and Country-men.'[171]

The ideology of the rule of law offered a way to organize the hostility to difference within a framework of accommodation built into an imperial enterprise. In each of these cases legal mechanisms failed – on their own terms – either to integrate difference or to expel it completely. The pamphlets and prints that expressed British fears of Gypsies and Jews allow us to look beyond the literate classes to show how race, nation, and religion played in British popular culture. Contrary to some scholarship on the eighteenth century, this evidence demonstrates that empire was a subject of real interest to ordinary people who identified

Figure 1.8 'The City Up and Down, or the Candidates Poiz'd'

with the imperial project even as they expressed anxieties about what it meant for them and about them. Taken together these cases give us purchase on contemporary ideas about race, nation, and empire in eighteenth-century Britain that allows us to interrogate and problematize the implications of what P. J. Marshall has called a 'nation defined by empire'.[172]

London's population in the second half of the eighteenth century included Africans. Some enjoyed free status, but many were enslaved. They had been brought to the metropole by their white colonial owners, many of whom sought to escape plantation life and take their place among London's elite circles. Their slaves sought freedom and the rights and privileges promised by the ideology of rule of law. We take up the vague and complicated parameters of their legal status in the next chapter.

Notes

1 John Brewer, *The Sinews of Power: War, Money and the English State, 1688–1783* (Cambridge: Cambridge University Press, 1990) and P. G. M. Dickson, *The Financial Revolution in England: A Study in the Development of Public Credit, 1688–1756* (New York: Macmillan, 1967). Steven Pincus argues that many of the financial

developments that took place in the decades after the Glorious Revolution originated earlier. Rather than being the result of 1688, they emerged from the strength of the English economy in the late seventeenth century and forces of modernity already at work. Steve Pincus, *1688: The First Modern Revolution* (New Haven, CT: Yale University Press, 2009), p. 6.
2 Dickson, *Financial Revolution*, p. 11.
3 The ideology of equality before the law is examined by Douglas Hay in 'Property, Authority, and the Criminal Law', in *Albion's Fatal Tree*; and Thompson, *Whigs and Hunters*, esp. pp. 258–269.
4 E. P. Thompson, *Customs in Common: Studies in Traditional Popular Culture* (New York: Merlin Press, 1991), p. 34.
5 Hay, 'Property, Authority, and the Criminal Law', in *Albion's Fatal Tree*, pp. 25 and 56.
6 Reeve Ballard, *The necessity of magistracy from the vices of mankind. An assize sermon, preached at Kingston upon Thames, August 16, 1745. Before the Right Honourable Sir William Lee, ... and the Honourable Mr. Justice Burnet* (London: H. Pemberton, 1745), p. 7.
7 Martin Madan, *Thoughts on executive justice: with respect to our criminal laws, particularly on the circuits: dedicated to the judges of Assize and recommended to the perusal of all magistrates and to all persons who are liable to serve on Crown juries* (London: J. Dodsley, 1785), p. 1.
8 James Bate, *The advantages of a national observance of divine and human laws. An assize sermon preach'd at Maidstone in Kent on the 13th of March 1733–4 before the Lord Chief Baron Reynolds* (London: John Whiston, 1734), p. 19; and Richard Green, *The benefit of oaths to civil society consider'd, in An assize sermon, Preach'd before The Hon. Martin Wright, Esq. One of the Justices of his Majesty's Court of King's Bench, The Hon. Sir Thomas Abney, Knt. One of the Justices of his Majesty's Court of Common Pleas, and The University of Oxford. July 5, 1744* (London: John and Paul Knapton, 1745), p. 22.
9 Green, *Benefit of oaths to civil society consider'd*, p. 13.
10 Ballard, *The necessity of magistracy from the vices of mankind*, p. 6.
11 David Lemmings, *Law and Government*, pp. 5–6.
12 The two acts were the Foreign and Protestants Naturalization Act 1709 (7 Anne c. 5) and the Jewish Naturalization Act 1753 (26 Geo II, c. 26).
13 Daniel Statt, *Foreigners and Englishmen*.
14 Alan Singer, 'Aliens and Citizens: Jewish and Protestant Naturalization in the Making of the Modern British Nation' (PhD dissertation, University of Missouri, Columbia, 1999), ch. 3 and Thomas Perry, *Public Opinion, Propaganda, and Politics in Eighteenth-Century England: A Study of the Jew Bill of 1753* (Cambridge, MA: Harvard University Press, 1962), pp. 31–44 enumerate the different naturalization bills preceding the Jew Bill. For more on the Act of 1709 and its aftermath, see H. T. Dickinson, 'The Poor Palatines and the Parties', *English Historical Review* 82 (1967), pp. 464–485.
15 John Toland, *Reasons for Naturalizing the Jews in Great Britain and Ireland, or the same foot with all other nations. Containing also, A defence of the Jews against all Vulgar prejudices in all countries* (London: J. Roberts, 1714), p. 7, emphasis original.
16 Rogers, *Mayhem*.
17 Rogers, *Mayhem*, pp. 4–5.
18 Wilson, *A Sense of the People*.
19 Nicholas Rogers, 'Confronting the Crime Wave: The Debate Over Social Reform and Regulation, 1749–1753', in *Stilling the Grumbling Hive: The Response to Social and Economic Problems in England, 1689–1750*, ed. Lee Davison, Tim Hitchcock, Tim Keirn, and Robert Shoemaker (New York: St. Martin's Press, 1992), pp. 77–98. See also Rogers, *Mayhem*. For more on the demobilization crisis, see J. M. Beattie, *Crime and the Courts*, and Douglas Hay, 'War, Dearth, and Theft in the Eighteenth Century: The Record of the English Courts', *Past and Present* 95 (1982), pp. 117–160.

INTERNAL OTHERS: JEWS, GYPSIES, AND JACOBITES

20 F. G. Stephens and Dorothy George, *Catalogue of Prints and Drawings in the British Museum*, 11 vols. (London: Trustees British Museum, 1870–1954), vol. 3, part 2, #3124, pp. 813–814.
21 Statt, *Foreigners and Englishmen*, pp. 194–214; Perry, *Public Opinion, Propaganda, and Politics*, pp. 31–44; and Singer, 'Aliens and Citizens', ch. 3.
22 AR 824, Jewish Museum of London. For more analysis of this image see Dana Rabin, 'Seeing Jews and Gypsies in 1753', *Cultural and Social History* 7 (2010), pp. 35–58.
23 The aborted Elibank Plot (1752), a Jacobite plan to coordinate a rebellion in Scotland simultaneous with attacks on St James and the Tower of London and restore the Stuart dynasty under the leadership of Charles Edward Stuart (the Young Pretender, 1720–1788), unravelled when Cameron was captured in Scotland in March 1753. His arraignment and sentence under the Act of Attainder passed in 1746 resulted from the intervention of Prime Minister Henry Pelham, who wished to conceal any knowledge of the Plot which he feared would destabilize the regime. The attainder was an instrument of law that declared the person or persons named 'attainted' of treason and guilty of the crime, necessitating no further legal proceedings or presentation of evidence and eliminating any contingency with regard to outcome. The proceeding involved only the testimony of witnesses to identify the defendant. Not wishing to draw attention to the persistence of a Jacobite cause, the government prosecuted Cameron for his role in the Jacobite Rebellion of 1745 in the quickest and least visible way and never mentioned Elibank. Cameron joined in the government's conspiracy of silence to protect the Jacobite cause and its followers. Charles Petrie, 'The Elibank Plot', *Transactions of the Royal Historical Society* 14 (1931), pp. 175–196.
24 Elizabeth Canning, *Old Bailey Sessions Papers* [hereafter OBSP], April 24–May 1, 1754, consulted online, t17540424-60.
25 Allan Ramsay, *A Letter to the Right Honorable the Earl of —* (1753) reprinted in *The investigator. Containing the following tracts: I. On ridicule. II. On Elizabeth Canning. III. On naturalization. IV. On taste.* (London, 1762), p. 38. More than fifty pamphlets and broadsides with either Canning or Squires in the title are listed in the British Library catalogue. The case has been the subject of several retellings for popular audiences including Josephine Tey, *The Franchise Affair* (London: Macmillan, 1948) and John Treherne, *The Canning Enigma* (London: Jonathan Cape, 1989). Scholarly examinations include: Amy Masciola, '"The unfortunate maid exemplified": Elizabeth Canning and Representations of Infanticide in Eighteenth-Century England', in *Infanticide: Historical Perspectives, 1550–2000*, ed. Mark Jackson (Aldershot: Ashgate, 2002), pp. 52–72; and Judith Moore, *The Appearance of Truth: The Story of Elizabeth Canning and Eighteenth-Century Narrative* (Newark, DE: University of Delaware Press, 1994).
26 Kristina Straub, 'Heteroanxiety and the Case of Elizabeth Canning', *Eighteenth-Century Studies* 30 (1997), pp. 296–303; and Straub, *Domestic Affairs: Intimacy, Eroticism, and Violence between Servants and Masters in Eighteenth-Century Britain* (Baltimore, MD: Johns Hopkins Press, 2009).
27 My interpretation follows on the pioneering work of Ann Stoler, *Carnal Knowledge and Imperial Power: Race and the Intimate in Colonial Rule* (Berkeley, CA: University of California Press, 1995); and Wilson, *A Sense of the People*; Wilson, *The Island Race*; and Wilson, *A New Imperial History*.
28 The discomfort with and ambivalence about empire is detailed in the remainder of this book. Others who have tracked this phenomenon in the second half of the eighteenth century include Michael Ragussis, *Theatrical Nation: Jews and Other 'Outlandish Englishmen' in Georgian Britain* (Philadelphia, PA: University of Pennsylvania Press, 2010); and P. J. Marshall, 'Empire and Authority in the Later Eighteenth-Century', *Journal of Imperial and Commonwealth History* 15 (1987), pp. 105–122, and P. J. Marshall, 'A Nation Defined by Empire, 1755–1776', in *Uniting the Kingdom: The Making of British History*, ed. Alexander Grand and Keith Stringer (London: Routledge, 1995), pp. 208–222. For more on single women, see Amy Froide,

Never Married: Singlewomen in Early Modern England (Oxford: Oxford University Press, 2007).

29 The definition of Gypsy is from the *Oxford English Dictionary*. On vagrancy, see Lee Beier, *Masterless Men: the Vagrancy Problem in England, 1560–1640* (London: Methuen, 1985); Paul Slack, 'Vagrants and vagrancy in England, 1598–1664', *Economic History Review* 27 (1974), pp. 360–379; Paul Slack, *Poverty and Policy in Tudor and Stuart England* (London: Longman, 1988). On migration in early modern England, see Peter Clark and David Souden, eds., *Migration and Society in Early Modern England* (London: Hutchinson, 1987); and Patricia Fumerton, *Unsettled: The Culture of Mobility and the Working Poor in Early Modern England* (Chicago, IL: University of Chicago: 2009). For more on Gypsies, see David Mayall, *Gypsy Identities 1500–2000: From Egipcyans and Moon-men to the Ethnic Romany* (London: Routledge, 2004). On place, honor, crime, and community, see Anthony Fletcher and John Stevenson, *Order and Disorder in Early Modern England* (Cambridge: Cambridge University Press, 1985); Robert Shoemaker, 'The Decline of Public Insult in London, 1660–1800', *Past and Present* 169 (2000), pp. 97–131; Garthine Walker, *Crime, Gender and the Social Order*; and Keith Wrightson, 'Two Concepts of Order: Justices, Constables and Jurymen in Seventeenth-century England', in *An Ungovernable People*, ed. Brewer and Styles, pp. 21–46.

30 Given what Charles Fleet called 'a guerrilla war' between smugglers and the government between 1740 and 1750, the proximity of Abbotsbury and Dorchester to the coast and the huge amount of tea smuggled into London sewn into outer garments not dissimilar to the capes and coats worn by Squires and her children, the connection would have been an easy one to make. 'Sussex Smugglers', in *Albion's Fatal Tree*, ed. Hay, Linebaugh, Rule, Thompson, and Winslow, pp. 119–166.

31 This discussion of the cultural meaning of place relies of Doreen Massey, *For Space* (London: SAGE Publications, 2005), esp. pp. 9–15, 64–68.

32 *London Evening Post*, February 15–17, 1753, p. 4.

33 *The Case of Elizabeth Canning* (London, 1753), reprinted in Ramsay, *A Letter*, p. 25.

34 Straub, 'Heteroanxiety', p. 296. Scholarship on race and nation in the eighteenth century includes Suvir Kaul, *Poems of Nation, Anthems of Empire: English Verse in the Long Eighteenth-Century* (Charlottesville, VA: University of Virginia Press, 2000); Catherine Molineux, *Faces of Perfect Ebony: Encountering Atlantic Slavery in Imperial Britain* (Cambridge, MA: Harvard University Press: 2012); Diana Paton, *No Bond but the Law*. Wahrman, *The Making of the Modern Self*; Wheeler, *The Complexion of Race*; and Wilson, *Island Race*, and *New Imperial History*. For the seventeenth century, see Traub, 'Mapping the Global Body'.

35 Henry Fielding, *A Clear State of the Case of Elizabeth Canning* (1753), in *An Enquiry into the Causes of the Late Increase of Robbers and Related Writings*, ed. Malvin Zirker (Oxford: Clarendon Press, 1988), p. 283.

36 Straub, 'Heteroanxiety', p. 299.

37 *London Daily Advertiser*, January 31, 1753, p. 2. For a study of newspapers in the eighteenth century, see Michael Harris, *London Newspapers in the Age of Walpole: A Study of the Origins of the Modern English Press* (Cranbury, NJ: Associated University Presses, 1987). The original maps of London and its surroundings can be found in Lillian de la Torre, *Elizabeth is Missing* (New York: Knopf, 1945).

38 *London Daily Advertiser*, January 31, 1753, p. 2. Stays are 'a laced underbodice, stiffened by the insertion of strips of whale-bone (sometimes of metal or wood) worn by women (sometimes by men) to give shape and support to the figure: a corset' (*OED*).

39 *London Daily Advertiser*, January 31, 1753, p. 2.

40 *Case of Elizabeth Canning*, reprinted in Ramsay, *A Letter*, p. 25.

41 *Case of Elizabeth Canning*, reprinted in Ramsay, *A Letter*, p. 26.

42 Straub, 'Heteroanxiety', pp. 296–297 and *Domestic Affairs*, pp. 47–82. For more on reading the body in the eighteenth century, Barbara Duden, *The Woman Beneath*

the Skin: A Doctor's Patients in Eighteenth-Century Germany (Cambridge, MA: Harvard University Press, 1991).
43 John Hill, The Story of Elizabeth Canning considered by Dr. Hill (London: G. Faulkner, 1753), p. 9.
44 Publications skeptical of Canning's veracity included The Truth of the Case, or, Canning and Squires fairly opposed (London: M. Cooper, W. Reeve, and C. Sympson, 1753), Ramsay, A Letter, and the ballad titled 'The Devil Outdone' (London, S. Wright, 1753).
45 Hill, Story of Elizabeth Canning, pp. 13–14.
46 Hill was the first to suggest that Canning had been with a lover, Story of Elizabeth Canning, p. 13. The author of The Imposture Detected; or, the Mystery and Iniquity of Elizabeth Canning's Story Displayed (London: M. Cooper, 1753) outlines other likely alternatives, pp. 23–33.
47 Daily Advertiser, January 6, 1753, p. 3. Mrs. Canning placed at least two other ads on January 4 and 20, 1753.
48 James Solas Dodd, A physical account of the case of Elizabeth Canning (London: G. Faulkner, 1753), p. 14. According to Dodd the obstruction was caused by 'her sleeping great Part of a Night, in a damp Stone Kitchen'.
49 Daniel Cox, An appeal to the public, in behalf of Elizabeth Canning (London: W. Meadows, 1753), p. 16.
50 David Mayall, 'Egyptians and Vagabonds: Representations of the Gypsy in Early Modern Official and Rogue Literature', Immigrants and Minorities 16 (1997), p. 62.
51 22 Henry VIII c. 10 (1530). John Raithby, ed., The Statutes of the Realm, 11 vols. (London: G. Eyre and A. Strahan, 1810–1828), vol. 3, p. 327.
52 1&2 Ph. & M. c. 4 (1554), Statutes of the Realm, vol. 4, p. 242; 5 Eliz. c. 20 (1562), Statutes of the Realm, vol. 4, p. 448.
53 Mayall, 'Egyptians and Vagabonds'. Mayall points out that their separateness is belied by the statute of 1562 which criminalizes associating with gypsies and points to intermixing.
54 Gwenda Morgan and Peter Rushton, Banishment in the Early Atlantic World: Convicts, Rebels and Slaves (London: Bloomsbury, 2013), p. 12.
55 London Evening Post, February 1–3, 1753, p. 4. An equally brief mention of Squires was made in the London Evening Post, February 8–10, 1753, p. 4.
56 Fielding, A Clear State, pp. 299–301.
57 London Evening Post, February 15–17, 1753, p. 4.
58 London Evening Post, February 15–17, 1753, p. 4.
59 Mary Squires and Susannah Wells, OBSP February 21, 1753, consulted online, t17530221-47.
60 David Mayall, 'The Making of British Gypsy Identities, c.1500–1980', Immigrants and Minorities 11 (1992), p. 26. In an unpublished paper presented in March 2014 at the Huntington Library titled 'Gypsies in Eighteenth-Century England: The Trials and Travels of Mary Squires', David Cressy examines the references to the Gypsy in Canning's 1754 trial for perjury. Despite copious references to their criminal nature, their cant, insinuations about their practice of passing fake coins, stealing, and telling fortunes, and the fears they inspired in witnesses, Cressy maintains that 'Gypsies were not specifically targeted by the authorities'.
61 Squires and Wells, OBSP, February 21, 1753.
62 Squires and Wells, OBSP, February 21, 1753. Lawn is a kind of fine linen, resembling cambric. Lawns were pieces of this linen. OED.
63 Squires and Wells, OBSP, February 21, 1753.
64 Squires and Wells, OBSP, February 21, 1753.
65 Squires and Wells, OBSP, February 21, 1753.
66 Ramsay, A Letter, pp. 3–4.
67 Ramsay, A Letter, pp. 20–21.
68 Freeman O'Donoghue and Henry M. Hake, Catalogue of Engraved British Portraits preserved in the Department of Prints and Drawings in the British Museum, 6 vols. (London: Trustees British Museum, 1908), vol. 1.

69 Fielding, *A Clear State*, pp. 309, 294.
70 Library of Congress.
71 *London Evening Post*, February 15–17, 1753, p. 4.
72 Squires and Wells, *OBSP*, February 21, 1753.
73 Squires and Wells, *OBSP*, February 21, 1753, Randolph Trumbach, *Sex and the Gender Revolution. Volume 1: Heterosexuality and the Third Gender in Enlightenment London* (Chicago, IL: University of Chicago Press, 1998), pp. 136–153, and Mayall, 'The Making of British Gypsy Identities', pp. 26–27.
74 Squires and Wells, *OBSP*, February 21, 1753. For more on prostitution in the eighteenth century, see Tony Henderson, *Disorderly Women in Eighteenth-Century London: Prostitution and Control in the Metropolis, 1730–1830* (London: Longman, 1999).
75 Fielding, *A Clear State*, p. 301.
76 Fielding, *A Clear State*, p. 301.
77 Fielding, *A Clear State*, p. 301.
78 Fielding, *A Clear State*, p. 302.
79 Fielding, *A Clear State*, p. 302.
80 Fielding, *A Clear State*, p. 302.
81 Fielding, *A Clear State*, p. 306.
82 Sir Crisp Gascoyne, *An Address to the Liverymen of the City of London* (London: James Hodges, 1754), p. 9.
83 Gascoyne, *Address*, p. 10. Fielding's tactics were made public by Virtue Hall on March 8, 1753. Hall explained that 'when she was at Mr. Fielding's she at first spoke the truth, but that she was told that that was not the truth, and was terrified and threatened to be sent to Newgate and prosecuted as a felon, unless she would speak the truth'. (Gascoyne, *Address*, p. 11).
84 *London Evening Post* August 13–15, 1751, Issue 3716, p. 1.
85 *London Daily Advertiser And Literary Gazette*, August 26, 1751, Issue 151, pp. 2–3; *General Advertiser*, October 25, 1751, Issue 5031, p. 1. Advertisements of the pamphlets recounting the story of the case appeared in newspapers throughout 1751, 1752, and 1753. The case was recounted again in 1767 in *The Cries of Blood, or Juryman's Monitor* (London: J. Cooke) which included ten cases of miscarriage of justice.
86 *London Evening Post* August 13–15, 1751, Issue 3716, p. 1.
87 Stephens and George, *Catalogue of Prints and Drawings*, vol. 3, part 2, #3214, p. 869.
88 John Styles, 'Sir John Fielding and the Problem of Criminal Investigation in Eighteenth-Century England', *Transactions of the Royal Historical Society* 33 (1983), pp. 127–149.
89 *A refutation of Sir Crisp Gascoyne's Address to the liverymen of London: by a clear state of the case of Elizabeth Canning, in a narrative of facts* (London: J. Payne, 1754), p. 29.
90 J. J. Hecht, *The Domestic Servant Class in the Eighteenth Century* (London: Routledge, 1955); Bridget Hill, *Women Alone: Spinsters in England, 1660–1850* (New Haven, CT: Yale University Press, 2001); D. A. Kent, 'Ubiquitous But Invisible: Female Domestic Servants in Mid-Eighteenth-Century London', *History Workshop Journal* 28 (1989), pp. 111–128; and Tim Meldrum, *Domestic Service, and Gender, 1660–1750: Life and Work in the London Household* (London: Longman, 2000).
91 Fielding, *A Clear State*, p. 292; Hill, *Story of Elizabeth Canning*, p. 30.
92 *London Evening Post*, February 15–17, 1753, p. 4
93 Thompson, *Whigs and Hunters*, pp. 258–269.
94 Gascoyne, *Address*, p. 3.
95 Ruth Frankenberg, *White Women*, p. 1.
96 Michael Fisher, *Counterflows to Colonialism: Indian Travelers and Settlers in Britain, 1600–1857* (Delhi: Permanent Black, 2004) demonstrates the diversity of Britain in the eighteenth century.

INTERNAL OTHERS: JEWS, GYPSIES, AND JACOBITES

97 26 Geo. II, c.26, 'The Act to permit Persons professing the Jewish Religion to be Naturalized by Parliament; and for other Purposes therein mentioned'. John Raithby and Thomas Edlyne, eds., *Statutes at Large, of England and of Great Britain: from Magna Carta to the union of the kingdoms of Great Britain and Ireland*, 20 vols. (London: G. Eyre and A. Strahan, 1811), vol. 11, p. 219.

98 The bill itself mentions as its objects the 'many Persons of considerable Substance, professing the Jewish Religion'.

99 Todd Endelman, *The Jews of Georgian England, 1714–1830* (Ann Arbor, MI: University of Michigan Press, 1999), p. 114. The details of the bill, its passage and repeal are detailed in Perry, *Public Opinion, Propaganda, and Politics*, and David Katz, *The Jews in the History of England, 1485–1850* (Oxford: Clarendon, 1994), ch. 6.

100 The act of repeal, 27 Geo. II, c.1, passed in the House of Lords on November 22 and the House of Commons on November 28. Raithby and Edlyne, *Statutes at Large*, vol. 11, p. 254.

101 Perry, *Public Opinion, Propaganda, and Politics* is a study of parliamentary practice and politics. Jewish historians who have discussed the controversy include Endelman, *Jews of Georgian England*, pp. 24–26, 30–33, 36–39, 59–64, 89–91, Todd Endelman, *The Jews of Britain, 1656–2000* (Berkeley, CA: University of California Press, 2001), pp. 68, 70, 74–76, Katz, *The Jews in the History of England*, and Cecil Roth, *A History of the Jews in England* (Oxford: Clarendon, 1941). Literary scholars have paid more attention to the anti-Semitic content of debates that surrounded the Jew Bill. See Frank Felsenstein, *Anti-Semitic Stereotypes: A Paradigm of Otherness in English Popular Culture, 1660–1830* (Baltimore, MD: Johns Hopkins University Press, 1995), ch. 8.

102 Linda Colley overlooks the episode entirely in *Britons: Forging the Nation, 1707–1837* (New Haven, CT: Yale University Press, 1992).

103 For trends in Anglo-Jewish historiography, see Endelman's preface to the 1999 edition of *Jews of Georgian England*, and Edelman, 'Writing English Jewish History', *Albion* 27 (1995), pp. 623–636.

104 All gentile discussions of Jews do this cultural work; however, each is differentiated by its geographical location and historical circumstance. Each discussion varies as any specific discourse about Jews is based on actual knowledge of and contact with Jews balanced with a Christian projection of Jews and Jewishness based on a small number of experiences and encounters with Jews and a heavy reliance on stories and stereotypes.

105 Statt, *Foreigners and Englishmen*, p. 31.

106 Endelman, *Jews of Britain*, 6. James Shapiro addresses issues of race and nation during the Jew Bill controversy in *Shakespeare and the Jews* (New York: Columbia University Press, 1996), ch. 7.

107 Singer, 'Aliens and Citizens', and Singer, 'Great Britain or Judea Nova? National Identity, Property, and the Jewish Naturalization Controversy of 1753', in *British Romanticism and the Jews: History, Culture, Literature*, ed. Sheila A. Spector (New York: Palgrave Macmillan, 2008), pp. 19–36.

108 J. A. Giuseppi, 'Early Jewish Holders of Bank of England Stock (1694–1725)', *Miscellanies of the Jewish Historical Society of England* 6 (1962), pp. 143–174; Dickson, *Financial Revolution*, pp. 259–260, 267–269, 282–283.

109 Harold Pollins, *Economic History of the Jews in England* (Rutherford, NJ: Fairleigh Dickinson University Press, 1982), pp. 53–58. The Bank of England Act 1696 (8 & 9 Will. 3 c. 20) limited the number of brokers to 100 and set the number of Jews allowed. The limit of 100 brokers was removed in 1709 (Bank of England Act 7 Ann c 30), but the number of Jewish brokers remained the same.

110 Gedalia Yogev, *Anglo-Dutch Jews and Eighteenth-Century Trade* (Leicester: Leicester University Press, 1978); Pollins, *Economic History of the Jews*, pp. 48–53; and Singer, 'Aliens and Citizens', ch. 2, pp. 66–73.

111 In Jamaica Jews made up 5 percent of the white population in 1680 rising to 9.5 percent in 1720 and 7.5 percent in 1740. In Barbados Jews made up 1.5 percent of

whites in 1680 and rose to 3 percent in 1750. Stephen Fortune, *Merchants and Jews: The Struggle for British West Indian Commerce, 1650–1750* (Gainsville, FL: University of Florida Press, 1984), pp. 47–49.
112 Fortune, *Merchants and Jews*; Singer, 'Aliens and Citizens', ch. 2, p. 72. In North America most Jews were shopkeepers, and the few who engaged in shipping restricted their trade to the West Indies.
113 Pollins, *Economic History*, pp. 50–53.
114 Endelman, *Jews of Georgian England*, p. 25. 7 Jac. I, c. 2., passed in 1609 allowing naturalization by private act of Parliament, attempted to enforce uniformity among non-Anglican sects. H. S. Q. Henriques, *The Jews and the English Law* (London: J. Jacobs, 1908), p. 238.
115 Jews became naturalized under this act, most of them residents of Jamaica. Perry, *Public Opinion, Propaganda, and Politics*, p. 15.
116 Alan Singer, 'Aliens and Citizens', ch. 2, pp. 50–54; Dickson, *Financial Revolution*, p. 514.
117 Philo-Patriae [J. Salvador], *Considerations on the bill to permit persons professing the Jewish religion to be naturalized by Parliament. In several letters from a merchant in town to his friend in the country. Wherein the motives of all parties interested therein are examined; the principles of Christianity, with regard to the admission of Jews, are fully discussed; and their utility in trade clearly proved* (London: R. Baldwin, 1753), p. 42.
118 An investigation of the lottery in 1753 concluded that Gideon had bought more than six thousand tickets from which he profited greatly. Lucy Sutherland, 'Samson Gideon: Eighteenth Century Jewish Financier', *Transactions of the Jewish Historical Society of England* 17 (1953), pp. 79–90; John Francis, *Chronicles and Characters of the Stock Exchange* (London: Willoughby, 1849), p. 90; and Edgar Samuel, 'Gideon, Samson (1699–1762)', ODNB (http://www.oxforddnb.com/view/article/10645, accessed February 24, 2016).
119 Samuel, 'Gideon, Samson (1699–1762)', ODNB.
120 Katz, *Jews in the History of England*, pp. 267–270.
121 Sutherland, 'Samson Gideon'.
122 Louis Hyman, *The Jews of Ireland from Earliest Times to the Year 1910* (Shannon: Irish University Press, 1972), ch. 8; Katz, *Jews in the History of England*, p. 243; and Robert Liberles, 'The Jews and their Bill: Jewish Motivation in the Controversy of 1753', *Jewish History* 2 (1987), pp. 29–36.
123 M. Woolf, 'Joseph Salvador, 1716–1786', *Transactions of the Jewish Historical Society of England* 21 (1962–7), pp. 104–137; and Edgar Samuel, 'Salvador, Joseph (1716–1786)', ODNB (http://www.oxforddnb.com/view/article/40772, accessed February, 24, 2016).
124 Philo-Patriae [J. Salvador], *Further considerations on the act to permit persons professing the Jewish religion, to be naturalized by Parliament. In a second letter from a merchant in town to his friend in the country. In this part, the utility of the Jews in trade, their situation in other nations; and the expediency of continuing them on the present footing, are fully considered and proved* (London: R. Baldwin, 1753), pp. 65–66.
125 It is important to note, however, that Locke's views on toleration were not generally accepted and were not embodied in the Revolution Settlement of 1689. The Toleration Act (1 Will. & Mary c. 18) did not apply to Jews, Catholics, or Unitarians, so the Glorious Revolution was in this sense profoundly anti-Lockean.
126 *Some thoughts upon a Bill for general naturalization: addressed to those of all denominations who act upon Whig-Principles* (London: M. Cooper, 1751), p. 3.
127 *Some thoughts upon a Bill*, pp. 4, 7.
128 Add MSS 35606 (Old Horace Walpole, Sen., to P. Yorke, Sept 29, 1753), f. 84.
129 Josiah Tucker, *A letter to a friend concerning naturalizations: shewing, I. What a naturalization is not; II. What it is ...* (London: Thomas Tyre, 1753), p. 6, emphasis original.
130 For more on Tucker, see Walter Ernest Clark, *Josiah Tucker, Economist; A Study in the History of Economics* (New York: Columbia University Press, 1903).

INTERNAL OTHERS: JEWS, GYPSIES, AND JACOBITES

131 Joseph Addison, *The Spectator* #495, September 12, 1712, in *The Spectator*, ed. Richard Steele and Joseph Addison, 6 vols. (London: I Walker, 1812–13), vol. 5, p. 228.
132 Toland, *Reasons for Naturalizing the Jews*, p. 14.
133 Philo-Patriae [J. Salvador], *Considerations on the bill* and *Further considerations*. For attribution of the pamphlets, see Woolf, 'Joseph Salvador, 1716–1786', pp. 105–106.
134 Philo-Patriae [J. Salvador], *Further Considerations*, pp. 12–16.
135 Philo-Patriae [J. Salvador], *Further Considerations*, pp. 84, 37.
136 Philo-Patriae [J. Salvador], *Further Considerations*, p. 37.
137 Philo-Patriae [J. Salvador], *Further Considerations*, p. 81.
138 Philo-Patriae [J. Salvador], *Further Considerations*, p. 53. Salvator's own experience bore this out. In 1746 as the warden of the Bevis Marks Synagogue, he wrote to the king of Sweden turning down his invitation to wealthy Portuguese Jews to move to Sweden. Woolf, 'Joseph Salvador, p. 105.
139 For an overview of the pamphlets produced during the Jew Bill controversy, see Albert M. Hyamson, 'The Jew Bill of 1753', *Transactions of the Jewish Historical Society of England* 6 (1912), pp. 156–188. An excellent analysis of newspaper coverage against the bill is found in G. A. Cranfield, 'The London Evening Post and the Jew Bill of 1753', *The Historical Journal* 8 (1965), pp. 16–30.
140 *Jackson's Oxford Journal*, No. 18, 1753, p. 3. For a good overview of the images that feature the Jew Bill, see I. Solomons, 'Satirical and Political Prints on the Jews Naturalisation Bill, 1753', *Transactions of the Jewish Historical Society of England* 6 (1912), pp. 205–233. The theme of circumcision in the prints is explored by Roy Wolper in 'Circumcision as Polemic in the Jew Bill of 1753: The Cutter Cut?' *Eighteenth Century Life* 7 (1982), pp. 28–36. For more on satirical prints, see Donald, *The Age of Caricature*. Mary Dorothy George provides analysis of 'The Cartoon in the Eighteenth Century', *History Today* 9 (1954), pp. 591–597.
141 *London Evening Post*, 4047, p. 1.
142 Genesis 34: 2–3.
143 Genesis 34: 9–10.
144 Genesis 34: 20, 23.
145 Genesis 34: 25, 27–29.
146 R.H., *The history of Genesis. Being an account of the Holy lives and actions of the Patriarchs; explained with pious and edifying explications, and illustrated with near forty figures* (London: J. D. for Andrew Bell, 1708), pp. 76–77.
147 Thomas Pyle, *A paraphrase with short and useful notes on the books of the Old Testament. Part I. In two volumes. Containing the five books of Moses. With Compleat index ... For the use of Families* (London: John Wyat, 1717), pp. 199–200.
148 Samuel Smith, *The family companion: or, annotations upon the Holy Bible. Together with the lives, ... of our blessed Saviour and his twelve apostles ...* (London, 1739), pp. 42, 43.
149 Felsenstein, *Anti-Semitic Stereotypes*. Nadia Valman sets out nineteenth-century English perceptions of Jewish masculinity in 'Muscular Jews: Young England, Gender, and Jewishness in Disraeli's "Political Trilogy"', *Jewish History* 10 (1996), pp. 57–88.
150 Stephens and George, *Catalogue of Prints and Drawings*, vol. 3, part 2, #3204, pp. 859–860.
151 Jonas Hanway, *A Review of the Proposed Naturalization of the Jews; Being an attempt at a dispassionate Enquiry into the present State of the Case, with some Reflexions on General Naturalization* (London: J. Waugh, 1753), p. 37, original emphasis.
152 Hanway, *A Review of the Proposed Naturalization of the Jews*, p. 33.
153 Hanway, *A Review of the Proposed Naturalization of the Jews*, p. 34.
154 Hanway, *A Review of the Proposed Naturalization of the Jews*, p. 36; original emphasis.
155 William Romaine, *An Answer to a Pamphlet, entitled, Considerations on the bill to permit persons ...* (London: H. Cooke, 1753), p. 10.
156 Romaine, *An Answer to a Pamphlet*, p. 45.

157 Add MSS 35606 (Old Horace Walpole, Sen., to P. Yorke, Sept 29, 1753), f. 84. A recent evaluation of the Jacobite movement argues that it was not truly defeated (nor was it believed to be defeated) until the Bay of Quiberon in 1759. Doron Zimmerman, *The Jacobite Movement in Scotland and in Exile, 1746–1759* (Houndmills: Palgrave Macmillan, 2003).
158 Philo-Patriae [J. Salvador], *Considerations*, p. 42.
159 Philo-Patriae [J. Salvador], *Considerations*, p. 41.
160 Philo-Patriae [J. Salvador], *Considerations*, p. 42.
161 Philo-Patriae [J. Salvador], *Considerations*, p. 47.
162 Philo-Patriae [J. Salvador], *Considerations*, p. 47.
163 *A looking-glass for the Jews: or, the credulous unbelievers* (London: B. Dickinson, 1753), p. iv.
164 Philo-Patriae [J. Salvador], *Considerations*, p. 79.
165 Tucker, *A letter to a friend*, p. 6.
166 Romaine, *Answer*, 60. David Feldman comes to a similar conclusion about the Bill in his article 'Conceiving Difference: Religion, Race and the Jews in Britain, c. 1750–1900', *History Workshop Journal* 76 (2013), pp. 160–186. His discussion of the Jew Bill is on pages 167–171.
167 Fisher, *Counterflows to Colonialism*.
168 London and Oxfordshire are the only two places that have been the subject of studies tracking the role of the Jew Bill in the elections of 1754. Joseph Grego, *A History of Parliamentary Elections and Electioneering* (London: Chatto and Windus, 1886), ch. 5; Ralph Robson, *The Oxfordshire election of 1754: a study in the interplay of city, county, and university politics* (Oxford: Oxford University Press, 1949); and Perry, *Public Opinion, Propaganda, and Politics*, ch. 9.
169 Peter Quennell, *Hogarth's Progress* (New York: Viking Press, 1955), ch. 13.
170 Robson, *Oxfordshire election of 1754*, pp. 101–103; and John Entick, *A new and accurate history and survey of London, Westminster, Southwark* (London: Edward and Charles Dilly, 1766), pp. 83–88.
171 Stephens and George, *Catalogue of Prints and Drawings*, vol. 3, part 2, #3265, pp. 909–910. As an MP Barnard was against the repeal of the Test Act (25 Car. II. c. 2) and voted against the naturalization of foreign Protestants and Jews. D. W. Hayton, 'Barnard, Sir John (c.1685–1764)', ODNB (http://www.oxforddnb.com/view/article/1456, accessed February 24, 2014).
172 Marshall, 'A Nation Defined by Empire'.

CHAPTER TWO

'In a country of liberty?':
Slavery, villeinage, and the making of
whiteness in the Somerset case (1772)

James Somerset was born in West Africa around 1741. When he was eight years old, he was bought by European slave traders and sold in Virginia to Charles Stewart, a Scottish merchant who later became Receiver General of Customs. Stewart (and Somerset as part of his household) frequently traveled among the northern American colonies, moved to Boston in 1764, and then relocated to England, specifically to Holborn's Baldwin Gardens in London in 1768. On October 1, 1771, Somerset, then about thirty years old, left his master's house and refused to return. He remained at large for two months before he was captured by slave hunters and, on Stewart's orders, delivered to the custody of one John Knowles, captain of the ship *Ann and Mary*. He was brought on board, confined in irons, and bound for sale in Jamaica. Abolitionists working on Somerset's behalf, calling themselves his godparents, publicized his situation and applied to William Murray, First Earl of Mansfield and Chief Justice of King's Bench, for a writ of habeas corpus. A writ of habeas corpus, Latin for 'you have the body', was issued by a court of justice to someone holding another person in his custody. The writ directs the detainer to bring his prisoner to a court at a specified time for a particular reason. Although there were many versions of the writ, the one issued in Somerset's case is best known as a legal instrument by which to correct violations of personal liberty by releasing an individual from unlawful detention. Eventually Somerset's case attracted the attention of the prominent abolitionist Granville Sharp.[1]

The case drew attention to the legality of slavery in eighteenth-century England and brought into prominent view two distinguishing and contradictory features of British life in the eighteenth century: liberty and property. In *Rex v. Knowles, ex parte Somersett* (1772) arguments about the nature and history of villeinage – the tenure by which a feudal villein held or occupied his land in exchange for bond-service rendered to the lord – played a crucial role.² Abolitionists, led by Sharp, maintained that English villeinage, a legal term for the labor regime under the English feudal land system in which unfree peasants, villeins, provided labor and services to their lord in return for holdings of land, became obsolete because English law favored freedom. Defenders of slavery mobilized the category of villeinage as slavery's logical precedent and analogue. The lawyers for James Somerset made part of their case against state support for domestic slavery by arguing that villeinage did not set a precedent because it was 'a slavery in blood and family, one uninterruptedly transmitted through a long line of ancestors'.³ This definition delineated villeinage as a specifically English status proven 'by other villeins of the same blood such as were descended from the same common male stock'.⁴ William Davy (d. 1780), sergeant-at-law and one of the lawyers representing Somerset, argued for Somerset's release on the grounds that as an institution villeinage was 'confined to Complexion and ... confined to a particular Quarter of the World'.⁵ In other words, villeins were English people with ties of family, whiteness, and place. Abducted Africans, without the requisite lineage or historical claim, could never inhabit this legal category. Mingling on the periphery and in the metropole had confusing implications for economic, political, and legal institutions as well as for individual physical bodies.⁶ The association of villeinage with whiteness that took place through the arguments presented in Somerset's case was necessary in order to distinguish between free and enslaved people, colonizers and colonized, English and African. The case provided an opportunity to clarify boundaries by creating and temporarily fixing legal categories.

Slavery in the colonies had legal sanction established through slave codes passed by colonial assemblies in North America and in the British Caribbean. Starting in the mid-seventeenth century colonial legislation defined slaves as property without any protection from the common law; these laws always referred to slaves' status through the color of their skin using words like negro, mulatto, and Indian.⁷ The British, world leaders in the slave trade, had by the 1780s shipped more than 1,250,000 Africans to Jamaica, Barbados, and the smaller West Indian 'sugar islands' while almost 300,000 had been sold in North America.⁸ Somerset's case was immediately seen as a test of the legality of slavery in England, and its proceedings were followed closely both by West Indian planters and abolitionists. Though some argued it was *immoral*, no English commentators claimed the practice of slavery was *illegal* at this time. Abolitionists worked to outlaw slavery precisely because they recognized and acknowledged the elaborate legal framework that had been established in colonial legislatures making it 'legal'. While the planters campaigned for a decision that would recognize colonial laws relating to slavery and enforce them in the metropole, Sharp advocated a ruling that would forbid slavery in England. Although it resulted in Somerset's discharge, Mansfield's ruling did not outlaw slavery in England. Instead, Mansfield resolved only the question of the writ of habeas corpus. He declared illegal the coerced transportation of slaves from England and remained silent on the general question of slavery in England and throughout the Empire.

The Somerset case has been the object of inquiry for scholars investigating the history of slavery, the African presence in Britain, labor conditions in the British Empire, and slavery in the American colonies.[9] Legal historians have pointed out the conservative nature of Mansfield's decision and its impact on slavery in the United States in the nineteenth century.[10] Most recently George Van Cleve has analyzed Somerset's case in terms of its impact on English law from an imperial perspective. He credits Mansfield with expanding freedom by protecting the '"rights of man" even for African slaves in England' and ultimately narrowing 'the legal authority for slavery' and circumscribing its moral and political legitimacy.[11] Van Cleve's innovation provides a 'conflict of laws' analysis of the case examining the inconsistencies between laws of different jurisdictions, but his Whiggish conclusion about the expansion of freedom assumes the abolition of the slave trade in 1807 and slavery in 1833. His conclusion begs the question of how the decreased legitimacy of slavery coexisted with Britain's leading role in the slave trade in the thirty-five years following the Somerset decision and of the role of law in this contradiction.

Much of the scholarship cited above either ignores or downplays the issue of race in the case. Some scholars assert that the equation of black and slave did not hold in English law and society, and that questions of race did not play a prominent role in the legal arguments or debates about Somerset.[12] I argue that the issue of race was indeed fundamental to the case. While blackness and property were not equated, whiteness and freedom were inextricably bound up in the arguments. In the staging of the case whiteness was constituted as race by both proponents and opponents of slavery arguing the precedent of villeinage. Again the legal setting reveals the law as a node in the imperial system in which ideas and experiences were generated and exchanged. Neither metropolitan nor colonial, or both, the law mediated these interactions, produced social categories, and attempted to fix cultural boundaries.

This chapter seeks to bring together fields that connect very selectively: slavery and empire. With important exceptions eighteenth-century scholarship touches on many similar threads, themes, and topics that seem to occur in segregated domains that do not engage each other directly.[13] Joining these areas of study gives us new and more nuanced ways to talk about race and the details of its production in specific historical circumstances. These discussions demonstrate that race is not a biological fact, but a category with very real, physical, social, and economic consequences; a category nonetheless constructed in, by and through interactions, experiences, and cultures.[14] In this particular context, merging an examination of empire and slavery makes more visible how the imperial state, through the jurisprudential process, contributed to the creation of whiteness in both the metropole and the colonies.

Somerset, a self-emancipated African slave, and the case, a legal event that generated printed commentary, again called attention to the tensions between the universal premise of equality before the law and Britain's promise of freedom and liberty and the realities of empire and slavery, property and profits. As in the Canning case and the debates over naturalization discussed in chapter 1, the Somerset case revisited the question of whether internal others should be bestowed the treatments and the rights implicitly promised to white Britons. The coverage of the case accentuated the entanglements of empire at home and the mess of legal and cultural inconsistencies both at home and in the colonies.

We will begin with a brief look at the cultural, physical, and legal entanglements of Britain and its colonial holdings on the eve of the Somerset case. Because these entanglements revealed the contradictions inherent in a legal system that condoned slavery and proclaimed everyone equal before the law, legal authorities were at times forced to create distinctions (sometimes against their own will) to try to reimpose order and coherence. The second half of the chapter examines the case itself and the ways in which lawyers on each side tried to reconcile the clear opposition of these two realities without sacrificing either. The conclusion analyzes the stakes of separation, the risks of a complete disentanglement, and how Mansfield's ruling negotiated this terrain.

Entanglements

England in the eighteenth century and London, in particular, was racially diverse. The most obvious evidence of the entanglement of colonial and metropolitan Britain was the presence of 10,000–15,000 blacks in the capital and the residence of up to 5000 blacks who lived in other parts of England, most of them concentrated in Bristol and Liverpool but also in the countryside.[15] Norma Myers has demonstrated that

England's black population was overwhelmingly young, male, and transient. While many black men worked as sailors and soldiers, they also appear in visual sources as footmen, coachmen, pageboys, street vendors, and musicians, and they people criminal records as pimps, prostitutes, highway robbers, and beggars. By no means segregated, blacks and whites lived in close proximity, socialized together, and intermarried. In addition to mixed social spaces, there were also black churches, pubs, and organizations that created a sense of community and provided poor relief and other forms of support for black Londoners.[16]

Eighteenth-century Britain's visual culture yields a rich record of black presence in England, especially the portraits of wealthy, absentee landlords surrounded by their families, servants, and slaves.[17] While these images show us a diverse England, some contemporaries resisted the incorporation of the colonial experience into the metropole. A letter reprinted in *The Gentleman's Magazine* in 1764 protested 'the practice of importing Negroe servants into these kingdoms'. The author complained that the phenomenon had resulted in an exaggerated black slave population of 20,000 in London. If in pictures of landed gentry the position of people of color was not only explicit, but made static, the author of the piece in *The Gentleman's Magazine* makes clear that in everyday life categories were more fluid. Explaining his 'grievance', the writer proclaimed that Africans 'cease to consider themselves as slaves in this free country, nor will they put up with an inequality of treatment, or more willingly perform the laborious offices of servitude than our own people, and if put to do it, are generally sullen, spiteful, treacherous, and revengeful'.[18] The author complained that residence in England changed the slave's status in fundamental and inappropriate ways, implying that the presence of slaves 'in this free country' interfered with the ordering mechanisms of status and power, upending established colonial hierarchies by bringing them to bear on metropolitan consciousness. The author attributed the slave's 'sullen, spiteful, treacherous, and revengeful' manner to his or her proximity to 'our own people', as if such attitudes manifested themselves only when slaves resided in England. Blacks in England, slave or free, disquieted and agitated white viewers who could not avoid seeing the slave's response to slavery made visible in the metropole.[19]

In 1768 justice of the peace and law-and-order advocate John Fielding (1721–1780) echoed the concerns about categories of free and slave in his comments on 20 Geo. II c. 19, an Act 'for the better adjusting and more easy Recovery of the Wages of certain Servants, and for the better Regulation of such Servants'. Fielding discussed the 'confusion' that resulted when West Indian slave owners brought their slaves to England 'as cheap servants, having no Right to Wages'.[20] He too characterized the black slaves as defiant and mutinous, accusing them of machinating for pay and for their freedom by making 'themselves ... troublesome and dangerous to the families' for whom they worked in order to get 'themselves discharged'. Upon achieving their individual freedom, they organized 'societies' that worked to 'corrupt and dissatisfy the Mind of every fresh black Servant that comes to England'.[21]

For Fielding the issue was not just one of categorization, but of political stability. In his view black slaves brought to England posed an even greater danger if they were returned to the colonies because 'after they have lived some Time in a Country of Liberty', they took leadership roles in 'those Insurrections that have lately caused and threatened such Mischiefs and Dangers to the Inhabitants of, and Planters in the Islands in the West-Indies'.[22] Beyond the hazards of slave resistance and violence in the colonies, Fielding described the bringing of slaves to England 'as a Species of Inhumanity to the Blacks themselves'. While abroad, they 'continue in a Degree of Ignorance ... contented with their Condition', with the result that they 'cheerfully submit to those severe Laws which the Government of such Persons makes necessary'. The transformations rendered by the 'sweets of Liberty and the Conversation with free Men and Christians, enlarge their Minds ... and imbitter their State of Slavery', leading to 'the blackest Conspiracies against their Governors and Masters'.[23] Like the writer of the letter in *The Gentleman's Magazine*, Fielding attributed the evaporation of the slave's imagined cheerfulness, submission, and contentment to the metropolitan setting and warned of bitterness, treachery, and violence as its result. Fielding ended his commentary by disavowing any responsibility as a justice of the peace for the capture of runaways, as in the case of slaves like Somerset who freed themselves by leaving their owners' homes and refusing to return to service. Fielding's analysis demonstrates the mid-eighteenth-century reality of constant mobility of ideas, people, and commodities across the Empire that collapsed the categories of home and away, free and slave. He clearly advocated more clear boundaries and regulated interactions.

If, for those like Fielding, the visible influx of blacks from the colonies was a source of apprehension, it might be understood at least in part as a displacement of the threat felt from wealthy plantation whites who returned to England. In contrast to North American colonists, wealthy West Indian landlords and their families were more tied to Britain and always aspired to 'going home'. They established large communities in London, Bath, and Bristol, they bought landed estates in the British countryside, and commissioned individual and family portraits that often featured their black slaves.[24] Brooke Newman has argued that after the Seven Years' War, the absentee planter slowly began to saturate English culture as a stock character, often the object of derision and scorn. An increasing number of West Indian planters became absentees after 1763 and returned to England with their slaves. These homecomings caused confusion and drew attention to the moral, social, and legal contradictions highlighted in Somerset's case, although Somerset's owner was not a planter himself.[25] In broadsides, newspapers, cartoons, novels, and plays returning planters were resented for their wealth and mocked for their social pretension.[26] Although ridiculed in the press, they also established strong organizations to lobby Parliament on their behalf.[27] The discomforts raised by the return of West Indian planters to the metropolis can be ascribed to their hybrid class status, the concrete reminders they provided of the realities of slave ownership, and the wealth created by the slave plantations, all of it unsettling metropolitan sensibilities. When the Empire came home, in the form of Nabobs, black slaves, or absentee landlords from the Caribbean, the difficulty of demarcating the colonial from the metropolitan became overwhelming. As visible difference, skin color became the critical element around which larger, more diffuse anxieties about influence, return, and change constellated.[28]

Judge Mansfield, the judge who would decide the Somerset case, was himself entangled in the imperial slave economy. His own household illustrates how slavery lay at the center of the imperial web that imbricated core and periphery on the eve of the Somerset case. Analysis of Mansfield's Somerset decision often discusses his Afro-British grandniece, Dido Elizabeth Belle (1761?–1804) also known as Elizabeth Dido Lindsay. Dido lived in Mansfield's home for thirty years starting in 1761. Her mother, a black, African slave called Maria Bell, was taken prisoner in an attack on a Spanish vessel in the West Indies by her father, Sir John Lindsay (1737–1788), Mansfield's nephew and a captain in the Royal Navy. After her capture, Maria was brought to England where she gave birth to Dido in June 1761. Maria disappeared from the historical record. Dido's father had little contact with his daughter, who lived with the childless Lord and Lady Mansfield, inhabiting (as one scholar put it) a space in the household 'between the family and the servants, not really fitting in with either group'.[29] Dido was in charge of the dairy and the poultry yard and she took her meals with the other servants, but her status as both a black servant and a member of the family gave her access to the drawing room after meals, famously shocking Thomas Hutchinson when he attended a family dinner in 1779.[30] We can only speculate about the influence that this domestic situation had on Mansfield's understanding of race, slavery, and servitude, but it is clear evidence that empire and nation were entwined in the eighteenth century. Dido lived in the very lack of separation between the colonies and the metropole. Her life speaks to the ways in which the two were enmeshed.

Making distinctions

It was this England that James Somerset entered in 1768. The details of Somerset's life illustrate the geographic mobility typical of Britain's imperial culture. He had lived on three continents; his owner was a Scotsman residing in Virginia, New England, and finally London. He was baptized at the church of St Andrew, Holborn on February 10, 1771, perhaps a step toward self-liberation as conversion to Christianity was believed (mistakenly) to bestow manumission.[31] Although a slave, he traveled freely on errands for his master, making deliveries and relaying messages in London and in the English countryside. A letter he delivered to Stewart in August 1771 included a note from its author, Michael Murray, explaining that 'This will be deliver [to] you by Somerset who sett of this evening and I suppose will be with you tomorrow night. I have given him a Guinea which he says will be sufficient to carry him down.' A few days later, Murray wrote to Stewart again asking 'you don't mention Somerset, but I take it for granted he got safe down'.[32]

Not surprisingly, the ambiguity of his position as an internal outsider – free to travel but not free; foreign and racially other; living in England but raised in the colonies and in Africa; slave and servant – reflects what one scholar has called an 'indeterminate', 'ambiguous', and 'equivocal' legal landscape of 'judge-made law' on the legality of slavery in England, dating back to in1569.[33] The rulings in such cases did not dispute the legality of colonial slavery and none resolved the contradiction between the ownership of human beings and an English legal system that claimed to favor liberty. The legal arguments emphasized the deep fundamental tension that slavery created between the English values of property and liberty.

The earliest mention of slavery in the English courts is Cartwright's Case (1569) an unreported case referenced in the Star Chamber trial of John Lillburne in 1637 during a discussion of the level of physical punishment, including whipping and flagellation, acceptable in England. Cartwright brought his slave from Russia to England 'and would scourge him'. When questioned about the physical punishment he inflicted on his slave, 'it was resolved That England was too pure an Air for Slaves to breath in'.[34] This conclusion was quoted and misquoted often in subsequent debates about slavery's legal status in England, misrepresented as an unequivocal statement of the illegal status of slavery in England instead of a comment on the limits of acceptable physical punishment addressed in its original context.

Beginning in the seventeenth century legal discussions of the status of slaves in England revolved around whether they considered villeinage a precedent for eighteenth-century chattel slavery. The argument for the legality of slavery in England was made on the basis of analogy between slavery and the 'complete subjection to a feudal lord or superior', known as villeinage.[35] Why turn to such an antiquated legal category? According to William Holdsworth, the last case of villeinage in the legal record was *Pigg. v. Caley* (1618).[36] In *Periodization and Sovereignty* Kathleen Davis shows how feudal historiography developed in England in the sixteenth and seventeenth centuries when legal scholars, whom she calls feudists, including most prominently John Selden (1584–1654) and Henry Spelman (1563/4–1641), 'began to "discover" that England had been "feudal"'.[37] Davis argues that this rediscovery of feudalism was necessary because 'at the very moment the colonial slave trade began to soar, feudal law and slavery were grouped together and identified as characteristic of Europe's past and of a non-European present'.[38] In the legal discussion of villeinage traced below the legal commentators and lawyers highlight the medieval law of villeinage to make a distinction between villeins and Africans caught in raced, chattel slavery, thereby whitening villeinage.

What did it mean to compare villeins with slaves in the eighteenth century?[39] On page 2 of his study Paul Hyams summarized the law of villeinage in 'the ideal world of a thirteenth century jurist's mind'.

> The lord owns his villein as chattel and may sell him like one. Consequently, the villein himself owns nothing; all his land and goods belong to the lord. He cannot leave his land or alienate it without the lord's permission, and he is unprotected by the royal courts against the lord raising his rent or ejecting him. Having no property of his own, he has nothing to transmit to an heir, and thus has no legal heir except – for certain purposes – the lord.[40]

The rest of Hyams' book is a reconstruction of the ways in which medieval legal practice diverged from this ideal. And it is those innovations, legal opportunities, and slippages integrated in William Blackstone's account of villeinage in his *Commentaries on the Laws of England* (1769) that enabled the lawyers in Somerset's trial to claim a distinction between slavery and villeinage. Although Blackstone detailed the villeins' servile condition which he attributed to the institution's Danish 'composition', he claimed that with the Norman Conquest the state of villeinage experienced 'sparks of enfranchisement' that admitted villeins to the oath of fealty, 'conferred a right of protection, and raised the tenant to a kind of estate superior to downright slavery, but inferior to every other condition'.[41]

In the fifteenth-century text *Tenures in England* Thomas Littleton (d.1481) defined a villein as one who 'holdeth of his lord, to whom he is a villein, certain lands or tenements according to the custom of the manner, or otherwise, as the will of his lord, and to do to his lord villein service'. Littleton is quite precise about the menial labor required of villeins 'as to carry and recarry the dung of his lord out of the city, or out of his lord's manor, unto the land of his lord, and to spread the same upon the land, and such like'.[42] Unlike eighteenth-century chattel slavery, entering into the state of villeinage necessitated consent either 'by title of prescription, to wit, that he and his ancestors have been villeins time out of mind of man; or he is a villein by his own confession in a court of record'.[43] Blackstone follows Littleton in designating two kinds of villeins: *regardant*, 'annexed to the manor or land' and *in gross*, 'at large, that is annexed to the person of the land'.[44] Although Blackstone distinguished them from slaves, he also explained that villeins had no physical autonomy: they required the lord's permission before they left the estate and 'if they ran away ... might be claimed and recovered by action, like beasts or other chattels'.[45]

In legal practice villeins ranked between free laborers and chattel slaves. Villeins owed labor to their lord who could impel them to do whatever labor he wanted. When not engaged in the labor owed the lord, the villeins' time was their own. Although villeins 'belonged' to their lords and had no rights in the face of their masters, Hyams has shown that over time they gained rights and privileges unknown in chattel slavery. They could purchase land or goods with the proviso that the lord could seize them at any time.[46] For a fee and their lord's consent, they could marry. Like noble status, a villein's status was hereditary.[47] If a male villein married a free woman, any children would inherit their father's status as villeins. Unlike slaves in the colonies, if a woman who was a villein married a free man, her children would be free.[48] Again unlike slaves in the colonies, the law recognized villeins as 'the king's subjects' and protected them 'against atrocious injuries of the lord'.[49] Female villeins 'had an appeal of rape, in case the lord violated them by force'.[50] As part of the narrative of 'Favor Libertatis', the bias to liberty, Blackstone pronounced the improvement in the villein's status: 'Villeins, by this and many other means, in process of time gained considerable ground on their lords; and in particular strengthened the tenure of their estates to that degree, that they came to have in them an interest in many places full as good, in others better than their lords.'[51] These rights created and claimed by villeins in the process of legal interactions limited the analogy of slavery to villeinage.

It was precisely this 'considerable ground' 'gained' by villeins 'on their lords' that could not be allowed to black slaves in the colonies or in the metropole.

In *Butts v. Penny* (1677) the Court of King's Bench affirmed a trover claim in ten blacks from Southeast Asia, the focus of a property dispute, citing the fact that 'the negroes were infidels, and the subjects of an infidel prince, and are usually bought and sold in America as merchandise, by the custom of merchants'.[52] Trover is a form of lawsuit for recovery of damages for wrongful taking of personal property; it is distinctive because the action is for recovery of the value of what was taken rather than the recovery of the property itself. In answer to the defendant's claim that 'there could be no property in the person of a man sufficient to maintain trover' and that 'no property could be in villains but by compact or conquest', the court reiterated its original point citing the regular buying and selling of 'negroes' as merchandise and their 'also being infidels'.[53] This is an important exchange because it references the contractual nature of villeinage, which assumed some consent on the part of the villein when he/she entered into the relationship. Although one can certainly argue about how free or coerced the level of consent, its mere mention, hypothetical or real, distinguished it from chattel slavery. The case resolved with a special (and vague) verdict: 'here could be no property in the plaintiff more than in villeins'.[54] The judges in this case had it both ways: they found for a claim of trover within the framework of a feudal system characterized by villeinage.

In contrast to the ruling in *Butts v. Penny* some jurists seemed to reject the legality of slavery in England and refused to accept the argument that slavery was a variation of villeinage. In decisions rendered in 1697, 1701, and 1706 Lord Chief Justice Holt (1642–1710) declared villeinage and slavery different and unrelated institutions, the former legally authorized though defunct, and the latter foreign and impermissible in Britain.[55] *Chamberline v. Harvey* (1697) involved a slave brought to England from Barbados. Chamberline sued Harvey for trespass and damages resulting from Harvey's friendship and employment of Chamberline's slave; Harvey claimed that by natural law no man could own another human being. Although the jury was sympathetic to the accusation of trespass, Holt seemed to side with Harvey when he ruled that 'by the laws of England one man cannot have an absolute property in the person of another man'.[56] Holt contradicted the finding of trover in *Butts v. Penny* and ruled instead that 'trover will not lie for a negro'.[57]

Chamberline v. Harvey (1697) is unusual because it included a more sustained discussion of the subject of villeinage. The lawyers arguing for the slave's freedom denied the analogy between villeinage and slavery, pointing out that villeins had more legal rights than slaves. More significantly for our purposes, they maintained that the slave's circumstances did not conform to the definitions of villeinage, particularly those having to do with the hereditary status of lord and villein. The slave could not be considered a *villein in gross* because he was not 'at large' but rather 'born of parents belonging to the plantation'. Nor could he be 'a *villein regardant* to the plantation' because that required that the plaintiff and his ancestors 'be seised of this negro and his ancestors time out of memory of man'. As the lawyers pointed out, Barbados 'was acquired to the English within time of memory'. Villeinage rested on an ancestral tie to the land shared by the lord and the villein from 'time out of memory of man'.[58] Aside from the constraints of time, place also entered the discussion because the lawyers claimed that the ordinance was 'adapted to that particular place ... and extends only to that country'.[59] This discussion of villeinage tied the institution to place and time, arguments that would be elaborated in Somerset's case.

The plaintiff in *Smith v. Brown and Cooper* (1701) appeared before King's Bench to recover the price of a 'negro' who, according to an agreement signed in Virginia, had previously been sold to the defendant. Holt declared that 'as soon as a negro comes into England, he becomes free, one may be a villein in England, but not a slave'. Rather than declaring all slavery illegal, Holt advised the slave's owner that he 'should have averred in the Declaration that the sale was in Virginia, and by the Laws of that Country, Negroes are saleable'. The decision acknowledged the existence of multiple jurisdictions in the Empire and the sometimes contradictory laws passed and enforced by colonial assemblies. Without commenting on those contradictions, Holt recognized Virginia's legalization of chattel slavery and claimed that 'the Laws of England do not extend to Virginia, being a conquered Country, their Law is what the King pleases; and we cannot take Notice of it but as set forth'. Holt 'directed' the plaintiff to change the wording of the declaration to reflect the fact that although the defendant 'was indebted to the Plaintiff for the Negro sold here in London', the sale had been made in Virginia where 'Negroes by the Laws and Statutes of Virginia, are saleable as Chattels' rather than in the parish of St Mary-le-Bow.[60] Regarding English law, servitude, slavery, and villeinage, the decision upheld the coerced servitude of a slave brought to England, but determined that in England his/her status was comparable to that of a villein rather than chattel.

Four years later *Smith v. Gould* (1705/6) again disallowed trover for a black slave, but strengthened the power of slave owners with a ruling that stated that 'villenage arose from captivity, and a man may have trespass'. The decision concluded with a declaration that 'the court seemed to think that in trespass ... the plaintiff might give in evidence that the party was his negro and bought him'. This acknowledgement that men could be bought gave slave owners a greater ability to sue for damages in an English court. The decision also stated that 'if I imprison my Negro, a *Habeas Corpus* will not lie to deliver him, for by Magna Charta he must be *Liber homo*'.[61] Later in the century in *Shanley v. Harvey* (1762), lord chancellor Robert Henley (1708–1772) reversed this conclusion proclaiming that 'As soon as a man sets foot on English ground he is free: a Negro may maintain an action against his master for ill usage, and may have a *Habeas Corpus* if restrained of his liberty.'[62] Ten years before Somerset's case, *Shanley v. Harvey* assumed the legitimacy of the writ of habeas corpus in a case of slavery.

In contrast to these cases, which equivocated on the equation of slaves as property, the Yorke–Talbot decision of 1729 declared that a slave's arrival in Great Britain had no liberating effect and no impact on a master's rights to his property. This 'opinion', was rendered by the Attorney General, Philip Yorke (1690–1764), and Solicitor General Charles Talbot (1685–1737) over coffee at Lincoln's Inn while in conversation with West Indian planters. After his promotion to Lord Chancellor, Yorke, now the First Earl of Hardwicke, averred in the *Pearne v. Lisle* decision of 1749 that a slave 'is as much property as [is] any other thing'.[63] *Pearne v. Lisle* adjudicated a debt owed for the rent of fourteen black slaves. The defendant, who withheld the two-year rental fee and refused to return the slaves to their owner, threatened to abscond to Antigua without paying: the plaintiff demanded a writ of *ne exeat regno*, to prevent Lisle from leaving the country. In his decision Yorke used the words villein and slave interchangeably, accepting a continuity because 'there are no laws that have destroyed servitude absolutely'.[64] The seamlessness of this analogy clarified the jurisdictional relationship between England and its colonies because 'all our colonies are subject to the laws of England, although as some purposes they have laws of their own'.[65] The decision suggested that it was precisely the mobility of eighteenth-century imperial subjects that necessitated a universal legal reach. The risk of sanctioning the opinion rendered by previous jurists that 'the moment a slave sets foot in England he becomes free', was that slaves or their advocates might apply that principle 'equally so when they set foot in Jamaica, or any other English plantation'.[66] Yorke's elision of villeinage and slavery sanctioned chattel slavery and recognized the legitimacy of colonial legislation pertaining to slavery in the metropole. Yorke–Talbot and *Pearne v. Lisle* resolved some of the contradictions between colonial and metropolitan statutes by allowing for chattel slavery. The universal acceptance of slavery imposed consistency by allowing for the recognition of different laws in different places in the Empire while sacrificing universal equality and freedom for African slaves.

Citing the *Butts v. Penny* case (1677), eighteenth-century legal historians and contemporary scholars quote Justice John Powell who said 'that the law takes no notice of a Negroe' and conclude that blackness played little or no role 'in the legal decisions concerning the status of black slaves in England'.[67] But legal discussions of villeinage did produce whiteness: the staging of the Somerset case was a moment in which race was made, through the 'albification' of villeinage.[68] Although not explicitly laid out in *Chamberline v. Harvey* (1697) as they would be at Somerset's trial, all of the relevant components were there: English law and subjectivity relied on the correlation of place and ancestry, which generated the inherited, privileged identities of 'genuine, natural-born subjects'. In the Somerset case, an ongoing discussion of the status of villeinage was thoroughly linked to whiteness through a definition of English heritage demonstrated in terms of longevity of family, continuous tenure 'in blood and family, one uninterruptedly transmitted through a long line of ancestors'.[69] Through villeinage the category of whiteness was produced in order to try to circumvent the ambiguous and contingent results of the mobility and co-mingling endemic of empire. In the Somerset case, a racially diverse London with a secure white majority met an empire of plantations with a majority of people of color. The albification of villeinage was necessary in order to make clear the boundary between free and enslaved people, colonizers and colonized, English and African. Villeins were English people with ties of family, whiteness, and place while abducted Africans, without the requisite lineage or historical claim, could never inhabit the legal category. Freedom and whiteness were metropolitan attributes while slavery and blackness were colonial.

In his preparation of a test case that would, he hoped, outlaw slavery in England, Granville Sharp was the first to argue systematically against the legal parity of villeinage and slavery. In *A Representation of the Injustice and Dangerous Tendency of Tolerating Slavery* (1769) he contended that the very resort to 'such obsolete customs' as villeinage by the proponents of slavery revealed its absolute incompatibility with the 'present constitution and customs of England'.[70] According to Sharp, even their medieval contemporaries found the constraints imposed by villeinage contrary to English law as evidenced by 'ancient lawyers ... [who] took all favorable opportunities to enfranchise the villein' and 'the King's courts ... [that] were so manifestly disposed in favor of liberty'.[71] Sharp catalogued the legal interventions that promoted the freedom of villeins and attributed the disappearance of villeinage by the sixteenth century to 'the repeated discouragements which Villeinage met with in the Courts of law'.[72]

Sharp invoked climate theory and the moral geography of the eighteenth century to explain that the only reason to tolerate 'this iniquitous and disgraceful bondage, *even in the West Indies,* is a presumed necessity, arising ... from the excessive heat of the climates where our colonies are situated'.[73] A caveat emphatically limited his tolerance for slavery to the colonial world beyond the metropole: 'but as the said supposed necessity is *merely local, so ought to be the toleration of it likewise'.*[74] Sharp reiterated his distinction of north and south, periphery and center, English and other by stating that 'the plantation laws and customs with respect to their source, temper and necessity, must certainly be esteemed as different and *distant'.* The distance to which he alluded 'is *so many degrees,* that the least right or title *to the inheritance of the old English Villeinage cannot possibly be admitted'.*[75] For Sharp, English law (which diminished although it never formally abolished villeinage) was irreconcilable with colonial chattel slavery. Sharp argued that plantation slave society was unworthy even of the weakest, least defensible English legal precedent, the institution of villeinage, which he had spent the chapter debunking. Through the repudiation of the analogy between villeinage and chattel slavery, law became the means of separating English from non-English and colonial from metropolitan.

Returning to his first priority, challenging metropolitan slavery, Sharp warned of the 'depravity' and 'corruption of manners' that would result 'if a state of bondage is likewise admitted even into old England itself!'[76] He concluded 'as soon as he [the slave] was removed out of the reach of those irreligious laws, *all obligation to service ceased,* together with the unjust authority of the master, who no longer has any power to compel his quondam Slave to serve him'.[77] English law would not uphold a colonial master's right to his slave while in England because 'the *law will protect him* (the Slave) *in the enjoyment of his person and his property'.*[78] To reconcile the discord between the English promise of rule of law and the social and economic realities of slavery, property, and profits Sharp advocated a strict separation between colonial and metropolitan legal channels. He concluded that 'plantation laws' can never infiltrate 'the mother country'.[79] Like Fielding, he warned against 'feedback', the forced return of former slaves to the colonies, because it furthered the interpenetration, intermingling, and co-shaping of metropole and colony. Sharp defined the links between colonies and metropole as discrete and unidirectional: 'I hope no one will presume to insinuate that their [colonial laws] influence can extend in the least degree to the mother country, howsoever they may have been confirmed for the use of the colonies.'[80] For Sharp, the center gave but never received law.

Mansfield himself contributed to the legal ambiguity surrounding the question of slavery's legality in England when he heard the case of *Rex v. Stapylton* in 1771.[81] The case involved a self-emancipated slave, Thomas Lewis, seized by slave catchers on the orders of Robert Stapylton, restrained on the *Captain Seward* at Gravesend, and bound for the slave market in Jamaica.[82] When he declared that 'the general question may be a very important one, and not in this shape ever considered that I know of' and that 'whether they have this kind of property or not in England [has] never been solemnly determined', Mansfield intentionally acted to reopen the question and to place it in the undecided category.[83] After these provocative remarks, Mansfield 'left to the Jury to find whether the Negro [was] the slave and property of Defendant Stapylton', making it a narrow question of one slave and an individual owner rather than slavery's legality. The case resolved when the jury found that Lewis did not belong to Stapylton.

Mansfield sought to avoid making the question of slavery's legality the focus of the trial. He said as much when at the end of the trial he reportedly told John Dunning (1731–1783), who served as counsel for Lewis, that:

> There are a great many opinions given upon it [that is, the legality of slavery in England]; I am aware of many of them: but perhaps it is much better it should never be finally discussed or settled. I don't know what the consequence may be, if the masters were to lose their property by accidentally bringing slaves to England. I hope it never will be finally discussed; for I would have all masters think them free, and all Negroes think they were not, because then they would both behave better.

Mansfield favored a vague settlement that satisfied neither the pro-slavery forces nor the abolitionists.[84] Rather than citing either Holt or Yorke as his authorities or acknowledging the sanction of slavery in the American colonies and Parliament's efforts to promote the slave trade, in his comments at the start of the trial Mansfield reframed the debate as inconclusive. His commitment to distancing himself and English law from case precedents resulted in his revisiting the same issues a year later in the Somerset case. In his determination not to rule on the case, Mansfield only put off the unwelcome task.

It was precisely this lack of division or separation and the arbitrariness of the lines that were drawn that prompted slave owners to organize in order to pursue a legal claim to their practice of moving their slaves between and among imperial sites, including London, Bristol, and Liverpool. The West Indian slave owners were just as interested in using Somerset as a test case as Granville Sharp. Somerset's owner Charles Stewart wrote to his friend James Murray in June 1772 that 'the West Indian Planters and Merchants have taken it off my hands, and I shall be entirely directed by them in the further defense of it'. They bankrolled the case and refused all offers to settle out of court in the hopes of finally resolving the question of slavery in England in their favor.[85] Sharp too seized the occasion of Somerset's arrest as the opportunity to deploy in court the arguments about villeinage he had developed in *A Representation of the Injustice and Dangerous Tendency of Tolerating Slavery in England.* Worried that his presence might adversely affect the trial's outcome, he passed his notes to Francis Hargrave (1741–1821), the leading lawyer on the case, and kept a low profile as the case made its way through the courts.

When Somerset's case finally came to trial in June 1772, the lawyers for Knowles, the captain of the *Ann and Mary* and the defendant in the case, contended that slavery was the eighteenth-century successor of villeinage and that it represented continuity in English practice. The lawyers for Somerset, conversely, defined villeinage as 'a slavery in blood and family, one uninterruptedly transmitted through a long line of ancestors'.[86] This definition delineated villeinage as a specifically English status proven 'by other villeins of the same blood such as were descended from the same common male stock'.[87] Villeinage then was a strictly domestic legal status and, by implication, English and white. Tied to English family and ancestry, it could not be conferred on a person whose birthplace and people were not English. It also had important repercussions for the definition of a lord, tacitly calling into question the status and legitimacy of returning Nabobs and West Indian planters.

This rather cursory reference to villeinage at the trial contrasts with a much more comprehensive discussion of the topic by William Davy, counsel for Somerset, at a pre-trial hearing before Mansfield in February 1772. He introduced the subject of 'Villeins regardant and Villeins engrossed': the former were 'not in such a miserable State ... and so much in the power of the Lord as the others for they were not subjected to do any Duty or perform any Subjection out of the Manors to which they belonged. The Villeins in Gross were those who had been severed from the Manor and became absolute Villeins'.[88] It was the Villeins in gross who might be considered the forbears of eighteenth-century slaves, and Davy's remarks attempted to disqualify and sever any continuity between these two categories. He insisted that there were only two ways by which a person could claim the status of villein: 'by Prescription or by Confession'. No slave would confess because Confession 'amounts to no more than this: an Admission that he was a Villein'.[89] More significantly, slaves were barred from Prescription because:

> no new families of the Man could ever be made Villeins. That no new Race of Men coming from where they may, being what they may Christians or Infidels ... be whom they may or come from where they may whatever was their Condition in their Native Country they never could become Villeins here for they must all be derived from the common Stock of Villeins.[90]

Reiterating his point Davy asserted that the set of villeins was closed, that 'no new Family could ever be introduced into the State of Villeinage in the Country' because 'it was necessary to prove a Man a Villein to show that he had been in his Stock and had been a Villein beyond all Memory'.[91] The legal category was fixed and visible as skin color: 'it is confined to Complexion[;] it is confined to a particular Quarter of the World'.[92] Bringing together place and race, Davy's assertion ties villeinage to family, whiteness, and England.

The comparison of villeinage and slavery clearly points to a much thornier problem: the question of jurisdictional boundaries and the relationship between colonial and metropolitan laws. As recorded in the legal reports, these murky, and perhaps deliberately confused, certainly contradictory, guidelines draw our attention again to the entangled bonds of center and periphery as recorded in earlier cases. In *Smith v. Brown and Cooper* (1706) Judge Holt declared that 'one may be a villein in England, but not a slave', and advised the slave's owner that he 'should have averred in the Declaration that the sale was in Virginia, and by the Laws of that Country, Negroes are saleable'. The decision recognized Virginia's legalization of chattel slavery and the laws that sustained the institution. Holt advised the plaintiff to change the wording of the declaration to reflect the fact that the sale had been made in Virginia where chattel slavery was legal.[93] Here we see the boundary between metropole and colony drawn and transgressed in the same short decision. The 'antislavery' position generally ascribed to Holt is actually a legal nicety. Sidestepping the legality of slavery in an English colony, he ruled that as long as the sale had been made in Virginia and that a distinction between villeinage and slavery was upheld through the rewritten declaration separating Virginia's laws from English law, the sale could stand. As mentioned above in *Pearne v. Lisle* (1749) Yorke declared that 'all our colonies are subject to the laws of England, although as some purposes they have laws of their own'.[94] Yorke's decision imposed uniformity: it elided villeinage and slavery, sanctioned chattel slavery, and recognized the legitimacy of colonial legislation pertaining to slavery in the metropole even if it contradicted metropolitan law or custom.

When Davy addressed issues of jurisdiction, his prose and diction conveyed frustration and consternation. He queried 'either this man remains upon his Arrival in England in the Condition he was abroad in Virginia or he does not. He does or does not so.' Evoking the shackle, Davy attributed to law a physical power to bind, explaining that 'if the Laws having attached upon him abroad are at all to affect him here it brings them all, either all the Laws of Virginia are to attach upon him here or not'.[95] Later he asked again: 'Then with regard to the Laws of Virginia do they bind here? Have the Laws of Virginia any more influence, power or Authority in this Country than the Laws of Japan?'[96] Throughout he seems preoccupied with mapping the reach of a set of laws and the scope of competing jurisdictions. Following the theme of law's portability and the extent of its 'attachment', he speculated about whether a master could bring his galley slaves to England and whether 'the Courts [would] permit him to exercise that power over them'.[97] When he asked 'where will they draw the line?' Davy expressed not idle curiosity but the high stakes adhered to these jurisdictional conflicts.[98]

Davy concluded his statement by emphatically declaring:

> whatever the Acts of Virginia are if they are Contradictory to the Fundamental Law of this Country – it is not my business to examine what effect they have there – This much I will say of the Laws of Virginia they cannot come to England – so they cannot affect our good and principal Maxims – for by our Laws they cannot be Slaves here, such Servitude cannot be acquired here and the Laws of Virginia can have no possible Effect upon our Laws here.[99]

With his words he acquiesced to jurisdictional differences with Virginia, 'a Branch of the British Empire', insisting that 'they can never make such Laws operate here that exist in that Country'.[100] Only by acknowledging segmentation, differentiation, and separation in the legal map could England retain both interest in and profits from the slave trade as well as claims to superior liberty. The exchange between colony and metropole had to be regulated to prevent 'feedback'. In other words laws, information, and physical bodies could be allowed to flow in only one direction, from metropole to periphery, because as noted above, 'they can never make such Laws operate here that exist in that Country and therefore ... there can be no pretence or Colour of Argument drawn from those Virginia Laws'.[101]

Davy's adamant rejection of slavery's legality in England merged two meanings of the word constitution to comment on the intersection of place, law, and race. Echoing many legal commentators, he distanced

England and English law not only from the toleration of slavery but even its countenance. He defined villeinage as 'entirely an oppression'. Its 'extinction' he attributed to 'a general Assertion of natural Rights of Mankind'. Davy traced the source of the 'assertion' to 'the Temper, Disposition, and Spirit of the People of this Country, its Climate, the Genius of the People and the Soil all which I look upon to be the ingredients to make up the English Constitution'.[102] Arguing for the legal, cultural, and physical incompatibility of the English disposition with slavery, Davy maintained that in the short time during which slavery had a statutory basis in English law (1 Edw. VI c. 3, passed in 1547) 'it was a State which an English mind revolts at. The English Constitution could not bear that any Set of Men under any Circumstances should be put in such a State in this Country'.[103] In response to the hypothetical situation in which a person 'confessed himself a villein in England', Davy declared: 'it is impossible any judge would hear more of it – they would be told that all England would revolt at it – that the Genius of the People would not suffer it'.[104] For Davy the rejection of slavery reflected a distinctive character and proclivity of the English. Slavery was completely at odds with his conception of English law and its ideological tenets and even the composition of the individual English male body. Davy depicts the national, institutional, and individual aversion to unfreedom as an irrevocable, immutable, and indisputably corporal element of an English man's 'Genius'.

Despite this condemnation of slavery's existence in England and his insistence on its incompatibility with the English constitution, William Davy had an aversion to racial mixing that echoed the author of the 1764 letter in *The Gentleman's Magazine*. His remarks included a thought exercise in which he imagined 'a West Indian coming here with half a Million in his Pocket [who] builds a fine House, but is Served entirely by Negroes, here is one upon his Coach Box and half a Dozen behind – some at the Plough some at the Carts some a sowing others reaping'.[105] With this scene in place, Davy, like John Fielding before him, called 'in God's Name' for 'an Act of Parliament to prevent the abominable Number of Negroes being brought here by those West Indian Planters ... before we have an Importation of them ... to prevent the abominable practice of bringing them over in such Numbers'.[106] Warning of the dangers of miscegenation, Davy worried that without a law against it, 'I don't know what our Progeny may be I mean of what Colour'. Further legal complications might arise if 'a Freeman of this Country may in the Course of time be the Grandfather of a half a Score of Slaves'. This was, of course, a familiar and common scenario in the colonies. Davy concluded that such a situation would 'be an immediate inconvenience in the Country' and that 'it would not be a pleasant Sight nor would be endured but would occasion a great deal of Heart Burn'.[107] Davy's views were not unique; those who worked to eliminate slavery often advocated racial separation born of racist opinions. Like John Fielding, Davy proposed that 'it would be full as pleasant and usefull to us if these Gentlemen did not bring over so many of them'.[108] Davy proposed closing off the slaveholding segments of the Empire from infecting, inconveniencing, and contaminating the metropole. The joining of villeinage to whiteness disaggregated slavery from villeinage and ensured the separation of England and its laws from colonial discoloration.

Mansfield's decision

Perhaps no 200 words have been subject to closer scrutiny than Mansfield's decision in the Somerset case rendered on June 22, 1772. By now it should be clear that the stakes were very high: not only was this a case about slavery's irreconcilability with both liberty and property, but it also pointed to the ambiguous jurisdictional boundaries between metropole and colonies, and to the hybrid legal, economic, social, and cultural relationships necessary for imperial expansion. The ruling did not end slavery in England legally or in practice (although Seymour Drescher has shown that many slaves and masters thought it had and acted accordingly).[109] Instead, as James Oldham and others have concluded, Mansfield decided the case narrowly around the question 'whether the cause of detention upon the return be sufficient'.[110] Mansfield restricted his opinion to resolving the writ of habeas corpus and whether it applied to the coerced transportation of blacks from England. Mansfield acknowledged Somerset's agency when he clarified that 'the Cause which is alleged is that the said James Somerset absented himself from his Master without his leave and against his consent and refused to serve him'.[111]

It is worth re-examining those words not only because they determined Somerset's fate, but also because they spoke to the legal partition between England, its colonies, and other countries. When Mansfield reflected on the circumstances of the case, Somerset's abduction and imprisonment on a ship bound for a Jamaican slave market, he averred that 'so high an Act of dominion and power must derive its Authority from the Law of the Country'.[112] With these words he echoed Hargrave's assertion at the trial that even if a continuity existed between villeinage and slavery, a key aspect of villeinage 'restrained a lord from forcing the villein out of England'.[113] The difference between villeinage and slavery, as elaborated by Sharp and acknowledged by the court, created only the slightest opening for a liberating result. Mansfield's comments affirmed the supremacy of English municipal institutions and conventions within the domain of England without nullifying colonial laws and regulations.

How much power English judges and legal process had in the colonies is a larger question. While it was perfectly within the purview of English justices to send a writ of habeas corpus to any of the colonies or dominions, Paul Halliday concedes that 'it was easy to send writs from Westminster, but harder to get them to come back'. Mathew Hale (1609–1676) wrote of the writ of habeas corpus as an instrument that could unify the fragments of empire and be equally effective in all of its parts. As the Empire grew in the eighteenth century, colonial courts were established to issue the writ. Even then, the cultural, ethnic, and racial diversity of the Empire caused the law to be 'increasingly fragmented' creating 'distinct kinds of subjects of greater and lesser kinds'. While this metropolitan tool was held up as the guarantor of English liberty in the colonies, habeas corpus was never available to slaves.[114]

Mansfield's opinion on the law and its reach addressed the question of a geographical definition that separated England from her colonies: 'A Foreigner can't be imprisoned here on any Law of his own Country'.[115] Mansfield again followed Hargrave by defining Somerset as a foreigner from Virginia, a different country. This sentence resonates for those of us interested in the British Empire in the eighteenth century and the rule of law. More specifically it allows us to speculate about how eighteenth-century contemporaries understood the relationship between those laws passed and enforced in England and the myriad legal authorities, assemblies, and statutes that comprised imperial law. Again we see legal lines drawn opportunistically: the legal relationship between colony and metropole depended on the circumstances. In this particular instance, it seems to have been important to think of Virginia and Jamaica as related peripheries: slaveholding locations repeatedly referred to by Somerset's attorneys as foreign places, where, as Mansfield put it, 'the power of a master over his servant is different in different Countries, in some it is more in others less extensive'. Mansfield concluded that 'it [the power of the master over his servants] must be regulated according to the Law of the place it is exercised', defining these colonial spaces where the imperial government, either through royal charter or Parliamentary statute, had intervened to facilitate and enable the ownership of slaves as foreign countries and distinguishing them as so different and distinct that the range of their law did not extend to England or vice versa.[116]

Imperial relationships would be continuously and repeatedly fraught with the tension and irregularity of the line drawn and constantly redrawn between English and foreign or colonial jurisdictions: in the case of Virginia and Britain this acknowledgement and toleration of legal differences would be considered quite differently a few years later. This tells us that consistency and regularity were not seen as imperative between colony and metropole or among colonial holdings. As Lauren Benton has observed, allowances for such variations were made repeatedly without ideological concessions.[117] But spatial distinctions were crucial for upholding the multiple systems that resulted. When accounting for different and at times contradictory legal practices such as slavery, contemporaries explained that vast distances and local conditions, which Sharp (as we have seen) referred to as 'necessity, arising ... from the excessive heat of the climates where our colonies are situated', created the need for different legal jurisdictions.[118] Attached to these jurisdictions, the law generated new co-constituted definitions of colonial and metropolitan, foreigner and English, black and white.

Calling again for a distinction between English law and laws currently promulgated outside of England, insisting on the separateness and dissimilarity between the colonial and the metropolitan contexts, and affirming the disaggregation of villeinage from eighteenth-century chattel slavery, Mansfield declared that 'No Master was ever allowed *here* to send his servant abroad because he absented himself from his service or for any other cause. No authority can be found for it in the Laws of *this Country*'.[119] With these words Mansfield concluded that 'James Somerset must be discharged'.[120]

Mansfield's dramatic pronouncement was greeted with elated if restrained responses from the blacks in the packed gallery, who 'bowed with profound respect to the Judges', followed by a celebration of the decision by '200 Blacks, with their ladies [who] gathered at a public house in Westminster to celebrate the triumph which their brother Somerset had obtained over Mr. Stuart his master'.[121] James Somerset left the courtroom, visited Granville Sharp 'to tell me that judgment was today given in his favor', and then disappeared from the historical record.[122] Mansfield's decision and its multiple interpretations and reverberations, needless to say, did not.

Conclusion

Somerset's case reminded Britons everywhere that much of Britain's wealth was built on the slave trade and slave labor. It revealed glaring contradictions within Britain's legal institutions. The English (later British) government had sanctioned slavery in the colonies for at least 200 years before the Somerset case came to court. In the eighteenth century, England's government accommodated an enormous engagement with the slave trade facilitating both slaveholding and slave-trading in ways that expanded the practices and maximized the profits garnered.[123]

The Somerset case revealed widespread contests about Britain's emerging imperial character, international trade networks, and cosmopolitanism. Mobility and comfort in many different spaces were suspected in an English setting and admired in an imperial one. The presence of outsiders in England exposed the fictive nature of a static and timeless imagined community and the futile attempt to distinguish home and away, insider and outsider. That this unease was raced, a product of racial anxieties and the desire to differentiate through the construction of a racial hierarchy that became whiter at the top, is clear in pro-slavery commentary on the case that appeared in June 1772 on the eve of the decision. While the writer wished to preserve the rights of planters to move their slaves around imperial sites and from colony to metropole, he advocated a heavy tax on such movement to discourage the practice and 'to preserve the beauty and fair complexion of our people, which otherwise is in a probable way of becoming Morisco, like the Spaniards and Portuguese'.[124] As noted above, this fear of a counterflow from the colonies into England was shared by lawyers on both sides of the case.[125]

Somerset's global mobility and autonomy called attention to the realities of empire and the unpredictable social relationship and cultural configurations that resulted from the collision of different religions, ethnicities, and races. Yet his relative comfort and integration into each of these different contexts (urban and rural, African, American, and English, slave and servant) and the acceptance of his presence by those whom he encountered provides evidence of a more flexible set of criteria for inclusion that in certain contexts or interactions accommodated newcomers who may have seemed strange or threatening at first and who did not have the same signs of belonging. This porous, intimate entanglement called out for fixity.

Through villeinage the legal category of whiteness was produced in order to try to circumvent the ambiguous and contingent results of mobility and commingling endemic in empire. There are moments when we observe contemporaries calling for the disaggregation of what they considered improperly coexisting contradictions: Somerset's case was a very public example of such an occasion. Certainly the case did not resolve these issues conclusively or permanently and more contradictions followed, but Mansfield's decision did temporarily allay disorder or the threat of disorder from both sides. Law balanced the messy, unpredictable mingling that was viewed as the very opposite of Enlightenment values of classification and ordering by claiming a logic and consistency 'in which political or civil liberty is the very end and scope of the constitution'.[126] According to William Blackstone, the law conformed to 'those equitable rules of action, by which the meanest individual is protected from the insults and oppression of the greatest'.[127] At the same time, law papered over the threatening differences, responding to the unknown by generating new definitions of subject, nation, and other.[128]

Certainly Mansfield postponed rendering his decision because it highlighted the contradictions between the ideology of equality before the law in the eighteenth century and the reality of the bodies bought and sold, disciplined and coerced in the name of Britain's Empire and Britons' profit. In Somerset's case Mansfield acted on his ambivalence in the run up to the trial when he 'strongly recommended to make it up, hinted at emancipating the slave, and advised the West India merchants, and so on to apply to Parliament for an act "for farther securing their property"'.[129] Although he did not convince the parties to settle out of court, his ambivalence carried into his decision as illustrated by the multiple misunderstandings of his opinion and the clarifications he issued over the next twenty years.[130]

Beyond the threat to profits and white slaveholders across the Empire, too strict a division between colonial and metropolitan law carried with it unintended consequences and high stakes. Making explicit the differences between jurisdictions risked exposing the fractures and fissures that divided the imperial system, or worse, imposing a formal rupture. An expansive ruling that spoke to broader issues like the lawfulness of slavery would be received as an antagonistic act and risked drawing attention to the differences between the legal systems. It could set the laws and the cultures that produced them, enmeshed as they were in 1772, against one another, radically changing them both in unforeseeable ways. Any decision that went beyond the narrow confines of the case would limit the ways in which the two could interact, and bring festering jurisdictional questions to the fore.

Although a complete disentanglement of colony and metropole would have been impossible and undesirable, the Mansfield decision did accomplish a limited severance of the ties between the two. By disallowing the forced return of former slaves to the colonies, the feedback loop was partially detached. The very narrowness of the decision accomplished a radical result: it allowed for the continuation of slaveholding and slave trading and the profits they realized, but it also created a measure of imaginary and physical distance so that those practices could coexist with English legal rhetoric about freedom and equality before the law. Benjamin Franklin (1706–1790) termed this 'the hypocrisy of this country, which encourages such a detestable commerce by laws for promoting the Guinea trade; while it piqued itself on its virtue, love of liberty, and the equity of its courts, in setting free a single negro'.[131] The decision continued (and nurtured) the fiction of an imperial regime separate from the domestic. It allowed maximum flexibility in terms of precedent because it accommodated both, with an eye to the various imperial contexts that existed in 1772 and those yet to come.

The legal opinion played an important and subtle role in maintaining British imperial ideology. Although Mansfield's judgment has been seen as the beginning of the end of unfree labor in the British Empire, especially as it related to the rise of the abolitionist movement and its attempts to outlaw the slave trade, what it really accomplished was to define unfree labor in terms of race and space. Freedom and whiteness were metropolitan attributes while slavery and blackness were colonial. The attention in the ruling to villeinage as raced, white, hereditary, and English relegated raced, black, chattel slavery to imperial sites. The ruling attempted to sharpen the binary that separated metropole and colony, insider and outsider, free and unfree; however, it could not reverse or undo the mixing about which there was so much anxiety. While both the distinctions drawn between villeinage and slavery helped Somerset's cause, it did not include him as part of the English nation nor did it free all those enslaved blacks who resided in England.

Blackness too may have been occluded by the decision. Mansfield's decision legitimated the right of blacks, both free and unfree, to habeas corpus in England although they themselves could not procure a writ.[132] The implication of this part of the decision was to make slavery's persistence (both colonial and metropolitan) and slaves themselves invisible in London and to erase race from the history of the Somerset case itself.[133] Deploying the exactitude of their technical training and the English tradition of rule of law, legal authorities obscured or at least minimized the inconsistencies that persisted. But the lines drawn were both unclear and partial. While the black body of a former slave was sometimes included in the imagined polity to serve ideological interests, allowing for slavery furthered imperial interests and English ones as well. The decision was a signal that this issue was not going away; Britain's leading role in the slave trade and in the practices of slavery was not ending.

In his *Memoirs of Granville Sharp* (1820) Prince Hoare reflected on the significance of the Somerset case. His words insistently remind us of the geographical and imaginative separation that the decision achieved. Hoare credited Sharp with securing the lives of Africans who 'ceased to be hunted in our streets as a beast of prey ... [and now] slept in security ... and feared no dangers'. But he claimed that the most important and visible consequences of the decision redounded to 'Englishmen' in that:

> we no longer see our public papers polluted by hateful advertisements of the sale of the human species; or that we are no longer distressed by the perusal of impious rewards for bringing back the poor and the helpless into slavery; or that we are prohibited the disgusting spectacle of seeing man bought by his fellow-man. To him, [Sharp] in short, we owe this restoration of the beauty of our constitution, this prevention of the continuance of our national disgrace.[134]

The physical removal of slaves and the manifestations of slavery such as slave advertisements and slave markets cleared the English air of these pollutants. The 'jurisprudence of England' earned an 'added tribute'. Hoare praised 'men of the highest talents and consummate legal knowledge' for their 'defence of injured human rights'. Mansfield's decision perpetuated a legal apparatus that ensured that human rights in Kingston, Jamaica and London, England would be relegated to different jurisdictions and tied to local rather than universal definitions. The Somerset case reinscribed key divisions while seeming to transcend them.[135]

Notes

1 Ruth Paley, 'Somerset, James (b. c.1741, d. in or after 1772)', ODNB (http://www.oxforddnb.com.proxy2.library.uiuc.edu/view/article/70057, accessed October 15, 2009). Habeas corpus determines only whether a prisoner has been afforded due process, not whether he or she is guilty: Somerset's case at King's Bench was argued against Captain Knowles, accused of unlawful detention. For more on habeas corpus, see Paul Halliday, *Habeas Corpus: From England to Empire* (Cambridge, MA: Harvard University Press, 2010). As Halliday points out, using habeas corpus in cases of slavery was an innovation of the 1770s led by Sharp (who used it to free the slave Thomas Lewis in 1770) who hoped to use the writ's prohibition of transporting someone against their will as an attack on slavery that went beyond the individual slave to the institution as a whole (pp. 174, 211). Sharp explained the applicability of habeas corpus to James Somerset even though he was born abroad by citing 32 Hen. VIII c. 16 'concerning strangers' (p. 418).
2 Somerset's name appears in various spellings. I have adopted the spelling used by Paley in the ODNB. I divert from that spelling only when the eighteenth-century sources spell it differently.
3 William Cobbett, Thomas Bayly Howell, Thomas Jones Howell, eds., *Cobbett's Complete Collection of State Trials and Proceedings for High Treason and other Crimes and Misdemeanors from the Earliest Period to the Present Time*, 34 vols. (London: R. Bagshaw, 1809–1828), vol. 20, p. 43.
4 Cobbett, Howell, and Howell, *State Trials*, vol. 20, p. 43. On the role of blood in legal cases in India in the eighteenth century, see Sudipta Sen, 'Imperial Subjects on Trial: On the Legal Identity of Britons in Late Eighteenth-Century India', *Journal of British Studies* 45 (2006), pp. 532–555.
5 'Proceedings, 7 Feb. 1772, in the court of the King's Bench, London, in the case of James Sommersett', New York Historical Society, microfilm, pp. 107–108.

6 On empire and nation as culturally, economically and legally bound and colony and metropole as mutually constituted see, Hall, *Civilising Subjects*; and Hall and Rose, *At Home with the Empire*. For the eighteenth century, see Wilson, *A Sense of the People*; Wilson, *The Island Race*; and Wilson, *A New Imperial History*. The legal relationship between colony and metropole is explored by Marshall in 'Britain and the World'; Greene, *Peripheries and Center*; and Bilder, *The Transatlantic Constitution*.

7 For a study of the legal codification of blackness in the colonies, see Brooke Newman, *A Dark Inheritance: Race, Sex, and Subjecthood in the British Atlantic* (New Haven, CT: Yale University Press, forthcoming); and Carmen Thompson, '"20. and odd negroes": Virginia and the international system of slavery, 1619–1660' (PhD dissertation, University of Illinois, Urbana-Champaign, 2012).

8 Kenneth Morgan, *Slavery and the British Empire: From Africa to America* (Oxford: Oxford University Press, 2007), pp. 111–114.

9 On Somerset as it relates to slavery, see David Brion Davis, *The Problem of Slavery in the Age of Revolution, 1770–1823* (Ithaca, NY: Cornell University Press, 1975). For the study of blacks in Britain, see Folarin Shyllon, *Black People in Britain, 1555–1833* (Oxford: Oxford University Press, 1977) and *Black Slaves in Britain* (Oxford: Oxford University Press, 1974); and James Walvin, *Black and White: the Negro and English Society, 1555–1945* (London: Penguin, 1973). On labor, see Seymour Drescher, *Capitalism and Antislavery* (Oxford: Oxford University Press, 1987) and *The Mighty Experiment: Free Labor versus Slavery in British Emancipation* (Oxford: Oxford University Press, 2002). For the case and its impact in the American colonies, see Patricia Bradley, *Slavery Propaganda and the American Revolution* (Jackson, MS: University of Mississippi Press, 1998); Gould, 'Zones of Law'; Rhys Isaac, 'Conspiracy and Consent in History and Culture', paper presented at the biannual symposium of the Milan-Montpellier Group for Early United States History in June 2009; and Simon Schama, *Rough Crossings: Britain, the Slaves and the American Revolution* (New York: Ecco, 2006).

10 Legal discussion of the case is cited throughout and includes Carol Phillips Bauer, 'Law, Slavery, and Sommersett's Case in Eighteenth-Century England: a Study of the Legal Status of Slavery' (PhD dissertation, New York University, 1973); W. R. Cotter, 'The Somerset Case and the Abolition of Slavery in England', *History* 79 (1994), pp. 31–56; James Oldham, 'New Light on Mansfield and Slavery', *Journal of British Studies* 27 (1988), pp. 45–68 and *English Common Law in the Age of Mansfield* (Chapel Hill, NC: University of North Carolina Press, 2004), ch. 17; and Ruth Paley, 'After Somerset: Mansfield, Slavery and the Law in England, 1772–1830', in *Law, Crime and English Society 1660–1830*, ed. Norma Landau (Cambridge: Cambridge University Press, 2002), pp. 165–184.

11 George Van Cleve, 'Somerset's Case and Its Antecedents in Imperial Perspective', *Law and History Review* 24 (2006), pp. 601–645. Van Cleve's article is part of a forum on the case that includes responses by Daniel Hulsebosch, 'Nothing But Liberty: Somerset's Case and the British Empire', and Ruth Paley, 'Imperial Politics and English Law: the Many Contexts of Somerset' both *Law and History Review* 24 (2006).

12 Prince Hoare, *Memoirs of Granville Sharp* (London: Henry Colburn, 1820), p. 59. Seymour Drescher argues that the science of race played a 'marginal role' in the 'debate over slavery' at the end of the eighteenth century: *Mighty Experiment*, p. 76.

13 Christopher Leslie Brown, *Moral Capital: Foundations of British Abolitionism* (Chapel Hill, NC: University of North Carolina Press, 2006); David Lambert, *White Creole Culture, Politics and Identity during the Age of Abolition* (Cambridge: Cambridge University Press, 2005); Peter Linebaugh and Marcus Rediker, *The Many Headed Hydra: Sailors, Slaves, Commoners, and the Hidden Story of the Revolutionary Atlantic* (Boston, MA: Beacon Press, 2000); Claire Midgley, *Women Against Slavery: the British Campaigns, 1780–1870* (London: Routledge, 1992) and *Feminism and Empire: Women Activists in Imperial Britain, 1790–1865* (London: Routledge,

2007). Charlotte Sussman discusses the colonial frame in *Consuming Anxieties: Consumer Protest, Gender, and British Slavery, 1713-1833* (Palo Alto, CA: Stanford University Press, 2000) as does Moira Ferguson in *Subject to Others: British Women Writers and Colonial Slavery, 1670-1834* (New York: Routledge, 1992).

14 Stuart Hall, *Race: The Floating Signifier*, DVD, prod. and dir. Sut Jhally (Northampton, MA: Media Education Foundation, 1996). Hall reminds us that race is relational and situational, created in specific historical circumstances through stories that draw on heritage, history, and culture. Uncertainties emerge from an understanding of race that is 'floating'. The very unfixed, contingent, and constantly changing meanings attached to difference force us to attend to it in specific contexts and to see its inconsistencies for what they are: a struggle to fasten that which cannot be fixed. The similarities with gender as a category of analysis are laid out in Joan Scott, 'Gender as a Category of Analysis', *American Historical Review* 91 (1986), pp. 1053-1075 and 'AHR Forum: Unanswered Questions', *American Historical Review* 113 (2008), pp. 1422-1430.

15 Philip Morgan, 'British Encounters with African and African Americans, 1600-1780', in *Strangers within the Realm: Cultural Margins of the First British Empire*, ed., Bernard Bailyn and Philip Morgan (Chapel Hill, NC: University of North Carolina Press, 1991), p. 159; Norma Myers, *Reconstructing the Black Past: Blacks in Britain, 1780-1830* (London: F. Cass, 1996), p. 35. In *Black London: Life Before Emancipation* (New Brunswick, NJ: Rutgers University Press, 1995), Gretchen Holbrook Gerzina leaves the realm of quantification to analyze black cultural presence in England from the sixteenth to the eighteenth centuries.

16 J. Jean Hecht, *Continental and Colonial Servants in Eighteenth Century England* (Northampton, MA: Department of History, Smith College, 1954), pp. 48-49; David Dabydeen, *Hogarth's Blacks: Images of Blacks in Eighteenth Century English Art* (Athens, GA: University of Georgia Press, 1987), pp. 19-20. For more on black life and experience in Britain in the eighteenth century, see Kathleen Chater, *Untold Histories: Black People in England and Wales during the period of the British slave trade, c.1660-1807* (Manchester: Manchester University Press, 2009); Paul Edwards and James Walvin, *Black Personalities in the Era of the Slave Trade* (London: Macmillan, 1983); Gretchen Holbrook Gerzina, 'Black Loyalists in London after the American Revolution', in *Moving On: Black Loyalists in the Afro-Atlantic World*, ed. John Pulis (New York: Garland Publishers, 1999), pp. 85-102; Jogdish S. Gundara and Ian Dufffield, eds., *Essays on the History of Blacks in Britain* (Aldershot: Averbury, 1992); Walvin, *Black and White*; Walvin, *England, Slaves and Freedom, 1776-1838* (Jackson, MS: University of Mississippi Press, 1986); and Walvin, *Making the Black Atlantic: Britain and the African Diaspora* (London: Cassell, 2000).

17 Blacks also feature in Hogarth's prints and engravings and on signboards and trade signs. Announcements offering rewards for runaway slaves and advertisements of public slave auctions appeared regularly in newspapers. Catherine Molineaux, *Faces of Perfect Ebony: Encountering Atlantic Slavery in Imperial Britain* (Cambridge, MA: Harvard University Press, 2012); Beth Fowkes Tobin, *Ficturing Imperial Power: Colonial Subjects in Eighteenth-century British Painting* (Chapel Hill, NC: University of North Carolina Press, 1999); Kay Dian Kriz, 'Marketing Mulàtresses in the Paintings and Prints of Agostino Brunias', in *The Global Eighteenth Century*, ed. Felicity Nussbaum (Baltimore, MD: Johns Hopkins Press, 2003), pp. 195-210; and Dabydeen, *Hogarth's Blacks*. Black characters peopled theatrical productions of Shakespeare's *Othello* and literary depictions like Aphra Behn's novella *Oroonoko: Or The Royal Slave* (1688) insistently reminded the British public of slavery and the black bodies among them. *Oroonoko* was so popular it was later adapted as a play by Thomas Southerne (1660-1746). See Diana Jaher, 'The Paradoxes of Slavery in Thomas Southerne's *Oroonoko*', *Comparative Drama* 42 (2008), pp. 51-72. For more on theatrical productions and racial, religious, and national differences, see Ragussis, 'Jews and other "Outlandish Englishmen": Ethnic Performance and the Invention of British Identity under the Georges', *Critical Inquiry* 26 (2000), pp. 773-797; Ragussis, *Theatrical Nation*; and Kathleen Wilson, 'Rowe's "Fair Penitent" as Global

History: Or, a Diversionary Voyage to New South Wales', *Eighteenth Century Studies* 41 (2008), pp. 231–251.
18 *The Gentleman's Magazine*, vol. 34 (1764), p. 493.
19 A letter voicing similar complaints about black servants brought to England authored by an 'Anglicanus' appeared in the *London Chronicle* in the same year (vol. 16, September 29–October 2, 1764, p. 317) and could be the inspiration for the selection quoted in *The Gentleman's Magazine*. Another letter signed F. Freeman expressing similar sentiments appeared the following year in the *London Chronicle* and Samuel Estwick echoed them in his *Considerations of the Negroe Cause Commonly So Called, Addressed to the Right Honourable Lord Mansfield, Lord Chief Justice of the Court of King's Bench* (London: J. Dodsley, 1772), esp. pp. 42–44.
20 John Fielding, *Extracts from such of the Penal Laws As Particularly Relate to the Peace and Good Order of this Metropolis* (London: H. Woodfall and W. Strahan, 1768), p. 144. For the full text of the Act passed in 1746, see Raithby and Edlyne, *Statutes at Large*, vol. 10, pp. 279–282.
21 Fielding, *Extracts*, p. 144.
22 Fielding, *Extracts*, p. 144.
23 Fielding, *Extracts*, p. 145. In his comments (p. 143) Fielding included a diatribe against foreign servants who 'obtained a Footing here by their Artifice and our own Caprice'. He blamed the mixing of English with foreign servants for 'Jealousies, Quarrels and Disturbances in the Families where they live' due to the unmerited favoritism enjoyed by those servants from abroad.
24 Tobin, *Picturing Imperial Power*; and Srinivas Aravamudan, *Tropicopolitans: Colonialism and Agency, 1688–1804* (Chapel Hill, NC: University of North Carolina Press, 1999), ch. 1.
25 Brooke Newman, 'Gender, Sexuality, and the Formation of Racial Identities in the Eighteenth-Century Anglo-Caribbean World', *Gender and History* 22 (2010), pp. 585–602.
26 Andrew Jackson O'Shaughnessy, *An Empire Divided: the American Revolution and the British Caribbean* (Philadelphia, PA: University of Pennsylvania Press, 2000), ch. 1, esp. pp. 2–18.
27 David Beck Ryden, *West Indian Slavery and British Abolition, 1783–1807* (Cambridge: Cambridge University Press, 2008), ch. 3.
28 There is debate in the scholarship about conceptions of race and color in the early modern period. Wheeler, *The Complexion of Race*; and Wahrman, *The Making of the Modern Self*, claim that metropolitan conceptions of race were defined by culture, civility, and commerce in the early modern period and that a fluid relationship existed between blackness and whiteness up until the last third of the eighteenth century. My own work draws on Kim Hall, *Things of Darkness: Economies of Race and Gender in Early Modern England* (Ithaca, NY: Cornell University Press, 1995); Ania Loomba, 'Periodization, Race, and Global Contact', *Journal of Medieval and Early Modern Studies* 37 (2007), pp. 595–620; and Traub, 'Mapping the Global Body', who trace the negative associations of blackness and the physical marking of race to a much earlier period. For more on the racialization of whiteness in the decades before and after the Somerset case, see Deirdre Coleman, 'Janet Schaw and the Complexions of Empire', *Eighteenth-Century Studies* 36 (2003), pp. 169–193.
29 Sarah Minney, 'The Search for Dido', *History Today* 55 (2005), p. 2; and Gene Adams, 'Dido Elizabeth Belle: a Black Girl at Kenwood', *Camden Historical Review* 12 (1984), pp. 10–14.
30 Thomas Hutchinson, *The Diary and Letters of His Excellency Thomas Hutchinson Esq.*, 2 vols. (Boston, MA: Houghton Mifflin, 1884–1886), vol. 2, p. 276.
31 Religious affiliation came to determine who might or might not be enslaved in Europe in the medieval period with Christians generally not enslaved by other Christians while legitimizing the enslavement of non-Christians. In the Atlantic World, however, starting in the seventeenth century legal codes specified that conversion to Christianity did not confer manumission. Seymour Drescher, 'From Consensus to Consensus: Slavery in International Law', *The Legal Understanding*

of Slavery: From the Historical to the Contemporary, ed. Jean Allain (Oxford: Oxford University Press, 2012), pp. 85–104. For more on slavery and Christianity in the colonies, see Travis Glasson, *Mastering Christianity: Missionary Anglicanism and Slavery in the Atlantic World* (Oxford: Oxford University Press, 2012).

32 Michael Murray to Stuart, August 4 and 10, 1771, Stuart Papers, ff. 16, 24–5. Quoted in Emma L. Powers, 'The Newsworthy Somerset Case: Repercussions in Virginia', *Colonial Williamsburg Interpreter* 23 (2002), p. 1.

33 William Wiecek, 'Somerset: Lord Mansfield and the Legitimacy of Slavery in the Anglo-American World', *University of Chicago Law Review* 42 (1974), p. 87.

34 John Rushworth, *Historical collections of private passages of state. Weighty matters in law. Remarkable proceedings in five Parliaments. Beginning the sixteenth year of King James, Anno 1618. And ending the fifth year of King Charles, Anno 1629*, 8 vols. (London: D. Browne, J. Walthoe, et al., 1721), vol. 2, p. 468. The unreported status of the case refers to the fact that it did not make it into the English Law Reports.

35 *OED*, villeinage.

36 74 English Law Reports, p. 997.

37 Kathleen Davis, *Periodization and Sovereignty: How Ideas of Feudalism and Secularization Govern the Politics of Time* (Philadelphia, PA: University of Pennsylvania Press, 2008), p. 52.

38 Davis, *Periodization and Sovereignty*, p. 8.

39 W. S. Holdsworth, *A History of English Law*, 7 vols. (London: Methuen, 1923), vol. 3, pp. 491–510. For more on medieval villeinage, see Paul Hyams, *King, Lords and Peasants in Medieval England: The Common Law of Villeinage in the Twelfth and Thirteenth Centuries* (Oxford: Clarendon, 1980); Alfred W. B. Simpson, *An Introduction to the History of the Land Law* (Oxford: Oxford University Press, 1961), p. 148; and Paul Vinogradoff, *Villainage in England: Essays in English Mediaeval History* (Oxford: Oxford University Press, 1892). On the comparison of villeinage and slavery in Somerset's case, see E. Washburn, 'Somerset's Case and the Extension of Villeinage and Slavery in England', *Proceedings of the Massachusetts Historical Society* 7 (1864), pp. 308–326.

40 Hyams, *King, Lord and Peasants*, p. 2.

41 Blackstone, *Commentaries*, vol. 2, p. 92.

42 Thomas Littleton, *Littleton's Tenures in English* (London: V&R Stevens and G. S. Norton, 1845), p. 73. Edward Coke (1552–1634) glossed Littleton in *The First Part of the Institutes of the Laws of England: Or, A Commentary upon Littleton* (London: Society of Stationers, 1628). Here I have used Thomas Coventry, *A readable edition of Coke upon Littleton* (London: Saunders and Benning, 1830).

43 Littleton, *Tenures*, p. 74.

44 Blackstone, *Commentaries*, vol. 2, p. 92; Littleton, *Tenures*, pp. 76–77. Littleton adds that all villeins *regardant* must have been so 'time out of mind of man' while those who become villeins in a court are *in gross* (p. 78). For an analysis of this distinction, see Vinogradoff, *Villainage in England*, pp. 48–57. He concludes 'I need hardly mention, after what has been said, that there is no such thing as this distinction in the thirteenth century law books.'

45 Blackstone, *Commentaries*, vol. 2, p. 92.

46 Littleton makes a distinction between goods purchased by the villein 'before the lord enter the town,' to which the lord had no claim, and those purchased after the lord entered, who could be seized by the lord at any time. Littleton, *Tenures*, p. 75. Blackstone, *Commentaries*, vol. 2, p. 93.

47 Littleton, *Tenures*, p. 74, Blackstone, *Commentaries*, vol. 2, p. 93.

48 Littleton, *Tenures*, p. 78.

49 According to Littleton, 'the lord may not maim his villein'. *Tenures*, p. 81. Blackstone, *Commentaries*, vol. 2, p. 93.

50 Littleton, *Tenures*, p. 79. Blackstone, *Commentaries*, vol. 2, p. 94.

51 Littleton describes the legal actions that villeins could take or were owed, *Tenures*, pp. 79–87. Blackstone, *Commentaries*, vol. 2, p. 95.

52 83 English Law Reports, p. 518. In the OED trover is 'The act of finding and assuming possession of any personal property; hence (in full, action of trover), an action at law to recover the value of personal property illegally converted by another to his own use.
53 83 English Law Reports, p. 518.
54 84 English Law Reports, p. 1011. Another case in the same year *Lowe v. Elton* had a similar result. Cited in John H. Baker, *Introduction to English Legal History* (London: Butterworths, 1990), p. 475.
55 *Chamberline v. Harvey* (1697), 87 English Law Reports, p. 598; *Smith v. Brown and Cooper* (1701), 90 English Law Reports, p. 1172; *Smith v. Gould* (1705/6), 91 English Law Reports, p. 566; and 92 English Law Reports, p. 338.
56 87 English Law Reports, p. 598.
57 91 English Law Reports, p. 994. The case is long and was heard on several occasions. See 87 English Law Reports, pp. 596–601; 90 English Law Reports, p. 830; 92 English Law Reports, p. 605. Holt's decision in 1697 also contradicted the findings that 'trover will lie for a negro boy' in the Court of Common Pleas case, *Gelly v. Cleve* (1694).
58 87 English Law Reports, p. 600.
59 87 English Law Reports, p. 600.
60 *Reports of cases adjudg'd in the Court of King's Bench; with some special cases in the courts of Chancery, Common Pleas and Exchequer, from the first year of K. William and Q. Mary, to the tenth year of Queen Anne. By William Salkeld*, 2 vols. (London: Elizabeth Nutt and R. Gosling, 1717), vol. 2, p. 666. For more detail on these cases, see Bauer, 'Law, Slavery, and Sommersett's Case', pp. 8–25.
61 *Reports of cases ... By William Salkeld*, vol. 2, p. 667.
62 This case involved Shanley who bought the slave, Harvey, to England in 1750 and gave the slave to his niece. When the niece gave Harvey £800 on her deathbed, Shanley sued Harvey to recover the money. 28 English Law Reports, p. 844.
63 Yorke's decision in *Pearne v. Lisle* is found in *Reports of cases argued and determined in the High Court of Chancery, with some few in other courts. By Charles Ambler* (London: A. Strahan and W. Woodfall, 1790), p. 75; 27 English Law Reports, p. 47.
64 *Reports of cases ... By Charles Ambler*, p. 77.
65 *Reports of cases ... By Charles Ambler*, p. 76.
66 *Reports of cases ... By Charles Ambler*, p. 76.
67 84 English Law Reports, p. 1011. Seymour Drescher, 'Manumission in a Society without Slave Law: Eighteenth-Century England', *Slavery and Abolition* 10 (1989), p. 89. In *Pearne v. Lisle*, Hardwicke echoes this when he states that 'being Negro did not necessarily imply slave'. *Reports of cases ... By Charles Ambler*, p. 76.
68 For more on the racialization of whiteness in the decades before and after the Somerset case, see Coleman, 'Janet Schaw'; more recently, Jones, *Engendering Whiteness*. and Newman, 'Gender, Sexuality, and the Formation of Racial Identities'.
69 Cobbett, Howell, and Howell, *State Trials*, vol. 20, p. 43.
70 Granville Sharp, *A Representation of the Injustice and Dangerous Tendency of Tolerating Slavery in England* (London: B. White and Robert Horsfield, 1769), p. 108.
71 Sharp, *Representation*, pp. 113, 114.
72 Sharp, *Representation*, p. 119. To support this claim Sharp quotes Blackstone who quotes Sir Thomas Smith (1513–1577) 'who testifies that in all his time (and he was secretary to Edward VI), he never knew any villein *in gross* throughout the realm'.
73 Sharp, *Representation*, p. 133, emphasis in the original.
74 Sharp, *Representation*, p. 133, emphasis in the original.
75 Sharp, *Representation*, p. 134, emphasis in the original. For more on the division of north and south, see Pat Rogers, 'North and South', *Eighteenth-Century Life* 12 (1988), pp. 101–111.

76 Sharp, *Representation*, p. 149.
77 Sharp, *Representation*, p. 152, emphasis in the original.
78 Sharp, *Representation*, p. 153, emphasis in the original.
79 Sharp, *Representation*, p. 153.
80 Sharp, *Representation*, p. 160.
81 Somerset was neither the first nor the last case in which Mansfield was confronted with the subject of slavery. On Mansfield's subsequent and most famous case, see Ian Baucom, *Specters of the Atlantic: Finance Capital, Slavery, and the Philosophy of History* (Durham, NC: Duke University Press, 2005); Jeremy Krikler, 'The Zong and the Lord Chief Justice', *History Workshop Journal* 64 (2008), pp. 29–47; and Anita Rupprecht, 'Excessive Memories: Slavery, Insurance and Resistance', *History Workshop Journal* 64 (2008), pp. 6–28.
82 James Oldham, *The Mansfield Manuscripts and the Growth of English Law in the Eighteenth Century*, 2 vols. (Chapel Hill: University of North Carolina Press, 1992), vol. 2, pp. 1225–1226, vol. 2, pp. 1242–1243. The details of the case along with some of the relevant primary sources are recounted by Hoare in *Memoirs*, pp. 52–61.
83 Hoare, *Memoirs*, p. 59.
84 Hoare, *Memoirs*, p. 60.
85 Charles Stewart to James Murray, June 15, 1772. James Murray Robbins Papers, Massachusetts Historical Society, *Proceedings of the Massachusetts Historical Society* 43 (1910), p. 451.
86 Cobbett, Howell, and Howell, *State Trials*, vol. 20, p. 43.
87 Cobbett, Howell, and Howell, *State Trials*, vol. 20, p. 43.
88 'Proceedings ... King's Bench ... Sommersett, Feb. 7, 1772', p. 14.
89 'Proceedings ... King's Bench ... Sommersett, Feb. 7, 1772', p. 15.
90 'Proceedings ... King's Bench ... Sommersett, Feb. 7, 1772', p. 15.
91 'Proceedings ... King's Bench ... Sommersett, Feb. 7, 1772', pp. 15–16.
92 'Proceedings ... King's Bench ... Sommersett, Feb. 7, 1772', pp. 107–108.
93 *Reports of cases ... By William Salkeld*, 2 vols., London, 1717, vol. 2, p. 666. For more detail on these cases, see Bauer, 'Law, Slavery, and Sommersett's Case', pp. 8–25.
94 *Reports of cases ... By Charles Ambler*, p. 76.
95 'Proceedings ... King's Bench ... Sommersett, Feb. 7, 1772', pp. 46–47.
96 'Proceedings ... King's Bench ... Sommersett, Feb. 7, 1772', p. 54.
97 'Proceedings ... King's Bench ... Sommersett, Feb. 7, 1772', p. 112.
98 'Proceedings ... King's Bench ... Sommersett, Feb. 7, 1772', p. 47.
99 'Proceedings ... King's Bench ... Sommersett, Feb. 7, 1772', pp. 116–117.
100 'Proceedings ... King's Bench ... Sommersett, Feb. 7, 1772', p. 115.
101 'Proceedings ... King's Bench ... Sommersett, Feb. 7, 1772', p. 117.
102 'Proceedings ... King's Bench ... Sommersett, Feb. 7, 1772', p. 27.
103 'Proceedings ... King's Bench ... Sommersett, Feb. 7, 1772', p. 32. For more on this statute, see C. S. L. Davies, 'Slavery and Protector Somerset: The Vagrancy Act of 1547', *Economic History Review* 19 (1966), pp. 533–549.
104 'Proceedings ... King's Bench ... Sommersett, Feb. 7, 1772', p. 35.
105 'Proceedings ... King's Bench ... Sommersett, Feb. 7, 1772', p. 58.
106 'Proceedings ... King's Bench ... Sommersett, Feb. 7, 1772', pp. 58–59.
107 'Proceedings ... King's Bench ... Sommersett, Feb. 7, 1772', p. 59. The term convenience recurs throughout Davy's remarks and in the trial transcript. I hope to examine its legal and cultural meanings in subsequent work.
108 'Proceedings ... King's Bench ... Sommersett, Feb. 7, 1772', p. 60.
109 Drescher, *Capitalism and Antislavery*, pp. 36–45 and 'Manumission in a Society without Slave Law'.
110 Oldham, 'New Light', pp. 45–68.
111 The Habeas Corpus Act 1697 (31 Cha. 2 c. 2) prohibited transportation of anyone outside the realm without their permission. For more on the active role of black slaves in their manumission, see Douglas Lorimer, 'Black Slaves and English Liberty:

a Re-examination of Racial Slavery in England', *Immigrants and Minorities* 3 (1984), pp. 121–150.
112 Mansfield's decision was recorded in four reports by different authors and is in itself a subject of much controversy. James Oldham has argued that Hill's manuscript 'is the most dependable report of the Somerset case', Oldham, 'New Light', p. 59. Van Cleve revisited the versions of the judgment, 'Somerset's Case and Its Antecedents', pp. 631–633. The quotations cited here are from Serjeant Hill's report, pp. 312–314. The original manuscript is in Lincoln's Inn Library. I used the microfiche cited in J. H. Baker, ed., *English Legal Manuscripts*, 2 vols. (Switzerland: Zug, 1975), MS 10, A-87, p. 314.
113 Cobbett, Howell, and Howell, *State Trials*, vol. 20, p. 66.
114 Halliday, *Habeas Corpus*, p. 261. Halliday treats the Imperial Writ in chapter 8.
115 Hill's manuscript, *English Legal Manuscripts*, MS 10, A-87, p. 314.
116 Hill's manuscript, *English Legal Manuscripts*, MS 10, A-87, p. 314.
117 Lauren Benton, *A Search for Sovereignty*.
118 Sharp, *Representation*, p. 133.
119 Hill's manuscript, *English Legal Manuscripts*, MS 10, A-87, p. 314.
120 Hill's manuscript, *English Legal Manuscripts*, MS 10, A-87, p. 314. Discharged refers to the writ of habeas corpus: the decision did not emancipate Somerset or any of the slaves living in England or in the colonies.
121 *London Chronicle*, June 20–23, 1772, vol. 31, p. 598; *London Packet*, #418, June 26–29, 1772.
122 Hoare, *Memoirs*, p. 91.
123 Some examples of statutory law that enabled and facilitated slavery include: 5 Geo. 2. c. 7 (1732); 23 Geo. 2 c. 31 (1750); 25 Geo. 2 c. 40 (1752). Each describes 'slaves' and 'negroes' as property. See Edward Fiddes, 'Lord Mansfield and the Sommersett Case', *Law Quarterly Review* 50 (1934), pp. 499–511; and Wiecek, 'Somerset: Lord Mansfield and the Legitimacy of Slavery', p. 97.
124 'Some Observations upon the Slavery of Negroes', *Scots Magazine* 34 (1772), p. 301. Similar sentiments are expressed in Estwick, *Considerations of the Negroe*.
125 Michael Fisher, *Counterflows to Colonialism*.
126 Blackstone, *Commentaries*, vol. 1, p. 6.
127 Blackstone, *Commentaries*, vol. 1, p. 6.
128 Elizabeth Kolsky examines the intersection of race, law, and violence in her masterful study *Colonial Justice in British India* (Cambridge: Cambridge University Press, 2010) revealing how law defined and constructed race in British India and facilitated violence.
129 Robbins Papers, Massachusetts Historical Society, *Proceedings*, p. 451; Wiecek, 'Somerset: Lord Mansfield and the Legitimacy of Slavery', p. 102; and Fiddes, 'Lord Mansfield and the Sommersett Case', p. 505.
130 Wiecek, 'Somerset: Lord Mansfield and the Legitimacy of Slavery', pp. 87–88, pp. 108–112.
131 Benjamin Franklin to Anthony Benezet, August 22, 1772, in George S. Brookes, *Friend Anthony Benezet* (Philadelphia, PA: University of Pennsylvania Press, 1937), p. 422.
132 Although not always effective there are several instances where habeas corpus was used to free individual slaves. Thomas Jones procured a writ of habeas corpus to free Little Ephraim Robin John and Ancona Robin Robin John in 1773. Sharp used a writ of habeas corpus to free Henry Demane in 1786.
133 Ruth Paley documents the persistence of slavery in London in 'Imperial Politics and English Law'. White slavery such as the enslavement of English mariners by Barbary pirates described by Linda Colley in *Captives* (New York: Pantheon Books, 2002) may also have been obscured by the distinctions drawn in the Somerset case.
134 Hoare, *Memoirs*, p. 93.
135 Although in the first half of the nineteenth century judges would work with abolitionists to end slavery in the colonies, the persistence of racial hierarchies and their relationship to coerced labor regimes did not eradicate the binary that associated

freedom with whiteness and oppression with color. Paton, *No Bond but the Law*; and Madhavi Kale, *Fragments of Empire: Capital, Slavery, and Indian Indentured Labor* (Philadelphia, PA: University of Pennsylvania Press, 1998). For more on judicial activism against slavery, see John McLaren, *Dewigged, Bothered, and Bewildered*; and Bridget Brereton, *Law, Justice, and Empire: the Colonial Career of John Gorrie* (Kingston: University of the West Indies Press, 1997).

CHAPTER THREE

Imperial disruptions: City, nation, and empire in the Gordon Riots

> What appeared most to excite public indignation was the criminal supineness of the Magistracy of London during these horrible commotions, apparently threatening to lay the Metropolis of the Empire level with the ground.[1]
>
> William Belsham, 1752–1827
>
> The mischief which had been perpetrated, and that which was evidently intended, were of so black an aspect, and involved so entirely the destruction of the empire.[2]
>
> Thomas Holcroft, 1745–1809

At ten o'clock on the night of Friday June 2, 1780 'a riotous set of people, who called themselves Protestants' stormed London's Sardinian Chapel in Duke Street, Lincoln's Inn Fields. The perpetrators 'entirely gutted it'.[3] Having 'pulled down the rails, seats, pews, communion table, etc', they carried them into the street, 'laid them against the doors, and set them on fire'.[4] The organ was destroyed and 'the altar piece alone, which was demolished, was executed by the Chevalier Casali, and is said to have cost £2500'.[5] The crowd barred anyone who tried to extinguish the flames, and by midnight 'the inside of the chapel was entirely consumed'.[6] The pregnant wife of the Sardinian Ambassador was 'so frightened when the rioters set fire to the Chapel, which joins his Excellency's dwelling-house, that she fainted away'.[7] A different set of rioters 'assembled round the chapel of the Bavarian Ambassador in Warwick street Golden Square, which they partly demolished'. Although some of the valuables were locked away before they could be taken, the mob 'broke open the box which contained the poor's money, and carried it all off, as well as many other things of value'.[8] Despite several attempts to set the chapel alight, 'the fire happily did not take effect'.[9]

The violence and destruction at the Catholic chapels began earlier in the day with the peaceful presentation to Parliament of the Protestant

Petition demanding the repeal of the Roman Catholic Relief Act 1778 (18 Geo. III c. 60). Spearheaded by the Protestant Association and its charismatic leader, Lord George Gordon (1751–1793), the campaign for repeal garnered 120,000 signatures followed by a march on Parliament 40,000 to 50,000 strong. Seventeen thousand stayed to witness the response to the petition in the House of Commons, which voted overwhelmingly (6 to 192) to deny the petition's request and adjourned. Frustrated by this response, the crowd regrouped in their initial gathering spot in Lincoln's Inn Fields and from there 'paraded off in different divisions from Palace yard' and attacked the Sardinian chapel nearby.[10]

For the next six days the Gordon Riots raged. Described by contemporaries as 'universal anarchy ... approaching desolation', the looting and destruction included attacks on Catholic chapels and homes in Moorfields, Wapping, and East Smithfield, the breaking of Newgate prison, the New Prison, Clerkenwell, King's Bench, and Fleet Prisons and the release of the prisoners in them. The Riots culminated in an attempt to destroy the Bank of England. The rioters initiated targeted strikes on the homes of prominent Londoners, such as Richard Challoner (1691–1781) the Catholic Bishop of London, justice of the peace John Fielding, MP George Savile (1726–1784) who introduced the Catholic Relief Act in Parliament, and William Murray, First Earl of Mansfield in retaliation for what was perceived as his Catholic sympathies.[11] Eventually quelled by 10,000 troops deployed throughout the city, the Riots subsided and 'peace and tranquility were restored' on the evening of Thursday June 8.[12] The exact number of lives lost during the Riots is unknown, with estimates ranging between 300 and 1000. Four hundred and fifty rioters were arrested; 160 people were brought to trial: 62 were sentenced to death and 26 were hanged. Gordon was arrested for treason and imprisoned in the Tower of London for eight months. His trial on February 5, 1781 ended with his acquittal. The physical damage and destruction cost thousands of pounds.[13]

Although some historians, notably Nicholas Rogers, discuss its international context, especially the unsuccessful state of the American War in 1780, the scholarship on the Gordon Riots generally casts the event as a domestic disruption.[14] In this chapter I argue that the Riots constituted an imperial disruption in two senses. The uneven and unwieldy expansion of the British Empire in the latter half of the eighteenth century necessitated the recalibration of certain legislation and policy precedents, such as the Quebec Act 1774 (14 Geo. III c. 83), and concessions, such as Catholic toleration, to colonial subjects that disrupted metropolitan ideas about English identity and culture.[15] The Riots were a response. Meanwhile the Riots disrupted the imagined relationship between nation and empire and rejected the vast networks of trade, colonialism, and bureaucracy supported by cosmopolitan imperial ideology seen in all renunciations of the Riots.

Like the controversies over Elizabeth Canning and James Somerset, the Gordon Riots and the pamphlets and images produced in their wake were a means of debating and resisting, as well as justifying and defending, the imperial policies of the British state. Contemporaries turned to newspapers as sources of information, and their circulation grew tremendously over the second half of the eighteenth century with annual sales increasing from 7 million in 1750 to 16 million in 1801.[16] The production and diffusion of print culture, including satirical prints, shaped perceptions of the government's authority and credibility and served as sites of information and opinion. Read and consumed by both men and women across the socio-economic scale, British print culture extended political consciousness, participation, and debate in the second half of the eighteenth century. Diana Donald argues for the broad geographical distribution of satirical prints. In addition to the hundreds or thousands of copies in any edition, Donald shows that the images circulated in London, throughout Britain, on the Continent, and in the British colonies through reissues, pirated cheap copies, woodcut versions, and in broadsides and ballads; they also appeared on coins, handkerchiefs, textiles, and ceramics.[17]

Again, law featured prominently in these debates. At least four legal events converged in the Gordon Riots: the four parliamentary acts, the Quebec Act 1774, the Roman Catholic Relief Act 1778 (18 Geo. III c. 60), the Catholic Relief Act in Ireland passed the same year, and the Scottish Catholic Relief Bill that prompted so much resistance that it was abandoned; the petition and its 120,000 signatures seeking the repeal of the Act of Relief, a legal means of appeal; the Riots themselves, including the breaking of prisoners from Newgate; and the imposition of martial law enforced by 10,000 troops – an act that contradicted Britain's longstanding aversion to a standing army in the metropole – that quelled the burning and looting across the city.[18] The law was enlisted by the authorities to justify and legitimate their new policies, and it was both the focus and the means of the crowd's resistance.

Anti-imperial sentiment was articulated by equating the British Empire with the Roman Catholic Church. Indeed, the Catholic Church, always a target of English fear and hatred, became in the commentary of the 1770s the dark mirror of empire. The antipathy to Catholics in the 1770s channeled discomfort and uncertainty about imperial policy, the financial strains of Britain's global presence, and the cultural implications of mixed communities, religions, nationalities, and ethnicities making their presence felt in England, especially in London.[19]

Animated by the opinion that imperial policy, and the seeming acceptance of Catholics and other internal others, endangered what they believed defined home, those who opposed the extension of the civil rights of Catholics lashed out. For them England was defined by Protestantism and the Riots served as a vehicle to resist what P. J. Marshall has called 'a nation defined by empire'.[20] In response, those who championed the rights of Catholics saw themselves as progressive cosmopolitan sophisticates, and relegated 'apprehensions, fears, and distressed mind' to the ranks of the lower orders: provincial, small minded, and 'vulgar'.[21] This chapter will use the Gordon Riots as a lens through which to examine the relationship between London, nation, and empire.

Historiography

Tracing the historiography of the Gordon Riots reveals several different interpretations that have prevailed since the 'riotous and tumultuous assembly' rocked the city for a week in June 1780. In 1795 the political writer and historian William Belsham (1752–1827) characterized those who joined the Protestant Association as 'men of the lowest orders of society, whose excess of zeal could be equaled only by the grossness of their ignorance'.[22] Belsham implied that the movement for repeal was a deliberate attempt to rouse the rabble evidenced by 'the pains [that] were taken by inflammatory harangues and pamphlets to prejudice the minds of the vulgar against the late wise and salutary relaxation of the penal code'.[23] Questioning Gordon's motives, Belsham accused him of 'address[ing] the mob without, in terms calculated to inflame their passions'.[24]

Modern interpretations of the Riots revived with John Paul de Castro's study published in 1926 detailing what happened and gathering the primary sources without suggesting a root cause. Christopher Hibbert's 1956 *King Mob* relied on anti-Catholicism as its explanatory mechanism. Blaming the Protestant Association for playing on these fears among London's poor and uneducated, Hibbert concluded that the Riots, sparked by anti-popery expressed 'anarchic violence' 'stimulated by alcohol and sheer destructiveness' with no larger motive or goal.[25] In the 1950s and 1960s a Marxist analysis of the Gordon Riots, associated most with George Rudé, replaced the rioters' anarchy and senseless violence with a political agenda fueled by economic and social grievances and borne of an emergent class consciousness.[26] E. P. Thompson also analyzed the Riots attributing to the crowd a political agenda inspired by John Wilkes and his campaign for parliamentary reform.[27]

In contrast to earlier depictions of the disorder and illegible anarchy of the Riots, Thompson described three phases: the first featured the tradesmen, orderly and well dressed. This phase ended when the House of Commons refused to debate the petition and initiated the second phase of 'licensed spontaneity' led by journeymen, apprentices, and servants. City officials who sided with the Protestant Association and took very little action to quell the Riots in these first two phases sprang into action in the third phase marked by the attack on the Bank of England and 'orgies, drunkenness, arson, and pick-pocketing'. Thompson sourced the crowd's agenda to 'the dissenting tradition of London artisans' and the debating clubs and tavern societies where London's plebeian culture circulated ideas and developed its political aspirations.[28] Both Rudé and Thompson argued that the crowd's attacks were organized and their targets, which included the prisons, houses of magistrates and judges, toll gates, and the Bank of England, carefully and rationally chosen, symbols of ruling class power.[29]

Most recently the Riots have been the subject of a collection of articles edited by Ian Haywood and John Seed who point out that the 'Gordon Riots are still a curiously unplaced event in British history and culture'. Haywood and Seed explain that the impact of the French Revolution may have 'displaced' the Riots, directing attention away from the specific social and political grievances they raised.[30] Conflating the Riots into the Jacobin cause in the 1790s may well have been intentional: radicalizing the protest may have provided the means to avoid granting it any legitimacy. As Carol Houlihan Flynn remarks, a silence enveloped the Riots. Their almost complete absence from literary depictions until 60 years later with Charles Dickens' *Barnaby Rudge* (1841) substantiates her claim that 'even before the Revolution, the Riots themselves produced an internalized terror connected to a notion of an Englishness under siege'.[31] Another explanation for the 'displacement' or shrouding of the Riots might be the discomfiting fact that they unabashedly contradict Whiggish narratives of increasing toleration and British exceptionalism.

Tying the legal events outlined above, seemingly domestic and metropolitan in their scope, to imperial history reveals the crucial place of law in the making and sustaining of empire. Empire and nation, center and periphery, intertwined through the physical bodies, ideas, languages, beliefs, and commodities that moved between and among imperial sites constituted each other in ideological and cultural terms.[32] Kathleen Wilson describes Britain's Empire in the eighteenth century as a network connecting people in the Atlantic, Pacific, and Indian Ocean worlds with knowledge, gossip, and ideas produced in and among these imperial nodes creating metropolitan 'conflicts, ambiguities, pleasures and desires'.[33] In the case of the Gordon Riots, laws passed in London about Quebec – discussed in pamphlets and newspapers on both sides of the Atlantic – inspired debate and resistance that eventually culminated in the relief acts in Ireland, Scotland, and England; the protests led by the Protestant Association in England and Scotland; and riots in Glasgow, Edinburgh, London, and provincial English towns and colonial sites.[34] Law operated as a network and a node in the circuits of empire, creating imperial infrastructure and expanding it, carrying Britain's legal ideology and discourse about rule of law and equality before the law in its institutional and documentary tracks.

Eighteenth-century contemporaries were well aware of the metropolitan side of the exchange of people, commodities, and ideas which moved between and among imperial sites: the diversity of London's population and the mixing of peoples perceived as racially and ethnically dissimilar was the cause of enormous anxiety, at times erupting into violence as in the anti-Irish riots that plagued London throughout the eighteenth century especially in the 1730s and in the 1760s and in the controversies and scandals analyzed in this book. London was the epicenter of support for the Protestant Association and its calls for the repeal of the Roman Catholic Relief Act. London's Court of Common Council, the City's primary decision-making body, had been a vigorous voice for the American colonists, against the American War, and for parliamentary reform. It urged its representatives in Parliament to repeal the Roman Catholic Relief Act.[35]

The alleviation of legal restraints on Catholics challenged imagined boundaries between 'colony' and 'metropole' and also among people in the metropole. These 'others' in London, different and mobile, destabilized an English geographical imagination secured by assuming a strict division of place as an authentic constant, home, and space as a signifier of contact, and interrelationships, anywhere that was not home.[36] Jane Jacobs has said that 'place-based struggles are also arenas in which various coalitions express their sense of self and their desires for the spaces which constitute their home'.[37] The English sense of home was disquieted by the small African, Jewish, Catholic, and Irish communities residing in London and calling London home despite the ambiguity of their status. Although scholars have written about the anxious assertion of Britishness at the margins of empire, where English Protestants were a minority, little attention has been paid to similar concerns in the Protestant metropole.[38] Ironically, at the center, in a population of which the vast majority was English and Protestant, a similar logic applied, and an insistent unease existed in a different register. The efforts to expand Catholic civil rights served as reminders of the messy, unpredictable networks and byways essential to empire. As demonstrated in chapters 1 and 2, the legal system caught Britain's internal others in its net: meting out punishment to the treasonous

Scot, Archibald Cameron and identifying and wrongly convicting the criminal Mary Squires, 'Gypsy'. The legal proceedings against these dangerous others were offset by the Jewish Naturalization Act and the Somerset case: in both instances internal others were drawn into the legal system seeking the fulfillment of its promises of rights and liberty.

We can observe contemporary calls for the disentanglement of what they considered improper proximities: like the Somerset case, the Gordon Riots constituted another, much louder and more insistent and violent occasion, again, not confined to the courtroom, but spilling out into London's streets. The debate about the place of empire in English politics and culture and its relationship to English nationality and national identity was ongoing throughout the eighteenth century. As this book argues, imperialists and their critics spoke up more vociferously in the aftermath of the Seven Years' War as sharply articulated in the pamphlets advocating the repeal of the Roman Catholic Relief Act and in their response to the Gordon Riots. The discourse that developed in the run up to the Riots and in their aftermath reveals a cultural preoccupation with Britain's imperial orientation and its effects on the metropolitan population.

The supporters of the Protestant Association used a nationalist language that relied on references to English rights, Protestantism, and nation. Their antagonism to Catholic toleration was based on a belief that England's imperial policies, which necessitated the integration and assimilation of difference, would erode the prominence of the Church of England and offer an alternative to the illusion of Anglican supremacy. In so doing, empire at home would destroy religious homogeneity and offer alternatives to the law's imagined white, male, Anglican property-holder as its normative subject. This cultural argument against Catholic toleration mobilized the familiar specter of potential, though unlikely, economic and political hardships, warning of a threat to two pillars of British life in the eighteenth century: liberty and property. Those who spoke against the rioters, in contrast, bemoaned the violence and destruction of property and attributed it to provincial and small-minded Londoners responding to an international reality. Britain served, in the words of Ignatius Sancho (1729?–1780), the Afro-British essayist, playwright, and musician, as a 'nurse of freedom! – Europe's fairest example, –the land of truth, bravery, loyalty, and of every heart-gladdening virtue',[39] and the benefits of global engagement outweighed any cultural and social changes caused by imperial 'feedback' in the metropole. While both sides acknowledged with nationalist pride that London was the 'metropolis of the Empire', those who spoke against Catholic toleration wished to separate the metropole from its imperial ties and obligations and warned of the dangerous implications of imperial policy for England. From this point of view cosmopolitans had to come to terms with an empire so diverse that it had provincialized London and its 'vulgar' populace.

The pamphlets and prints that recount events surrounding the Gordon Riots allow us to look beyond the literate classes to see how race, religion, ethnicity, and nationality functioned in British popular culture. While many Londoners prided themselves on the capital as the showcase of English global reach, imperial difference was not welcomed by everyone. The violent and disorderly rejection of imperial difference, exemplified by attacks on the otherwise indistinguishable Catholics, show a provincial London. The Riots left leaders at Court and in Parliament scrambling to regain their sophisticated poise in the 'Metropolis of Empire'.[40]

An empire defined by religion

The notion of England as a Protestant and anti-papal empire was not new in the eighteenth century. The Act in Restraint of Appeals 1533 declared 'this realm of England is an empire ... governed by one supreme head and king'.[41] It was an empire created in explicit opposition to the Catholic Church 'furnished by the goodness and sufferance of Almighty God'.[42] The king of England possessed 'whole and entire power, pre-eminence, authority, prerogative and jurisdiction ... in all causes manners debates and contentions ... without restraint or provocation to any foreign princes or potentates of the world'.[43] Citing the precedent of former rulers, the statute (attributed to Thomas Cromwell) appropriated to the king the right to make 'ordinances, laws, statutes and provisions' for the 'conservation of the prerogatives, liberties and pre-eminences of the said imperial crown ... to keep it from the annoyance as well as the see of Rome as from the authority of other foreign potentates attempting the diminution or violation thereof'.[44] Asserting the self-sufficiency of the Church of England and its severance from the papacy, this statute officially staked English autonomy on anti-popery. Any reconciliation or integration of the two would be deemed impossible and oxymoronic.

By the eighteenth century, many in England were convinced that Protestantism ensured their liberties, freedoms, and rights. Despite the reality of poverty in Britain, high taxes, and the harsh 'Bloody Code' that prescribed the death penalty for over 200 crimes, Britons believed that their Protestantism made them 'richer in every sense than other peoples'.[45] They associated Catholicism with religious superstition, but also with an elaborated set of oppressive traditions that translated into fundamental unfreedoms, including absolutism, tyranny, and slavery. Protestant rulership, established by the Revolution of 1688 and confirmed by the Act of Settlement in 1701 (12 & 13 Will. III c. 2) produced a government that would uphold the English constitution and guarantee rule of law. At the core was Parliament, the source and guarantor of English rights and freedoms. Educated elites and middling men and women venerated what Linda Colley has called 'the cult of Parliament', and considered this institution 'unique, splendid and sovereign, the hard one prerogative of a free and Protestant people'.[46]

Legal restrictions on Roman Catholics in Britain date back to the Henrician Reformation. Elizabethan legislation attempted to enforce outward conformity (1 Eliz. I c. 1 and 2), limited Catholic emigration (13 Eliz. I c. 3), and barred priests and Jesuits from England (27 Eliz. I c. 2). James affirmed all of the statutes passed under Elizabeth and after the Gunpowder Plot, he passed laws requiring Catholic recusants to communicate at least once a year in the Church of England (3 Jac. I c. 5). After the Restoration, the Corporation Act (13 Car. II, st. 2, c. 1) disqualified from municipal office anyone who did not take the Oaths of Allegiance and Supremacy. In 1673 Parliament passed that Test Act (25 Car. II c. 2) requiring all officers, civil and military, to take the Oaths of Allegiance and Supremacy. After the Revolution of 1688, further legislation constrained Catholics. The preamble of 'An Act for the further preventing the growth of popery' (11 & 12 Will. III c. 4) explained that 'there has beene of late a much greater Resort into this Kingdom than formerly of Popish Bishops Priests and Jesuits and they doe very openly and in insolent Manner affront the Laws and daily endeavour to pervert His Majesties naturally borne Subjects'. The language of the statute blamed 'treasonable and execrable Designes and Conspiracies against His majesties Person and Government and the Established religion' on the 'Neglect of the due Execution of the Laws already in Force'. The Act rewarded anyone who caught a Catholic priest 'saying Mass or of exerciseing any other Part of the Office or Function of a Popish Bishop or Priest' with £100 and barred Catholic priests from opening schools. Among its harsh measures it prohibited Catholics from sitting in Parliament, purchasing land, or holding civil or military offices. Catholics could not inherit property or practice their religion freely.[47] In Ireland the Roman Catholic majority could not vote in parliamentary elections and Catholic landowners could be readily dispossessed of their land by their Protestant relatives.

Colin Haydon's work tracking anti-Catholic sentiment in the eighteenth century argues that despite the legal restrictions, elite opinions about Catholics shifted toward toleration in the second half of the century, certainly after the Seven Years' War and Quiberon Bay in

1759.[48] Recent work shows pretty convincingly that this move to toleration was not the relentless unidirectional march to toleration and eventual Catholic Emancipation that some scholars of the Enlightenment have asserted.[49] Instead Robert Donovan demonstrates that Catholic Relief was a direct consequence of the military needs of Britain's growing Empire.[50] Karen Stanbridge builds on Donovan's findings by examining the processes that created more rights for Catholics. She argues that 'movement' toward Catholic emancipation was neither unobstructed nor driven inexorably by the spread of liberal values. Instead of the growth of toleration or Enlightenment, military necessity and imperial needs forced the expansion of Catholic rights, always a site of struggle and contestation.[51]

The dramatic increase in the vociferous expression of anti-Catholicism between 1778 and 1780 can be traced to the religious toleration extended by the Quebec Act, English losses in the American War, the entrance of Spain and France on the side of the North American colonies, and the Roman Catholic Relief Act 1778.[52] Many in England feared that Britain's colonial projects were seriously eroding the nation, its wealth, and its moral direction. They defined the core values of English identity by what threatened them. While anti-Catholic feeling in the earlier period expressed concern about subjugation at the hands of tyrannical Catholic rulers, those who stood against Catholic toleration in the latter part of the 1770s feared foreign invasion alongside a cultural penetration voluntarily introduced into the metropole by deliberate governmental policy.

The Quebec Act and the Roman Catholic Relief Act embedded within them imperial assumptions that promised inclusion and tolerance of difference: it was precisely those provisions that became the focus of debate and discussion.[53] The Quebec Act nullified governing strictures for the 65,000 professed Catholics of French Canada and declared that 'his Majesty's Subjects, professing the Religion of Rome, of and in the said Province of Quebec, may have, hold, and enjoy the free Exercise of the Religion of the Church of Rome'. In addition to tolerating Catholic belief and ritual observance, the act allowed the Roman Catholic clergy to 'hold, receive, and enjoy, their accustomed Dues and Rights'. By providing an alternative to the Elizabethan Protestant oath, Catholics could declare their loyalty to George III. In exchange the Act extended full civil rights pertaining to 'Property and Possessions', 'Customs and Usages' and 'Civil Rights' to all of 'his Majesty's Canadian Subjects'. The Act allowed Quebec's Catholics to will their property as they wished and afforded them the 'Certainty and Lenity' of English criminal law.[54] This mechanism of integration welcomed those Catholics living in Canada into the ranks of other loyal English colonial subjects, granting

Catholics abroad many more rights than those Catholics living in England. This expansion of rights for Catholics in Quebec stood in stark contrast to the expansion of slavery and its legal infrastructure that so constrained people of color outside of England. Again the lines of inclusion shifted and the Quebec Act incorporated Catholic French colonists as normative white free legal subjects.

Commentary on the Quebec Act worried about the effects of Catholic toleration on English rights, pointing to the negative consequences of integrating vastly different perspectives and values into the British Constitution. A newspaper article from August 1774 decried the Act as 'dangerous' because of the 'inconsistency and self-contradiction' that will result from it.[55] Couched as a defense of the king, the piece depicted the Act as the work of evil advisors whom the author accused of 'virtual Treason'. The writer professed concern about the incompatibility of the king's role as the supreme head of the 'Popish Church in Canada' and the Head of the Church of England. He listed the opposing beliefs and tenets that the king must uphold 'here' and disavow 'there', protect 'there' while he rejected them 'here'.[56] The pragmatics of empire integrated seemingly opposed systems of belief, and Catholic toleration imperiled the integrity of the Church of England and its supreme head. More than just a personal affront that disrespected the king's 'dignity' and 'character', the argument of its opponents was that the Act, and by extension the toleration of difference that accompanied imperial expansion, became a chink in Britain's armor eroding English personal liberties and heralding the geopolitical resurgence of France and the papacy.

What prompted the government to pass this legislation? Quite simply, imperial demands. The victories of the Seven Years' War in Canada brought Quebec's majority Catholic population under British rule. Forced conversion was out of the question and forbidden by treaty. The only option was a certain amount of toleration. The same phenomena motivated the Acts for Catholic Relief. Catholic recruits already made up 20 percent of the British army by the start of the American war, an increase of 14 percent since the 1750s.[57] The American victory at Saratoga and the military campaigns of Warren Hastings, governor-general of India, created pressing new imperial obligations in the 1770s. Frederick North, Second Earl of Guilford, struggling to staff the increasing number of military outposts, turned to Catholic recruits. Through his envoy, Sir John Dalrymple, in 1778 North offered Roman Catholic Bishop George Hay, Vicar Apostolic of the Lowland district of Scotland (encompassing St Andrews and Edinburgh), a secret agreement promising to repeal the laws against Catholics hearing or saying mass, to expand the rights of Catholics to hold and transfer land, and to amend the attestation oath allowing military recruits to swear allegiance to the sovereign rather than the Church of England. Despite the caution urged by Bishop Richard Challoner and Matthew Duane, a Catholic lawyer, the government moved forward with strategic toleration.[58]

In June 1778 the Roman Catholic Relief Act (18 Geo. III c. 60) passed easily and extended many of the privileges granted in the Quebec Act even closer to home. The 1778 Act repealed 'certain Provisions' of the 'Act for the further preventing the Growth of Popery'. It lifted restrictions on Catholic clergy with regards to activities related to education, reversed the ban on Catholic inheritance of land which had given 'to the next of Kin, being a Protestant, a Right to have and enjoy such Lands, Tenements, and Hereditaments', and explicitly allowed Catholics the purchase of 'Manors, Lands, Profits out of Lands, Tenements, Rents, Terms or Hereditaments' within England and Wales.[59] To the Act's opponents, the ability of Catholics to buy land in England and to inherit land unimpeded threatened the rights that had hitherto been defined as belonging exclusively to English Protestants. The objections of the Protestant Association and others who opposed the bill are reminiscent of the arguments made against the Jewish Naturalization Act and echoed some of the same concerns about access to English land and birthright.

To add cultural insult to material injury, the Relief Act contained an oath of loyalty to the king and to the succession that omitted all reference to the Anglican Church or the king's role as leader of the Church of England. The same year the Irish Parliament also passed a Catholic Relief Act constituting the first significant alleviation of the system of the legal discrimination against Ireland's Catholic majority. Its provisions were very similar to the English Act.[60] To make matters worse, Catholics in Scotland were also promised measures of relief similar to those contained in the Act already passed in England. To these critics of the Quebec Act, the English Roman Catholic Relief Act, the Irish Catholic Relief Act, and the proposed Scottish Catholic Relief Act certainly looked like 'the inroads of Popery'.[61] Taken together, the Acts expanded those qualifying characteristics of English subjects in unprecedented ways.

This new legal landscape may very well have struck English observers as confusing, erasing as it did the legal line between Protestants and Catholics. A letter first published in *The London Magazine* in 1774 and reprinted in *The Gentleman's Magazine* echoed this sentiment worrying that the Quebec Act heralded the restoration of the 'golden age of popery to the British empire – connected with the abolishing juries for the decision of property, setting aside the *habeas corpus* act, and other old ... English laws'.[62] Horace Walpole opposed the Quebec

Act as one of many complaints about the government's policies and urged a vigorous campaign to defeat the Catholic Relief Bill when it was proposed. In 1775 Walpole called on Charles Lennox, the Third Duke of Richmond, in October 1775 to lead a 'very active Opposition' to the English bill proposed in Parliament and offered strategies, 'motions and grievances' that would 'pelt and harass them with questions and delays'.[63] In the campaign of obstruction he suggested that Richmond 'Ask what the Catholics in Canada have done in return for the restoration of the religion and the abolition of juries? ... is abolition of juries part of the spirit of toleration?'[64] Walpole's question implied that Catholics did not understand English liberties, that they could not appreciate or carry out the rights and responsibilities of Englishmen, and that they ought not enjoy the rights extended to them in Canada in London. Both of these examples appealed to English Protestants to oppose toleration based on claims that the extension of civil rights to Catholics would redefine English rights and curtail them.

Disrupting the metropole

Despite this opposition, the English Catholic Relief Act became law in 1778. In Scotland too, Catholics looked forward to measures of relief similar to those in the English Act. In October 1778 the movement against the proposed Scottish Catholic Relief Act created the Committee for the Protestant Interest, publicizing their stance against the bill and gathering supporters through newspaper advertisements, pamphlets, and resolutions. The opponents of Catholic relief gathered momentum throughout the end of 1778 and January 1779 leading the Catholic leadership in Scotland 'resolved of their own accord, to give up all further thoughts of applying to Parliament for the wished for Indulgence'.[65] Despite these attempts to head off 'what Excess the fury of the populace might go in raising Sedition and Disturbance in the Country', animosity toward Catholic toleration erupted in violent riots in Edinburgh and Glasgow in February 1779 destroying houses and chapels and intimidating Catholic residents.[66] After the riots subsided, a 'Proclamation from the Lord Provost and Magistrates' announced in the Edinburgh papers that the bill for Catholic relief 'is totally laid aside'.[67]

A sympathetic author of a pamphlet written after the Scottish riots replied to the anti-Catholicism with expressions of cosmopolitan concern: 'What a disgrace to this country! What a tarnish to the British glory! But alas: How is it possible to conceal it? Already the voice of fame has carried it to foreign Countries! Already our public papers are spreading it through all the Nations of Europe!'[68] Commenting on the inextricable link forged by the Union of England and Scotland, the author posited the question about what responsibility England would bear for the Scottish riots in the eyes of the world: 'But tho' the English Nation had no hand in this affair, will foreign nations make the distinction? Are England and Scotland now a days two separate nations in the eyes of Europe? Are they not united in one body under the same King and the same Parliament of Great Britain?'[69] Acknowledging the realities of a global empire comprised of diverse religious practices, the author commented that 'they had presumed to look for that relief from the severity of the laws, which had already been granted to their brethren in all other parts of the British dominions'.[70] The pamphlet expressed an expectation of equality before the law and acute disappointment and indignation when the law failed to provide consistent treatment of everyone in the same category, in this case Catholics across the Empire. The arguments made on both sides rehearsed many of the same concerns about the effects of empire on British life as articulated eighteen months later in commentary published to justify, explain, and condemn the Gordon Riots.

Inspired by the successful anti-relief efforts in Scotland, the Protestant Association in London gathered signatures on its petition to repeal England's Catholic Relief Act. The propaganda that comprised its campaign revealed widespread unease with Britain's imperial character, international trade networks, military recruiting, and cosmopolitanism. Prints published in response to the Relief Act reflect disquiet about the Court and its policies. 'The Times' (Figure 3.1), published on February 26, 1780, expressed a cacophonous myriad of anxieties about Britain's imperial competition with other European empires. In the center the pope is pictured on a dais whose three steps are labeled 'superstition', 'ignorance', and 'absolute power'. Among these familiar insults, the company closest to the pope indicates a different target of English Protestant antagonism. Seated immediately next to Pius VI (1775–1799) are Louie XVI of France (1754–1793), Charles III of Spain (1716–1788) and Joseph II, the Holy Roman Emperor (1740–1791). Each displays an imperial symbol: the king of Spain holds a circular shield displaying a globe, the French king, a paper inscribed 'Grande Alliance', and the Hapsburg emperor's scepter features the eagle.[71] A dog urinating on Magna Carta in the front of the print foregrounds the threats to England's law and its constitution. Those supporting repeal deemed remaining a powerful empire, important but above all else they valued retaining England's distinguishing constitutional characteristics as a kingdom ruled by law and an empire created in opposition to 'the see of Rome ... and the authority of other foreign potentates'.[72]

BRITAIN AND ITS INTERNAL OTHERS, 1750–1800

Figure 3.1 'The Times'

The internal imperial threat is often represented in terms of Scottish influence and infiltration at the highest levels of England's government. In 'Argus' (Figure 3.2), which appeared in May 1780, several of the king's closest advisors stand over him as he sleeps. William Murray, First Earl of Mansfield and a man dressed as a Scottish Jacobite both reach for the king's crown while John Stuart, the Third Earl of Bute (1713–1792) looks on holding the scepter he has taken from the king. Mansfield suggests that Bute 'Wear it Your sel my Leard'. Britannia and the British lion lay asleep intimating that the Scottish members of the king's inner circle have bewitched England's leaders and that the Scots at the king's side deserved none of the trust and confidence they enjoyed. The image unambiguously renders the results of the treachery and infiltration: the impoverished representative of the commercial classes says 'I have let them quietly strip me of every Thing'; the Irishman declares 'I'le take care of Myself and Family'; while a Dutchman absconds with two beehives. The message is clear: Britain is weakened and vulnerable, the English victimized by policies that integrated the Scots, inviting them into the halls of power, only to suffer at their foreign hands and those of other interlopers, the Dutch

Figure 3.2 'Argus'

and the Irish among them. Like the commentary on the rape of Dinah discussed in chapter 1, this print is another example of the theme of insidious internal enemies, cloaked in familiar garb, members of the elite with access to the highest levers of power, stealing and threatening, directing and misdirecting policy.[73] 'Ecclesiastical and Political state of the Nation' (Figure 3.3) appeared on June 2, 1780, the day that the Protestant Petition was presented to Parliament and the Riots began. It shows the misdirection of government policy literally. A blindfolded George III plows ahead with policy designed by Lord North.[74]

While questioning Scottish loyalty, legitimacy, and intentions, the prints clearly place some of the blame on English toleration and integration of outsiders. The Scots have encamped in the metropole, at Court, and at the heart of the Empire; their presence symbolic of cosmopolitan ease with (or at least acceptance of) certain differences. But this ease or acceptance was not an attitude universally shared as demonstrated by other members of the polity who remained skeptical and suspicious, threatened and alienated from these scenes and their implications.

Horace Walpole discussed the causes of 'the great combustion' in a letter to the Reverend William Mason (1725–1797) written on June 29, 1780.[75] Walpole rejected anti-Catholicism as the main motivation for

Figure 3.3 'Ecclesiastical and Political state of the Nation'

the Riots and quickly pointed to 'a thousand discontents' that resulted in 'the late tumults'. He dismissed rumors that placed the blame on 'a plot' devised by France, Spain, and the Americans. Instead, his analysis elaborated on the themes highlighted in the visual evidence discussed above. Walpole emphasized the internal 'dissention' that permeated the Court and concluded that 'a necessity for calling the army together to suppress an insurrection was no very disagreeable opportunity'.[76] He went so far as to say that 'the Court wished insurrections' as a pretext 'to suppress them, and the suppression would unite all the military and militia, and all under one standard'.[77] Blaming the government's disunity and the fissured polity for the misdirection he identified as the root cause of the Riots, Walpole declared that the state of the nation 'is at its dregs and the men that do think and act from principle are ... few ... and have no one general system in common'.[78] He predicted pessimistically that 'anarchy will reign for some time, and despotism succeed'.[79] What emerges from his somewhat incoherent assessment is an emphasis on the centrality of the military and a lamentation about the disagreements and conflicts that existed within the government. Elsewhere he referred to the 'confusion of jarring interests and opinions that cross one another in every possible direction', and he averred 'Well, here is a religious war added to all our civil and foreign wars.'[80] Walpole's analysis points to 'an universal *anarchy of opinion*' as a cultural thematic and to internal contradictions, infiltrations, and tensions about who might be recognized as a good leader and who identified as a traitor.[81]

Scholars have examined the social status of those who joined the rioting mobs, concluding that the Protestant cause found supporters among all social and political ranks. 'An exact representation of the Burning, Plundering and Destruction of Newgate' (Figure 3.4) includes at least two black faces among the raucous throng and draws our attention to the racial and ethnic mix of the crowd.[82] These men may be Benjamin Bowsey and John Glover. Bowsey, described as a 'blackmoor', was indicted at the Old Bailey on June 28, 1780 for 'disturbance of the public peace' and for attempting to 'demolish and pull down the dwelling house of Richard Akerman, the warden at Newgate prison'.[83] He was found guilty and sentenced to death. John Glover also participated in the looting of Akerman's house accused of 'standing on the steps, thumping ... against the gate'. He too was convicted and sentenced to

Figure 3.4 'An exact representation of the Burning, Plundering and Destruction of Newgate'

death.[84] At least one of the female defendants charged with breaking the peace during the Riots was raced as black. Witnesses described Charlotte Gardiner as a 'black girl' and a 'black woman'. She worked with Mary Roberts, described as 'white', 'pulling the house [belonging to John Lebarty] all to pieces, both inside and out, and throwing the things out at the window'. Gardiner apparently joined those who carried goods and furniture out to the top of Towerhill to burn them. Gardiner and Roberts were found guilty and sentenced to death and hanged. Glover and Bowsey were pardoned.[85]

Samuel Solomons, a Jewish pencil maker from Whitechapel, represented religious diversity among the rioters. He was tried and convicted at the Old Bailey for attacking the house of Christopher Connor, the publican at the Red Lion in the parish of St Mary's Whitechapel. According to Connor's testimony, the mob returned to his house on the night of June 8 at about 10 o'clock. Solomons 'was the third or fourth man that entered my house; he began pulling down the boxes as fast as he could'. When Solomons and two or three other men ran up the stairs, Connor pursued the intruders begging them 'for God's sake not to tear my place to pieces'. In response the accused held Connor 'by the colar and his comrade held a pistol to my head'. The victim ran down the stairs, hitting his arm and fracturing the bone.[86]

As discussed in chapter 2 England in the eighteenth century and London in particular was racially, ethnically, and religiously diverse. The significant black presence in London including many South Asian and African seamen passing through the Docks – has led historians to suggest that perhaps as many as 8000, 10,000 or even 15,000 blacks called London home, and there are estimates that up to 5000 blacks lived in other parts of England, most of them concentrated in Bristol and Liverpool but also in the countryside.[87] England's Jewish population has been estimated at 8000 in the time of the Jewish Naturalization Act in 1753. Jewish immigration from the Netherlands, the German states, and Poland over the second half of the eighteenth century increased London's Jewish population to an estimated 11,000 in 1791.[88] By no means segregated, the different communities lived in close proximity, socialized together, and intermarried.[89] In the context of the Gordon Riots John Glover, Benjamin Bowsey, Charlotte Gardiner, and Samuel Solomons defined themselves as British insiders, accepted, at least by some, as fellow rioters. According to witnesses as she carried 'a great deal of furniture' out of Akerman's house to the fire, Gardiner was heard 'swearing and crying, "More wood for the fire, damn your eyes you bouger, more wood for the fire."'[90] These African and Jewish Londoners blended in as part of the crowd signaling their identification with the rioters and the cause for which they agitated. Isaac Land describes a similar phenomenon in his discussion of 'street citizenship' best exemplified by Joseph Johnson, a black man who walked London's streets in the 1780's singing patriotic songs and wearing a wooden model ship on his head. Like Johnson, Bowsey, Glover, Solomons, and Gardiner performed their street citizenship through their participation in street acts, in this case the Riots.[91]

While none of these defendants explicitly articulated their argument against empire, their 'street citizenship' suggests an association of their freedom and way of life in London with England and Britishness. Their participation in the Riots suggests an awareness of a link between their status as free people and the law of the land in which they lived. One might speculate that the ambiguity in the law and the insecurities that surrounded their freedom (especially given Britain's complicity and leadership in the slave trade and the recapture and sale of self-emancipating slaves like Somerset), contributed to the identification of these black citizens with London and 'the cause' of the Gordon Riots.[92] The collaboration of black and white rioters, Protestants and Jews, seems like precisely the sort of metropolitan mixing represented as threatening to opponents of the Relief Bill and presumably what the Riots set out to stop. From this perspective, the comments of Thomas Holcroft (1745–1809) about 'the mischief ... perpetrated' and their 'black ... aspect' in the service of 'the destruction of the empire'[93] allow for a different interpretation of the two sides in the conflict and what they thought they stood for.

The language in the trials provides some evidence about white opinion of interracial London. While questioning one of his witnesses, the prosecutor in Glover's case asked a witness if he had ever been outside of England. When he replied that his travels had only taken him as far as the Isle of Wight, the attorney replied 'you have never been in a country where Blacks are the inhabitants ... Then you are only accustomed to see Blacks by accident as I am'.[94] The prosecutor's question reveals his perception of London as a white city with only an irregular and infrequent black presence. Is this an example of the occlusion of blackness mentioned as a consequence of the Somerset decision in chapter 2? Rose Jennings, a witness in the Bowsey case, said that 'when I first saw the black I turned to a lady and said, this is a motley crew, and of every colour'.[95] Her choice of the word motley, referring to 'an incongruous, multifarious, or confused mixture or assembly' (OED), indicates a disordered combination, out of place. No mention of Solomon's Judaism was made at his trial, but the newspaper reports from the scene of his execution did. One article called him 'Samuel Solomons, a Jew', while another mentioned that 'a priest of his own profession, who attended him in Newgate, got up into the cart, and prayed to him for about half an hour, in which he joined with the greatest devotion'. After his hanging, Solomon's 'body was delivered to some of his brethren, who were waiting to receive it for interment'.[96]

In contrast with these perceptions of London's fitful and rare diversity, pro-slavery planter Samuel Estwick described pervasive interracial mixing in London in 1772 on the eve of the Somerset decision: 'scarce is there a street in London that does not give many examples of that [that is, Estwick's reference to 15,000 blacks in England]'.[97] An anonymous writer in the *Scots Journal* recommended a limit to the number of blacks in England 'to preserve the beauty and fair complexion of our people, which otherwise is in a probable way of becoming Morisco, like the Spaniards and Portuguese'.[98] Twenty years later in 1802, Hester Piozzi wrote:

> I am haunted by *black shadows*. Men of colour in the rank of gentlemen; a black Lady, cover'd with finery, in the Pit at the Opera, and tawny children playing in the Squares, – the gardens of the Squares I mean, – with their Nurses, afford ample proofs of Hannah More and Mr. Wilberforce's success toward breaking down the *wall of separation*. Oh! How it falls on every side! And spreads its tumbling ruins on the world! Learning all ranks, all customs, all colours, all religions *jumbled together*, till like the old craters of an exhausted volcano, Time closes and covers with fallacious green each ancient breach of distinction.[99]

According to these sources, mixing and mingling of races, nationalities, ethnicities, and religions characterized London life in the eighteenth century. Their authors' less than enthusiastic assessments of London's racial, religious, ethnic, and cultural diversity speak to the specter of 'black shadows' that herald the removal of what Piozzi names 'the wall of separation'. Piozzi seems most concerned that the result will be the erasure of any marks of 'distinction' and the eradication of any condemnation of their transgression. Even by the last quarter of the eighteenth century some white Londoners imagined the metropole as separate from imperial networks and expressed a hope that they could remain unconnected to mobile colonial bodies and disappointment when 'all ranks, all customs, all colours, all religions jumbled together'.

In contrast, blacks living in England claimed British citizenship and rights and considered them a scarce commodity, tied very locally to English soil. In his copious correspondence Ignatius Sancho, the former slave, often articulated his patriotism, his concern for his country, and his loyalty to the monarchy, especially regarding the American war. As an independent male householder in Westminster, he is the only Afro-Briton known to have voted in parliamentary elections to select representatives for Westminster in 1774 and 1778.¹⁰⁰ He mentioned the racial discrimination he and other blacks in London faced and he did not avoid the topic of slavery. Initiating a correspondence with Laurence Sterne in July 1766, Sancho distinguished Sterne, 'of all my favorite authors, not one has drawn a tear in favor of my miserable black brethren – excepting yourself, and the humane author of Sir George Ellison'. Urging Sterne to continue to write in favor of the alleviation of slavery's oppression of Africans he said: 'I think you will forgive me; – and I am sure you will applaud me for beseeching you to give one half-hour's attention to slavery, as it is at this day practiced in our West Indies – That subject, handled in your striking manner, would ease the yoke (perhaps) of many – but if only of one – Gracious God! – what a feast to a benevolent heart!'¹⁰¹ He summarized his cosmopolitan outlook in a letter to John Meheux in July 1777:

> We will mix, my boy, with all countries, colours, faiths, – see the countless multitudes of the first world – the myriads descended from the Ark – the Patriarchs, – Sages – Prophets – and Heroes! My head turns round at the vast idea! – We will mingle with them and to untwist the vast chain of blessed Providence – which puzzles and baffles human understanding.¹⁰²

The Afro-Briton Charlotte Gardiner's participation in the Riots seems to have been motivated by anti-Catholicism. Witnesses testified that she and those around her pulling down John Lebarty's house cried 'down with Popery, down with Popery'. According to Sancho 'the Sardinian ambassador offered 500 guineas to the rabble, to save a painting of our Saviour from the flames, and 1000 guineas not to destroy an exceeding fine organ: the gentry told him, they would burn him if they could get at him, and destroyed the picture and organ directly'.¹⁰³ The record of these negotiations reflects a determination on the part of the crowd not to be swayed by bargaining, no matter how lucrative. Yet this anti-Catholicism did not insist on a specific Protestant denomination, perhaps indicating the acceptance of a more capacious set of Protestants including those who were not members of the Church of England.

However, not everyone cited religion as their motive for rioting: for some the anti-Catholic sentiment that animated the Gordon Riots was a palimpsest overwritten with anxieties about these very real imperial connections and the losses associated with the presence of difference. Walpole's refusal to cite religion as the root cause of the Riots is echoed in some of the testimony of defendants prosecuted for riot at London's Old Bailey. Despite repeated mention of 'Papists' and references to rioters checking the bibles in the homes they raided, Thomas Haycock disavowed religion when asked 'what could induce him to do all this? He said the cause. I said, do you mean a religious cause? He said no; for he was of no religion'. Another witness asked him on the night of the riot 'Tom, what harm has the poor old fellow done, you have had many a guinea of his money. Is that religion?' The prisoner replied, 'D – n my eyes I have no religion, but I love to keep it up for the good of the cause.'[104] Similarly, the Protestant Association's *Appeal* claimed that 'If the doctrines held by Papists were confined to matters of opinion in religion, and did not include political tenets of the most dangerous tendency, they might expect the same connivance, which has generally been extended to other erroneous sects.'[105] This evidence suggests that what disturbed the crowd, and what held it together across lines of class and race, was not only the belief that religious pluralism would undermine Protestant faith or practice. Many of the rioters feared that Catholic relief brought with it the acceptance of ideas that would ultimately infuse England's 'political tenets' with a 'dangerous tendency' that implied disorder and unruliness. Although he would never align himself with the Protestant Association, Haycock's comments echo Walpole's foreboding prediction that 'anarchy will reign for some time, and despotism succeed'.[106] Together these sources suggest the perception that Protestantism, and Anglicanism in particular, bound the nation together and that universal English membership in its ranks – even by those who claimed they 'have no religion' – protected the values of 'the cause' from unraveling.

One need look no further than the first places attacked, the Sardinian embassy chapel in Lincoln's Inn Fields followed by the Bavarian embassy in Golden Square, to see the disquieting imprint of xenophobic attitudes merged with anti-Catholicism. Some of the witness testimony at the Old Bailey expressed similar sentiments. Charlotte Gardiner's victim, John Lebarty, declared himself 'an Italian' who kept 'a publick-house and a stop shop'.[107] At Gardiner's trial Lebarty testified that 'After the mob had pulled down the ambassador's house, she (Mary) came by my house, and said, "You outlandish bouger, I will have your house down; you outlandish Papist, I will have your house down."' Thomas Morris told the court that Roberts 'called him [Lebarty] an old Portuguese bouger'.[108] Several references to Lebarty's religion accompanied these damning mentions of his foreignness.

In addition to Catholic targets, legal institutions also found themselves in the sights of the rioters. On Tuesday evening June 7 the mob attacked jails throughout London. Ignatius Sancho's letters, purportedly written in close proximity to these events, reported that 'The Fleet Prison, the Marshalsea, King's Bench, both Compters, Clerkenwell, and Tothill Fields, with Newgate, are all flung open; – Newgate partly burned, and

300 felons from thence only let loose upon the world'.[109] What do we make of this attack on Newgate, rebuilt between 1770 and 1778, newly reopened only two years when the Riots burned it and other prisons? Historians of crime have argued convincingly that the rioters were resisting England's 'bloody' criminal code marked by harsh punishments for relatively minor property offenses.[110] There is much truth to this explanation, but perhaps the crowd's action denounced other legal institutions as well. If the Riots were also a critique of a parliament and legislative process unresponsive to and unrepresentative of popular opinion, specifically but not exclusively in regard to the passage of the Relief Act, all law may have come under fire. The Riots implicitly and explicitly rejected equality before the law for Catholics. The attack on the prisons suggests a connection between the rejection of the legislation and a rejection of the legal process that resulted in the jail sentences interrupted by the crowd.

That same night the attacks on the jails were followed by an attack on Lord Chief Justice Mansfield's house. The *Whitehall Evening Post* reported that 'About half past two they had got to his Lordship's law library, etc. And destroyed some thousand volumes, with many capital manuscripts, mortgages, papers, and other deeds, etc'.[111] Mansfield had already suffered an attack by the marchers delivering the petition to Parliament on June 2 when the windows of his carriage were broken and his wig was torn off. Mansfield may have been targeted for at least three reasons. Although he had left Scotland as an adolescent, his family had supported the Jacobites in the rebellion of 1715. He too was among the king's inner circle pictured in 'Argus', considered an interloper, responsible for the Court's poor choices and policies. But it is noteworthy that the attack targeted Mansfield's law library. Reflecting back on events of Tuesday night, Sancho remarked 'shall we call it a judgement? – or what shall we call it? The thunder of their vengeance has fallen upon gin and law – the two most inflammatory things in the Christian world.'[112] The crowd's assault on the prominent judge's house and his legal archive suggests discontent with the legal apparatus that created and sustained empire, arbitrating the legal status of internal others like Somerset and meeting out harsh punishments while espousing the ideology of rule of law and equality before the law.

The Bank of England was as powerful a symbol of empire as any of the sites attacked by the mob. On Wednesday, the mob 'not only declared their resolution of firing the prisons, and some private houses, but had avowed their intention to destroy the Bank'. A guard was sent to the Royal Exchange for the protection of the Bank 'as nothing perhaps could have equaled the national desolation, had the diabolical purposes of the insurgents upon this place succeeded'.[113] When Holcroft justified the government's use of the military to suppress the Riots, he explained that the troops secured 'those places, on the safety of which the very existence of the empire might be said to depend'.[114] Fourteen years after he published his account of the Gordon Riots, Holcroft was arrested for high treason, a target of the government's anti-republican policies for his support of the French Revolution and reformist politics. But in 1780 in the wake of the Riots he defended the government's actions against the rioters, citing the rioters' targets as imperial assets whose protection necessitated the unusual, controversial, indeed what might be called the most un-English, imposition of martial law.

The Bank of England represented financial networks, commercial endeavors, and circuits of goods and people. Although some considered these the core components of the imperial mission, many in England felt threatened by the mobility they enabled and the mixing that resulted from them, especially in the metropole. Yet the relatively successful integration of Catholic communities in eighteenth-century England, and their integral place in every site and aspect of the Empire, attested to the affluence, comfort, and acceptance enjoyed by some Catholics in England and across the British Empire. Indeed by the end of the eighteenth century some Catholics were fundamental to the British imperial project and many lived their lives enjoying almost complete toleration.[115] From their positions of wealth and power, having experienced some limited acceptance, Catholics, like English Jews during the furor over the Jewish Naturalization Act 1753–1754, sought the provisions of the Relief Act and their demands seemed consistent with the ideology of rule of law. The British government, keenly aware of the Empire's dire need for troops and the demands of security in its global outposts, responded with a measure of relief in order to integrate different ethnic and religious groups, like Catholics in Quebec and Ireland, to ensure the defense and continued expansion of the Empire.

The threat posed by empire at home came from the very competence and success, sameness and assimilation of those defined as 'other'. As a result of this sameness, 'in order that they might know their friends from their enemies',[116] supporters of the Protestant Association were urged to mark their allegiance to the cause by wearing 'blue cockades in their hats, to distinguish themselves from the Papists, and those who approve of the late act in favour of Popery'.[117] Ribbons and cockades were often used to herald a political position and were part of the sartorial performance of politics in this period, and the Protestant Association supplied blue cockades to those who did not have them.[118] On Monday June 5 when the Riots raged and the bonfires were set, 'all ranks of people began to be exceedingly terrified at the lawless proceedings of this day'. Erasing the marks of difference between those who supported the Riots and those who did not and between rioters and their targets, 'numbers put blue cockades in their hats, although it might now be said to be the ensign of rebellion, on purpose to avoid personal injury and insult', donning the marks of difference as signs of solidarity and similarity.[119]

By Thursday the militia had been engaged and 'the whole city had the appearance of a place that every moment expected to be stormed, and was so well defended that nothing less than a regular army could have endangered it'.[120] Despite martial law and the heavy troop presence, 'the inhabitants could by no means persuade themselves they were entirely secure'. City dwellers took protective measures 'their doors all scrawled with chalk, intimating that they were no Papists, and their windows decorated with blue flags or ribbands'.[121] Subverting all attempts to mark difference, 'Jews, in Houndsditch and Duke's Place, were so terrified that they followed the general example, and, unintentionally, gave an air of ridicule to what they understood in a very serious light, by writing on their shutters, "This house is a true Protestant."'[122] For the Jews who wrote this, the word Protestant represented their identification with England and Englishness. With this label, a survival tactic, they marked themselves claiming an ethnicity (or a lack of ethnicity) that they associated with a fictive indigenous culture.

Later in the week in response to the association of criminality with the blue cockade, a handbill 'requested of all peaceable and well-disposed persons (as well Protestants associated as others) that they will abstain from wearing BLUE COCKADES, as these ensigns are now assumed by a set of miscreants'. In the space of a few days, the blue cockade, initially a sign belonging to the supporters of Protestantism, order, English law, and civil rights had become, according to the handbill, a deliberate ruse by those criminals 'whose purpose it is to burn this city, and plunder its inhabitants' to blend in among the city's law-abiding populace 'by distributing among better-disposed persons, and prevailing on them to wear these marks and distinctions, to screen themselves from the detestation and punishment due to their enormous crimes'.[123] Reframing the events of June 2–8, 1780, a retrospective on the causes of the Riots redrew the boundaries of insiders and outsiders defining those 'who could plan or attempt to execute such dreadful excesses' as 'a combination of our foreign enemies, acting by means of their emissaries, and by means of our own internal enemies'.[124] In an ironic turn of events, this account redrew the lines of inclusion and exclusion defining rioters as 'internal enemies', questioning their allegiance and pushing these white, English Protestants outside the bounds of the normative legal subject.

Disrupting the Empire

Those who spoke in favor of toleration used a nationalist rhetoric to defend their position and condemn that of the rioters, but their nationalism was always couched in an international frame that muted internal differences while it emphasized cosmopolitan values of inclusion. A commentator who wrote in the midst of the furor over the proposed Scottish Relief Bill appealed to national pride as a way to shame the rioters. He lamented the attacks on Catholics whose 'only crime, [had been] the daring to be good subjects'.[125] An anonymous pamphlet about the Gordon Riots attributed to Ignatius Sancho condemned the Protestant Association's revival of anti-Catholic sentiment. Sancho declared it an anachronism, which 'the general benevolence of the age had almost consigned to oblivion'.[126] The writer accused the Protestant Association of hypocrisy because while 'they proclaim their loyalty to the throne ... and attachment to the happy constitution, the preserver of the rights liberties and privileges they enjoy', they are 'so jealous of these rights', that they 'would deprive others of enjoying the same, lest they should lose the satisfaction of indulging in the comparison between luxury and oppression'.[127] Citing liberty of conscience as a frequently practiced English right, the author called on those living 'in an age so enlightened as the present, when every one maintains the right of thinking freely for themselves' to spread the 'spirit of benevolence' through toleration.[128]

On its surface the pamphlet reads as a condemnation of anti-Catholicism, a defense of coexistence, and a brief 'to show that there is nothing to be apprehended from the Toleration in question'.[129] But the pamphlet also posited the Act as an explanation of the necessities and realities of a culture fully immersed in imperial concerns and priorities. The author pointed to the diversity of ethnic and religious life in London, including 'Pagans, Mahomedans, Infidels of every denomination' who 'are good and worthy members of society'.[130] Conversely, he reminded his readers that 'a very considerable number of English and other Protestant merchants, have long resided in every trading town throughout the Papal dominions', attesting to the pragmatic, mutual toleration that greased the wheels of trade and empire.[131] He acknowledged the existence of multiple legal jurisdictions, but he insisted that they did not imperil the authority of the civil law. Highlighting the civilizing mission of the British Empire, he maintained that 'benevolence' must start in the metropole and 'will soon diffuse her genial warmth to the most distant regions of his [majesty's] empire'.[132] In a retort to those who feared relying on a military force staffed by Scottish Catholics, the author argued for the strength and success of the imperial relationship between England and North Britons whose 'interests are so blended with our own, that the support of each becomes a common cause'.[133]

Aware of the global gaze on an imperial center in flames, the pseudonymous author 'Pensive', writing in the *St James Chronicle or the British Evening Post* on June 3, recounted a meeting with an artist who asked him 'What will Foreigners think of us when they are told of the Brutality of our People? We shall with Justice be called the Savages of Europe!' 'Pensive' responded 'These barbarians seem to make War with the fine Arts as much as with the Papists; they have destroyed two beautiful Altar Pieces, which cost an immense Sum of Money.'[134]

Despite his seemingly liberal leanings, the anonymous author does not advocate the inclusion of Catholics at the highest reaches of political power. He supports the exclusion of non-Protestants from 'sitting in Parliament or serving in any office of civil magistracy under the crown'.[135] The spirit of competitive imperial aspiration and conquest explicitly animates the end of the pamphlet in which the author sets out the stakes for Britain. Claiming that 'the leading maxim of the House of Bourbon is universal empire', he warns his readers that 'the present contest is, who shall ride the seas triumphant. Our title to it is disputed, and time only will decide this important event, big with the fate of Europe'.[136] Denying Catholics religious toleration risked Britain's 'title' while religious toleration served imperial goals. The choice was clear: benevolence, enlightenment, and limited inclusion served the strategic and political ends of imperial policy. In a letter to his friend the banker John Spink, Sancho recommended a similar course 'Let us convert by our example and conquer by our meekness and brotherly love'.[137]

Ignatius Sancho voiced his aversion for prejudice against Catholics and attacks on them, and he connected his concerns to the law and its supposed protection for all. 'This – this – is liberty! Genuine British liberty! – This instant about two thousand liberty boys are wearing and swaggering by with large sticks – thus armed in hopes of meeting with Irish chairmen and labourers'.[138] Here Sancho leaves toleration and maps the Riots onto the grid of civility and barbarity drawing a clear distinction between the barbarity of the rioters and the civility of the cosmopolitans, leaving Sancho to recommend 'an universal toleration'.[139] Although he implied an affirmation of the British Empire as a vehicle to greater emancipation and rights, Sancho embraced the declaration of martial law without remarking on its contradiction of English rights and liberties.

The question of race is never far from the distinction drawn between barbarity and cosmopolitan tolerance as articulated by Sancho who called 'the insanity of Ld. G. G. ... worse than [the] Negro barbarity of the populace'.[140] Calling attention to his own blackness, Sancho condemned the Riots and averred 'I am not sorry I was born in Afric'.[141] While Dissenters insisted on their inclusion in the nation and the absolute exclusion of Catholics, Sancho relied on the possibility of Catholic Emancipation and the extension of rights to Catholics. If there was no hope for Catholics to be included in the nation and afforded all the rights of white British subjects, surely black Britons and black slaves all over the Empire had no chance of enjoying the rights and liberties promised by the rule of law. Unlike the blacks who participated in the Riots, the educated Afro-Briton Sancho identified with the political project of empire. He suggests that it is Britain's imperial mission, its 'genial warmth' that affords inclusion to those like himself by mitigating the exclusionary attributes of Englishness and expanding the definition of 'good and worthy members of society'.

Conclusion

Ignatius Sancho said it best when he wrote 'It is thought by many who discern deeply, that there is more at the bottom of this business than merely the repeal of an act'.[142] What was really going on in the Gordon Riots and how do they relate to the larger themes of empire and law traced in this book? What is evident throughout is the flexible and permeable line between insiders and outsiders and the opportunistic ways in which it operated. Authorities enlisted the law to legitimize these boundaries, keeping the gates closed for some while opening them for others. The rule of law and its promise of equality before the law were at the heart of this story, motivating all sides with promises of liberty and equality and property and pushing them to act to grab those rights and actualize the promises or to oppose their extension.

The triangulation between various groups of internal others is also quite striking and begs for more analysis. The blacks, John Glover, Benjamin Bowsey, and Charlotte Gardiner, and the Jew, Samuel Solomons, joined in the rioting and identified themselves as rights-bearing Londoners who opposed Catholic toleration. The cooperation between Charlotte Gardiner and Mary Roberts indicates that at least in that instance, the white woman and the black woman partnered in their endeavors and imagined themselves both within the boundaries of nation. Their behavior suggests that they believed they had every right to protect themselves and their position while restricting those of others. Dissenting Protestants felt the same way, adamantly opposing Catholic toleration and insistently reminding their co-petitioners of the wrongs done them by the Catholic-leaning Stuarts. The Riots made Dissenters, ever the internal others, deprived of rights by oaths of loyalty to the Church of England that they refused to take, into the consummate insiders, urging the exclusion of Catholic rights. Unlike the Jewish Naturalization Act in which Jewish toleration was opposed because it would necessitate the toleration of Catholics, the Catholic Relief Act shifted the line of acceptance to include 'papists'. The rioters redrew that line uniting Protestants, no matter what denomination, against Catholics. Unlike the Jewish Naturalization Act 1753, however, Parliament did not repeal the Relief Act. The naturalization of individual Jews in exchange for their supposed talent for circulating imperial goods and generating both commerce and taxes, stood in stark contrast to the state's need for an increasing number of men to staff its global military forces.

Both the supporters of Gordon and those who spoke for Catholic toleration equated Protestantism, Englishness, and liberty. The debates that culminated in the Gordon Riots divided those Londoners who believed that the benefits of Englishness could only be enjoyed by a limited number in a confined space from those with a more expansive economy of rights. For those who opposed Catholic toleration, the maintenance of these rights relied on the exclusion of foreign influence from the indigenous setting because external influences threatened to dilute or circumscribe the rights in question or worse, to change them to reflect the values of those new populations. Although those who opposed the Relief Act supported the expansion of British power and influence beyond England's borders, they did not want those circuits of empire to thread through the metropole. Their opponents, conversely, perceived any obstruction of the imperial networks running in, through, and around the metropole as a disruptive force whose implications could have sweeping, negative effects.

In the cultural conversation about the relationship between nation and empire, London emerged as an important symbol. The place of London in the imperial imagination revealed a tension between those who defined it as an English city, free of imperial influences, and those for whom it served as a showcase of a global empire. Samuel Johnson described London as 'a great city ... the school for studying life'[143] providing an inexhaustible breadth of experiences and people such that 'when a man is tired of London, he is tired of life; for there is in London all that life can afford'.[144] Johnson's words encapsulated the cosmopolitan pride in London. Although many sought the sophistication and anonymity of the 'school for studying life', they rejected the reality of an imperial metropole, seeking instead homogeneity, in this case religious uniformity. No longer the most worldly wise in the kingdom, the London rioters refused to acknowledge the diversity of their neighbors and the imperial influences shot through the metropole. When faced with the destruction, violence, and disorder of the Gordon Riots, the pamphleteers who condemned the Protestant Association and its work against Catholic toleration wrote in favor of migration, movement, and comfort in many changing spaces, including and most especially in the metropole: the unacceptable alternative was a provincialized London.

Debates about what freedom and equality really meant, and for whom, continued and became louder and more vociferous in the next two decades. William Cowper expressed anxiety about the Gordon Riots and the extent of English liberty in his poem 'Table Talk' (1782). He implicated liberty as their cause: 'Too apt to play the wanton with her pow'rs. Grow freakish, and o'er leaping ev'ry mound Spread anarchy and terror all around.' Cowper's poem referred to disruption and riot as the 'effects like these she [Liberty] should produce' calling them 'worse than the deeds of galley-slaves broke loose'.[145] This stark and negative image of emancipated slaves questioned the extension of liberties to those who lacked them, not only slaves and people of color but also England's white, working classes. Cowper's poem highlighted fears about safety, property, and possession.

In her poem 'Slavery, A Poem' (1788) Hannah More responded to Cowper's depiction of freedom and its resulting mayhem. She declared that liberty was 'Not that unlicens'd monster of the crowd whose roar terrific bursts in peals so loud, Deaf'ning the ear of Peace; fierce Faction's tool, Of rash Sedition born, and mad Misrule; Whose stubborn mouth, rejecting Reason's reign, No strength can govern, and no skills restrain.'[146] The opportunistic lines of inclusion and exclusion relied on the discourse of liberty and equality and rule of law. Their dangerous and threatening implications vied with their palliative promises. For these conservative patriots, Britain's Empire was sometimes proposed as the answer to the unbridled nature of secular liberty as it was by the leaders of the Society for the Promotion of Christian Knowledge and its proposal to send children to schools and missions in imperial holdings to convert and missionize colonial subjects while inculcating religious values among the English children of the lower orders while removing their potentially disorderly bodies from the metropole.[147] Chapter 4 examines the impact of debates about the expansion of rights and the social order among Britain's working classes, specifically its sailors. The 1797 mutinies at the Spithead and the Nore pivoted on the contradiction between the navy's mission, summarized in 'Rule Britannia's' famous line 'Britons never, ever, ever shall be slaves' and the brutal conditions on board its ships.

Notes

1 William Belsham, *Memoirs of the reign of George III to the session of Parliament ending AD 1793*, 3 vols. (Dublin: J. Milliken, 1796), vol. 3, p. 22.

CITY, NATION, AND EMPIRE IN THE GORDON RIOTS

2 Thomas Holcroft, *A Plain and Succinct Narrative of the late riots and disturbances in the cities of London and Westminster, and borough of Southwark* (London: Fielding and Walker, 1780), p. 44.
3 *Morning Chronicle and London Advertiser*, June 3, 1780, issue 3446.
4 *The Political Magazine, and Parliamentary, Naval, Military, and Literary Journal*, 1 (1780), p. 421.
5 The artist is probably Italian Andrea Cavaliere Casali (1705–1784) who worked in England for 25 years starting from 1741 until 1766. His work in the Sardinian embassy is dated 1761. He also painted for the Bavarian embassy. John Ingamells, 'Casali, Andrea (1705–1784)', ODNB (http://www.oxforddnb.com.proxy2.library.uiuc.edu/view/article/4849, accessed April 14, 2010); and Jane Turner, ed., *The Dictionary of Art*, 34 vols. (New York: Grove, 1996), vol. 5, pp. 906–907.
6 *Political Magazine*, p. 421.
7 *London Chronicle*, June 3, 1780, issue 3667.
8 *Political Magazine*, p. 421.
9 *Gazetteer and New Daily Advertiser*, June 5, 1780, issue 16010.
10 *Annual Register* 23 (1780), p. 259.
11 For a detailed description of the Riots, see the *Annual Register* 23 (1780), pp. 254–287.
12 *Annual Register* 23 (1780), p. 263. According to Ignatius Sancho 'If any body of people above ten in number are seen together, and refuse to disperse, they are to be fired at without any further ceremony.' Ignatius Sancho, *Letters of the Late Ignatius Sancho, An African*, ed. Vincent Carretta (London: Penguin,1998), p. 221. For more on the imposition of martial law during the Gordon Riots, see Anthony Babington, *Military Intervention in Britain* (London: Routledge, 1990), pp. 21–31; and Tony Hayter, *The Army and the Crowd in Mid-Georgian England* (Totowa, NJ: Rowan and Littlefield, 1978), pp. 147–161.
13 John Archer, *Social Unrest and Popular Protest in England, 1780–1840* (Cambridge: Cambridge University Press, 2000), p. 59. For more on the Gordon Riots, see Ian Gilmour, *Riot, Risings and Revolution: Governance and Violence in Eighteenth-Century England* (London: Hutchinson, 1992); Colin Haydon, *Anti-Catholicism in Eighteenth-Century England, c. 1714–1780: A Political and Social Study* (Manchester: Manchester University Press, 1993); Adrian Randall, *Riotous Assemblies: Popular Protest in Hanoverian England* (Oxford: Oxford University Press, 2006); Nicholas Rogers, *Crowds, Culture and Politics in Georgian Britain* (Oxford: Clarendon, 1998); George Rudé, 'The Gordon Riots: A Study of the Rioters and their Victims: The Alexander Prize Essay', *Transactions of the Royal Historical Society*, 5th series, 6 (1956), pp. 93–114; and Matthew White, ' "For the Safety of the City": The Geography and Social Politics of Public Execution after the Gordon Riots', in *The Gordon Riots: Politics, Cultures and Insurrection in Late Eighteenth-Century Britain*, ed. Ian Haywood and John Seed (Cambridge: Cambridge University Press, 2012), pp. 204–225.
14 Nicholas Rogers, 'The Gordon Riots and the politics of war', in *Gordon Riots*, ed. Haywood and Seed, pp. 21–45; and Nicholas Rogers, 'Nights of Fire: The Gordon Riots of 1780 and the Politics of War', in *Crowd Actions in Britain and France from the Middle Ages to the Modern World*, ed. Michael Davis (Houndmills: Palgrave Macmillan, 2015), pp. 124–145. Carol Houlihan Flynn, 'Whatever Happened to the Gordon Riots', in *A Companion to the Eighteenth-Century English Novel and Culture*, ed. Paula Backscheider and Catherine Ingrassia (Malden, MA: Blackwell Publishers, 2005), pp. 459–480 analyzes the targets of the mob's attacks as 'spaces of commerce and empire' p. 466.
15 Disputes about what rights would be accorded to French Catholics in Grenada had been raging since 1763 when the island was ceded to Britain by the Treaty of Paris. For more, see Hannah Weiss Muller, 'Bonds of Belonging: Subjecthood and the British Empire', *Journal of British Studies* 53 (2014), pp. 29–58.
16 Donna T. Andrew, *Aristocratic Vice: The Attack on Duelling, Suicide, Adultery, and Gambling in Eighteenth-Century England* (New Haven, CT: Yale University

Press, 2013), pp. 9–10, 37–41; and H. T. Dickinson, *Caricatures and the Constitution, 1760–1832* (Cambridge: Chadwyck-Healey, 1986).
17 Diana Donald, *The Age of Caricature*, pp. 1–21. For more on caricature, see Amelia Rauser, *Caricature Unmasked*.
18 For more on petitions and their place as a legal means of appealing to the government, see Mark Knights, 'The 1780 Protestant Petitions and the Culture of Petitioning', in *Gordon Riots*, ed. Haywood and Seed, pp. 46–68. Matthew McCormack describes how the troops worked with civilians to quell the riots in 'Supporting the Civil Power: Citizen Soldiers and the Gordon Riots', *London Journal* 37 (2012), pp. 27–41.
19 Michael Ragussis, *Theatrical Nation*, p. 3.
20 P. J. Marshall, 'A Nation Defined by Empire, 1755–1776'.
21 Belsham, *Memoirs*, vol. 3, p. 22.
22 Belsham, *Memoirs*, vol. 3, p. 19.
23 Belsham, *Memoirs*, vol. 3, p. 19.
24 Belsham, *Memoirs*, vol. 3, p. 20.
25 John Paul De Castro, *The Gordon Riots* (Oxford: Oxford University Press, 1926); Christopher Hibbert, *King Mob: The Story of Lord George Gordon and the London Riots of 1780* (Cleveland, OH: World Publishing Company, 1958).
26 George Rudé, *Paris and London in the Eighteenth Century* (New York: Viking, 1970); George Rudé, *The Crowd in History: A Study of Popular Disturbances in France and England 1730–1848* (New York: Wiley, 1964).
27 E. P. Thompson, *The Making of the English Working Class* (New York: Pantheon, 1966), pp. 71–73.
28 For an analysis of London's Dissenters, see John Seed, '"The Fall of Romish Babylon Anticipated": Plebeian Dissenters and anti-popery in the Gordon Riots', in *Gordon Riots*, ed. Haywood and Seed, pp. 69–92.
29 Work on the Riots since Rudé and Thompson has qualified many of their conclusions. Randall, *Riotous Assemblies*; Nicholas Rogers, 'Crowd and People in the Gordon Riots', in *The Transformation of Political Culture: England and Germany in the late Eighteenth Century*, ed. E. Hellmuth (London: German Historical Institute, 1990), pp. 39–55; Nicholas Rogers, 'The Gordon Riots Revisited', *Historical Papers* 23 (1988), pp. 16–34; Nicholas Rogers, 'Plebeians and Proletarians in Eighteenth-century Britain', *Labour* 33 (1994), pp. 253–262; Robert Shoemaker, *The London Mob: Violence and Disorder in Eighteenth Century England* (London: Hambledon, 2004) and 'Streets of Shame? The Crowd and Public Punishments in London, 1700–1820', in *Penal Practice and Culture: Punishing the English, 1500–1900*, ed. Simon Devereaux and Paul Griffiths (New York: Palgrave Macmillan, 2004), pp. 232–257; and John Stevenson, *Popular Disturbances in England, 1700–1870* (New York: Longman, 1992).
30 Ian Haywood and John Seed, 'Introduction', in *Gordon Riots*, ed. Haywood and Seed, p. 12.
31 Flynn, 'Whatever Happened to the Gordon Riots', p. 460.
32 Hall, *Civilising Subjects*; Hall and Rose, *At Home with the Empire*; Wilson, *A Sense of the People*; Wilson, *The Island Race*; and Wilson, *A New Imperial History*. The legal relationship between colony and metropole is explored in Marshall, 'Britain and the World'; Greene, *Peripheries and Center*; Bilder, *The Transatlantic Constitution*.
33 Wilson, *Island Race*, pp. 15–18; and Wilson, 'Introduction: histories, empires, modernities', in *New Imperial History*, pp. 17–19.
34 For the impact beyond London, see Colin Haydon, 'The Gordon Riots in the English Provinces', *Historical Research* 16 (1990), pp. 354–359. For more on Scottish resistance to Catholic relief, see Eugene Black, 'The Tumultuous Petitioners: The Protestant Association in Scotland, 1778–1780', *Review of Politics* 25 (1963), pp. 183–211; and Robert Donovan, 'Voices of Distrust: The Expression of Anti-Catholic Feeling in Scotland, 1778–1781', *Innes Review* 30 (1979), pp. 62–76. For imperial sites, see Brad Jones, '"In Favour of Popery": Patriotism, Protestantism, and the Gordon Riots

in the Revolutionary British Atlantic', *Journal of British Studies* 52 (2013), pp. 79–102.
35 Haywood and Seed, 'Introduction', in *Gordon Riots*, ed. Haywood and Seed, p. 2.
36 This discussion of the cultural meaning of place relies on Massey, *For Space*, esp. pp. 9–15, 64–68.
37 Jane Jacobs, *Edge of Empire: Postcolonialism and the City* (New York: Routledge, 1996), p. 2.
38 Most recently, Jones, *Engendering Whiteness*; Newman, 'Gender, Sexuality, and the Formation of Racial Identities'.
39 Sancho, *Letters*, ed. Carretta, p. 227.
40 Belsham, *Memoirs*, vol. 3, p. 22.
41 The Act of Restraint in Appeals, 24 Hen. VIII c. 12. For the full text of the Act, see Raithby, *The Statutes of the Realm*, vol. 3, pp. 427–429.
42 *Statutes of the Realm*, vol. 3, pp. 427–429.
43 *Statutes of the Realm*, vol. 3, pp. 427–429.
44 *Statutes of the Realm*, vol. 3, pp. 427–429.
45 Colley, *Britons*, p. 33.
46 Colley, *Britons*, p. 50.
47 *Statutes of the Realm*, vol. 7, pp. 586–587. This statute was extended by Anne in 1719 (12 Anne, st. 2, c. 14). During the reign of George I statutes were passed to ensure that Catholics affirmed the Hanoverian succession. After the Jacobite Rebellion in 1715 several statutes were passed allowing surveillance of Catholics and their property and increasing the taxes Catholics paid.
48 Haydon, *Anti-Catholicism in Eighteenth-Century England* and Haydon, ' "Popery at St. James": The Conspiracy Theses of William Payne Thomas Holis and Lord George Gordon', in *Conspiracies and Conspiracy Theory in Early Modern Europe: From the Waldensians to the French Revolution*, ed. Barry Coward and Julian Swann (Burlintgon, VT: Ashgate, 2004), pp. 174–177.
49 On toleration and the Enlightenment, see Martin Fitzpatrick, 'Toleration and the Enlightenment Movement', in *Toleration in Enlightenment Europe*, ed. Ole Peter Grell and Roy Porter (Cambridge: Cambridge University Press, 2000), pp. 23–68.
50 Robert Donovan, 'The military Origins of the Roman Catholic Relief Programme of 1778', *The Historical Journal* 28 (1985), pp. 79–102.
51 Karen Stanbridge, 'Quebec and the Irish Catholic Relief Act of 1778: An Institutional Approach', *Journal of Historical Sociology* 16 (2003), pp. 375–404. In 'The Catholic Question in the Eighteenth Century', *History Ireland* 1 (1993): 17–21, Thomas Bartlett points out that the British government used the specter of expanding Catholic rights to contain the aspirations of Irish Protestants for self rule.
52 For more on anti-Catholic responses in 1778, see Jones, 'In Favour of Popery'.
53 For more on the Act, see Philip Lawson, *The Imperial Challenge: Quebec and Britain in the Age of the American Revolution* (Montreal: McGill-Queen's University Press, 1990).
54 Raithby and Edlyne, *Statutes at Large*, vol. 13, pp. 789–794.
55 *Public Advertiser*, 12 June 1774.
56 *Public Advertiser*, 12 June 1774.
57 David Dixon, *New Foundations: Ireland 1660–1800* (Dublin: Irish Academic Press, 2000), p. 161.
58 Nigel Abercrombie, 'The First Relief Act', in *Challoner and his Church: A Catholic Bishop in Georgian England*, ed. Eamon Duffy (London: Darton, Longman, and Todd, 1981), pp. 174–194.
59 Raithby and Edlyne, *Statutes at Large*, vol. 14, pp. 389–391.
60 Robert Burns, 'The Catholic Relief Act in Ireland, 1778', *Church History* 32 (1963), pp. 181–206.
61 *Whitehall Evening Post*, April 11, 1780. Black, 'The Tumultuous Petitioners', and Donovan, 'Voices of Distrust'.
62 *The London Magazine, or, Gentleman's monthly intelligencer*, 63 (1774), p. 487.

63 Lewis, W. S., ed., *Horace Walpole's Correspondence*, 48 vols. (New Haven, CT: Yale University Press, 1983), vol. 41, pp. 315.
64 *Walpole's Correspondence*, vol. 41, p. 312.
65 *A Memorial to the Public in behalf of the Roman Catholics of Edinburgh and Glasgow; containing an account of the late riot against them on the second and following days of Feb. 1779* (London: J. P. Coghlan, 1779), p. 11.
66 The damage done in Scotland is recounted in selections from William Forbes-Leith, ed., *Memoirs of Scottish Catholics during the Seventeenth and Eighteenth Centuries*, 2 vols. (London: Longman's, Green and Co, 1909), vol. 2, pp. 374–380.
67 *Memorial ... in behalf of the Roman Catholics of Edinburgh and Glasgow*, p. 28.
68 *Memorial ... in behalf of the Roman Catholics of Edinburgh and Glasgow*, pp. 37–38.
69 *Memorial ... in behalf of the Roman Catholics of Edinburgh and Glasgow*, p. 39.
70 *Memorial ... in behalf of the Roman Catholics of Edinburgh and Glasgow*, p. 37.
71 Stephens and George, *Catalogue of Prints and Drawings*, vol. 5, #5643, pp. 381–382. The theme of misdirection is depicted repeatedly in the images that warn against the Act for Catholic Relief. See also 'The Royal Ass', #5669 and 'Father Peters leading his mangy whelp to be touched for the evil', #5670.
72 The Act of Restraint in Appeals, 24 Hen. VIII c. 12.
73 Stephens and George, *Catalogue of Prints and Drawings*, vol. 5, #5667, p. 399. Argus refers to the character from Greek mythology said to possess an unusual number of eyes. This is a much more dangerous and threatening interaction than the 'Family quarrel' described by Ragussis, *Theatrical Nation*.
74 Stephens and George, *Catalogue of Prints and Drawings*, vol. 5, #5678, pp. 406–407.
75 *Walpole's Correspondence*, vol. 29, pp. 61–65.
76 *Walpole's Correspondence*, vol. 29, p. 62.
77 *Walpole's Correspondence*, vol. 29, p. 63.
78 *Walpole's Correspondence*, vol. 29, p. 64.
79 *Walpole's Correspondence*, vol. 29, p. 64.
80 *Walpole's Correspondence*, vol. 29, p. 54.
81 *Walpole's Correspondence*, vol. 29, p. 63, emphasis original.
82 Stephens and George, *Catalogue of Prints and Drawings*, vol. 5, #5844, p. 509. For more on black participation in the Riots, see Kathleen Chater, *Untold Histories: Black People in England and Wales during the Period of the British Slave Trade, c. 1660–1807* (Manchester: Manchester University Press, 2009); and Marika Sherwood, 'Blacks in the Gordon Riots', *History Today* 47 (1997), pp. 24–28.
83 Benjamin Bowsey, OBSP, June 28, 1780, consulted online, t17800628–33. Bowsey avoided execution: he wrote to his former employer Lord Earlsbury and to Alderman Woolridge seeking their help. On August 9, 1780 after several attempts by Woolridge and even the Lord Mayor, Brackley Kennet, he received a respite. Sherwood, 'Blacks in the Gordon Riots', p. 27.
84 John Glover, OBSP, June 28, 1780, consulted online, t17800628–94. Glover's employer, John Philips, a lawyer, for whom Glover had worked as a servant for twelve years, testified on his behalf at the trial. After Glover's conviction, Philips petitioned the king arguing that two of the men who had testified against Glover, William Sheppard and William Lee, had criminal records which should have disqualified them from serving as witnesses. Glover was reprieved and pardoned. Sherwood, 'Blacks in the Gordon Riots', p. 26.
85 Mary Roberts and Charlotte Gardiner, OBSP, June 28, 1780, consulted online, t17800628–65. Although Gardiner, Bowsey, and Glover were all convicted and sentenced to death, only Gardiner was executed. News of the pardons received by Glover and Bowsey was carried in several newspapers including *Craftsman or Say's Weekly Journal*, Saturday July 22, 1780, issue 1075. Although the newspapers all mention that Glover and Bowsey were black, they do so only in the articles that report on their trials. No mention is made of their color in the announcement of their pardons.

86 Samuel Solomons, OBSP, June 28, 1780, consulted online, t17800628-23.
87 Morgan, 'British Encounters', p. 159; Myers, *Reconstructing the Black Past*, p. 35.
88 Endelman, *The Jews of Georgian England*, pp. 171–178. The influx of Jews in the eighteenth century was highest in the 1770s. The rate dropped in the later eighteenth century slowed by the Revolutionary and Napoleonic wars.
89 Hecht, *Continental and Colonial Servants*, pp. 48–49; and Dabydeen, *Hogarth's Blacks*, pp. 19–20. For more on black life and experience in Britain in the eighteenth century, see Gerzina, 'Black Loyalists in London'; Shyllon, *Black People in Britain*; Walvin, *Black and White*.
90 Mary Roberts and Charlotte Gardiner, OBSP, June 28, 1780, consulted online, t17800628-65. Bouger is another spelling for the derogatory term bugger.
91 Isaac Land, 'Bread and Arsenic: Citizenship from the Bottom Up in Georgian England', *Journal of Social History* 39 (2005), pp. 89–110, esp. 100–102.
92 Lorimer, 'Black Slaves and English Liberty'; and Drescher, 'Manumission'.
93 Holcroft, *A Plain and Succinct Narrative*, p. 44.
94 John Glover, OBSP, June 28, 1780, consulted online, t17800628-94.
95 Benjamin Bowsey, OBSP, June 28, 1780, consulted online, t17800628-33.
96 *London Packet or New Lloyd's Evening Post*, July 19, 1780–July 21, 1780, issue 1575; *General Evening Post*, July 20, 1780–July 22, 1780, issue 7239, p. 1. The *London Chronicle*, July 20, 1780–July 22, 1780, issue 3688, p. 1, contradicted the *General Evening Post* reporting that 'It is very remarkable, that although there are such numbers of Jews live in Whitechapel, not one person of that sect was seen out during the execution in that neighborhood'.
97 Estwick, *Considerations of the Negroe*, p. 43.
98 'Some Observations upon the Slavery of Negroes', *Scots Magazine*, 34 (1772), p. 301. Similar sentiments are expressed in Edward Long, *Candid Reflections Upon the Judgment Lately Awarded by the Court of King's Bench in Westmister Hall on What is Commonly Called the Negroe Cause* (London: T. Lowndes, 1772).
99 Oswald G. Knapp, ed. *The Intimate Letters of Hester Piozzi and Penelope Pennington, 1788–1822* (London: John Lane, 1914), pp. 243–244, emphasis original.
100 Vincent Carretta, 'Sancho (Charles) Ignatius (1729?–1780)', ODNB (http://www.oxforddnb.com/view/article/24609, accessed April 12, 2016).
101 Carretta, ed., *Letters*, p. 74.
102 Carretta, ed., *Letters*, p. 86.
103 Carretta, ed., *Letters*, p. 219.
104 Thomas Haycock, OBSP, June 28, 1780, consulted online, t17800628-34. Connivance here means a willingness to secretly allow. OED.
105 *An Appeal from the Protestant Association to the people of Great Britain* (London: J. Dodsley, 1779), p. 4.
106 *Walpole's Correspondence*, vol. 29, p. 64.
107 Mary Roberts and Charlotte Gardiner, OBSP, June 28, 1780, consulted online, t17800628-65.
108 Mary Roberts and Charlotte Gardiner, OBSP, June 28, 1780, consulted online, t17800628-65.
109 Carretta ed., *Letters*, p. 220. For a critical assessment of Sancho's letters and when they were written, see Brychhan Carey, '"The Worse than Negro Barbarity of the Populace": Ignatius Sancho Witnesses the Gordon Riots', in *Gordon Riots*, ed. Haywood and Seed, pp. 144–161.
110 Tim Hitchcock, 'Re-negotiating the Bloody Code: the Gordon Riots and the Transformation of Popular Attitudes to the Criminal Justice System', in *Gordon Riots*, ed. Haywood and Seed, pp. 185–203.
111 *Whitehall Evening Post*, June 6, 1780.
112 Carretta, ed., *Letters*, p. 222.
113 Holcroft, *A Plain and Succinct Narrative*, p. 32.
114 Holcroft, *A Plain and Succinct Narrative*, p. 33.
115 The life of William Mawhood provides ample evidence of middling Catholic life in the eighteenth century. E. E. Reynolds, ed., *The Mawhood Diary: Selections from*

the Diary Notebooks of William Mawhood, woolen draper of London, for the years 1764–1780 (London: Publications of the London Catholic Record Society, 1956).

116 *A Narrative of the proceedings of Lord George Gordon, and the persons assembled under the denomination of the Protestant Association, from their last meeting at coach makers hall, to the final commitment of his lordship to the tower* (London: J. Wallis, 1780), p. 3.
117 Holcroft, *A Plain and Succinct Narrative*, p. 14.
118 For more on ribbons and cockades see, Andrea McKenzie, ' "God's Hat" and the highwayman's Shoes: A Gestural and Sartorial History of Seventeenth- and Eighteenth-Century English Trial and Execution', *Canadian Journal of History* 47 (2012), pp. 231–257.
119 Holcroft, *A Plain and Succinct Narrative*, p. 26.
120 Holcroft, *A Plain and Succinct Narrative*, p. 37.
121 Holcroft, *A Plain and Succinct Narrative*, p. 37.
122 Holcroft, *A Plain and Succinct Narrative*, p. 38.
123 Holcroft, *A Plain and Succinct Narrative*, p. 43. Another pamphlet urged employers not to hire anyone wearing a blue cockade.
124 *The Political Magazine, and Parliamentary, Naval, Military, and Literary Journal*, 1 (1780), p. 438.
125 *Memorial to ... Roman Catholics of Edinburgh and Glasgow*, pp. 37–38.
126 *A Reply to an appeal from the Protestant Association to the People of Great Britain wherein the fallacious arguments of that pamphlet are sufficiently exposed and candidly refuted* (London: Dilly, 1780), p. vii.
127 *A Reply to an appeal*, p. viii.
128 *A Reply to an appeal*, pp. 16, 21, 19.
129 *A Reply to an appeal*, p. xi.
130 *A Reply to an appeal*, p. 2.
131 *A Reply to an appeal*, p. 4. For more on the tolerance shown by English merchants in various global sites in the fifteenth and sixteenth centuries, see Allison Games, *The Web of Empire English Cosmopolitans in an Age of Expansion, 1560–1660* (Oxford: Oxford University Press, 2008).
132 *A Reply to an appeal*, p. 19.
133 *A Reply to an appeal*, p. 20.
134 *St James Chronicle or the British Evening Post*, June 3, 1780.
135 *A Reply to an appeal*, p. 22.
136 *A Reply to an appeal*, p. 25.
137 Carretta, ed., *Letters*, p. 220.
138 Carretta, ed., *Letters*, p. 218.
139 Carretta, ed., *Letters*, pp. 219–220.
140 Carretta, ed., *Letters*, p. 217.
141 Carretta, ed., *Letters*, p. 219.
142 Carretta, ed., *Letters*, p. 219.
143 Roger Ingpen, ed., *The Life of Samuel Johnson*, 2 vols. (Boston: Charles E. Lauriat Co., 1907), vol. 2, p. 764.
144 Ingpen, *Life of Samuel Johnson*, vol. 2, p. 720.
145 William Cowper, *Poems by William Cowper of the Inner Temple* (London: J. Johnson, 1782), p. 16. The conservative response to the Riots is discussed in Susan Matthews, ' "Mad Misrule": the Gordon Riots and conservative memory', in *Gordon Riots*, ed. Haywood and Seed, pp. 226–242.
146 Hannah More, *The Works of Hannah More*, 8 vols. (London: A. Strahan, 1801), vol. 1: 98.
147 Susan Matthews, 'Mad Misrule', in *Gordon Riots*, ed. Haywood and Seed, p. 236.

CHAPTER FOUR

'This fleet is not yet republican': Conceptions of law in the mutinies of 1797

The *Memoirs of Richard Parker*, published shortly after his execution on June 30, 1797, for his participation in the work action at the Nore, portrayed Parker's as a good death. The pamphlet reported that the prisoner 'arose with cheerfulness', on the day of his execution, asked for a barber, and dressed in a mourning suit. He 'lamented the misfortune that had been brought on the country by the mutiny, but solemnly denied having any connection or correspondence with any disaffected persons ashore; and declared that it was chiefly owing to him that the ships had not been carried into the enemy's ports'. Although he looked 'a little paler than common', he 'soon recovered his usual complexion' and 'imploring forgiveness' he asked God for mercy.[1]

In front of many spectators on shore and those in 'a considerable number of yachts, cutters, and other crafts' a procession led Parker from the quarter deck to the forecastle where they heard the warrant for his execution read aloud. Parker 'heard [it] with great attention, and bowed his head, as if in assent, at the close of it'. The prisoner asked to speak, promising not to address the ship's company. 'I wish only to declare, that I acknowledge the justice of the sentence under which I suffer, and I hope my death will be deemed a sufficient atonement, and save the lives of others!' The pamphlet declared that he went to his death willingly.[2] Or did he?

In a letter to a friend on June 28, 1797, just two days before his execution, Parker wrote, 'The ignorant and violent will call me a criminal, but when it is remembered what were the demands which I made for [upon] my unprincipled employers, I know the discreet part of mankind will acquit me of criminality.' He continued: 'By the Laws of War I acknowledge myself to be legally convicted, but by the Laws of Humanity, which should be the basis of all laws, I die illegally.'[3]

In their letters and petitions describing events at the Spithead (April–May 1797) and the Nore (May–June 1797) the sailors drew on the language of Thomas Paine (1737–1809) and appealed to what Parker called the 'Laws of Humanity', but they also related their rights to Britishness and masculinity. Most insistently they asserted a distinction between sailors and African slaves implicitly claiming whiteness as a possession that bestowed legal privilege and access to freedom and liberty. The government responded to the work actions at the Spithead and the Nore by accommodating the former and by ignoring and then harshly punishing the latter. The Admiralty and Prime Minister William Pitt's government acknowledged the sailors' rights to demand the redress of their grievances and enlisted various dimensions of the law including new legislation, martial law, and courts martial to reinscribe hierarchies of status and re-establish order in the naval ranks. They read the crews' actions as a dangerous combination of insubordination and republican ideas.

'Rule Britannia' originating from the poem written by James Thomson glorified Britain, its sailors, and the navy's place in British culture and society. The famous chorus declared that Britannia would 'rule the waves' and that 'Britons never, ever, ever shall be slaves'. The song compared Great Britain's superiority to other 'nations, not so blest as thee' who 'to tyrants fall' while Britain 'shalt flourish great and free'. The song, published, in 1740, at the start of the War of Austrian Succession, tells of the 'dreadful' 'foreign stroke' and repeated 'attempts' by Britannia's foes 'to bend thee down'. Despite these challenges and setbacks Britannia prevails, inspired by 'The Muses still with Freedom found', and thanks to the protection of 'manly hearts to guard the fair'. At the forefront of Britain's defense was the Royal Navy. Indispensable to empire, the navy fought Britain's imperial wars, protecting hearth and home as well as far flung trade routes. Manning the ships were the sailors, often known as Jack Tar. 'Rule Britannia' clearly named the values and way of life that the mariners worked to defend – freedom from slavery and tyranny – they included themselves among those free men represented by British law.[4]

In stark contrast to the discourse of liberty and freedom that resounded in 'Rule Britannia' was the common practice of impressment that filled the Royal Navy's ships with forced recruits.[5] David Hume remarked in an essay originally published in 1742 that 'the sailors, who are alone affected by it, find no body to support them, in claiming the rights and privileges, which the law grants, without distinction, to all English subjects'.[6] The tension between the navy's mission to uphold law and freedom and the 'irregular power' of forced conscription 'a practice seemingly the most absurd and unaccountable' complicated the place of the British sailor and ideals of national virtue and rule of law.[7]

CONCEPTIONS OF LAW IN THE MUTINIES OF 1797

This chapter will examine the chain of events at Spithead and then at the Nore to see how each set of incidents shaped the other and how their relationship to each other defined the limits of change. Although similar, the two episodes resolved differently: the very successful resolution of the first led to escalating rhetorical exchanges and the ultimate failure of the second.[8] The attitude toward the two events was summarized by James William who wrote in 1837, 40 years after the mutinies:

> The complaints of the Portsmouth mutineers having been, for the most part, founded on justice, the sympathy of the nation went with them ... On the other hand, the mutineers at Sheerness and Yarmouth [the Nore] had no solid nor even plausible ground of complaint. They appear to have been actuated by a mere mischief-making spirit, with scarcely a knowledge of the object they had in view. The nation, therefore ... came at once to the resolution of making a firm stand against it.[9]

Contemporary sources convey the uncertainty and insecurity that surrounded these remarkable events, revealing conflicting conceptions of law and justice circulating in Britain at the end of the eighteenth century. The rule of law sat uncomfortably beside the jurisprudence of emergency; Edmund Burke's conservative ideology articulated in *Reflections on the Revolution in France* (1790) defined by the preservation of hierarchy, social order, and tradition contrasted with the universal rights described in Thomas Paine's *Rights of Man* (1791, 1792) and the insistence that sovereignty lay in the nation; traditional ideas about the negotiation between ordinary sailors and their officers stood against a broader set of human rights; slavery and impressment juxtaposed freedom and whiteness; English and British rivaled foreign, nation differentiated from empire.

An analysis of contemporary interpretations of these events illustrates the relationship between law, nation, and empire during the tumultuous global wars between Britain and France in the aftermath of the French Revolution. In their negotiations with the Admiralty the sailors at the Spithead and the Nore, a multinational and multiethnic workforce at the Empire's front lines, drew on the naval tradition of negotiation between sailors and their superiors to protest low wages and harsh working conditions. In so doing they harnessed a new language of liberty, reason, and justice to support their claims. The law formed the bedrock of many discussions of these events both for the sailors and the British government and each side resorted to law in order to explain and justify their actions.[10] This chapter seeks to understand the language of law and the context, symbols, and values embedded within it. More specifically I aim to show that by drawing events into the legal sphere through statute and criminal trial, the government reimposed hierarchies of class and power within the navy using the jurisprudence of emergency with the veneer of lawful process. The government argued that the passions stirred by republican ideology invited treason and insubordination that upended practices of discipline and deference. Although not traditionally discussed as part of the benevolent definition of rule of law, the kinds of legal acts implemented by the British government in the late eighteenth century need to be included in our accounts of law and empire because they reveal the co-constituted nature of rule of law and the jurisprudence of emergency that suspended it.

The mutinies at Spithead and the Nore took place in metropolitan spaces, domesticating a 'crime' that usually played out in faraway oceans. Instead of news of mutinous events reaching home weeks, months, or years after the fact, England's regional newspapers covered stories of the Spithead and the Nore closely and insistently, disturbing domestic spaces with discomfiting questions about law, liberty, and labor disputes in the armed forces during a time of war.[11] Often gendered, these discussions of disorder implied that the sailors' resistance imperiled British strength and masculinity. Given the special place held by the navy and its sailors in the British imagination, the public may have found these events especially disturbing because they forced onlookers to choose between several equally compelling ideals. Both Whigs and Tories agreed that the House of Commons must 'provide for the safety of the empire'.[12] That very clear directive proved 'the necessity of Laws and Government – of Magistrates and Governors, and those various though partial and incomplete curbs by which human wisdom has endeavored to confine and control the impetuosity of inflamed and corrupt appetites'.[13] While the French Revolution had first garnered British sympathy for the cause of rights and liberties that the English believed they already enjoyed, the sailors at the Spithead and the Nore called attention to the limits of those rights. In the context of war and an imperial rivalry between Britain and France they were determined to win, Pitt's government resorted to the jurisprudence of emergency to ensure the quickest and most complete suppression of these acts of resistance.

Questions of race and ethnicity permeated these discussions in important and underappreciated ways. Although far less diverse than merchant ships, Nicholas Frykman characterized 'naval crews ... among the most cosmopolitan and multinational assemblies of workers to be found anywhere in the Atlantic World'.[14] The 4000 crewmen involved at the Spithead and the Nore included 58.3 percent English, 16.3 percent Irish, 13.9 percent Scottish, 2.8 percent Welsh, and 1.8 percent from other parts of the British Empire. Of the remaining men 4 percent came from the rest of the world and the origins of 2.9 percent are unknown.[15]

The mostly British origins of those involved may have emboldened the men to act in the name of English liberty. In any case the actions at Spithead and the Nore, located in the English seaways, focused attention on the complicated and intimate relationship between nation and empire, a relationship that discomfited many in England and one they preferred would operate in distinct, segregated, and distant realms. Again legal ideas and institutions were central to efforts to define those distinctions and attempts to segment, detach, and separate nation from empire. Ironically, the law, an institution claimed as the very essence of Englishness, worked in precisely opposite ways suturing together networks of information, surveillance, and governance in disparate colonial realms.

What should we make of these events? Were they mutinies? As Ann Coats notes in her overview of the events at Spithead in 1797, calling it a mutiny 'is to view the event through the eyes of the authorities'.[16] However, contemporaries, including authorities, disagreed on this question. A letter from one V. V. to Lord Chancellor Thurlow (1731–1806) dated June 8, 1797 admitted that 'Mutiny it cannot be called; for there was neither mutiny nor riot', but the author pronounced that 'never was there so serious an example of the uncertainty of human affairs as this conduct of the Navy'.[17] Many strained to define these events citing the sailors' 'grievances' as meriting some response and redress from the Admiralty. This ambivalence may have turned on the strict discipline that the sailors maintained in their ranks during the tense standoff. Rather than anarchy, bloodshed, or violence, the Spithead and the Nore saw the transfer of authority from naval officers to delegates elected by the sailors. In many ways that phenomenon may have been more frightening than open revolt and rebellion. The sailors organized themselves, creating a counter-authority to that of the naval hierarchy. Historical circumstance, specifically events surrounding the French Revolution, produced fears of radical reform agendas that many believed threatened Britain's security, its commercial networks, and the future of its Empire.[18] The sailors' discipline and order seemed menacingly efficient, effective, and potentially successful.

The acts of resistance coordinated and initiated by the crews of two of Britain's fleets in English waters during a time of war have captured the imagination of historians and other writers since they took place. E. P. Thompson called these events 'the greatest revolutionary portents for England ... There is no doubt that appalling conditions of food, pay and discipline precipitated the mutinies, but there is also some evidence of direct Jacobin instigation.'[19] Thompson argued that the blockade of the Thames for a week in June 1797 paralyzed 'the British fleet – the most important instrument of European expansion, and the only shield between revolutionary France and her greatest rival'.[20] While some historians have disputed the 'world wide significance' of the mutinies and the extent of Jacobin ideas among the sailors, other scholars have demonstrated that reports of events at the Spithead and the Nore traveled very quickly throughout the British fleet and that they inspired similar work actions as far away as southern Africa.[21]

Interpretations of what happened at Spithead and the Nore fall into two broad categories. One school of historians, led by G. E. Manwaring and Bonamy Dobree, argues that Republican ideas and spreading radicalism motivated events on board.[22] Historians of the navy like N. A. M. Rodger maintain instead that the sailors agitated for the redress of a narrow set of grievances based on a long maritime tradition of consultation and collective decision making with superior officers.[23]

Contemporary context and reactions blamed these events on the influence of 'outsiders'. They included Quota Men, landsmen impressed by the Quota Acts – three Acts passed in 1795 and 1796 that mandated that local authorities deliver a certain number of recruits to the navy and in some cases to the army.[24] These explanations attributed events at the Spithead and the Nore to the landsmen's education, republican ideas, and active membership in the London Corresponding Societies or the Society for Constitutional Information. Others implicated Irish sailors politicized by the Society of United Irishmen and the cause of Irish nationalism and French revolutionaries spreading the ideology of liberty, equality, and fraternity.[25] Since the publication of these early works, some historians have found evidence to source the mutinies in a proletarian ethos, others cite a mariners' code while still others have concluded that republican ideas drove all of the mutinies.[26]

Given the uncertainties surrounding the events and the dangerous implications of the organized grievances presented as lawful by the sailors to the Admiralty, the government responded by defining these events as treasonous. They classified the petitioning as a mutiny associated with and inspired by Jacobin ideas circulated in the French Revolution, by its very essence a crime they attributed to republican ideas, sedition, riot, and France. Defining these events as crimes allowed the authorities to employ legal mechanisms to contain the damage to naval discipline, the war effort, and the social order. Criminalizing these events as mutiny muted the sailors' economic demands and limited the use of similar tactics by others within the army and the navy.

Most of the studies cited above have searched for the motives of the mutinies using many of the same terms and categories as contemporary MPs and other eighteenth-century commentators. Rather than rehearse these arguments again to trace the infiltration of revolutionary ideas in and among English sailors, I want to read the rich sources generated by the 'mutinies' for different understandings of law among the sailors, government authorities, and other contemporary observers. While the government balanced an urgent desire to palliate the sailors, control the specter of republicanism, and reimpose order in a sailing force on which they desperately depended in a time of war, my analysis shows a growing alarm among the sailors about impressment and harsh conditions on board navy ships. The sailors claimed that their treatment bore resemblance to the raced and chattel slavery of the Atlantic slave trade. The sailors' comparison of their plight with that of enslaved Africans was not new in the late eighteenth century, but it took on a particularly shrill tone in the context of the rising discourse of abolition that brought more attention to slavery and the slave trade at the end of the eighteenth century. The sailors' rhetoric referenced English liberty and freedom in an attempt to draw a very firm boundary between the sailor's life and that of a slave. In exchange for loyalty and service, they insisted they could not be treated like black slaves and claimed whiteness as a privileged legal category that entitled them to the rights of man.

Events at Spithead: April–May, 1797

The events at Spithead and the Nore are well known. Although one author called them 'shockingly understudied', their general outline and details have been chronicled since the first retelling in the early nineteenth century.[27] Located between the entrance to Portsmouth harbor and the Isle of Wight, Spithead stood at the eastern most part of the Solent, the strait of the English Channel that separates the Isle of Wight from England, and provided a safe and spacious anchorage. Sheltered from the enemy and from westerly winds, crews could perform repairs on the ships and restock both men and provisions. Portsmouth's proximity to Spithead and to the Royal Naval Dockyard made it the main military embankment for the Channel Fleet during the French Wars of the eighteenth century. Eighty ships crewed by 30,000 men were at Spithead in April and May 1797.[28]

In February and March 1797 members of the Channel Fleet at Spithead sent eleven anonymous petitions to Admiral Richard Howe (1726–1799) asking for a pay raise. When the ships returned from blockading French ports on March 30, the sailors still had no response from Howe. Two weeks later, on April 14, the ships notified the Admiralty that they refused to fulfill their duties 'till their wages is increased'.[29] On April 16 the ships refused their orders to go to sea. The Spithead sailors elected two delegates from each of the 16 ships as their governing body and charged them with composing regulations for the sailors' behavior and comportment. Representatives from the Board of Admiralty arrived in Spithead on April 18, led by Earl George Spencer (1758–1834), the First Lord of the Admiralty. By April 20 the Admiralty had agreed to most of the mariners' conditions and demands including a pay raise, provisions for care of the sick and wounded, shore leave, and prize money. Before they resumed their navigational duties, however, the sailors insisted on a royal pardon. Spencer left for London where he met with Pitt and the Privy Council to arrange the pardon, which was read to the men on April 23 while Parliament passed an Act (37 Geo. III c. 53) on May 9 securing the pay raise the sailors had demanded. Howe visited the ships on May 14–15 and presided over a celebration in Portsmouth. The ships of the Channel Fleet sailed on May 17, on the whole a peaceful, organized, and relatively smooth resolution to the situation.[30]

Dichotomous views: rights, justice, and law

Responses to the actions initiated by sailors at Spithead in the spring of 1797 highlight many of the themes of eighteenth-century politics and life. The context, symbols, and values deployed in the discourse surrounding these events reveal several crucial sites of contestation that had real implications for the discussion of law, justice, and difference we have traced throughout this book. The polarities of opinion that emerged in these debates did not have a resolution, nor did they originate in a well-established cannon. The oppositions themselves defined new orthodoxies in the shifting political and cultural landscape of the 1790s.

Edmund Burke and Tom Paine: law and revolution

The debate between Edmund Burke (1729–1797) and Thomas Paine over the meaning of the French Revolution for Britons centered on questions of rights, representation, nation, law, and empire echoed through the reactions to events at Spithead. Never limited to politicians and intellectuals, the debate between these two men and their ideas about government, its power and authority, permeated English culture and society in the 1790s providing each side in our story a deep well of rhetoric on which to draw. Paine's *Rights of Man* responded directly to Burke's *Reflections on the Revolution in France* and referenced Burke throughout. Other authors quickly penned their own responses and within a year of each pamphlet's publication almost a hundred printed pamphlets had appeared. By 1793, an anthology featured extracts from each work as well as the opinions of leading writers and commentators. The London Corresponding Society (1792–1799) and the Society for Constitutional Information (founded in 1780), organizations dedicated to democratic ideals, the promotion of parliamentary reform, and the distribution of information about politics, collaborated in their efforts to make Paine's work available cheaply.[31] Sales of these published works were brisk and the pricing meant the works circulated to a broad readership. The number of Paine's pamphlets in circulation by 1793 reached one-quarter of a million, and one-half a million by the end of the decade. Satirical prints depicting either Burke or Paine or reception of their work captured the dynamics of the debate and the broad participation it provoked.[32]

Richard Price provided Burke's initial impetus for the *Reflections*, as Burke wrote to refute Price's contention that 'by the principles of the [French] Revolution the people of England have acquired three fundamental rights ... 1. To choose our own governors, 2. To cashier them for misconduct, 3. To frame a government for ourselves.'[33] This is exactly what the mariners were doing. In contrast Burke insisted that the preservation of 'Good order is the foundation of all good things. To be enabled to acquire, the people, without being servile, must be tractable and obedient. The magistrate must have his reverence, the laws their authority. The body of the people must not find the principles of natural subordination by art rooted out of the minds.'[34] Burke reiterated the virtue and necessity of subordination throughout the *Reflections*. Property ownership bestowed power and authority while the growing discourse of equality and inalienable rights threatened every aspect of life especially the military where 'the principle of obedience ... [is] the great essential critical link between the officer and the soldier, just where the chain of military subordination commences, and on which the whole of that system depends'.[35] Burke cautioned that the new doctrine of universal rights would confuse soldiers, disturbing indisputable hierarchies.

> The soldier is told, he is a citizen, and has the rights of man and citizen. The right of a man, he is told, is to be his own governor, and to be ruled only by those to whom he delegates that self-government. It is very natural he should think, that he ought most of all to have his choice where he is to yield the greatest degree of obedience.[36]

Repudiating the need for parliamentary reform, Burke warned that 'when antient opinions and rules of life are taken away, the loss cannot possibly be estimated. From that moment we have no compass to govern us; nor can we know distinctly to what port we steer.'[37] For Burke, law upheld hierarchy, inheritance, and an aristocratic order secured in 'the Revolution of 1688, made to preserve our antient indisputable laws and liberties, and that antient constitution of government which is our only security for law and liberty'.[38] In the face of the unregulated brutality exercised on men in the military, Burke's reference to law and liberty ensured by the constitution may have raised questions in the minds of many soldiers and sailors.

Throughout the *Reflections* and until his death Burke expressed deep concerns about the infiltration of Britain by destructive French republican ideas. Although Burke acknowledged that 'France has always more or less influenced manners in England',[39] he advised his readers that:

> we ought not, on the other side of the water, to suffer ourselves to be imposed upon by the counterfeit wares which some persons, by a double fraud, export to you in illicit bottoms, as raw commodities of British growth though wholly alien to our soil, in order afterwards to smuggle them back again into this country, manufactured after the newest Paris fashion of an improved liberty.[40]

Burke's preoccupation with cross cultural influence and its negative effects was not an idle one given the circulation of ideas, people, and texts between and among empires and peoples in the late eighteenth century. With his references to conspiracy in his parliamentary speeches discussed below, Pitt seems to have shared this Burkean perspective.

Thomas Paine clearly embodied this susceptibility to 'foreign' influence and as the author of *The Rights of Man* acted as its agent. In response to Burke's axiom that Parliament in 1688 changed things forever making further political reforms unnecessary, Paine pronounced that 'every age and generation must be as free to act for itself, in all cases, as the ages and generations which preceded it'.[41] The capacity to participate in this process derived from 'the illuminating and divine principle of the equal rights of man (for it has its origin from the Maker of man)' and 'the unity of man; by which I mean, that men are all of one degree, and consequently that all men are born equal, and with equal natural right'.[42] These equal rights bestowed responsibilities and 'place[d] him in a close connection with all his duties'.[43] Paine's pronouncements about universal male rights and responsibilities concerned political engagement with 'Sovereignty, as a matter of right', which he clarified 'appertains to the Nation only, and not to any individual; and a Nation has at all times an inherent indefeasible right to abolish any form of Government it finds inconvenient, and establish such as accords with its interest, disposition, and happiness'. Within the nation 'Every citizen is a member of the sovereignty, and, as such, can acknowledge no personal subjection; and his obedience can be only to the laws.'[44] The law provided the connection between the individual and his political participation because when confronted with bad laws, 'it is a duty which every man owes to society to point them out. When those defects, and the means of remedying them are generally seen by a nation, that nation will reform its government or its constitution in the one case, as the government repealed or reformed the law in the other.'[45] These prescriptions for men as the agents of change stand in stark opposition to Burke's instructions about continuity, stability, and hierarchy.

A right to petition or human rights?

In his comparison of the army and navy Blackstone described the maritime state as 'much more agreeable to the principles of our free constitution'.[46] Unlike the disparagement of a standing army and its association with a despotic and absolutist state, 'The royal navy of England hath ever been its greatest defence and ornament: it is its antient and natural strength; the floating bulwark of the island; an army, from which, however strong and powerful, no danger can ever be apprehended to liberty.'[47] Blackstone credited the Navigation Acts, particularly the Act passed in 1651 with its stipulation that 'the master and three fourths of the mariners shall also be English subjects' for the growth of the navy and the cultivation of mariners' skills among Englishmen.[48] Blackstone praised the 'rules, articles and orders' that bound the navy and its sailors because 'every possible offence is set down, and the punishment thereof annexed: in which respect the seamen have much the advantage over their brethren in the land service; whose articles of war are not enacted by parliament, but framed from time to time at the pleasure of the crown'.[49]

Sailors, the government, and the Admiralty acknowledged a tradition of negotiation and concession common in the navy. Sailors communicated their complaints and requests by petitioning their superiors to open a dialogue between the two sides. The sailors exchanged their service, sacrifice, and loyalty for the limited right to grieve and petition.[50] While the sailors and the Admiralty agreed on the place of negotiation and concession throughout most of the eighteenth century, the French Revolution and particularly the writings of Thomas Paine changed the balance of the equation for some sailors. According to Horace Walpole in a letter to Mary Berry dated July 21, 1791 'vast numbers of Paine's pamphlet [*The Rights of Man*, Part I] were distributed both to regiments and ships', although he also admitted that they 'were given up voluntarily to the officers' when requested.[51] The naval tradition of cooperation and limited consultation and the political context in which these events unfolded combined to prompt the sailors to resist their working conditions and insist on changes in working regimes and pay informed by Paine's conception of the *Rights of Man*.[52] The sailors used the language of law and justice to articulate their demands, and they often couched their grievances in the context of the navy's mission to uphold British law and freedom throughout the Empire. The response of the government and even the Admiralty was framed in Burkean terms, arguing for the need to uphold the traditional social order, hierarchy, and deference in the face of a serious threat to the English way of life, its law, and constitution.

Superior officers sometimes appealed to the Admiralty on behalf of their sailors. On September 25, 1629, Sir Henry Mervin (1583–1646) wrote to the Lords Commissioners of the Admiralty imploring them to provide for sailors suffering 'foul winter weather, naked backs, and empty bellies' who 'voice the King's service worse than a galley slavery'. Mervin warned the admiralty that 'necessitous wants together with famine pleading the cause of their disorders, lays open a way to what they are too prone already to – mutinous disobedience and contempt of all commands, for necessity hath no law'.[53] Another letter to the Admiralty written in July 1653 spoke of the complaints among the sailors regarding withheld wages and the 'wives and children ... who suffer much hardship', impressment, and bad provisions at sea.[54] These passages reveal the difficult conditions on board naval ships and the implicit and explicit relationship between supplies, obedience, and order.

Historians trace the tradition of petitioning as a form of communication between the sailors who staffed the navy and the British government to *The humble Petition of the Sea-men, belonging to the Ships of the Commonwealth of England* written to Oliver Cromwell in 1654.[55] In this modest petition the sailors framed their requests using a simple rhetorical equation: they presented their dedication and loyalty in terms of tremendously hard work and sacrifice, and in exchange they asked the government to abandon impressment and to adopt a system of regular payment. To support their requests, they cited English 'Principles of Freedom and Liberty'. The sailors 'suffered great hardship ... having sacrificed themselves' 'limbs mangled', 'blood spilt', enduring 'great diseases and distempers' along with 'bad Victual'. Citing Parliament's promise 'to maintain and enlarge the Liberties of the free people of England where infringed', they called attention to the 'very great burthens' of 'being impressed'. They described being 'haled on board the Commonwealth's Ships, turned over and confined there, under a degree of thralldom and bondage', unpaid for months and sometimes years, 'to the utter ruin' of their families and themselves, their suffering exacerbated by the uncertainty of foreign service in the Dutch wars. In their short list of demands the sailors mentioned the 'Liberties and Priviledges due' to them as 'freemen of England'. They used the word free and freedom four times in the short paragraph and demanded that the terms of employment 'shall be agreeable with justice'. The petition ended with the sailors' promise to 'faithfully serve and pray' reiterating the bargain of hard work and sacrifice in exchange for a recognition of certain privileges and rights.[56]

In response a Council of War held on HMS *Swifsure* in October 1654 considered the petition and found that 'the points complained of were real grievances, and that the Vice-Admiral should send the petition and these resolutions to the Protector'. More significantly for this discussion of the lawfulness and acceptability of such communication between sailors and their superior officers, the Council 'resolved unanimously that it was lawful for the seamen to present their grievances by way of petition'.[57]

According to N. A. M. Rodger the navy had no defined or official means by which sailors could lodge complaints during the middle decades of the eighteenth century. As a result, sailors used a variety of methods to communicate with their superiors about their dissatisfaction with provisioning, living conditions on board, or ill treatment at the hands of their commanding officers. One way sailors objected to their circumstances was by speaking directly to their captain or admiral: the captains would forward these grievances to their senior officers or to the Admiralty. Sailors often used petitioning to relay their criticism. Evidence of petition writers who sought clients by hanging around the gates of the Admiralty speaks to the frequency of this form of negotiation. Usually sailors shared their petitions with their captain before sending it up. Once received by a senior officer, two or three junior flag officers or senior captains would be assigned to investigate the grievance. The practice of complaint and investigation documented by Rodger comprised the custom of negotiation between sailors and their superiors. It was predicated on the sailors' expectation of a hearing – even if it did not result in a satisfactory resolution to the problem they identified.[58] Beyond this internal process sailors had advocates working for them on shore who publicized their living and working conditions and spoke out for redress. *The Sailors Advocate* written by James Oglethorpe in 1728 is one example of external pressure brought to bear on the sailors' behalf.[59]

As events unfolded at Spithead, each side tried to shape the representation of their actions in the public eye. The sailors remained adamant that their comportment fell within acceptable and traditional parameters of negotiation, adhering strictly to the exchange of service and loyalty for a hearing from their superiors. Letters appeared in *The Times* written by delegates to Lord Bridport wishing 'to convince your Lordships and the Nation in general of our moderation'. In a letter dated April 19 and published on April 24 the sailors addressed their motives directly protesting that 'we are not actuated by a spirit of contradiction, but that we earnestly wish to put a speedy end to the present affair'. They argued for their 'disinterestedness and moderation', offering as proof their support of a pay raise for the Marines on board. In addition they promised to contribute to the pensions from Greenwich College and suggested including among the beneficiaries those who served the East India Company.[60]

The proximity of these events to the metropole resulted in a fast pace of communication. The production and circulation of print culture shaped perceptions of the sailors' work action sparking discussion and debate which often found its way into the next edition of the paper allowing each side to rehearse different points of view and interpretations of events while enlisting public opinion. We see in the recounting of the 'mutinies' that the very process of publication and discussion contributed to their rapid transformation making, reflecting, and remaking popular opinion. On April 20 the sailors responded with lament to an article in which 'we are accused of those crimes which disgrace the name of a British Seaman, and which may prejudice the minds of our country men against us'.[61] This prompted a retelling of events at Spithead including the petitions presented to Howe, the lack of a response from him or the Admiralty, followed by an adamant denial of 'anywise the least spark of republican spirit'.[62] They insisted on their patriotic loyalty, claiming 'we have our country's good as much at heart as any other description of men whatever, and that our request is nowise injurious to our country'.[63]

As Paine reminded his readers several times in *Rights of Man*, the pay of the army, navy, and revenue officers had remained the same since the reign of Charles II (d.1685). Paine advocated more equitable taxation and economic justice with the sailors and soldiers in mind, imploring his readers that 'the persons who have devoted themselves to these services, and have thereby unfittd themselves for other lines of life, are not to be sufferers by the means that make others happy'.[64] In a similar register the sailors, declaring the simplicity and purity of their motives and requests, 'ask[ed] for that comfortable subsistence which our country can easily bestow, and that the barbarities which are practiced by some ... be erased out of this well instituted service'.[65] They urged their audience 'to come forward in a fair and manly way, in your real and corporeal state' to try to live on 'the scanty allowance' provided 'to keep you in the spirited state which men of our description require'. They deplored the conditions of their 'wives and families languishing in want while this country, that abounds with plenty, ought to be ashamed at the word want!'[66] In a postscript the sailors referred to 'the clamours of justice' from 'Loyal Tars' who 'have made Britannia Rule the Main [and] know also their duty to their Sovereign'.[67] This last sentence asserted the mutineers' discipline and hard work arguing that they deserved to have their demands met. Given that even most officers did not always abide by all of the navy's strict rules, this postscript explicitly linked masculinity, military prowess, loyalty, and patriotism laying claim to those superior virtues for the hard working sailors.[68]

In a letter to Admiral Lord Bridport, dated April 18, the officers who met with the sailors at Spithead determined that 'the only chance of bringing back the fleet to subordination and the seamen to their duty, was by complying with the demands made in their petitions'. With an almost solicitous tone, they explained that they reached this conclusion 'having taken into our consideration the petitions transmitted by your Lordship from the crews of several of H.M. Ships under your command, and having the strongest desire to attend to all the complaints of the seamen in H.M. Navy, and to grant them very just and reasonable redress'.[69] Despite internal debates among those on the Admiralty Board about whether to meet all of the demands and how to re-establish order, the Admiralty, like their sailors, sought to frame the dispute at Spithead within the trope of the customary negotiation between the sailors and their superiors in order to re-establish hierarchy, order, and control.

The conversation in the Admiralty about how to respond to the sailors' demands echoed in the halls of Parliament. In debates held between May 8 and May 10, 1797 concerning legislation to increase the pay of naval personnel (passed as 37 Geo. III c. 53) as demanded by the mariners at Spithead, Charles Fox (1749–1806) and Richard Brinsley Sheridan (1751–1816) led the opposition Whigs in condemning Pitt and his administration for the delays and secrecy surrounding events at Spithead and the government's negotiations. In his case for Pitt's censure on May 8, Sheridan claimed that 'what was now proposed to be granted to them [the sailors] was nothing more than justice', although he expressed his 'disapprobation for the mode in which these demands were insisted upon'. He averred that 'however just their complaints were, they ought to complain in a regular way'.[70] Here Sheridan recognized the traditional mariners' code regarding rights but stopped short of acknowledging the universal rights of man.

On May 10, in a rejoinder to Pitt's defense of his government's tactics, Fox minimized the presence of 'Jacobins' among the sailors and denied the need for an aggressive response asserting that 'there are not in this country a sufficient number of such persons to make us waver in our determination to adhere to our Constitution'. Fox blamed the sailors' continued refusal to go back to work on the government's slow response to events at Spithead.[71] In addition to accusing the ministry of mismanagement, he signaled his disapproval of the legislation passed earlier in the decade that had suspended habeas corpus and limited the right of assembly.[72] Warning of the larger implications of the government's response he asked whether 'the popular part of the Constitution had been sacrificed to the influence of the executive?'.[73] Fox and Sheridan employed a heightened rhetoric to condemn the ministry and Pitt's government. They emphasized the themes of justice, rule of law, and Parliament's protections of the constitution and pushed back against the majority's contention that justified according the government unbridled authority in times of war.

Henry Dundas (1742–1811), the king's close advisor and at the time the secretary of state for war, responded to the rumored republican contamination of the British navy by asserting 'that he had experienced great satisfaction from one circumstance connected with the last disturbances at Portsmouth. That satisfaction arose from a conviction that the seamen were not infected with Jacobinism'. When he 'declared that they would not suffer the Crown of England to be imposed upon, nor the glory of the British fleet to be tarnished', he pronounced that the sailors viewed their rights in a traditional manner and that they had no further aspirations beyond an exchange of service and loyalty for the right to express their grievances. He told his fellow MPs that he firmly believed 'if any attempt had been made to detach them from those principles of loyalty and affection to their Sovereign, which had always distinguished British seamen, they would not have yielded to any such attempt'. To explain the delay in resolving the issues at Spithead, Dundas accused 'some persons ... for whom he could not find a name, whether Jacobin or any other, sufficiently descriptive of their wickedness [who] soon sought to mislead them'.[74] In his rejoinder to Fox and Sheridan Dundas defended the government and its response to the mutiny. He hoped to redeem the reputation of British mariners, their loyalty, and their service in order to restore confidence in the sailors, the navy, and the government.[75]

Replying to 'unjust aspersions thrown on our characters as British Seamen', *The Address to the Nation, by the Seamen at St. Helen's,* dated May 13, 1797, spoke from 'the loyal and humane tars' to their 'dear' and 'grateful countrymen', so they 'might not be deceived, or ourselves prejudiced by false reports'.[76] The pamphlet set out the sailors' grievances on HMS *London* at Spithead asserting their traditional rights to negotiate better terms for themselves and listing 'just and moderate requests – Grievances which were promised to be redressed' including a modest raise in wages, the elimination of 'the purser's eighths' from food rations, spirits, and beer, and a pardon 'to exempt our Brethren from having any punishment inflicted on them for trivial misdemeanor, and our non-compliance to the order given for going to Sea'.[77] The

Address defended the sailors' decision to leave Spithead for St Helen's rather than accepting the pardon and discharging their duties as they awaited passage of the Act of Parliament (37 Geo. III c. 53), discussed above, that would raise their wages.

In particular the pamphlet sought to reframe a violent incident on HMS *London* that defied the sailors' claims of peaceful and reasonable discussion within a customary maritime tradition of negotiation. The pamphlet mentioned 'private murmurings' on board that exacerbated the 'state of suspence' engulfing the fleet. This tension 'burst forth' on May 7 when some of the crew heard rumors of schemes for a continuation of the mutiny they believed would 'sacrifice some of the brightest gems that ever adorned this or any other country'.[78] The ship's captain, John Colpoys (c.1742–1821) tried to keep order by confining all the men below deck in a vain attempt to seal up the ship. When the crew resisted, Colpoys ordered the ship's officers to open fire, killing three sailors, wounding one marine, and seriously wounding two officers. Colpoys called for a ceasefire, and the crew took charge of the ship restricting Colpoys and two other officers to their cabins. The ship sailed to St Helen's anchorage (Isle of Wright) to join the other mutinous ships.

The pamphlet cast the sailors' actions as a performance of republican democracy. Each ship's company voted on the fate of the captain. The secret ballot returned twelve votes 'in his favour, at least that he should be left to his own ship's company's mode of punishment' and five 'for immediate execution'.[79] With that Colpoys and 'his officers were delivered up to the Portsmouth Magistrate'. The sailors expressed indignant surprise that in the aftermath of this violent altercation followed by their performance of democracy: 'no sooner was that pardon granted, but, in direct contradiction to that his Royal Proclamation, were individuals selected for the express purpose of sacrificing them to malice and private resentment'.[80]

The pamphlet re-told the story and represented the sailors' determined effort to appear transparent, democratic, orderly, and fair. Their process of decision making modeled the kind of treatment they wished to receive from those in positions of authority over them and rested at its core on mutual respect. The mutineers expressed a desire to be taken seriously as moral and upstanding men with legitimate complaints and unquestioned loyalty to Britain. They claimed that their behavior fell within customary means of communication with their superiors and traditional rights of arbitration.[81] While they acknowledged that the crew in question 'were more headstrong than those of other ships', they explicitly disavowed 'treachery or republican principles'.[82] Echoing Paine's formulation that 'The duty of man ... It is plain and simple ...

with respect to his neighbor, to do as he would be done by', their very words articulated a new understanding and expression of their rights.[83] The sailors demanded respect and expressed their desire to be treated as equals. While they distanced themselves from explicitly republican ideas and an association with France asserting that events at Spithead fell squarely within a traditional, allowable, and legal means of communicating between ordinary sailors and their superior officers, their strategies, language, and perspective revealed the influence of contemporary politics that offered a more expansive, egalitarian definition of the rights of men.

The *Address* related promises made and broken, lives lost 'for the mere sport of tyrants'. This reference evoked descriptions of English sovereigns like Charles I and James II or French absolutism before the revolution and even English conservative descriptions of French Revolutionary radicals. Most immediately, the tyrant could be William Pitt who presided over his government's 'reign of terror', which included the suspension of habeas corpus in 1794.[84] In contrast to these vague and threatening alternatives, the author(s) pivoted back to nationalist and British imperial ideology, specifically the rule of law as the model for all forms of governance, asserting that the lives of 'poor, but loyal individuals' may not be 'sacrificed', 'according to the laws of civilized nations'. Protesting the injustice of retributive action in light of the 'meritorious service tendered to their amiable sovereign and benevolent nation', the author(s) sought 'protection' but found none 'since all laws, human and divine, are trampled under foot'.[85] The sailors words again recall Paine's admonition that 'All the European governments are constructed not on the principle of universal civilization, but on the reverse of it ... they are in the same condition as we conceive of savage, uncivilized life; they put themselves beyond the law as well of God as man.'[86]

Coverage of the incident on HMS *London*, so widely discussed in the media, undermined the mutineers' credibility. An extract from a 'private letter' that appeared in *The Times* on May 12 insisted that 'the conduct of the Delegates, while they were on board, proved that they had no *real grievances*'. Instead the author argued that 'they were men instigated solely by turbulence and passion, which appeared to be got to such a height, as to be attended with danger even to attempt to reason on the business, much more to come forward with manly firmness to oppose them'. Commenting on what the sailors said about Captain Colpoys as well as their future plans, the anonymous writer described their language as 'really indecent, and the effect of madness or some diabolical intention'. Describing St Helen's 'where all is anarchy and confusion' and referencing 'the madness of the Delegates of the Fleet', this inflammatory language constructed a disorderly crime scene in which no space remained for those who wished to abide by the law.[87] The letter associated the sailors' insubordination with a lack of reason and insufficient emotional control calling into question their masculinity.

Despite this setback, events at Spithead generally met with public sympathy. 'The Floating Republic', a song written at the time, reiterated the understanding between the sailors and their superiors that 'he who danger braves Should scud in freedom o'er the waves, That sailors should no more be slaves'. The lyrics recounted the story of the sailors' refusal to work, their negotiations with Whitehall, and Spencer's mediating role. The song's title referred to the representative and orderly organization of the sailors' resistance and conceded that 'the captains then, all struck with fear, quaked such a loud complaint to hear, for well they knew the facts were clear'. In describing the resolution of the crisis, the song echoed the themes and some of the exact words of 'Rule Britannia' proclaiming that 'Now Jack, no more a tyrant's slave ... teaches Britons that the brave, May if they will, be free.'[88]

Events at the Nore, May–June, 1797

The Nore action began on May 12 when the sailors, in support of Spithead, vented three cheers and raised a red flag. Their elected delegates then immediately met to strategize on what they called the Parliament ship, HMS *Sandwich*. They elected Richard Parker (1767–1797) as their president.

Much smaller than the Spithead action, the Nore Mutiny involved only three capital ships and 3500 sailors. The Nore, an anchorage in the Thames Estuary closest to the town of Sheerness in Kent, served as a reserve squadron and a second line of seaborne defense for London and southeast England as well as a source of reinforcements of the North Sea Fleet of Admiral Adam Duncan (1731–1804). In the earliest days, those involved in the Nore saw themselves primarily as advocates of the Spithead. But events at the Nore soon took a different turn.

Hearing of the resolutions reached at Spithead, the delegates abandoned their supportive role and instead set a more ambitious agenda defined by a list of eight grievances handed to Vice Admiral Charles Buckner (1735–1811) by Parker on May 20. The list demanded that the Nore receive 'every indulgence granted to the fleet at Portsmouth', that 'upon coming into harbor', every man 'shall have liberty ... to go and see their friends and family', that 'all arrears of wages' be paid, and that no officer 'turned out of any of his Majesty's ships shall be employed in the same ship again, without the consent of the ship's company'.[89]

Buckner referred the grievances to the Board of Admiralty in London, but the Admiralty lords refused to fulfill any of the grievances and rejected the mutineers' request for a meeting at Sheerness. When the Board did agree to a brief meeting with the sailors' delegates on May 22, its members affirmed their stance against any concessions. They then disallowed food supplies to ships in active mutiny, and increased military presence in the area including strengthening the fort at Sheerness and patrolling the coast line.[90]

In contrast to the negotiations with the representatives at Spithead, the Admiralty responded to the actions at the Nore more aggressively. They deployed martial law to try to lock down the sailors on board ship and intimidate them. Soldiers lined the shores of the estuaries where the ships anchored to bar the sailors from leaving the ships and to prevent anyone on shore from aiding or communicating with those on board. The military granted only limited access to Sheerness and increased surveillance and security.[91] Tensions ran high and reports circulated of violence on all sides. The lack of communication between the ships and residents living on shore nearby and the government's refusal to negotiate with the delegates caused two ships to cut their cables and rejoin naval forces on May 31. This loss seemed to herald the end of the action, but everything changed just a few hours later on June 1 when Admiral Duncan's ships arrived from Yarmouth to join the Nore mutiny. The added infusion of men and supplies re-energized the sailors' efforts. With the Yarmouth ships the crews moved to blockade the Thames, posing a serious threat to London and its commerce.

The Admiralty and Pitt's government refused to negotiate with the sailors or to accede to their demands. Seeking to isolate the mutineers further they removed navigational buoys from the Thames estuary to prevent the ships from escaping to other ports, foreign or local. Despite a high degree of loyalty among the sailors and more or less uniform discipline, disagreements began to break their determination, and the work action disintegrated. By the end of the day on June 1 all of the vessels had surrendered. Swift and harsh retribution followed: 400 sailors were detained (although most were released). Fifty-two men were condemned to death, of whom twenty-nine were hanged. Another twenty-nine were imprisoned and nine flogged. As recounted above, Richard Parker, as their leader, was court martialed between June 22 and June 26 and hanged from the yardarm of HMS *Sandwich* on June 30.[92]

The sailors' demands at the Nore did not fit easily into the customary exchange of hard work and sacrifice for the expression of grievances that had led to a resolution at Spithead. The call and response escalated the rhetoric, intensifying the positions taken on both sides. The sailors' more expansive and insistent demands met the government's harsh retort defining the limits of possible change.[93]

The rule of law and the jurisprudence of emergency

In 'A New Song Called True Blue' the sailors declared that 'No faction seperates our love, From British and her laws; For with our lives we strive to prove; The justice of our cause'.[94] The song enunciates justice and law as the core values for which the sailors believed they fought. David Garrick's 'Hearts of Oak' (written in 1776) pronounced 'Jolly Tars' 'freemen not slaves, For who are as free as the sons of the waves?'[95] A later version, adopted as the official song of the Royal Navy, proclaimed Britain's military and moral ascendance as 'Britannia triumphant, her ships sweep the sea, Her standard is Justice – her watchword, "be free."'[96] We hear in these words a special pride in the work of the navy inseparable from freedom, justice, and law. The special relationship between the sailors, equality, and rights seems to provide a higher mission to their imperial work and an identity as freemen, not slaves. How did the British understand the legal status of Britain's military forces in a time of war?

Blackstone summarized the government's policy and attitude toward the army and the navy in the first volume of his *Commentaries on the Laws of England* (1769). At the center of his analysis lay the lack of a distinction between civilians and those who staffed the military.

> In a land of liberty it is extremely dangerous to make a distinct order of the profession of arms. ... no man should take up arms, but with a view to defend his country and its laws: he puts not off the citizen when he enters the camp; but it is because he is a citizen, and would wish to continue so, that he makes himself for a while a soldier. The laws therefore and constitution of these kingdoms know no such state as that of a perpetual standing soldier, bred up to no other profession than that of war.[97]

Like the sailors' songs, Blackstone twinned the mission of the military with the protection of liberty, law, and the constitution.

During the English Civil War many asked 'how far the power of the militia did inherently reside in the king?' Parliament found only a vague and unsatisfactory answer: it 'being unsupported by any statute, and founded only upon immemorial usage'.[98] Laws passed during the restoration of Charles II recognized 'the sole right of the crown to govern and command' the army whose members lived under martial law during times of war.[99] Blackstone averred that 'martial law, which is built upon no settled principles, but is entirely arbitrary in its decision, is ... in truth and reality no law, but something indulged, rather than

[165]

allowed as a law: the necessity of order and discipline in an army is the only thing which can give it countenance'.[100] He went so far as to declare that 'it ought not to be permitted in time of peace, when the king's courts are open for all persons to receive justice according to the laws of the land'. The large armed forces kept by Charles II and James II led to the stipulation in the Bill of Rights 'That raising or keeping a standing army within the kingdom in time of peace, unless it be with the consent of parliament, is against the law.'[101] The annual legislation that reinstated the army each year allowed the maintenance of the fiction that Great Britain did not have a standing army. Balancing his discomfort with martial law with what he perceived as the necessities of state security and imperial competition, Blackstone walked a fine line that allowed martial law as an exception while insisting that it contradicted the very definition of rule of law.

Blackstone criticized the powers granted to the king in relationship to the army and 'regretted that a set of men, whose bravery has so often preserved the liberties of their country, should be reduced to a state of servitude in the midst of a nation of freemen'. Clarifying his definition of servitude with reference to Edward Coke's principle that identified 'genuine' servitude with a 'concealed or precarious' law, Blackstone warned against the specter of slavery and the 'perpetual envy and hatred' which divides the community and threatens violence and revolt by those who might 'indulge a malignant pleasure ... to destroy those privileges, to which they can never be admitted'.[102]

Events in the last half of the eighteenth century, particularly the American War of Independence (1775–1783) and the Gordon Riots, tested Britain's government to maintain order within the strictures of rule of law, but the ideas generated by the French Revolution presented a much more radical set of challenges as they reverberated through the Britain and Ireland. Fearing the outbreak of an internal revolution or at least an insistent movement for extensive parliamentary reform that many perceived as a threat to aristocratic society and the hierarchies defined in the constitution, the British government enlisted the jurisprudence of emergency to stem the flow of radical ideas, mobilization, and association. Parliament suspended habeas corpus in 1794, allowing for the arrest and detention of those considered enemies of the government and banned meetings and publications dedicated to political reform in 1796.[103] The repressive legislation passed between 1793 and 1800 to inhibit, restrain, and intimidate reformers and radicals raised questions among many about the nature of British freedom and liberty and what remained of it during what has been called 'Pitt's reign of terror.'[104]

Parliament debated a statutory response to the sailors' work action at the Nore on June 1, 1797. The session began with Dundas reading a letter from the king expressing his concerns about the 'violent and treasonable acts' at the Nore. The king urged Parliament to take 'every measure which can tend, at this important conjuncture, to provide for the public security'.[105] In particular the king suggested consideration of a measure against those 'attempts to excite sedition and mutiny in His Majesty's naval service', because they deterred the 'obedience and discipline which are so important to the prosperity and safety of the British Empire'. The king's message referenced the latest rumors about the efforts among the mutineers to blockade the Thames warning about the 'heinous nature of the offences by them committed' including the 'threatened and taken measures for stopping the commerce of the kingdom, passing to and from the port of London'.[106] The message paired the disruption of hierarchy and the dissipation of naval discipline and obedience with a concern about trade. A foreboding tone implied the ever-present possibility of violence.

Aware how effectively the sailors at Spithead had used the press and their communication with those on shore to rally public opinion in their favor, Pitt proposed two bills in Parliament to sever existing ties between ship and shore and to prevent new relationships from developing between the ships at the Nore and the towns on the nearby banks of the Thames, especially Sheerness. The 'Act for more effectually restraining Intercourse with the Crews of certain of His Majesty's Ships now in a State of Mutiny and Rebellion and for the more effectual Suppression of such Mutiny and Rebellion' (37 Geo. III c. 71) defined any communication with a ship in mutiny as a felony punishable by death without benefit of clergy. The vague 'Act for the better Prevention and Punishment of Attempts to seduce Persons serving in his Majesty's Forces, by Sea or Land, from their Duty and Allegiance to His Majesty, or to incite them to Mutiny or Disobedience' (37 Geo. III c. 70) passed on the same day. It classified as a felon anyone who acted to 'incite or stir up ... to commit any Act of Mutiny ... or to make, or endeavor to make, any mutinous Assembly, or to commit any traitorous or mutinous Practice'. The punishment again was death without benefit of clergy.[107]

Perhaps to temper the harsh provisions and vague wording in the bills, Home Secretary, William Henry Cavendish, Duke of Portland (1738–1809), raised the possibility that among the sailors there might be men who wanted to break with their mutinous colleagues 'desirous of returning to their obedience' who had been 'prevented from so doing by violence'. He advocated passage, urging the public to 'use their utmost endeavours, according to law, to suppress all such mutinous and treasonable proceedings, and to use all lawful means to bring the persons concerned therein, their aiders and abettors, to justice'.[108]

Pitt argued to his colleagues in the House of Commons on June 2 that the best way forward for the government 'was to shew to the world, that there was no public difficulty which they were not ready to meet with that firmness, with that courage, with that zeal for the public welfare, which alone would extricate the country from its present distress'. Reminding his fellow MPs that they worked for 'a great, a brave, and a free people', Pitt asserted that passage of the bill would provide 'the Throne the assurances of their unanimous determination of affording to His majesty every support in their power, to enable him to put an end to this resistance of regular authority and to counteract the effects of so fatal an example'. Pitt acknowledged that the representatives might have reservations about the bill's sweeping provisions that could circumscribe certain liberties, but he argued for their necessity based on his assertion that external forces motivated the mutiny because 'it could not be in the hearts of British seamen that such sentiments originated'.[109]

For Pitt, the use of law as a technology to stem the spread of republican ideas demonstrated loyalty and patriotism. Explicitly tying radical ideas to mutiny and treason, Pitt argued:

> that every man who boasted, and who was worthy of the name of an Englishman, would stand forth, in the metropolis, and in every part of the kingdom, to maintain the authority of the laws, and enforce obedience to them; to oppose and counteract the machinations of the disaffected; and to preserve a due principle of submission to legal authority.[110]

In his speech Pitt associated these efforts with 'national defence', 'security in the kingdom at large', and 'public safety'. Pitt sought to reinscribe the military hierarchy and restore the navy's chain of command. The British often called on such 'jurisprudence of emergency' in colonial spaces far from home when political or economic security seemed imperiled – including for example British controlled Trinidad.[111] But employing the latitude to act outside the law based on necessity in the metropole was far more unusual and risky: it drew attention to the government's weakness and vulnerability and undermined its signatory achievement, the rule of law and its most vaunted claim – the 'freedom' of its people. More significantly, it exposed the co-constituted nature of rule of law and its suspension by jurisprudence of emergency.

The bill elicited a mixed reaction from MPs. Whigs expressed their support for the proposed legislation while defending the existence of an opposition to the government that was neither seditious nor treasonous. William Jolliffe (1745–1802), who often sided with the opposition Whigs, expressed reservations about giving 'his assent to any alteration in the laws of the country' despite proclaiming that 'without discipline and subordination in the army and navy, no Government could exist'.¹¹²

Sheridan expressed his disappointment in the mariners and the 'delusion [that] operated on their minds' and worried about the implications of the mutiny for Britain's war against France and for its 'national commerce'. Nevertheless, Sheridan argued that he could not support the legislation under consideration. He disapproved of the Admiralty's seemingly inconsistent negotiations with the mutineers at the Nore, but his more serious critique compared the bills under discussion with the Treason and Sedition Bills of 1795 (later passed as 36 Geo. III c. 7) which he had strongly opposed. Cautioning against 'any measure of the Legislature, which went to increase the number of sanguinary penal laws', Sheridan implored his fellow ministers to consider whether 'present laws were deficient for the attainment of the ends proposed in the address'. He refused to assent to 'that mode of legislation ... continually and systematically increased under the present Administration' on the grounds that 'it had uniformly produced the very evil which it was intended to prevent'.¹¹³ This comment referred to the large number of statutes that prescribed capital punishment and the debate over their efficacy in the third quarter of the eighteenth century. Those who advocated law reform argued that England's harsh 'Bloody Code' and its irregular application did not deter crime and that in fact the very unpredictable nature of the criminal legal process might promote transgressive acts. Instead they called for more moderate punishments applied more systematically.¹¹⁴

Sheridan queried those assembled 'was not the present mutiny a proof that the spirit of sedition had increased, notwithstanding the bills which had been introduced by His Majesty's Ministers?'¹¹⁵ He reminded his audience of the new barracks built with 'millions of the public money' on the assurance that 'a system would keep the soldiers out of the way of seduction, and prevent them from being exposed to the intrigues of the emissaries of faction'. He quipped that 'If the people could not be made dumb, the soldiers should be made deaf.'¹¹⁶

In his response to Sheridan, Pitt described a conspiracy of radicals as working within well organized, coordinated, and far flung networks. On land, sailors found support in 'the engines of sedition ... busily and unremittingly persevering on shore' whose 'emissaries begin at work at secret hours, by the handbills which had been industriously circulated and dispersed in every part where they were likely to attract the attention of the soldiers in the army'. Although Pitt admitted that these efforts to identify radical recruits had failed in the army, their success among the navy's ranks proved the strength of these radical networks, unimpeded by the distance between ship and shore. Pitt contended that the 'sedition was extensive enough to prove it to be systematic, and dangerous enough to make precaution requisite' and that this 'treacherous conspiracy' justified the legislative measures he so vehemently supported. Pitt also protested that these ideas were 'least congenial to the natural disposition of the persons who professed them', evoking a national British character that instinctively recoiled from Jacobin ideas.[117]

Having rhetorically established the strength and organization of a seditious conspiracy, Pitt moved on to address concerns about the need for new legislation and to refute Sheridan's assertion that England's 'sanguinary laws' did not require any more elaboration. In Pitt's mind, the crime in question 'united all the malignity, all the heinousness which could excite resentment, with all that danger and importance which could demand the immediate interference of the Legislature'. He argued that the very fact that the crimes took place proved that 'the laws in force were not sufficient'. Given that all English legislation did not originate in a 'deliberate systematic code' but instead resulted from 'an accumulation of provisions made to suit offences as they occurred, and their character and complexion distinguished them to be the produce of different periods', he opined that Parliament responded appropriately by promulgating new laws.[118] In contrast to the movement for law reform that called for measured punishments and their predictable enforcement, Pitt supported a vague set of punishments that would leave many of the consequences of a guilty verdict to the judge's discretion; possible punishments would include imprisonment, banishment, and transportation.[119]

Both acts passed on June 6, 1797 – only one person was ever indicted for inciting mutiny in the armed forces.[120] Again we see the government enlisting law to gird the underbelly of empire, maintain order, and reinstate conformity to traditional hierarchies. Parliament deployed these legal interventions somewhat haphazardly to try, often unsuccessfully, to connect and to sever, to gather and to disperse, opportunistically attempting to separate what was allowed in and what was not, who was included and who was excluded.

Slavery and impressment, freedom and whiteness

Despite his condemnation of martial law as a kind of servitude, Blackstone did not condemn impressment, calling it 'a matter of some dispute'. Instead he relied on its longevity as a justification for considering the practice as a 'part of the common law'. Citing legislation that both allowed and constrained the power to impress, Blackstone concluded that 'all which do most evidently imply a power of impressing to reside somewhere; and, if any where, it must from the spirit of our constitution, as well as from the frequent mention of the king's commission, reside in the crown alone'.[121] Acknowledging the problematic nature of impressment 'only defensible from public necessity', he suggested incentivizing English recruits by offering them higher wages while 'every foreign seaman, who during a war shall serve two years in any man of war, merchantman, or privateer, is naturalized *ipso facto*'.[122] The comparison with slavery recurred when Blackstone recounted the statute passed to create a 'register of seamen ... for a constant and regular supply of the king's fleet; with great privileges to the registered men, and ... heavy penalties in case of their non-appearance ... but this registry, being judged to be rather a badge of slavery, was abolished'.[123]

Many made the comparison between slavery and impressment. The abolitionist Granville Sharp had written against the press gang in the 1770s and early 1780s.[124] Riots protesting the practice of pulling men off the streets and out of taverns and forcing them into naval service took place around England and in Canada in the 1790s.[125] Nicholas Rogers has found an instance of rioters disrupting the work of press gangs in black face.[126] Some compared the life of sailors to slavery outside the immediate context of impressment: Thomas Pasley, a captain in the navy, wrote in 1780 that 'you are the only class of being in our famed Country of Liberty really Slaves'.[127] This observation recognized that impressment did not fit within the exchange of service and loyalty for a hearing of grievances and suggested that the oppressive working conditions on most naval ships did not either. Life on a ship was difficult, the food scarce, and the violence of naval discipline brutal. In his account of life in the navy between 1780 and 1819 William Richardson described it as 'Horrid work! Could any one bear to see a beast used so, let alone a fellow creature?' Making an explicit comparison to abolitionist arguments, he continued 'People may talk of negro slavery and the whip, but let them look nearer home, and see a poor sailor arrived from a long voyage ... if he complains he is likely to be seized up and flogged with a cat, much more severe than the negro driver's whip, and if he deserts he is flogged round the fleet nearly to death.'[128] In June 1800, Richard Hall wrote to his wife from HMS *Zealand* at the Nore describing 'where I live it is as a prison ... we are looked upon as a dog and not so good ... there is so much Arbatory Paower that a man must not say [h]is Soul is [h]is Own. It is worse than a prison'.[129]

Songs composed during the action at the Nore declared the mariners' loyalty to the king and promised 'still their country's cause they would maintain', but when 'the Nore the lions boldly roused', they 'swore ... all the tyrants would subdue, Their gallant hearts the chains of bondage broke No to revolt but to evade the yoke'. Sung from the sailors' perspective, the song related how 'each broke his chains and off the panic shook ... Oh Britons free, usurp no tyrant sway, Protect your tars, and then they'll you obey'.[130] Another song made the comparison of the lives of sailors with that of slaves more explicit. The song enjoined its listeners to 'view the tender's loathsome hold Where droops your injured seamen; Dragged by Oppression's savage grasp From every dear connection. 'Midst putrid air, oh! See them gasp'. The song then demanded:

> If Liberty be ours, oh say why are not all protected? Why is the hand of ruffian sway 'Gainst seamen thus directed? Is this your proof of British rights? Is this rewarding bravery? Oh shame to boast your tars' exploits, Then doom these tars to slavery.[131]

These lyrics rewrote the legal understanding of the mariner's culture, the trade of work and loyalty for good treatment. The references to rights, liberty, and freemen suggest an expansion of sailors' expectations in terms of what they hoped to earn in the exchange of hard work and service for their country. Their words insisted that their status did not and must not bear any similarity to slavery. Here the word slavery is not an abstraction or a metaphor: the song calls out 'ye minions of a court Who prate at Freedom's blessing ... And vindicate impressing'.[132]

The references to slavery in these songs were not the only time the sailors mentioned the topic. In the midst of the crisis at the Nore the sailors raised the subject of slavery. On June 7, Evan Napean (1752–1822), secretary of the Admiralty under Lord Spencer and an important figure in foreign and home secret service, received a document intended to set the public straight about the 'falsehood and misrepresentations' circulating about the mutiny. This text from the Nore sought to reframe the debate by explaining the sailors' true motives. The document declared:

> Far from our very ideas to subvert the Government of our beloved country we have the highest opinion of our beloved sovereign and have to hope that none of the measures taken to deprive us of our Common Rights have been instigated by him. You cannot, countrymen, have the smallest idea of the slavery under which we have for many years labored ... Labour under every disagreement and affliction which African slaves cannot endure.[133]

What exactly did the sailors mean when they claimed that their 'disagreement and affliction' exceeded those suffered by African slaves? Sailors were quite familiar with the brutality of chattel and raced slavery. During their time in ports around the globe they witnessed the dehumanizing loading and unloading of human cargo. Some sailors in the navy had learned their trade on slave ships while others worked beside freed slaves on merchant ships; some freed black sailors served in the British navy.[134] The simultaneity of the French Revolution, the *Rights of Man*, the peak of the slave trade, and the campaign for abolition did not elude the mariners at the Nore. In this message they proclaimed their distinction from African slaves by asserting their inherent rights and entitlements – the absence of which defined a slave. The sailors suggested that the men who fought for England's freedom and liberty suffered 'every disagreement and affliction', more than slaves who lacked humanity and freedom. Undoubtedly it was more acceptable for sailors to claim rights through an abolitionist idiom instead of an explicitly republican discourse the government found both threatening and destabilizing. Through their discussion of slavery the sailors articulated a desire to prevent an erosion of their status especially in the context of abolitionist debates and the prospect of black emancipation. In the process they honed a definition of Englishness that twinned expanded rights with whiteness.

Britons or foreigners, nation or empire

In his lengthy sermon at Trinity House on June 2, 1797 Thomas Rennell (1754–1840), the dean of Winchester, delivered a Burkean interpretation of events at Spithead and the Nore. Rennell sought refuge in the nation which he considered an alternative to a transnational ideology of rights and a means of preserving a traditional social order based on hierarchy and embedded in law. Rennell's presentation of Britons as cohesive, homogeneous, and in accord allowed for the creation of villainous outsiders, atheists, Irishmen, Frenchmen, and republicans on whom to blame the rebellious mutinies. This shielded 'British seamen' as loyal protectors and allowed the law and government free rein to take whatever measures were necessary to forestall complete chaos and disintegration.[135]

In his sermon Rennell savagely attacked the mutineers and the 'present disgraceful conduct of some of the Seamen of your Majesty's Fleet', who, he speculated:

> instigated, no doubt by the wicked insinuations of some evil disposed persons, enemies alike to your Majesty's Royal Person, and to their country, have been betrayed into acts of insubordination and outrage, degrading to the character of British Seamen, hitherto as highly distinguished for loyalty and good conduct, as for intrepidity in vanquishing their enemies.[136]

Like all of those who searched for the motives of the mutinies, Rennell answered his own question. 'Who aimed this blow?' he demanded. Taking the onus off of 'the body of English Seamen', he declared that 'it is impossible to suppose that a beloved and favourite child should strike at the heart of its parent!'. Rennell argued that given the 'hereditary virtues of that body of men from the earliest periods of our naval power to the very commencement of this disastrous disaffection', responsibility for these 'acts of insubordination and outrage' lay with outside influences.[137] Speaking of events at the Nore in particular, he refused to believe that 'without a single grievance to complain of, and in the moment of kindest concessions, they should add to plunder, mutiny, and murder, the language of insolence, and the tone and terms of republican menace'.[138] Here he recognized the traditional exchange of loyalty and service from the sailors for negotiation and consideration from their superiors, and he affirmed that the sailors by their behavior had broken the traditional terms allowed by mariner culture. Rennell concluded that the sailors, either suffered 'under the delusion of artful misrepresentation', or they 'remain[ed] under the tyranny' of external foes 'for the purposes of sedition and revolt'.[139]

Rennell identified the French as the culprits who 'contaminated' the sailors. In what might be a reference to the London Corresponding Society or the other moderate English organizations that advocated parliamentary reform, he pointed to 'those innocent associations of men, who under different pretexts have been long meditating the destruction of their native land' and those who have 'furthered and promoted the word of murder and devastation in Ireland'.[140] At stake for Rennell was 'our free and happy Constitution' threatened by those who 'under pretexts of reform' have 'employed every artifice, to foment a civil war both in this country and Ireland'.[141] Those who collaborated with this agenda, 'seduced ... into a momentary, though tremendous error', Rennell warned, would 'perish by premature violence in the midst of the perpetration of crime' or 'subject themselves, as well as their countrymen, to be hewers of wood and drawers of water to their ancient and inveterate foe the French'.[142] Bringing his warnings into the legal realm of the 'constitution' underlined the severity of the threat of the 'republican menace' which Rennell cautioned would bring 'violence', 'crime', and 'civil war': the complete dismemberment of British law and social order.

Rennell's nationalist theme carried an imperial message.[143] He asked 'if the navy of this country is destroyed, and its Commerce the prey of our foes, where will be found those rich and inexhaustible resources which dispense the means of industrious exertion and plentiful subsistence?'.[144] The navy functioned as an indispensable arm of Britain's Empire, discovering resources, delivering them 'to our numerous manufacturers', and enabling Britain to acquire great wealth. The navy provided employment 'peculiarly to our mariners, pilots, and every species of naval artificers, and in short to all those who "go down to the sea" in ships, and occupy their business in great waters'.[145] In terms of an imperial rivalry, Rennell posited France as Britain's constant 'enemy', an 'inveterate pest'. Emphasizing the sea-centered parameters of Britain's imperial project and the global dimensions of the threat posed by acts of resistance among mariners, he declared that by Britain's 'naval superiority ALONE they are now prevented from the plunder and subjugation of the whole habitable globe!'.[146]

Following Burke's thesis Rennell defined law and government as the bulwarks against 'the passions [which] are by nature savage and ferocious, and stand in need of perpetual check and coercion'. Hence the need for 'Laws and Government – of Magistrates and Governors, and those various though partial and incomplete curbs by which human wisdom has endeavoured to confine and control the impetuosity of inflamed and corrupt appetites.'[147] Only the 'perpetual check and coercion' of the 'passions', contained 'that long list of crime and misery which have ... deluged and desolated the earth!'.[148] Given the enormous challenges presented by the passions and their criminal consequences, Rennell's sermon empowered the government and by extension its laws to 'confine and control'. The sermon implied that as the vehicle of suppression and restraint, the law and those who enforced it should have very few limits and directed the government to use its powers to restore order.[149]

Rennell expressed only contempt for the 'French' emphasis on liberty and equality. Quoting Corinthians he contrasted a Christian belief 'that where the spirit of God is, there is liberty', with 'a petulant spirit of equality, which leads every man to be the little tyrant over his fellow creatures'.[150] He urged a Christian posture of 'meekness and humility' instead of 'captiously and turbulently insisting upon visionary and abstract rights'.[151] He dismissed all of the values propagated by the revolution as 'delusion', 'flattering to the corruptions, the pride, and frenzy of man'. He compared the period of English Republicanism in the seventeenth century as far superior to the moment of the mutiny in 1797. As bad as the English Civil War and the Republic had been, he promised that 'the prevalence of the present principles of sedition and atheism would be ... infinitely sharper' because in the former case 'the only contest was among BRITONS – no foreign power interfered, at least visibly – no troops of a foreign nation were attempted to be introduced'.[152] If as P. J. Marshall has asserted Britain in the eighteenth century was a 'nation defined by empire', by the end of the century nation emerged as a separate entity and a solution to the republican threat.[153]

Conclusion

In a letter written to Alexander Carlyle on June 3, 1797 immediately after the resolution of the crisis at the Nore, Admiral Lord Cuthbert

Collingwood (1748–1810) compared Britain's ongoing campaign to blockade Cadiz with the mutinies. He predicted that even if the campaign failed, it would not be as bad as the Spithead and the Nore because 'we are in no danger of being disgraced. For this fleet is not yet republican; we have no delegates to determine what our movement shall be, or whether we shall move at all'.[154] By the time he wrote to his sister on August 7, 1797 answering her questions about what happened at the anchorages, Collingwood seemed determined to frame the events within traditional hierarchies. He enumerated those factors he considered the 'concurrent causes which made the thing practicable', but he never used the word mutiny in his text; instead, he spoke of 'convulsions', 'irruption', 'the spirit of insurrection', and 'popular tumults spread with the violence of a conflagration'.[155] Describing 'this great national calamity which has shook the constitution of England, and given a wound to naval discipline', he blamed Howe for 'not having taken proper notice of the memorials and petitions of the seamen which were sent to him' and considered his 'neglect was the sole cause'.[156] Collingwood conceded that the pay raise awarded to the army, militia, and naval officers in 1795 may have caused resentment among sailors denied a similar raise. In combination with the press 'trumping their (sailors') praises in nonsensical paragraphs' and 'calling them England's best hope', some mariners may have believed that the Admiralty would quickly acquiesce to their demands.[157] Nonetheless, Collingwood insisted that 'without being powerfully instigated by the arts of others they wou'd not have engaged in so disgraceful an undertaking'.[158] Determined to minimize the effect of the events and dismiss any significant changes they might herald, Collingwood presented a familiar trope: his acceptance of the sailors long established right to petition the Admiralty and even an admission that the lack of an official response exacerbated tensions in the ranks. He supported the Admiralty's ultimate decision to circumscribe the concessions they made to the sailors and dismissed any larger republican agenda on the part of the sailors as the consequence of outside forces. Collingwood's evolving assessment of events at Spithead and the Nore reveal his unsettled conclusion that the sailors had indeed contested hierarchies and disrupted traditional forms of negotiation.

In 'The Delegates in Council or Beggars on Horseback' (Figure 4.1) dated June 7, 1797 Isaac Cruikshank (1764–1811) captured all of the contradictions and oppositions surveyed above.[159] The glaring mutineers stand or sit around a table. At one end of the table is Admiral Buckner with whom they negotiate terms. The representations of the mutineers discredit them as rough and ready characters: one man smokes, another chews tobacco, a third aims a pistol in the air, and several others display

Figure 4.1 'The Delegates in Council or Beggars on Horseback'

their weapons. One of the men sitting at the table rests his hand on a sheet of paper titled 'Resolutions', a reference to their claims to choose representatives and make decisions. The crowded room, teeming with discontent, conveys toppled hierarchies of power and deference. Their leader, Richard Parker, undermines their professed egalitarian values by sitting on a chair that is slightly higher than the others.

A print of Britannia hangs upside down, near two torn scraps of paper with the words of two well-known naval ballads. One of the ballads, 'True Blue an old Song' proclaimed the sailors' loyalty. The second, 'Hearts of Oak', undermined that claim. In the first stanza 'Hearts of Oak are our Ships Jolly Tars are our men We always are Ready' the word 'ready' is crossed out, presumably a reference to the sailors' refusal to obey their orders to sail. Despite Cruikshank's negative opinion of the mutiny, the reference to 'Hearts of Oak' calls our attention (and that of his viewers) to the bedrock of British ideology – honor, freedom, and liberty, precisely those values the sailors believed they maintained on the waves and across the globe and those they believed the imperial government owed them.

The chaotic scene confirms its title, a reference to the proverb, 'set a beggar on horseback and he will ride to the devil'. Shortened to 'a beggar on horseback', the idiom warns of a poor person made arrogant or corrupt by rising above his/her station, violating traditional hierarchies. The image implies that the Admiralty erred by entering into negotiations with the mutineers because doing so afforded the mutinous sailors too strong a voice and cast the delegates as equals with their naval officers. Most seriously it legitimated the crime of mutiny. The cartoon condemned the mere fact of opening a dialogue with the mutineers, arguing that nothing positive or lawful could result from a criminal act.

Standing next to the delegation's president Parker is John Thelwall (1764–1834) the political radical with ties to many reform organizations including the Society of the Friends of the Liberty of the Press, the Friends of the People at Southwark, the Society for Constitutional Information, and the London Corresponding Society. Thelwall, a frequent speaker on the reform lecture circuit, called in his speeches (one of which hangs out of his pocket in this print) for universal manhood suffrage and an end to the war with France. In the image he advises Parker to 'Tell him we intend to be Masters, I'll read him a Lecture'. Hiding under the table Cruikshank depicts five presumptive masterminds of the mutiny dressed in more expensive clothes and wearing wigs: James Maitland Eighth Earl of Lauderdale (1759–1839) holds a piece of paper titled 'Letter from Sheerness to Ld L——le', and beside him kneel John Horne Tooke (1736–1812), Charles Stanhope, Third Earl Stanhope (1753–1816), Fox, and Sheridan. On them falls the blame for inspiring and initiating the mutinies. No doubt of this fact remains when Fox declares his complicity and leadership: 'Aye, Aye, we are at the bottom of it.' The few prints that mention the mutinies at Spithead and the Nore all point to the Whigs or other radical reformers as the source of the sailors' demands and their inspiration. Like other contemporary observers, the conservative Cruikshank print divested the mutineers of agency, originality, and a vision of their future. At one level the print reiterated Burke's advice 'at once to preserve and to reform', to proceed with 'circumspection and caution' in order to maintain tradition, hierarchy, and property.[160] But by capturing the ideological shift of the late eighteenth century, the unresolved and disruptive dichotomies and their discomfiting results, the print suggested at least some doubt about the feasibility of Burke's solution.

Although the sailors' demands did not necessarily articulate an agenda that aimed to destroy or radically change the Britain they knew, the revolutionary rhetoric posed new challenges to the British nation and its Empire. The men who participated in the mutiny, the very sinews of empire, drew on Paine's paradigm – especially what he said about the role of government and its relationship to the alleviation of poverty

– to make demands that had real implications for the conduct of the war and Britain's success or failure in that effort. They answered Paine's call to action when he said 'There is no such thing as the idea of a compact between the people on the one side, and the government on the other. The compact was that of the people with each other to produce and constitute a government.'[161] The last words of a sailor named Smart, executed on July 18 for his participation in the mutiny on HMS *Grampus*, attest to Paine's influence: 'a few minutes before Smart was run up, he said, that reading Pain's [sic] works had brought him to so untimely an end'.[162]

The sailors' participation in this discussion of rights, freedoms, and governance pointed to larger themes and demands such as parliamentary reform and universal manhood suffrage that Pitt and his government did not wish to engage – and certainly not with maritime workers. The British government resorted to tactics it had used before, enlisting the law to intervene, prevent, suppress, and redirect. The government's responses operationalized Burke's view of the law as the instrument by which to maintain hierarchy and the aristocratic social order. Legislators and commentators argued that using the law to circumscribe liberties would reimpose order. By controlling the passions inflamed by these negative and damaging influences, a jurisprudence of emergency would reinvigorate a masculinity damaged by insubordination and re-establish confidence in the navy as an effective military force of both nation and empire in a time of war.

Epilogue

The Memoirs of Richard Parker begins with a biographical overview that follows Parker from his 'wild and extravagant' youth, intemperate excess, debt, and consequent impressment, through the mutiny at the Nore, and his hanging. His 'nocturnal revels' and his association with 'men who he suspected were disaffected to the King and Constitution' culminated in a visit to France in the 'time of Robespierre' which 'led to a suspicion, that, during the Mutiny, he might open a correspondence with the enemy'.[163] When asked about the origin of the mutiny and 'whether any persons in London were in league with him[,] He declared to those gentlemen that the Mutiny originated, and was conducted, solely on board the ship'.[164] This crisp denial of any connection to a larger movement served the government's desire to represent the mutinies as isolated incidents, the work of one man, his troubled youth, and his time in France. One stark difference between the Spithead and the Nore was the fact that in the latter there was an elected leader who could be named, blamed, and punished. Parker's presidency may in a small way account for the very different outcomes of the two events.

The pamphlet ended with a wish for 'PEACE TO HIS REPENTANT ASHES!' describing Parker as possessing 'progressive traits of heroism, which best demonstrate a firm and gallant mind'. Although mention of his 'very violent ... temper' moderated the praise, Parker's 'decent contrition, and candid acknowledgement of the justice of his sentence have proved the best atonement within his power for his national offence'. His execution redeemed him as 'a man of genteel manners, shrewd understanding, keen and vehement in his observations, ... and generous to the extreme'. Through his execution the navy achieved collective redemption, his punishment restoring the institution's disciplinary hierarchies through Parker's acquiescence, submission, and deference: 'His last words of manly submission cannot fail to have a proper influence on the minds of British seamen, delivered by the leader of their common, but desperate cause.'[165] His execution following court marital, at sea, yet so close to English soil, expunged him from the nation and relegated him, and by extension all sailors, to the imperial realm.

As J. A. Sharpe explained, a convicted felon who performed a good death upheld the conviction and affirmed the truth-finding capacity of England's legal system as a whole.[166] In the case of treason during a time of war when grave concerns about security and infiltration abounded, Parker's good death allowed for the redemption of the navy as a fighting body and for a reconciliation with the sailors who, reclaimed through Parker's death, 'the brave, generous and open character of British seamen'.[167] The pamphlet's discursive work buttressed the British state, muted the passions that ignited the mutiny, and vindicated the Admiralty and the navy, its organization, and the conduct of its officers. It provided closure and resolution to all of the contradictory responses to events at the Spithead and the Nore. Empire, nation, and whiteness emerged as the resolution to the disruption and instability represented by Thomas Paine, the *Right of Man*, and the conflict between the sailors' customary and legal rights. The pamphlet lacked all subtlety in what it set out to achieve: 'it was not the exit of a Desperado, nor of a discomfited Pretender; but that of a man who, conscious of the enormity of his offences, was resolved at the same time to maintain his fortitude to the last, which had led him to pre-eminence in the choice of those fellow seamen, who were now to witness his last exertions!'.[168] With its self-congratulatory tone, the pamphlet attempted to shut down any dangers and threats posed by the mutinies by representing them, their motives and aspirations as the work of a moment in the past of one man.

As norming and restorative of accepted hierarchies as Parker's execution looked to some, a different, more critical message may have been discerned by other observers or those who read the widely reported newspaper accounts. *Bell's Weekly* attributed to Parker 'progressive traits of heroism, which best demonstrate a firm and gallant mind'.[169] He combined this brave and courageous aspect with manly resignation and a willingness to take the blame and to suffer for others:

> I have heard your sentence – I shall submit to it without a struggle – I feel myself thus, because I am sensible of the rectitude of my intentions. Whatever offences may have been committed, I hope my life will be the only sacrifice – I trust it will be thought a sufficient atonement. Pardon I beseech you, the other men – I know they will return with alacrity to their duty.[170]

Parker's acknowledgement of and submission to authority performed an implicit criticism of the judicial response to the sailors' demands. As Andrea McKenzie's work on the dying 'game' demonstrates, a condemned man's acceptance of his fate and godly comportment at the scaffold could serve as social commentary.[171] The newspaper accounts attest to Parker's efficacious moral one-upsmanship:

> It is but common justice, however, to his character, to acknowledge, that his descent contrition, and candid acknowledgement of the justice of his sentence, have proved the best atonement within his power for his national offence. His last words of manly submission cannot fail to have a proper influence on the minds of British Seamen, delivered by the Leader of their common, but desperate cause; and that neither through hopes of mercy, nor fear of death.[172]

Parker's emotional control and his canny choreography of everything he did on his last day displayed a moral superiority that vied with or even morally upstaged the state's execution rituals and their conventional meanings. Moreover, in speaking of the rectitude of his intentions Parker rejected the rightfulness of his conviction and upheld his innocence according to the 'laws of humanity'.

Competing interpretations of the law and its intention played out in the next and final legal event we will examine, the English and Irish Acts of Union, 1800 (39 & 40 Geo. III c. 67 and 40 Geo. III c. 38). As Protestant elites debated the proposal to shut down the Irish Parliament between 1798 and 1800, they challenged English understandings of the constitution and the powers of Parliament. While Westminster hoped to consolidate imperial governance and eliminate colonial challenges, the Irish elite resisted, asserting a superior knowledge of English law and the British constitution.

Notes

1 *Memoirs of Richard Parker, The Mutineer; Together with an Account at large of his Trial by Court Martial, Defense, Sentence, and Execution and a Narrative of the Mutiny at the Nore and Sheerness from Commencement to its Final Termination* (London: G. Cawthorn, 1797), p. 7.
2 *Memoirs of Richard Parker*, p. 9.
3 'The Dying Declaration of the late unfortunate Richard Parker written two days previous to his execution, in a letter to a person who had known him from his earliest infancy'. TNA ADM 1/5339. Printed in G. E. Manwaring and Bonamy Dobrée, *Mutiny: The Floating Republic* (London: G. Bles, 1935), pp. 273–276.
4 James Thomson, 'Rule Britannia' (1740), consulted online, http://www.songandpraize.org/rule-brittania-lyrics.htm.
5 Impressment is discussed at length later in this chapter. Along with other works cited in footnotes below, see Nicholas Rogers, *The Press Gang: Naval Impressment and its opponents in Georgian Britain* (London: Continuum, 2007).
6 David Hume, 'Of Some Remarkable Customs', in *Essays and Treatises on Several Subjects*, 2 vols. (Edinburgh: T. Cadell, A. Donaldson, and W. Creech, 1784), vol. 1, p. 395.
7 Hume, *Essays and Treatises*, vol. 1, p. 396. For more on sailors and the place of the navy in British society, see Linda Colley, *Britons: Forging the Nation*; Isaac Land, *War, Nationalism and the British Sailor, 1750–1850* (New York: Palgrave Macmillan, 2009); Margarette Lincoln, *Representing the Royal Navy: British Sea Power, 1750–1815* (Aldershot: Ashgate, 2002); Marcus Rediker, *Between the Devil and the Deep Blue Sea: Merchant Seamen, Pirates, and the Anglo-American Maritime World, 1700–1750* (Cambridge: Cambridge University Press, 1987); N. A. M. Rodger, *The Wooden World: An Anatomy of the Georgian Navy* (London: Collins, 1986), and N. A. M. Rodger, *The Command of the Ocean: A Naval History of Britain, 1649–1815* (New York: Norton, 2004).
8 My analysis here takes inspiration from William Sewell, 'Historical Events as Transformations of Structures: Inventing Revolution at the Bastille', *Theory and Society* 25 (1996), pp. 841–881.
9 James William, *The Naval History of Great Britain*, 2 vols. (London: R. Bentley, 1837), vol. 2, p. 63.
10 James Oldham and Su Jin Kim discuss the 'creative legal fictions' and judicial rationalizations that developed during the Napoleonic Wars in 'Insuring Maritime Trade with the Enemy in the Napoleonic Era', *Texas International Law Journal* 47 (2012), pp. 561–586 and James Oldham, 'Some Effects of War on the Law in late Eighteenth- and early Nineteenth-Century England', unpublished paper shared with the author.
11 Philip MacDougall, 'Reporting the Mutinies in the Provincial Press', in *The Naval Mutinies of 1797: Unity and Perseverance*, ed. Ann Veronica Coats and Philip MacDougall (Woodbridge: Boydell Press, 2011), pp. 161–178. For more on English newspapers at this time, see Lucyle Werkmeister, *A Newspaper History of England, 1792–1793* (Lincoln, NE: University of Nebraska Press, 1967).
12 Eighteenth Parliament of Great Britain: first session (27 September 1796–20 July 1797), *The Parliamentary Register; or, History of the Proceedings and Debates of the House of Commons*, 12 vols. (London: J. Debrett, 1797–1802), vol. 2, p. 439.
13 Thomas Rennell, *The ruinous effects of faction, discord, and mutiny, A sermon, preached before the Corporation of Trinity-House, at St. Nicholas Church, Deptford, on Trinity Monday, 1797* (London: Master and the Corporation, 1797), p. 7. The fiery language points to the history of emotions. Although not a subject of this chapter, I hope to analyze the affective dimensions of this rhetoric in a separate essay.
14 Nicholas Frykman, 'The Mutiny on the *Hermione*: Warfare, Revolution and Treason in the Royal Navy', *Journal of Social History* 44 (2010), p. 169. Frykman details the composition of the HMS *Hermione* whose crew he speculates at 180 men. Half of

them were English, one-fifth were from the British Empire including Scotland, Wales, Canada, and the British West Indies, one-fifth from Ireland. One-tenth came from Prussia, Sweden, Norway, Denmark, the Low Countries, Portugal, Italy, Switzerland, the United States, and the Danish West Indies. At least two men, a little over one percent, were of African descent.

15 Jeffrey Glasco, 'The Seaman Feels Him-self a Man', *International Labor and Working-Class History* 66 (2004), pp. 44, 53.
16 Coats, 'Spithead Mutiny: Introduction', in Coats and MacDougall, *Naval Mutinies of 1797*, p. 27. The OED defines mutiny as 'open revolt against constituted authority; (now usually) *spec.* rebellion on the part of a body of people normally subject to strict discipline, such as soldiers or sailors; behaviour which flouts or shows disregard for discipline; mutinous conduct'.
17 Alan Miles, 'A Letter on the Naval Mutinies of 1797', *Mariners Mirror* 78 (1992), p. 200.
18 There is a vast literature on Britain during the French Revolution. See Ian R. Christie, *Stress and Stability in late Eighteenth-Century Britain: Reflections on the British Avoidance of Revolution* (Oxford: Clarendon, 1984); Seamus Deane, *The French Revolution and Enlightenment in England, 1789–1832* (Cambridge, MA: Harvard University Press, 1988); H. T. Dickinson, ed., *Britain and the French Revolution, 1789–1815* (New York: St. Martin's Press, 1989); Emma Vincent Macleod, *A War of Ideas: British Attitudes to the Wars against Revolutionary France 1792–1802* (Aldershot: Ashgate, 1998); Jennifer Mori, *Britain in the Age of the French Revolution* (Harlow: Longman, 2000); Mark Philp, ed., *The French Revolution and British Popular Politics* (Cambridge: Cambridge University Press, 1991); and Malcolm Thomis and Peter Holt, *Threats of Revolution in Britain, 1789–1848* (London: Macmillan, 1977). For visual representations, see David Bindman, *The Shadow of the Guillotine: Britain and the French Revolution* (London: Trustees British Museum, 1989).
19 A Jacobin was 'a sympathizer with the principles of the Jacobins of the French Revolution; an extreme radical in politics or social organization' OED. Thompson, *Making*, p. 167.
20 Thompson, *Making*, p. 168.
21 Nicole Ulrich, 'International Radicalism, Local Solidarities: The 1797 British Naval Mutinies in Southern African Waters', *International Review of Social History* 58 (2013), pp. 51–85; and Niklas Frykman, 'Connections between Mutinies in European Navies', *International Review of Social History* 58 (2013), pp. 87–107. The editors of this special issue argue for a 'geographically connected process' they call 'maritime radicalism' during the age of revolution (1760s–1840s).
22 Manwaring and Dobrée, *Mutiny*, led this school followed by a more popular retelling by James Dugan in *The Great Mutiny* (New York: Putnam, 1965). More recent scholarship that traces the mutiny to the influence of the French Revolution and Republican ideas includes Joseph Price Moore III, '"The greatest Enormity That Prevails": Direct Democracy and Workers' Self Management in the British naval Mutinies of 1797', in *Jack Tar in History: Essays in the History of Maritime Life and Labour*, ed. Colin Howell and William Twomey (Fredericton, NS: Acadiensis Press, 1991), pp. 76–104; Anthony Brown, 'The Nore Mutiny – Sedition or Ships' Biscuits? A Reappraisal', *Mariners Mirror* 92 (2006), pp. 60–74; and D. Featherstone, 'Counter-Insurgency, Subalternity, and Spatial Relations: Interrogating Court-Martial Narratives of the Nore Mutiny of 1797', *South African Historical Journal* 61 (2009), pp. 766–787. In *Insurrection: The British Experience 1795–1803* (Gloucester: A Sutton, 1983) Roger Wells attributes the mutinies to a peace movement among the sailors.
23 N. A. M. Rodger, 'Mutiny or Subversion? Spithead and the Nore', in *1798: A Bicentenary Perspective*, ed. Thomas Bartlett, David Dickson, Dáire Keogh, and Kevin Whelan (Dublin: Four Courts, 2003), pp. 549–564.
24 35 Geo. III c. 5, applied to English and Welsh counties; 35 Geo. III c. 9, English, Welsh and Scottish ports for the navy; 35 Geo. III c. 29, Scottish counties, cities and burghs for the navy; 37 Geo. III c. 4 English and Welsh counties for both army

and navy; 37 Geo. III c. 5 Scottish counties and cities for army or navy. Rodger, *Command of the Ocean*, p. 443.

25 The London Corresponding Society (hereafter LCS) founded by Thomas Hardy in 1792 dedicated itself to parliamentary reform, specifically annual parliaments and universal manhood suffrage. Repressive government policies, including the Treason and Sedition Acts (36 Geo. III c. 7) and (36 Geo. III c. 8) (1795) targeted its members. The Society of Constitutional Information, founded in 1780, reported on parliamentary reform and advocated annual parliaments and universal manhood suffrage. They anticipated much of the radical agenda of the 1790s.

26 Coats and MacDougall posit the first in *Naval Mutinies*, p. 22 while Rodger cites the latter in 'Mutiny or Subversion', p. 563.

27 Rodger, 'Mutiny or Subversion'. The earliest historian to take up the subject was W. Johnson Neale, *History of the Mutiny at Spithead and the Nore: With an Enquiry into Its Origin and Treatment and the Suggestions for the Prevention of Future Discontent in the Royal Navy* (London: Thomas Tegg, 1842) and in the modern period Conrad Gill, *The Naval Mutinies of 1797* (Manchester: Manchester University Press, 1913). Recently the most comprehensive treatment is *The Naval Mutinies of 1797: Unity and Perseverance* edited by Coats and MacDougall.

28 Coats, 'Spithead Mutiny: Introduction', in *Naval Mutinies*, ed. Coats and MacDougall, pp. 31, 36. There were just over 500 ships in the British navy in 1797 and 123,000 men.

29 TNA, ADM 1/1022.

30 This cursory reconstruction of events is drawn from Coats, 'Spithead Mutiny, Introduction', in *Naval Mutinies of 1797*, ed. Coats and MacDougall, pp. 22–26. For the full text of the Act, see Raithby and Edlyne, *Statutes at Large*, vol. 19, pp. 301–303.

31 Jon Mee, 'Popular Radical Culture', in *British Literature of the French Revolution in the 1790s*, ed. Pamela Clemit (Cambridge: Cambridge University Press, 2012), p. 118. Both Burke's *Reflections* and Paine's *Rights of Man* (Part I) cost three shillings. When sold with part II each sold at 6 pence. Kathryn Sutherland, '"Events … have made us a world of readers": Reader Relations 1780–1830', in *The Penguin History of Literature*, Volume V: *The Romantic Period*, ed. David Pirie (London: Penguin, 1994), p. 19. For more on the satirical prints, see Donald, *The Age of Caricature*.

32 According to David Duff 'In the wake of the *Reflections* and *Rights of Man*, reading was no longer a passive, private process but an act of public engagement in which every citizen was required to participate, and for which each could be held publicly accountable. The stakes in this great national scene of reading were nothing less than the political future of the country', Duff, 'Burke and Paine: Contrasts', in *The Cambridge Companion to British Literature of the French Revolution in the 1790s*, ed. Clemit, p. 56. Duff discusses the images depicting reading Burke and Paine on pp. 50–55.

33 Edmund Burke, *Reflections on the Revolution in France* (Oxford: Oxford University Press, 2009), p. 16.

34 Burke, *Reflections*, pp. 245–246.

35 Burke, *Reflections*, p. 221.

36 Burke, *Reflections*, p. 221.

37 Burke, *Reflections*, p. 78.

38 Burke, *Reflections*, p. 31.

39 Burke, *Reflections*, p. 80.

40 Burke, *Reflections*, pp. 25–26.

41 Thomas Paine, *Rights of Man, Common Sense, and Other Political Writing* (Oxford: Oxford University Press, 2009), pp. 91–92. The irrevocable abolition of the Irish Parliament by the Act of Union (1800) was an issue of much debate and contention that related directly to Paine's point about posterity. For more on the Act, see chapter 6.

42 Paine, *Rights of Man*, p. 117.

43 Paine, *Rights of Man*, p. 118.

44 Paine, *Rights of Man*, pp. 193–194.
45 Paine, *Rights of Man*, p. 206.
46 Blackstone, *Commentaries*, vol. 1, p. 405.
47 Blackstone, *Commentaries*, vol. 1, p. 405.
48 12 Car. II. c. 18. Blackstone, *Commentaries*, vol. 1, p. 406.
49 Blackstone, *Commentaries*, vol. 1, p. 408.
50 Rodger details the forms of communication between officers and sailors about complaints and grievances in *The Wooden World*, pp. 229–237.
51 Lewis, ed., *Horace Walpole's Correspondence*, vol. 11, p. 318. For more on Paine's *Rights of Man*, see Clemit, ed., *British Literature of the French Revolution*. For the circulation of these radical ideas, see James Epstein, '"Our real constitution": Trial Defence and Radical Memory in the Age of Revolution', in *Re-reading the Constitution: New Narratives in the Political History of England's Long Nineteenth Century*, ed. James Vernon (Cambridge: Cambridge University Press, 1996), pp. 22–51; and Gillian Russell and Clara Tuite, eds., *Romantic Sociability: Social Networks and Literary Culture in Britain* (Cambridge: Cambridge University Press, 2002).
52 Sailors may have also taken inspiration for their actions from the 'democratic' practice that Marcus Rediker argues prevailed on pirate ships, *Villains of All Nations: Atlantic Pirates in the Golden Age* (Boston, MA: Beacon, 2004). For more on the navy in this period, there is no more comprehensive account or knowledgeable author than Rodger, *Command of the Ocean*. See also Brian Lavery ed., *Shipboard Life and Organisation, 1731–1815* (Aldershot: Ashgate, 1998) and Brian Lavery, *Royal Tars: The Lower Deck of the Royal Navy, 875–1850* (Annapolis, MD: Naval Institute Press, 2010).
53 Harold Winter Hodges, ed., *Select Naval Documents* (Cambridge: Cambridge University Press, 1922), p. 49.
54 Hodges, *Select Naval Documents*, pp. 67–68.
55 *To his Highness the Lord Protector: The Humble Petition of the Sea-men, belonging to the Ships of the Commonwealth of England* (London, 1654).
56 *To his Highness the Lord Protector*. The sailors goaded the government asking that they 'may be as free as the Dutch Seamen', against whom they have fought. For more, see John Donoghue, *Fire under the Ashes: An Atlantic History of the English Revolution* (Chicago, IL: University of Chicago Press, 2013).
57 Hodges, *Select Naval Documents*, p. 68.
58 Sometimes the officers initiated the process and consulted the men about military decisions. Rodger, *The Wooden World*, pp. 229–237.
59 Julie Anne Sweet, 'The British Sailors' Advocate: James Oglethorpe's First Philanthropic Venture', *Georgia Historical Quarterly* 91 (2007), pp. 1–27.
60 *The Times*, Issue 3877, April 24, 1797, p. 2.
61 *The Times*, Issue 3877, April 24, 1797, p. 2.
62 *The Times*, Issue 3877, April 24, 1797, p. 2.
63 *The Times*, Issue 3877, April 24, 1797, p. 2. The sailors' insistence on their lawful, moderate, and customary behavior is reminiscent of the argument made by reformers who organized the Manchester reform meeting that ended in the Peterloo massacre in 1819. Robert Poole, 'The March to Peterloo: Politics and Festivity in Late Georgian England', *Past and Present* 192 (2006), pp. 109–153.
64 Paine, *Rights of Man*, p. 301.
65 *The Times*, Issue 3877, April 24, 1797, p. 3. A song called 'Mutiny at Portsmouth' published in *The Morning Post* on April 25, 1797, reiterated similar themes about the exchange of service from the sailors for the respect and negotiation of their superiors. Britannia visited the HMS *Charlotte* and found 'Fair Freedom was there, True Loyalty sat by her side'. The sailors 'assur'd her that, if they were treated like men, they would still guard her favourite Isle'. Betty Bennett, *British War Poetry in the Age of Romanticism: 1793–1815* (New York: Garland Publishers, 1976), p. 190.
66 *The Times*, Issue 3877, April 24, 1797, p. 3. Margaret Hunt demonstrates that sailors' wives effectively organized to claim the pay and benefits owed to their husbands

in 'Women and the fiscal-imperial state in late seventeenth and early eighteenth centuries', in *A New Imperial History* Kathleen Wilson, pp. 29–47. The men's agitation and petitioning on board ship may have been prompted by the severe restrictions on organization and protest placed on their wives by the legislation passed at the end of the eighteenth century (see below note 76).

67 *The Times*, Issue 3877, April 24, 1797, p. 3.
68 *The Times*, Issue 3877, April 24, 1797, p. 3. The sailors addressed their letter to 'Admiral Kempenfeldt's Ghost'. Kempenfeldt (1718–1782) had advocated strict discipline throughout the navy and warned that the only alternative to the rigorous enforcement of naval discipline for both the crew and their officers was insubordination and mutiny. David W. London, 'The Spirit of Kempenfeldt', in *Naval Mutinies*, ed. Coates and MacDougall, pp. 79–97. In the Parliamentary debates in June 1797 over 37 Geo. III c. 70 and 37 Geo. III c 71, discussed below, note 107, Richard Sheridan made a similar statement opining that among the mutineers 'a rooted spirit of disobedience had taken place of those manly and loyal sentiments with which they had been on former occasion constantly animated': Eighteenth Parliament of Great Britain: first session (27 September 1796–20 July 1797), *The Parliamentary Register*, vol. 2, p. 692. On gender, see Margaret S. Creighton and Lisa Norling, eds., *Iron Men, Wooden Women: Gender and Seafaring in the Atlantic World, 1700–1920* (Baltimore, MD: Johns Hopkins University Press, 1996).
69 Cited in Gill, *The Naval Mutinies*, p. 368.
70 Eighteenth Parliament of Great Britain: first session (27 September 1796–20 July 1797), *The Parliamentary Register*, vol. 2, p. 432.
71 Eighteenth Parliament of Great Britain: first session (27 September 1796–20 July 1797), *The Parliamentary Register*, vol. 2, p. 449.
72 The legislation included the Suspension of Habeas Corpus Act (34 Geo. III c. 54), the Treasonable and Seditious Practices Act (36 Geo. III c. 7), The Seditious Meeting and Assemblies Act (36 Geo. III c. 8), the Seduction from Duty and Allegiance Act (37 Geo. III c. 70), the act prohibiting Administering Unlawful Oaths (37 Geo. III c. 123), the Act in Suppression of Seditious and Treasonable Societies (39 Geo. III c. 79), and the Combination Act (39 Geo. III c. 81 and 39 and 40 Geo. III c. 106). The Treasonable and Seditious Practices Act was passed in 1795 in response to the government's failure to secure convictions in the Treason Trials of 1794. In the Treason Trials the government had unsuccessfully relied on the Statute of Laborers passed in 1351.
73 Eighteenth Parliament of Great Britain: first session (27 September 1796–20 July 1797), *The Parliamentary Register*, vol. 2, p. 452.
74 Eighteenth Parliament of Great Britain: first session (27 September 1796–20 July 1797), *The Parliamentary Register*, vol. 2, p. 454.
75 For more on the image of the navy and the army in British culture and society, see Gillian Russell, *The Theatres of War: Performance, Politics, and Society, 1793–1815* (Oxford: Clarendon, 1995).
76 *The Address to the Nation, by the Seamen at St. Helen's* (London: B. Crosby, 1797), p. 2.
77 *The Address to the Nation*, p. 3. The purser's eighth refers to a tradition that issued mariners seven eighths of their rations and awarded the last eighth to the purser to compensate for waste and loss. Janet MacDonald explains the efforts made in the wake of events at Spithead to redesign the navy's provisioning in *The British Navy's Victualling Board, 1793–1815: Management and Competence and Incompetence* (Woodbridge: Boydell, 2010), p. 104.
78 *Address to the Nation*, p. 4.
79 *Address to the Nation*, pp. 6–7.
80 *Address to the Nation*, p. 4. For more on this incident, see David London, 'What Really Happened on Board HMS *London*?' in *Naval Mutinies*, ed. Coates and MacDougall, pp. 61–78.
81 For more on custom, see Thompson, *Customs in Common*; and Douglas Hay and Nicholas Rodger, *Eighteenth-Century English Society* (Oxford: Oxford University

Press, 1997), esp. chs. 6 and 7. Thompson concentrates on continuities in the understanding of custom while my discussion is grounded more specifically in the turn to an understanding of rights emerging in the revolutionary moment.
82 *Address to the Nation*, p. 7.
83 Paine, *Rights of Man*, p. 119.
84 Clive Emsley, 'Repression, "Terror" and the Rule of Law in England during the Decade of the French Revolution', *The English Historical Review* 100 (1985), pp. 801–825; and Michael Lobban, 'Treason, Sedition and the Radical Movement in the Age of the French Revolution', *Liverpool Law Review* 22 (2000), pp. 205–234. See also the works cited in notes 103 and 104, this chapter.
85 *The Address to the Nation*, p. 4.
86 Paine, *Rights of Man*, p. 264.
87 *The Times*, Issue 3893, May 12, 1797, p. 3, emphasis original.
88 Roy Palmer, ed., *The Valiant Sailor: Sea Songs and ballads and prose passages illustrating life on the lower deck in Nelson's Navy* (Cambridge: Cambridge University Press, 1973), pp. 28–29.
89 *A Narrative of the Mutiny* in *Memoirs of Richard Parker*, p. 14.
90 *A Narrative of the Mutiny* in *Memoirs of Richard Parker*, pp. 15–16.
91 *A Narrative of the Mutiny* in *Memoirs of Richard Parker*, pp. 17–18.
92 MacDougall, 'The Nore Mutiny: Introduction', in *Naval Mutinies of 1797*, ed. Coates and MacDougall, pp. 142–146.
93 Sewell, 'Historical Events'.
94 'A New Song called True Blue' (London, 1780). *Eighteenth Century Collections Online*. Gale. University of Illinois Urbana Champaign. 14 May 2013<http://find.galegroup.com/ecco/infomark.do?&source=gale&prodId=ECCO&userGroupName=uiuc_uc&tabID=T001&docId=CB130522282&type=multipage&contentSet=ECCOArticles&version=1.0&docLevel=FASCIMILE>.
95 David Garrick, *Hearts of Oak* (Edinburgh, 1776).
96 Garrick, *Hearts*.
97 Blackstone, *Commentaries*, vol. 1, p. 395.
98 Blackstone, *Commentaries*, vol. 1, p. 399.
99 Blackstone, *Commentaries*, vol. 1, pp. 399–400.
100 Blackstone, *Commentaries*, vol. 1, p. 400.
101 Blackstone, *Commentaries*, vol. 1, p. 401.
102 Blackstone, *Commentaries*, vol. 1, p. 404.
103 The treason trials have received extensive treatment from John Barrell, *Imagining the King's Death: Figurative Treason, Fantasies of Regicide, 1793-1796* (Oxford: Oxford University Press, 2000). For more on the history of habeas corpus, see Halliday, *Habeas Corpus*. For more on the movement for parliamentary reform, see Albert Goodwin, *The Friends of Liberty: The English Democratic Movement in the Age of the French Revolution* (Cambridge, MA: Harvard University Press, 1979); and H. T. Dickinson, *British Radicalism and the French Revolution* (Oxford: Blackwell, 1985).
104 Although there remain apologists for the British government who argue that liberty and the rule of law were unhindered by the events of the French Revolution, most recent scholarship demonstrates quite convincingly that Pitt's government did use the law to repress political activity deemed threatening to Britain's constitution with varying degrees of success. Clive Emsley, '"An Aspect of Pitt's Terror": Prosecutions for Sedition during the 1790s', *Social History* 6 (1981), pp. 155–184 and Emsley, 'Repression, "Terror"' and the Rule of Law'; Lobban, 'Treason, Sedition and the Radical Movement'; James Measell, 'William Pitt and Suspension of *Habeas Corpus*', *Quarterly Journal of Speech* 60 (1974), pp. 468–476; and Jennifer Mori, *William Pitt and the French Revolution, 1785–1795* (Edinburgh: Keele University Press, 1997).
105 Eighteenth Parliament of Great Britain: first session (27 September 1796–20 July 1797), *The Parliamentary Register*, vol. 2, p. 675.
106 Eighteenth Parliament of Great Britain: first session (27 September 1796–20 July 1797), *The Parliamentary Register*, vol. 2, p. 676.

107 Benefit of clergy was the privilege of exemption from trial by a secular court, allowed to or claimed by clergymen arraigned for felony. By the eighteenth century, the privilege of exemption from the sentence, which, in the case of certain offences, might be pleaded on his first conviction by everyone who could read – OED. The full text of the statutes is in Raithby and Edlyne, *Statutes at Large*, vol. 19, pp. 334–337.
108 Eighteenth Parliament of Great Britain: first session (27 September 1796–20 July 1797), *The Parliamentary Register*, vol. 2, p. 678.
109 Eighteenth Parliament of Great Britain: first session (27 September 1796–20 July 1797) *The Parliamentary Register*, vol. 2, p. 688.
110 Eighteenth Parliament of Great Britain: first session (27 September 1796–20 July 1797) *The Parliamentary Register*, vol. 2, pp. 689–690.
111 Hussain, *Jurisprudence of Emergency*.
112 Eighteenth Parliament of Great Britain: first session (27 September 1796–20 July 1797) *The Parliamentary Register*, vol. 2, p. 691.
113 Eighteenth Parliament of Great Britain: first session (27 September 1796–20 July 1797) *The Parliamentary Register*, vol. 2, p. 693.
114 Beattie, *Crime and the Courts in England*, pp. 554–559.
115 Eighteenth Parliament of Great Britain: first session (27 September 1796–20 July 1797) *The Parliamentary Register*, vol. 2, p. 693. A letter from one V. V. to Lord Chancellor Thurlow (1731–1806) dated June 8, 1797 expressed a similar sentiment. The letter's author called 'This bill in Parliament ... premature; coertion in a declaration without the means, is a greater proof of distraction than discretion. Miles, 'A Letter', *Mariner's Mirror*, p. 200.
116 Eighteenth Parliament of Great Britain: first session (27 September 1796–20 July 1797) *The Parliamentary Register*, vol. 2, p. 694. Despite his objections to these provisions in the bill, Sheridan did not vote against it. He abstained in order 'not to interrupt [Parliament's] unanimity' 'on a subject ... of the most serious importance' (p. 694). On the first barracks, see T. H. McGuffie, 'Early Barrack Life', *The Army Quarterly* 54 (1947), pp. 65–68.
117 Eighteenth Parliament of Great Britain: first session (27 September 1796–20 July 1797) *The Parliamentary Register*, vol. 2, pp. 699–700.
118 Eighteenth Parliament of Great Britain: first session (27 September 1796–20 July 1797) *The Parliamentary Register*, vol. 2, p. 700.
119 Eighteenth Parliament of Great Britain: first session (27 September 1796–20 July 1797) *The Parliamentary Register*, vol. 2, p. 701. Sheridan's argument and Pitt's response were part of a much larger discussion of law making and legal reform of the 'Bloody Code' in the late eighteenth century. For more see, Radzinowicz, *History of English Criminal Law*; Beattie, *Crime and the Courts*; and Hay, 'Property, Authority, and the Criminal Law', in *Albion's Fatal Tree*.
120 H. T. Dickinson, 'The Political Context', in *Cambridge Companion*, ed. Clemit, p. 13.
121 Blackstone, *Commentaries*, vol. 1, p. 407.
122 13 Geo. II c. 3. Blackstone, *Commentaries*, vol. 1, p. 407.
123 7&8 Will. III c. 21 abolished by 9 Ann c.21. Blackstone, *Commentaries*, vol. 1, pp. 407–408.
124 Paul Conner, '"Maynard" Unmasked: Oglethorpe and Sharp versus the Press Gangs', *Proceedings of the American Philosophical Society* 111 (1967), pp. 199–211.
125 Christopher Magra, 'Anti-Impressment Riots and the Origins of the Age of Revolution', *International Review of Social History* 58 (2013), pp. 131–151. For more on impressment and resistance to it, see Denver Alexander Brunsman, *The Evil Necessity: British Naval Impressment in the Eighteenth-Century Atlantic World* (Charlottesville, VA: University of Virginia Press, 2013); Robert Burroughs, 'Sailors and Slaves: The "Poor Enslaved Tar" in Naval Reform and Nautical Melodrama', *Journal of Victorian Culture* 16 (2011), pp. 305–322; Keith Mercer, 'Northern Exposure: Resistance to Naval Impressment in British North America, 1775–1815', *The Canadian Historical Review* 91 (2010), pp. 199–232; and Rogers, *Press Gang*.

126 Nicholas Rogers, 'Vagrancy, Impressment and the Regulation of Labour in Eighteenth-Century Britain', *Slavery and Abolition* 15 (1994), p. 109.
127 R. M. S. Pasley, *Private Sea Journals, 1778–1782* (London: J. M. Dent and Sons, 1931), p. 61.
128 Spencer Childers, ed., *A mariner of England: an account of the career of William Richardson from cabin boy in the merchant service to warrant officer in the royal navy (1780 to 1819) as told by himself* (London: J. Murray, 1908), pp. 292–293. I am grateful to Emma Goldsmith for this reference.
129 Christopher Lloyd, *The British Seaman, 1200–1860: A Social Survey* (London: Collins, 1968), p. 294.
130 'The Muse's Friendly Aid', in Gill, *The Naval Mutinies*, p. 387.
131 'Song', in *The Oxford Book of Sea Songs*, ed. Roy Palmer (Oxford: Oxford University Press, 1986), p. 164. Another version with slightly different wording appears in Bennett, *British War Poetry in the Age of Romanticism*, pp. 122–123.
132 'Whilst Landsmen Wander', in Gill, *The Naval Mutinies*. pp. 388–389.
133 TNA, ADM 1/5125, Address by the representatives of the mutineers at the Nore, 7 June 1797.
134 Emma Christopher, *Slave Ship Sailors and Their Captive Cargoes, 1730–1807* (Cambridge: Cambridge University Press, 2006); and Marcus Rediker, *The Slave Ship: A Human History* (New York: Viking, 2007).
135 Rennell, *The ruinous effects of faction, discord, and mutiny*. In *The World in Play: Portraits of a Victorian Concept* (Palo Alto: Stanford University Press, 2012) Matthew Kaiser argues that in the early nineteenth century nautical melodrama expressed both extreme patriotism and a critique of the bureaucratic state and the abuses suffered by sailors. Chapter 2, especially p. 71.
136 Rennell, *The ruinous effects of faction, discord, and mutiny*, p. 7.
137 Rennell, *The ruinous effects of faction, discord, and mutiny*, p. 18.
138 Rennell, *The ruinous effects of faction, discord, and mutiny*, p. 19.
139 Rennell, *The ruinous effects of faction, discord, and mutiny*, p. 19.
140 Rennell, *The ruinous effects of faction, discord, and mutiny*, p 19.
141 Rennell, *The ruinous effects of faction, discord, and mutiny*, p. 20.
142 Rennell, *The ruinous effects of faction, discord, and mutiny*, pp. 21, 22.
143 For a study of European nationalism at this time, see Otto Dann and John Dinwiddy, eds., *Nationalism in the Age of the French Revolution* (London: Hambeldon, 1988).
144 Rennell, *The ruinous effects of faction, discord, and mutiny*, p. 21.
145 Rennell, *The ruinous effects of faction, discord, and mutiny*, p. 21.
146 Rennell, *The ruinous effects of faction, discord, and mutiny*, p. 29.
147 Rennell, *The ruinous effects of faction, discord, and mutiny*, p. 9.
148 Rennell, *The ruinous effects of faction, discord, and mutiny*, p. 9.
149 For more on the ways in which the government restricted liberties and intruded on private lives in this period, see John Barrell, *The Spirit of Despotism: Invasions of Privacy in the 1790s* (Oxford: Oxford University Press, 2006). Rennell saw religion as another effective means of containing the passions. Although he had long objected to any British measures for Catholic Emancipation and his opinions on the subject remained steadfast during the French Revolution, Rennell, like Burke, defended Catholic priests who took refuge in England during the Revolution and warned of the dangers of atheism, 'the most certain road to anarchy'. He predicted that removing the framework of Christianity and its emphasis on 'obedience to Kings and Magistrates' would result in the 'utter subversion of civil society' (p. 14). Burke's defense of the Catholic Church earned him an accusation as a crypto Catholic, Burke, *Reflections*, pp. 145–149.
150 Rennell, *The ruinous effects of faction, discord, and mutiny*, p. 14.
151 Rennell, *The ruinous effects of faction, discord, and mutiny*, pp. 14–15.
152 Rennell, *The ruinous effects of faction, discord, and mutiny*, p. 29. Rennell's words here are printed in an appendix to his sermon where he quoted his own sermon from 1796. The passage conveniently overlooked the religious disagreements with

the Scots which erupted in war in the early 1640s as well as the large number of 'foreigners' who staffed Britain's army and navy at this time

153 Marshall, 'A Nation Defined by Empire'.
154 Edward Hughes, ed. *The Private Correspondence of Admiral Lord Collingwood* (London: Naval Records Society, 1957), p. 82.
155 Hughes, *Collingwood*, p. 85.
156 Hughes, *Collingwood*, p. 85.
157 Hughes, *Collingwood*, p. 85.
158 Hughes, *Collingwood*, p. 85.
159 Stephens and George, *Catalogue of Prints and Drawings*, vol. 7, #9021, p. 354.
160 Burke, *Reflections*, p. 169.
161 Paine, *Rights of Man*, pp. 241–242.
162 *The Trials of Davis, who stiled himself the Captain, and 16 Delegates, Who on Thursday last received Sentence of Death, For Mutiny at Sheerness* (London, 1797), p. 6. I am grateful to Mary Shiavone for this reference.
163 *Memoirs of Richard Parker*, p. 3.
164 *Memoirs of Richard Parker*, p. 5.
165 *Memoirs of Richard Parker*, p. 9.
166 J. A. Sharpe, '"Last Dying Speeches": Religion, Ideology and Public Execution in Seventeenth-Century England', *Past and Present* 107 (1985), pp. 144–167.
167 Eighteenth Parliament of Great Britain: first session (27 September 1796–20 July 1797), *The Parliamentary Register*, vol. 2, p. 432.
168 *Memoirs of Richard Parker*, p. 9.
169 *Bell's Weekly Messenger* (London, England), Sunday, July 2, 1797; Issue 62.
170 *Sussex Weekly Advertiser or Lewes Journal*, Monday, July 3, 1797; Issue 2654.
171 Andrea McKenzie, *Tyburn's Martyrs: Execution in England, 1675–1775* (London: Hambledon, 2007), esp. ch. 7 and McKenzie, 'Martyrs in Low Life? Dying "Game" in Augustan England', *Journal of British Studies* 42 (2003), pp. 167–205.
172 *Bell's Weekly Messenger* (London, England), Sunday, July 2, 1797; Issue 62.

CHAPTER FIVE

Wedding and Bedding: Making the Union with Ireland, 1800

With the passage of the Act of Union (Ireland) (40 Geo. III c. 38) on July 2, 1800 the Irish Parliament abolished itself.[1] Initiated by Britain's Prime Minister William Pitt (1759–1806) in response to British fears of Irish insurrection and the threat of a permanent separation, the Union was precipitated most immediately by the Irish Rebellion of 1798. Even today discussion of the Union is freighted with the complicated, painful, violent, and impassioned relationship between Ireland, England, and the United Kingdom. Up to this point Ireland was a separate kingdom, part of a composite monarchy in personal union with England. As a separate kingdom, it had the privilege of a separate parliament. So while it is perfectly reasonable to describe Ireland as England's first colony, legally it was a separate kingdom with its own parliament, which housed male, Anglo-Irish, Protestant legislators.

The American, French, Irish, and Haitian revolutions of the last three decades of the eighteenth century disrupted imperial expansion, trade, and security and contributed to the urgency with which Britain pursued a union. The mutinies of 1797, discussed in chapter 4, serve as important but by no means unique examples of social and cultural tensions that ignited around the discourse of rights. The French Revolution in particular exacerbated political and sectarian divisions in Ireland and contributed to a cycle of violence, rebellion, and reprisal. Many in the British government concluded that the only effective way to restrain the threat of Irish insurrection was to take full control through union.[2]

The outbreak of war with France in 1793 forced a new perspective on Whitehall. Britain's military throughout the Empire and in the Continental war depended on Irish Catholic troops. In 1797 Pitt began to investigate the possibility of a formal legislative union. With the outbreak of the Irish Rebellion in 1798, George III encouraged his ministers to leverage the bloody Irish uprising into support among

Protestant elites for a formal union.³ Employing the vocabulary of contract, discussions of the Union animated an analogy with marriage.⁴

The Bill that was passed in 1800 was Britain's second attempt to effect union with Ireland. The first plan for union, proposed in the summer of 1798 was modeled on Scotland's Acts of Union passed by the English and Scottish Parliaments in 1706 and 1707 (6 Ann c. 11 and 7 Ann c. 7). It would have appointed commissioners in each county to design the terms of union. Pitt hoped for quick passage and planned to spend as little as possible to ensure its success. Before he could direct the organization of commissions, in January 1799 opponents of union in the Irish Parliament voiced their vociferous hostility to merging Britain and Ireland's legislatures. On January 24, 1799 the Irish House of Commons voted 109 to 104 to purge mention of the king's recommendation of union.⁵

Faced with the humiliation of defeat, Prime Minister Pitt pursued a new strategy. Discarding the commissioners, he designed the Union as a bill that would be passed first by the Irish Parliament and then by the British Parliament. Pitt also abandoned his earlier parsimonious approach: now money was no object. In addition to a fierce propaganda campaign, the government used patronage, borough compensation, and secret service funds to ensure the Bill's passage through monetary rewards and bribes. In a spectacular reversal, a mere 18 months after the first failed attempt, the opposition, which had been so vocal and successful in the first round of the debate, could not disrupt the government's organized and well subsidized efforts.⁶

The Union took effect on January 1, 1801. It shuttered Dublin's Parliament and in exchange expanded London's Parliament by 100 seats reserved for Irish MPs. Ireland's 'Protestant Ascendancy' already barred Catholics from public office, and so all of the new members of London's expanded Parliament were Anglican.⁷ Despite Ireland's Catholic majority, the Act recognized the Anglican Church as the official Church of Ireland. Although Pitt originally hoped to include in the bill the expansion of legal and political rights for Irish Catholics or its promise, Irish Protestants, joined in their opposition by George III, quashed Catholic Emancipation.⁸

A cultural analysis of the debate surrounding the Union in newspapers, pamphlets, literary sources, and images produced between 1798 and 1800 reveals the Union as a defensive effort by the British government hoping to stave off further losses and contain the disorderly mess of an expanding empire grappling with the ideological, imperial, and military implications of the French Revolution. Despite the Bill's eventual passage, the debates it produced gave voice to an active Irish resistance to assimilation as well as a skeptical British public opinion. For most of the Protestant elite involved, these debates did not signal Irish nationalism or a movement for independence. What they did represent is a phenomenological campaign to preserve the space occupied by the Protestant ascendancy in Ireland, a settler colonial hegemony they feared would disappear once the Irish Parliament was folded into Westminster.

These responses pivoted on a debate about Ireland's consent to union with Great Britain quite deliberately framed as a marriage. The metaphor of marriage and family presented the only acceptable language with which to describe the political situation because in the era of the French Revolution the language of sovereignty, nation, and the will of the people summoned radical democracy, precisely what the advocates of union sought to avoid. The language of union, moreover, constituted the queering moment, mapping onto matrimony the political integration of the highest jurisdictions, Ireland's Parliament and the United Kingdom's Westminster, peopled by the male elites of both societies, each the source of law and privilege. Followed to its logical conclusion, this could mean a marriage between two men (Figure 5.1).[9]

I argue that Irish opponents of Union claimed a superior knowledge and understanding of English law and the British constitution. By

Figure 5.1 'An Irish Union!'

asserting its better comprehension of British law, Irish opposition queered the Union by exacerbating the very problems that Pitt's government hoped to resolve with union. My analysis has been guided by queer theory, seeking to destabilize categories and trouble binary oppositions often unsettled by desire. In the debates about the Act of Union desire is omnipresent: Britain's desire for control, order, regularity, and predictability contrasts with Ireland's desire for autonomy and agency. Queer theory materializes the uncontained, overlapping, and untamed contradictions in the story shining a light on precisely those cultural developments absent from the political histories of the Act of Union which often miss the multilayered tensions and contradictions.[10] Teasing out meaning from the sources that record the interactions between nation, colony, and empire, an examination of the Union reveals that their impact was never unidirectional: the very contingent flow of ideas and their unpredictable momentum and direction confused normative relationships and upset power dynamics, calling into question axiomatic truths about who could make law and on what basis.[11]

Just as the analogy of slavery to villeinage rested on consent (see chapter 2), so too did the viability of a comparison between the Union with Ireland and a marriage. In the Somerset case of 1771–1772, the comparison of villeinage and slavery failed because while villeins were said to enter into the feudal arrangement with some measure of consent, even proponents of slavery in the eighteenth century could not argue that anyone would consent to chattel slavery. In the case of Irish Union, the Act's passage would speak Ireland's consent. Even after it was achieved, Union did not resolve the relationship between Britain and Ireland: by closing the Irish Parliament and bringing 100 Irish MPs to London, the British government brought the 'Irish Question' to the metropolitan heart of the Empire with its final outcome still unresolved.[12]

For Irish historians, the Union is the fulcrum of modern Irish history.[13] According to James Kelly 'the historiography of the Act of Union remains one of the most controversial areas of Irish history, and is likely to remain so for at least as long as the Union exists'.[14] Unsurprising given Irish history and politics, most of these political histories square unionists against nationalists. The nationalist historians began to recount the story of union as the ink on the act dried, characterizing it as coerced, forced on the Irish against the will of the people. This interpretation explained that resistance to union among Irish Protestant elites, the failure of the measure in 1799, and the British government's conviction about the urgency of union caused Pitt's British government to resort to bribery and corruption, with the goal of 'extinguishing' a nation.[15] Some of the earliest nationalist histories accused Britain of planning the Union in response to the constitutional developments of 1782 that had granted Dublin parliamentary autonomy for the first time since the fifteenth century. The most extreme accused Pitt of fomenting the rebellion of 1798 in order to frighten Irish aristocrats into giving up the Irish parliament. Most of the nationalist histories of the Act downplayed Catholic support for it.[16]

Unionist historians writing in the nineteenth and twentieth centuries argued that the Act was vital to Ireland's economic and strategic well-being and that in contrast to Protestant opposition to the Bill, Catholic public opinion favored union with Britain. These chroniclers point out that both sides engaged in corruption and that in terms of rights, Catholics enjoyed better treatment after the Act of Union. Regarding security, union represented a defense against internal faction and rebellion as well as the external threat of French encroachment. The unionist authors emphasized the tremendous benefits of Ireland's ties to Britain and the myriad opportunities afforded Irish men and women by the connections of union, especially as a part of the Empire.[17]

G. C. Bolton's landmark study, *The passing of the Irish Act of Union: a study in parliamentary politics* (1966), reframed the discussion of corruption by 'right sizing' the place of patronage, reminding readers and fellow historians of its normative presence in eighteenth-century society and politics. Bolton's work changed the terms of the debate between unionists and nationalists by qualifying the acts of corruption and bribery that facilitated union – including eighteen creations (offices of state often with titles), fifteen promotions in the peerage, seventy-four MPs given jobs, eleven lawyers advanced, ten ecclesiastics advanced, sixteen annuities, boroughs compensated, and parliamentary seats bought – as typical tools of the political process that also expedited union.[18] After 30 years in ascendance, Bolton's thesis faces challenges from discoveries by David Wilkinson of secret service expenditure and evidence of the British government's attempts to hide the monies. The question of the legality of the Act has re-entered the debate.[19]

This chapter focuses on the liminal moment, between the failed first attempt to pass the Act in January 1799 and its eventual passage in June 1800, 18 months later. I consider the legal questions about the legitimacy of the Act of Union from two different perspectives: the first concerns the issue of consent, specifically Ireland's consent to the Union seen as analogous to consent to a contract of marriage. Deliberately framing the Act as a 'union', like a marriage dependent on even the most nominal consent, created the possibility that this consent would be denied. Even the possibility of a rejection revealed the contingency of the situation, allowing a colonial legislature to thwart the Empire, further destabilizing the very hierarchy, domination, and supremacy that Britain sought through the Act. The second part of the chapter analyzes the arguments made about the constitutional legitimacy of the Act, which posited Irish claims to superior knowledge and understanding of English constitutional law. Both views demonstrate the mutually constitutive relationship between law and empire and how metropolitan authorities hoped to use the law to fix relationships of power that would build imperial networks to buttress the Empire.

The failure to pass the Union in 1799 reversed the normal power relationship between metropole and colony. It opened up a space in the eighteen months that followed for the production and circulation of alternative ways of thinking about British authority, sovereignty, and power. These challenges took place through language and imagery taken from a heteronormative context, specifically images and metaphors of marriage, which relied on notions of potency and impotence.

Ireland and England on the eve of Union

Any discussion of the Act of Union must consider the French Revolution as its larger historical context. Republican ideas about rights, representativeness, and the meaning and role of legislative assemblies detailed in chapter 4 permeated both British and Irish popular culture in the 1790s. A new discourse of inherent human rights upended previous conceptions of rights as bestowed by monarchs or social superiors. These ideas circulated through pan-British debating societies that connected radicals in England, Ireland, Scotland, continental Europe, and the Americas. The debates about the *Rights of Man* carried particular resonances in the Irish setting given the history of English colonial violence, land appropriation, and anti-Irish prejudice and discrimination.[20]

The uncertainties surrounding Ireland's economic and constitutional relationship with Britain in the second half of the eighteenth century unsettled Pitt and his administration. As tensions mounted between Britain and its North American colonies before the American War of Independence, Ireland strongly supported the American colonies and especially the rights of colonial legislatures. On the eve of Britain's loss of the thirteen colonies in 1782 the Irish Parliament's demand for legislative independence led to the repeal of Poynings' Law (10 Hen. VII c. 22); Poynings' Law, passed in 1494, had made it unlawful to call the Irish Parliament without the English king's approval and made passage and repeal of any law for Ireland subject to similar royal consent.[21] The Renunciation Act (23 Geo. III c. 28) passed the following year repealed the Declaratory Act (6 Geo. I c. 5) passed in 1719 and acknowledged the exclusive right of Ireland's parliament to legislate for Ireland, granting Irish courts exclusive jurisdiction in Ireland.[22]

This series of events referred to as the 'Constitutional Crisis of 1782' and the new political configuration of ties between Ireland and Britain seemed to indicate a growing separation between the two marked by Ireland's economic prosperity and legislative independence. Irish support for the American colonies over shared grievances about trade and sovereignty precipitated concern about Britain's diminishing political control over Irish policy and apprehension that Ireland would pursue independent policies that might impede British profits. Pitt responded with his 'commercial proposals' in 1784–1785, an attempt to create a more binding relationship, but negotiations about the new fiscal relationship between Britain and Ireland ended in an impasse.[23]

In 1788–1789 the Regency Crisis gave rise to renewed British panic about the possible contingencies of an independent legislature in Dublin. Late in 1788 George III became mentally incapacitated by the effects of porphyria. The Irish opposition, taking its lead from the English Whigs, championed the cause of George, Prince of Wales, and argued for an immediate transfer of all governing power to him. (Pitt too advocated a Regency, but one which limited the powers of the Regent.) For the Whigs in London this would have been a chance to form the ministry; the Irish opposition meanwhile contemplated a more permanent, constitutional separation between Ireland and Great Britain. The situation resolved itself when George III regained his mental capacities in March 1789, but the Crisis evidenced the hazards of an untethered Irish legislature and potentially disruptive political consequences that could intrude on England's domestic situation.[24]

Britain's design for a union with Ireland mirrored similar political integrations or dismemberments taking place across Europe between 1770 and 1815. Tensions between executive powers and representative assemblies led to revolutions in Poland, Belgium, and the Dutch Republic before the outbreak of the French Revolution in 1789. The French Revolution so threatened regimes across Europe that they abolished provincial legislatures in order to eliminate their resistance. Metropolitan centers Geneva, Venice, and Brabant lost their representative bodies as well.[25] James Liversey points out that 'the language of ancient constitutionalism' had become a 'total anachronism' in the face of the expansion of global empires whose executives wished to eliminate intermediary bodies that could interfere with efforts to centralize power.[26] Meanwhile the language of inherent human rights and English liberty popularized by Thomas Paine among others seemed more current, relevant, and effective in securing greater liberties for those individuals and groups to whom they had previously been denied.

The French Revolution intensified conflict between Ireland and Britain.[27] With the outbreak of war in 1793 the radical cause suffered a conservative backlash that forcibly curtailed discussions of political and constitutional reform while economic hardship, political turmoil, and deepening sectarian rifts once again underlined the need to define the parameters of the relationship with Ireland and to ensure Britain's advantage. In 1797 Pitt sent Robert Smith, First Lord Carrington (1752–1838) to Ireland to consult with John Pratt, Earl of Camden (1759–1840) serving as lord lieutenant of Ireland, to investigate possible plans for legislative union.[28]

Then the Irish Rebellion of 1798 broke out in scattered campaigns concentrated in the Down and Antrim in northeast and Kildare and Wexford in the southeast. Between May and September the rebellion claimed 30,000 lives and reconfigured Irish politics and history. Its historiography has evolved over the past forty years: explanations that relied on religious and sectarian divisions have been displaced by evidence of agrarian discontent while other historians have cited mass politicization inspired by the Enlightenment and revolutionary ideology. Recently historians have abandoned these unitary explanatory frameworks and have pointed instead to the multilayered discontents alive within Ireland and between different constituencies as well as the global context of imperial rivalries among European powers during the wars of the French Revolution.[29] As summed up by Ian McBride, the Rebellion 'saw the explosion of all the tensions – Catholic disaffection, Presbyterian radicalism, anti-English patriotism, agrarian discontent, middle-class liberalism, loyalist anxiety, popular sectarianism' – all of the conflicts and divisions that characterized eighteenth-century Ireland.[30]

The 1790s saw the emergence of the Society of United Irishmen under the leadership of Theobald Wolfe Tone who hoped to inaugurate an inclusive Irish nationalism that would bind Catholics, Protestants, and Dissenters.[31] The United Irishmen succeeded in joining forces with the Defenders, a Catholic agrarian society that formed earlier in the eighteenth century to counter economic grievances. However, religious difference ultimately intervened to sever cross-denominational ties. Membership in the Orange Order, which defended Protestant supremacy, the British monarchy, and the Anglican Church, grew to 30,000 by 1797.[32] This mass politicization presented several challenges to Britain's imperial regime. Irish nationalism and separatism undermined the project of Great Britain, while the political groups in Ireland confronted each other with opposing agendas and goals that portended civil war. Irish revolutionaries and reactionaries endangered Britain's imperial aspirations and weakened its war efforts. This risk was embodied by Britain's reliance on Irish men to staff its military forces: one in five Irish men served in the British army between 1793 and 1815. In this context the Act of Union became 'the ultimate security response by the British state to the security crisis of the 1790s'.[33]

In the summer of 1798, in the aftermath of the Irish Rebellion, Pitt and his foreign secretary William Wyndham Grenville (1759–1834) proposed a plan for union that left its design to appointed county commissioners. Acquiescing to the objections of Irish Protestant politicians eager to preserve their legal privileges by maintaining existing limits on Catholic rights, the provision for Catholic Emancipation was purged. Although doing so lost the Pitt administration any support for the Bill among Ireland's Catholics, union without emancipation preserved its biggest appeal for Ireland's Protestant elite: namely their coalition with the Protestant majorities in England, Scotland, and Wales. The measure's failure in January 1799 has been attributed to the lack of specifics about the terms of the agreement, the lack of compensation promised to borough proprietors for their seats, and the disrespectful way in which Pitt and his ministry handled their limited consultation with Irish MPs in the autumn of 1798.[34]

When union failed in January 1799, Pitt replaced the commissioners with union in two Acts. In addition to patronage, borough compensation, and secret service funds, the government funded an aggressive propaganda campaign that produced and circulated pamphlets, broadsides, songs, and cartoons, flooding the publishing markets in London and Dublin. The pamphlets, penned by prominent members of the Irish Protestant elite and including some Catholic voices, argued the merits of union. This deliberate pamphlet war, instigated by the British government's agents in Ireland and funded by Westminster, touted the legal, economic, political, and diplomatic advantages of union.[35]

Marriage and evidence of consent

While some scholarship has argued that Britain preferred informal colonial rule, the Act of Union demonstrates a forceful initiative to solve the problem of colonial legislative authority, competition, and resistance through integration. As long as Ireland, a colonial space, retained even a modicum of legislative independence, the possibility remained that it could wreak havoc on Britain's interests. Like the many-headed hydra, the disruption could emerge from one of several arenas.[36] Based just on the thirty years before Union, Irish manufacturing might threaten British economic interests. Irish republican affinities might spark further rebellion, or the Irish Parliament could threaten the government's balance of power as had so nearly happened during the Regency Crisis of 1788. The Act's name then – the Union – offers the analogy to marriage and suggests the solution to these centripetal forces.

The Act's Preamble promised to 'strengthen and consolidate the connection between the two kingdoms' and to 'promote and secure the essential interests of Great Britain and Ireland, and to consolidate the strength, power, and resources of the British Empire'.[37] To effect the merger of the British and Irish Parliaments so necessary for Britain's imperial project and so desired by some Irish elites, the legal instrument to which the architects of the Act turned was contract. All contracts rested on the principle of consent, so the problem remained: how to obtain the consent of the Irish Parliament? Securing Irish consent would require the Irish Parliament to vote itself out of existence at a time when ideas about representativeness, inherent human rights, and national sovereignty were expanding. This context made the consent sought in the contract more contingent, with the very real possibility of refusal.

Contemporaries often referred to the Union with Scotland in 1707 when debating the Union of Ireland with Great Britain. Despite the different historical circumstances surrounding these two instances of early modern incorporation, they shared important similarities. Westminster initiated both of the final attempts at union prompted by economic competition that interfered with English dominance in manufacturing and shipping. In both the threat posed by France spurred action, and war with France formed the background of the negotiations. Like Ireland, Scotland too was perceived by England as interfering in the royal succession when in 1701 they resisted the Act of Settlement (12 & 13 Will. III c. 2), which assured the Hanoverian succession. In both cases union depended on the collaboration of indigenous advocates who cooperated with London's agents to force the union through with the help of financial and political incentives and extensive propaganda campaigns. Both Unions failed on their first try, at least in part as a consequence of English inattention to detail and disrespect; but in each case, the opposition forces successful in the first instance suffered from disorganization and an inability to resist union once the British government threw its superior resources into the project. Accusations of corruption and illegitimacy tainted both.[38]

Political union with Scotland created tense ties between England and the kingdom to the north that often frayed as religious, cultural, and economic differences pulled the English and the Scots in different directions.[39] Throughout the first half-century of the Union with England many Scots believed that they had the worst part of the bargain, and some Scots turned to the Jacobites, espousing support for the restitution of the Stuart dynasty under the leadership of first the Old Pretender

(James Francis Edward Stuart, 1688–1766) and then Charles Edward Stuart (the Young Pretender, 1720–1788). This resistance coalesced in the risings of 1715 and even more dramatically during the reign of George II in the 1745 rebellion, as Jacobite troops came within 140 miles of London before their defeat at Culloden.[40] But a lot had changed by the end of the century and in the discussions of union with Ireland, these historical details of conflict and resentment were occluded, replaced with images of Scottish economic success, imperial achievement, and political access and influence at the highest levels of government.

After the failure of union in Ireland's Parliament, the Scotsman Henry Dundas, Pitt's close friend and advisor, as well as a fellow politician and a strong supporter of union, addressed the House of Commons in Westminster. In his speech on February 7, 1799 Dundas reminded his colleagues that:

> When Gentlemen pretended to think lightly of the sacrifices of Scotland compared with those of Ireland, let them recollect, that Ireland had not for many centuries been free or independent of England, but that Scotland never was completely subdued or under the control of England; – that Scotland gave up, what Ireland cannot give up, an independent Parliament of King, Lords, and Commons; – and that Scotland gave up what Ireland *cannot* give up, an *independent* and *separate* crown![41]

Dundas accentuated the biggest perceived difference between the two Unions: in comparison to Ireland, Scotland emerged more independent, civilized, and powerful.[42] While not exactly England's co-equal in the negotiations for union, Dundas' rise to power in the English cabinet and his proximity to Pitt and to the king (along with a group of other Scots discussed in chapter 3) supported the contention that Scotland suffered no loss of power through union.

Dundas is ubiquitous in the images surveyed here, and he represents the perceived successes of Union with Scotland. As a member of Pitt's administration, he served as secretary of state for war, treasurer of the navy, and chairman of the Board of Control, which carried almost all of the responsibilities of the secretary of state for India. Throughout these images in support of Irish union, he peddles privileges and patronage, always favoring Scottish interests. In many of the prints Dundas urges the Irish to Union on the grounds that it will redound to their benefit the way it already has for the Scots. His frequent appearances in the prints suggest imperial rivalry, tension, and competition with a comparison of the two unions a pervasive referent. Dundas heralds his complicity with the British government like other colonial elites who benefitted from the imperial project. He remains for an English audience the interloper who beckons other undeserving outsiders to enjoy the fruits of British prosperity. To an Irish reader he might very well have discredited his own advice about the benefits of union, signaling a pecking order within the British hierarchy that placed the Irish in a subordinate role, at best an aspirational realm of prosperity and power.[43]

The iconographic representations of the two Unions are strikingly different: absent from the depictions of Union with Scotland is the conjugal imagery so pervasive in depictions of the Act of Union with Ireland that we will examine below. Instead references to the Scottish Union feature on coins and medals that portray Queen Anne as the defender of the new United Kingdom. Dundas did not frame the Union with Scotland around the question of Scotland's consent, nor did he mention English appropriation of Irish land, the establishment of the Ulster plantations in the seventeenth century, or the encouragement of Protestant migration to Ireland. This contentious and violent historical context accounted for some of the differences between the two Unions. Dundas and by extension the comparisons with the Scottish Union signaled the power differentials surrounding the Union between Great Britain and Ireland and Ireland's consent to the match.

In contrast the pamphleteers commissioned by Pitt's government during this pivotal eighteen-month period compared the Irish Union to marriage promising disingenuously that a merger would strengthen each of the parties. One pamphlet written in 1799 as a letter to John Foster (1740–1828) who led the opposition to union in the Irish Parliament, described the two, Britain and Ireland, as 'divided and distinct'. The author claimed that:

> union alone by consolidating the interests of both, each conceding and each embracing, can substantiate the power of either; resembling two flames, that by meeting become one, and burn the stronger and the brighter for their union. Such, Sir, would be the marriage of Great Britain and Ireland, who would then form one family living in one house, and having but one interest, with that interest directed to their common advantage.[44]

The analogy to family is a familiar trope and one that had great portability.[45] The quotation reveals the anxiety surrounding this particular relationship in 1799 gesturing at the dangerous contingencies that would result if each member of this union behaved independently, unconfined by a framework of family, its hierarchies, shared obligations, and responsibilities. Marriage would provide this framework. Everyone at the time would have understood that according to legal theory marriage suspended a wife's independent existence: when a woman married, she became a *feme covert* and she ceased to exist as a legal actor.[46] While Irish constituents may have balked at the prospect of their coverture,

English prejudices against the Irish and their inherently inferior intelligence, indolence, and incivility fueled apprehensions about union. Both sides then met the prospect of union and the blended family with hostility at worst, ambivalence at best.

However, to be legally binding a marriage contract relied on the consent of both parties. Legal commentators discussed the relationship between marriage and consent at some length. In his discussion of 'Espousals ... a mutual Promise of a future Marriage', John Ayliffe explained in 1726 that:

> this Promise must be mutual ... 'tis not sufficient for either of the Parties to promise alone singly: And, therefore (for Example) if the Man says to the Woman, I promise that I will marry thee; and the Woman does not promise the like to a Man, this is a Contract that walks upon one Leg; and consequently, not of any Force in Law. And so vice versa, if the Woman promises, and not the Man, it shall be deem'd a lame Contract, Nor is the silent Party in this Case presum'd to consent; unless such Consent appears either by Words, or (at least) by sufficient Conjectures.[47]

Ayliffe expounded on this point when he listed among the conditions that limit the 'Effects of Espousals' 'want of Consent, occasion'd by Fear, Madness, Drunkenness, and so on I say in these and the like Cases Espousals have no Effect'.[48] A contract created an obligation between the parties. In order for a contract to be both legal and binding, both parties had to enter it voluntarily, without compulsion or coercion. Children, drunks, and the mentally ill or incapacitated were considered unable to enter a contract because of their impaired ability to understand the obligation to which the contract bound them.[49] Given changing attitudes about affect and marriage and the expansion of the discourse of rights, by the end of the eighteenth century a woman's nominal consent was considered essential to legitimate a marriage contract.[50] In seeking the passage of the Act from the Irish Parliament, Pitt's government opened a space in which the subordinate party might speak and introduce contingencies that changed the terms of negotiation in unpredictable ways.

In March 1799 in the wake of the failure of the first attempt at union, *The Times* of London published a fabricated letter to John Bull considering how Britain might secure Ireland's consent. Dated February 6, 1799 (a week after the measure's failure), the letter promised to respond to Bull's request for advice on 'selecting a partner for life'. His friend concluded that John had been 'too precipitate in this affair'. Although moved by 'love for the beautiful Orphan, and the generous wish that she should possess an equal share in your estate, money, and rank in life', the friend told John 'You should first have secured her affections, and then have solicited her permission to apply to her guardians for their consent.'⁵¹ In the face of Bull's rejection 'by the young and haughty fair' and the government's failure to push Union through the Irish Parliament, the writer advised him to 'break off the match at once' and 'wait one year longer'. In the meantime the author reassured Bull that Charles Cornwallis (1738–1805), former military leader of the British forces in the American war, who had served as governor-general of India before assuming the position of lord lieutenant of Ireland, will 'continue to prevent the approach of your rival'. This last reference to a French invasion reminds us that war loomed in the background of the debate about union – many believed that Britain had only the most tenuous hold on law and order in Ireland, where the memory of rebellion was fresh and rumors circulated about the possible revitalization of the United Irishmen and their cause.

The letter concluded with a caution:

> An Atheist, professed Libertine, Polygamist, or one who claims a right to divorce his wives *ad libtum*, can never be chosen partner of the innocent and delicate Irene. It must appear to all the world that in this marriage you can have no interested views, since your bride will bring you no acquisition of fortune, since it will be settled on her and her heirs, whilst she will share all your immense riches, power, and consequence.⁵²

The author counseled perseverance. In order to secure Ireland's assent, Britain was to preserve the appearance of disinterest and maintain the fiction that Britain would gain nothing from union and that Ireland brought no wealth or 'acquisition of fortune', to the match. Only such a posture would elicit Ireland's sincere and uncoerced consent.

The title of this chapter is taken from a poem by T. Canning published in 1800 after the Act had passed: *The Wedding and Bedding: or, John Bull and his bride fast asleep. A satirical poem. Containing, an history of the happy pair, From their Infancy to the present Period. With Reasons for, and Means used to accomplish their Union. Also, the matchmakers matched; with their rueful lamentation for the loss of the bride cake.* The groom, introduced as John Bull, 'a man of trade', 'of a copious race', has so many biological connections 'there's scarce a family, or name, with which he may not kindred claim'.⁵³ Despite his general longstanding good health, the poem explained that 'his late intrigues' have 'impair'd' him and 'matters are not right within'. In contrast to the thriftiness that characterized him in the past when he was 'rich in health in wealth and fame',⁵⁴ recent financial problems have beset him because of 'clerks, who have a bankrupt made him'.⁵⁵ The poem accounts for this reversal of fortune as a consequence of the ill advice of 'greedy Fav'rites', excessive spending, 'pride', and the pursuit of 'new farms on every side' clarified in the footnote as 'passions for colonization and foreign conquests',[56] including the establishment of an English colony in Ireland.[57] According to the poem, Britain's loss of the American colonies, the push for parliamentary reform, and Pitt's ministerial career exacerbated Bull's financial misfortunes even before the French Revolution and war with France.[58]

John Bull's longstanding 'mistress', Ireland, who 'possess'd some fertile lands. On which he hop'd to lay his hands', 'often shar'd her bed' but had 'hitherto refus'd to wed'.[59] A footnote provides a gloss of the metaphor: 'invaded, and submitted to the introduction of colonies, but retained her own legislature'.[60] A quick summary of England's relationship with Ireland concludes that 'though he (John Bull) thus became ascendant, She'd (Ireland) fain continue independent'.[61] According to the poem the constitutional changes of 1782, referred to as Erin's liberation, brought prosperity and the peaceful coexistence between Catholics, English Protestants, and Presbyterians.[62] Ireland seemed to have all of the advantages at this point: 'fertile fields', 'corn and cattle all around No better land is to be found', 'her grain, her butter, pork and beef', along with an 'abundant' supply of milk, fowl, eggs, and fish.[63]

Meanwhile John Bull, 'Deceiv'd in every thing attempted His credit sunk and coffers emty'd', 'fixes on the present marriage To compensate his past miscarriage'.[64] John Bull eyed 'the bride's possessions;' and schemes to 'make her So poor that no gallant will take her'.[65] Despite Irish protestations, the union was made through Pitt's 'cunning' with the slogan 'divide and conquer'.[66] The poem attributed the rise of sectarianism and the resulting Irish Rebellion of 1798 to Pitt and the desire for union. The Union, riddled with bribes and personal vote buying deals, has Erin so 'Scar'd night and day, with these pretences' that she 'almost lost her senses'.[67] In her depressed and fearful state, concerned for her health and her financial well-being, she acquiesced, explaining that 'By marriage might be all reliev'd; Her faithful Bull's protecting arms Would save her from impending harms; Return her children to their duty, And renovate her health and beauty.'[68]

Union forces 'Resolve to drown her feeble voice; and just for form, with answer ready, They put the question to the lady. She shudders, groans, attempts a nay; The vast Rotunda rings with AYE!'[69] The poem makes explicit Ireland's forced consent: 'This fatal word [referring to AYE], with instant blow, For ever lays her glories low.' Her submission secured, Erin's 'death-struck hand they seize, and lead To sign and seal the nuptial deed'.[70]

Stripping Erin of both material wealth and political agency, the marriage initiates an appropriation of property and sovereignty: 'They Erin's moveables secure; And take, as she no more will need 'em, The seals and badges of her freedom.'[71] All of her assets now confiscated by John Bull 'trophies of her ancient house, Must now be quartere'd by her spouse;' 'And ev'ry think that's worth a Crown They carry to his house in town.' As in any literary tragedy, the winners suffer for their crimes: John Bull 'listless' as the French Wars continued, Pitt's success in union followed by his resignation.[72] These hardships foreshadow the image that concludes the poem: a funeral pyre to which 'the victim fair is urg'd along'. As the flames engulf her, she 'yields her charms to her dead husband's putrid arms'.[73]

This is by no means a story of a marriage that followed full consent. At every turn the author reminds the reader about Britain's desire to seize and control Ireland's wealth, the corruption that brought about the Union, and the coercion that precipitated Ireland's ultimate assent. The references to Erin's confusion and her 'almost lost senses' introduce questions about her state of mind and the clarity of her thinking that gesture at discussions in the legal scholarship about whether a person who is *non compos mentis* can enter into a contract or be bound by one. The poem ultimately predicts that a forced union will result in Ireland's annihilation and Britain's decline and destabilization.

A series of broadsides published in the format of playbills in early 1800 also commented negatively on the union as a marriage. The first, advertising a 'Pantomimical, Serio-Comic olio' titled 'The Forced Marriage; or, the Humbugged Islanders', promised a performance 'for the benefit of Mrs. Ireland' on January 15.[74] The title clearly heralded the Union as an act of British aggression with Ireland as its victim. The Irish people have been tricked into cooperating by a hoax: the false promise of advancement.

The playbill series continues with the promise of a second performance on February 5 featuring 'An entirely new Change of Amusements, with several new Performers' in 'a grand Serio-Comic Pastichio, called, the Rape of Ierne or Fidelity Betrayed'. This entertainment 'for the benefit of the Great Mrs. Britain featured Tarquinius Brutus played by Mr. Bull (from the British Theater)' while Mr. Reaycastle, a clear transposition of the syllables in Robert Stewart, Viscount Castlereagh and Second Marquis of Londonderry (1769–1822), an Irish MP and a strong proponent of union, 'performs Filius Falsus'.[75] The February performance cast Britain as the unambiguous dominatrix; the references to rape and betrayal produce a harsh tone leaving little doubt about who controlled the process and who the beneficiary of union would be. Ireland is silenced and the question of consent overridden by coercion. The show promised to conclude with 'a grand Display of the new Political Steam-Engine; or, Civilizing Machine, for Britainizing the wild Irish' that would end with 'a harsh Concert of Woeful and Detrimental Music'.[76]

The series of playbills culminated with the 'great Mrs. Britain's second benefit', a performance called 'Self-Immolation, or, the Wise Men of Gotham' scheduled for a week later on February 12, 1800. Gesturing to the imperial context and competitive colonial jockeying, the segment, titled 'Erin Lie Down' by Mr. Macfarlane, would feature highland bagpipes accompanied by the Welch harp while 'Mrs. Senate will sing the Plaintive Song of "Dublin Farewell".' The performance would end with 'splendid pantomime called Ambition at all Risks, or the Emperor of the Western Isles' featuring 'A Triumphal Entry and Procession of Khan Logg mounted on an Elephant, Receiving the Homage of his Western Vassals, and a Striking Perspective seen, finely executed in fret work of Rome in Flames and Nero, playing on his lyre'.[77] Casting indignant outrage on Britain's imperial reach and it domination and oppression of its colonial subjects, this last performance, like the conclusion of *Wedding and Bedding*, foreshadowed Britain's undoing, predicting that the Empire would share Rome's doomed fate, a well-known and frequently circulated trope. Absent any pretense of consent on Ireland's part, the playbills instead announce Ireland as a victim of deception, rape, and suicide.

Visual evidence of consent

The sources examined so far have represented the metaphor of union between Ireland and England as a conventional marriage between a man and a woman cast in traditional heteronormative gender roles with Ireland's consent secured as a combination of English 'cunning'[78] and Irish fear and anxiety which resulted in a 'Forced Marriage'.[79] An analysis of gender and sexuality as deployed in the visual evidence lends another perspective to the issue of consent.[80] Britain is usually featured as a man, a sailor and soldier in 'The Mad Music Master' (1799?–1801) (Figure 5.2),[81] as John Bull an uncouth host in 'Miss Hibernia at John Bull's Family Dinner' (March 18, 1799),[82] or as a lecherous and grotesque male figure in 'Marriage Against Inclination: A Step to Separation' (March 1, 1800).[83] Erin, or Miss Hibernia as she is sometimes called, performs Ireland with reserve or indignation, well dressed and statuesque in 'The Mad Music Master'; a helpless and passive bride in 'Carrying the Union' (1800) (Figure 5.3),[84] a simple housewife in 'John Bull Shewing his Intended Bride the Parliament House' (April 30, 1800) (Figure 5.4).[85]

But the images are supple and their creators often bend gender expectations and roles. For instance, in the James Gillray (1756–1815) print 'Horrors of the Irish-Union' (1798) (Figure 5.5), a female Britain entices Pat as a seductive woman or as a willing servant maid in

Figure 5.2 'The Mad Music Master'

Figure 5.3 'Carrying the Union'

Figure 5.4 'John Bull Shewing his Intended Bride the Parliament House'

BRITAIN AND ITS INTERNAL OTHERS, 1750–1800

Figure 5.5 'Horrors of the Irish-Union'

'Union between England and Ireland' (Figure 5.6) (February 20, 1799).[86] When Ireland is male, he is a stout and simple Paddy in 'Horrors of the Irish Union', a soldier who has lost one leg in 'Union between England and Ireland', an impoverished and sad looking young man in *Party's Not Agreed* (1800) (Figure 5.7), or an enormous but seemingly sympathetic figure in 'An English Twig and an Irish Shillelee!!' (March 1800) (Figure 5.8).[87] According to one couplet called 'Impromptu on the Irish Union' quoted in *The Times* on January 31, 1799 (presumably to explain why the Irish Parliament rejected union) Paddy is such a simpleton that 'when you talk about Union, it Paddy perplexes: He knows of no union – but that of the Sexes!'[88] This depiction of Paddy signals a question of competence and his fitness to enter into a contract.[89]

Although 'Union between England and Ireland' published in February 1799 portrays Ireland as lustfully and happily engaged, most of the prints picture Ireland spurning Britain's affections while Britain plays the aggressor who initiates and strives to control the process.[90] This is especially true in the four images published in the *Hibernian Magazine* between January 1799 and April 1800: 'The Union Olio', *Hibernian Magazine*, February 1799; 'The Children of Erin Seeking Protection from their Foster Father', *Hibernian Magazine*, April 1799; 'Ways and Means or Vox Populi!!', *Hibernian Magazine*, February 1800; and

[210]

Figure 5.6 'Union between England and Ireland'

Figure 5.7 'Party's Not Agreed'

'Marriage Against Inclination: A Step to Separation', *Hibernian Magazine*, April 1800. According to Dorothy George, 'the opposition to the Union by the *Hibernian Magazine* was almost confined to its plates'.[91] Nonetheless, the images from the *Hibernian Magazine* convey unabashed opinions through a raw artistic style. Rendered with less artifice, they seem deliberately less sophisticated than the English prints, the individuals depicted less attractive and more crudely drawn. No pretense is made of the art – the very ugliness of the images and those who peopled it may have captured the eye and ensured that the copious words that appear in each image received the reader's full attention. The style adopted by these artists suggests an unvarnished, less mediated message that communicates the urgency of the political question in a dramatic contrast with the refined and more distant style of the English prints.

Most of the artists held generally conservative views, especially on the question of constitutional reform. While they did not necessarily express their own opinions in their work, they summarized popular opinion and presented it to political elites in the prints.[92] What we see in the images of the Act of Union corroborates H. T. Dickinson's claim that illustrators, including those with more conservative views, sought to convey the perception that Irish union was accomplished through

Figure 5.8 'An English Twig and an Irish Shillelee!!'

a sleight of hand. In some of the images the union is portrayed as an event thrust on an unknowing people while in others the Irish actively resist it. When Irish opinion of the union is represented, it is decidedly negative.

Most of the visual sources, satiric prints produced in 1798–1800 as the debates over the Union unfolded, were published first in English newspapers (which also circulated in Ireland); many had Irish counterparts and a minority appeared only in Irish newspapers. According to Dickinson the prints produced in England at the end of the eighteenth century spoke to political elites and the literate middling sorts. The number in circulation was quite modest – especially those published as broadsides – with 500–1500 a typical run. Those that appeared in newspapers and magazines circulated more widely: newspaper circulation grew tremendously over the second half of the eighteenth century with annual sales increasing from 7 million in 1750 to 16 million in 1801.[93]

This assessment of caricatures and their somewhat modest influence and impact has been revised by Diane Donald who argues for their global circulation in print and in material culture. Read and consumed by both men and women across the socio-economic scale, caricatures extended political consciousness, participation, and debate in the second half of the eighteenth century and especially in the 1790s.[94] We get an idea of the diversity of the readership, the method of delivery, and its reception in the 'Caricature Shop' (1801) (Figure 5.9).[95] The mixed audience includes white men and women, old and young, a person of color, rich and poor, able bodied and disabled. The image confirms Donald's contention that 'the caricature prints once formed a living part of everyday experience in Georgian Britain' and that they 'permeated the national consciousness far more widely and deeply than has been suspected'.[96]

With the tremendous growth in newspapers and their circulation at the end of the eighteenth century scholars credit the press with broadening the discussion of politics and facilitating public debate of policy. Contemporaries valued newspapers as sources of information and as venues for debating the significant issues of the day; they considered England's free press (along with the jury) fundamental to English liberties.[97] The press shaped public opinion which by the 1790s 'had acquired a pronounced and legitimate role' in political discourse.[98] The popularity and currency of caricature prints, 'a quintessentially British art form', increased with the expansion of the press, parliamentary reporting, and a growing political awareness. They amplified the circulation of news as well as opinion among their consumers.[99] As in the 'Caricature Shop', the images were often viewed collectively.

Figure 5.9 'Caricature Shop'

Although this kind of communal readership included newspapers, pamphlets, and magazines that circulated in private clubs, libraries, taverns, and debating societies, I want to think specifically about masculine spaces where mostly men would have seen and interacted with these images: taverns, barbers' shops, brothels, smoking and billiard rooms, men's dressing rooms, bog-houses, domestic male privies, and especially coffeehouses.[100] These images engaged the wealthy Protestants who frequented English coffeehouses: explicitly homosocial spaces populated by elite men denounced as debauched dandies and rakes beset with accusations of effeminacy, foppery, gossip, disrespect for authority, and a frivolous preoccupation with fashion. These men, Irish and English, would have seen themselves in the satiric prints: Protestant elites considering the merger of the highest political bodies in Dublin and London. These renditions of the Act of Union suggest a range of possible responses including discomfort at the power dynamics in the heterosexual marriages of Erin and John Bull; laughter at the ridiculous depiction of Paddy and John Bull at the altar, and ultimately concern that union might disadvantage one or both partners.

The image of a heteronormative and possibly reproductive marriage recurs throughout these images, even as they raise doubts about Hibernia's consent by illustrating her resistance and trepidation. In 'Marriage against inclination' she pulls away from the grotesque image of John Bull, but she is so hemmed in on all sides that there is nowhere to run; a metaphor for Ireland's eventual grudging or coerced consent to union. Perhaps the print's creator saw the handwriting on the wall – this print was published just two months before the Union was passed. Ireland's consent would be secured through the legislative process of passing the Act.

The images of a single-sex union between Paddy and John Bull – so far I have found four – published in the liminal period between the first attempt at union in 1799 and its successful passage in 1800, expressed a very different message about the union as a certain failure because it was pictured as inconceivable and ludicrous. These images reframed heteronormative questions of consent: they represent Britain's quest for consent as not just insincere but unnatural. Calling out union and marriage as a sham, not at all what it claimed to be, these images liken union to joining two partners who cannot be joined.

In 'Paddy's Escape from the Union Net' (1799) (Figure 5.10) Pitt stands holding a net in which Paddy and John Bull are caught. Paddy crawls out of a hole at one end saying 'Good bye Billy honey. Old birds are not caught with chaff.' The implication is that an emasculated Pitt, unable to consummate the marriage, allowed Ireland to escape the confines of the agreement known as the union. While Pitt looks on anxiously, John Bull appears completely unconcerned suggesting indifference or the knowledge that he will eventually prevail.[101]

'An Irish Union!' published on January 30, 1799 just days after the union's first failure, represents the marriage between Pat, who looks suspicious and hostile, and a surprised and confused John Bull. Pitt performs the wedding, putting their hands together and pronouncing 'I join your hands in Friendship and one Interest – and whom I put together – let no man put asunder.' Dundas promises Paddy, who is dressed as a farmer, that 'you will be much happier – and mair independent than ever'. Paddy scowls, looking leery, while John Bull says 'This may be Nation good Fun – but dang my buttons, if I know what it is about! And Cousin Paddy don't seem quite clear in the Case neither.' Nicholas Robinson speculates that the man nearby who holds blankets labeled 'tax on income' may be Pitt's private secretary, Joseph

MAKING THE UNION WITH IRELAND, 1800

Figure 5.10 'Paddy's Escape from the Union Net' (watermarked image)

Smith. In any case, we see displayed Britain's bald pursuit of Ireland as revenue.[102]

Isaac Cruikshank, who drew 'An Irish Union!' in 1799 subtitled it with a reference to Shakespeare: 'If there be no great love in the beginning – Yet heaven may decrease it upon better acquaintance, vide Shakespeare.'[103] To this quotation from the first act of *The Merry Wives of Windsor* (1602) he added a dark prediction: 'when we are married and have more occasion to know one another: I hope, upon familiarity will grow more contempt'.[104] Cruikshank's criticism of union is clear: rather than ameliorating the situation, the subtitle declares in no uncertain terms that a forced marriage between two unwilling partners will only increase the antipathy between them. As if in answer to this accusation, another image depicting two men shows an emaciated Pitt reaching out to 'My Dear Pat' in 'Party's Not Agreed' (1800) asking for his friendship. 'You know what happiness it will be to me to have an Union with you.' Like a besotted lover, he promises that union will bring economic prosperity and offspring: 'I will make you Rich and give you plenty of money and provide for your Children.'[105]

These images of an emasculated Pitt reflected badly on England's masculinity as a whole and signaled self-doubt about Britain's

[217]

feminization through the Union and empire. William Drennan (1754–1820), an Irish Patriot, a founder of the Society of United Irishmen before the Rebellion, and a life-long supporter of parliamentary reform and Catholic Emancipation, expressed similar anxieties about Ireland's masculinity where he referred to Ireland as a 'base Posterior of the world', 'at the back of Europe, hurl'd'.[106] In *A Letter to the Right Honourable William Pitt* (1799), he worried specifically about the Union 'making a capon of our country – an Eunuch of Ireland'. He continued 'Such an insidious and impudent proposal, to swell the loins of the country at the expense of its virility, I think, and I say, should be revolting to the nation, as to a man.'[107] These images suggest a fear of subordination and mutual dependence. In each instance, England's fear of rejection and Ireland's loss of autonomy, inverted gender expectations raised alarm because they signaled weakness.

The homosexual marriage scenes suggest some of the reasons for the failure of the Union in 1799. The reference to cousin Paddy implies an incestuous union too close to be fruitful or generative. Rather than interrogating the actuality and sincerity of consent and the unequal power dynamics inherent in a marriage between a man and a woman, the images eliminate a female figure altogether. Questioning the viability of such a match, they designate the marriage as misguided and improbable. Ireland's resistance of Britain's imperial power is portrayed as successful: a close escape in the one print and a clear rejection of Pitt's offer in the second. Within a discourse of colonialism, the images suggest that this Union is sterile, that is cannot and will not result in the normal outcome of marriage, reproduction, sought from an imperial relationship between metropole and colony. Even with the law attempting to forge these ties in the guise of contract and marriage, the images suggest that these connections will prove fruitless and unproductive. They destabilize and deconstruct the myths of imperial power.

Clearly the images published on both sides of the Irish Sea signaled both British and Irish ambivalence about the contract and the Union. Ireland's participation in the contract assigned her agency and implied her consent, and once the Union passed, even its harshest critics accepted the outcome and did not discuss its annulment or dissolution until later in the nineteenth century.[108] So this was a moment when Britain simultaneously solicited and eliminated Ireland's consent. Securing Ireland's consent was the last occasion on which her opinion would be sought: abolishing the Parliament was supposed to ensure Ireland's subordination. The questions that swirled around this event, this Union, marriage, and contract, and the persistence of Ireland's grudging stance on union reveal Britain's self-doubt and the tradeoffs between contingencies foreclosed and those foreshadowed.

Consent and constitution

The republican ideas and Jacobin discourse that fueled the French Revolution sparked a debate in Britain during the 1790s about governance and the definition of the constitution. Like the images that set the Union in a domestic setting, Edmund Burke too used the analogy of family when he characterized the constitution as an 'inheritance'. He elevated both when he spoke of 'binding up the constitution of our country with our dearest domestic ties; adopting our fundamental laws into the bosom of our family affections'.[109]

Burke and the conservative anti-revolutionaries defended Britain's governing structure and argued against the need for reform because 'in justice to that old-fashioned constitution, under which we have long prospered ... our representation has been found perfectly adequate to all the purposes for which a representation of the people can be desired or devised'.[110] Burke opined that 'from the Magna Carta to the Declaration of Right, it has been the uniform policy of our constitution to claim and assert our liberties ... By this means our constitution preserves an unity in so great a diversity of its parts'.[111] In his defense of the French Parliaments, threatened with 'utter abolition', Burke described these 'venerable bodies' that 'they composed permanent bodies politic, constituted to resist arbitrary innovation; and ... they were well calculated to afford both certainty and stability to the laws'. They provided 'a safe asylum to secure these laws' and 'they kept alive the memory and record of the constitution'.[112]

In contrast Thomas Paine who advocated reform presented a very different assessment of the place of both constitution and parliament. According to Paine 'a constitution of a country is not the act of its government, but of the people constituting a government'.[113] He asserted that 'there never did, there never will, and there never can exist a parliament, or any description of men, or any generation of men, in any country, possessed of the right or the power of binding and controuling posterity to the "end of time," or of commanding for ever how the world shall be governed, or who shall govern it'.[114] The trials of Thomas Paine in 1792 and John Reeves in 1796 rehearsed the unsettled state of constitutional doctrine in the 1790s, destabilizing William Blackstone's platitudes on the subject. Discussion of the ideological and political ramifications of these debates appeared frequently in the satirical prints of the period.[115]

It is in this context that Irish resistance to the Union offered an even more radical and profound critique of union from a legal and constitutional perspective that called into question the legitimacy of any merger or combination of the two parliaments. While marriage was an easily imagined analogy for the Act of Union, necessitating only each party's consent for its validity, the 'constitutionalists' declared that analogy invalid because the very idea of abolishing one legislative body and merging its members into another presented Ireland a preposterous, unnatural, and false choice that could never exist constitutionally. This thornier, more existential question raised by Irish and even some English lawyers destabilized British rule by asserting a superior legal understanding of the spirit of the British constitution among colonial subjects who reversed the narrative flow by speaking back to metropolitan authorities.[116] Just as the images make visual the contingency and instability of imperial power, so the language of the pamphlets plays with notions of potency and unmanning through the violation of legal doctrine implicit in the signing of Union.

On January 26, 1799 *The Times* published an explication of the ideas and radical politics of Lord Charles Stanhope, Third Earl Stanhope as voiced in his pamphlet *An Address to the Nations of Great Britain and Ireland on the Projected Union* (1799). Stanhope decried union as 'one of the most extraordinary and unconstitutional measures that ever has been agitated, in this, or in any other country, which has any pretence to term itself a free nation' because it would deprive 'the people of Ireland of their separate legislature, by substituting for that national Parliament ... a few votes in a foreign Parliament'. Stanhope's claim that 'a foreign Parliament can never be equally apprised of the feelings, of the sentiments, and the wishes of the Irish nation' insisted on the preservation of an Irish Parliament, exposing his reform agenda, one that was very much influenced by French republican ideas about human rights and national sovereignty.[117]

In a letter to an unnamed MP written in 1799 Henry Maddock (d.1824) an English lawyer, described the Union as 'no less a despotic, than an irrevocable Act ... most unreasonable, most absurd and highly unconstitutional'.[118] He stated quite unequivocally that 'to the Absolute Power of Parliament there is necessarily the following notable exception: it cannot do what it cannot undo. It cannot give validity to an irrevocable Act'.[119] Maddock argued that a law by which 'a Parliament pretends to destroy itself' is no law: consequently, the very Act of Union was illegitimate.[120]

Referencing John Locke on *Civil Government*, Maddock defined the 'power of making laws' as 'a delegated power from the people' and one that cannot and does not transfer.[121] Two concerns propel Maddock's text: the reversibility (or more precisely the irreversibility) of unmaking a legislative body and the transfer of representation from one parliamentary body to another. He asserted that:

> when the people have said, we will submit to rules, and be governed by laws made by such men, and in such forms, nobody else can say other men shall make laws for them; nor can the people be bound by any laws, but such as are enacted by those whom they have chosen, and authorised to make laws for them.[122]

For Maddock the stakes of the discussion were high indeed: the very constitution, its strength, legitimacy, and operability hung in the balance. The constitution bestowed power on legislators, and if they changed it, they threatened the foundation of their own authority. While Maddock acknowledged that Parliament had the legal right to change or amend all but the 'fundamental laws' such as Magna Carta, the Petition of Right, and the Habeas Corpus Act, 'they shall not commit an act *felo de se* and for ever resign their delegated Trust'.[123] To Maddock, such a self-destructive act would imperil a government, 'acting on itself, or attempting to nullify its own essential Constitution'.[124] Quoting legal commentators Edward Coke (1552–1634), Locke, Emmerich de Vattel (1714–1767), and Richard Wooddeson (1745–1822) Maddock declared that they confined the power of Parliament 'to making laws. Can then', he asks 'an act, destroying the Legislature, be denominated a law!'[125]

Citing the changes Parliament had made both to religion and to the royal succession, Maddock acknowledged Westminster's power as arbitrary and capacious, but he insisted on its limit: all acts must be revocable, and this included those of the Irish Parliament. Maddock conceded in his letter that 'means there are, I think, by which the Union may constitutionally proceed to maturity. Let it then be your object to support the Union, but also to respect the Constitution'.[126] Given the Irish Parliament's inability to make an irreversible decision, he advised that 'if you urge the Union forwards, you cannot too cautiously avoid suffering it to flourish on the Ruins of First Principles'.[127] Maddock concluded by declaring the Act of Union illegitimate because a piece of legislation by which 'a Parliament pretends to destroy itself' is no law. He dismissed any analogy with Wales, 'subdued into a Union' or Scotland, whose government he called 'but an Aristocracy, with a spice of Monarchy' and whose 'Constitution, in its bearings and its tendencies' did not at all resemble those of the Irish or British.[128]

Maddock's opinion on the Union fit quite consistently with conservative arguments about constitutional reform made throughout the second half of the eighteenth century. While his focus in this instance was the Act of Union, his position resonated with the conservative position that cautioned against any radical changes and urged instead that all constitutional reforms proceed systemically and slowly in order to ensure the most consistent and legally valid outcome.[129]

Matthew Weld's pamphlet on *Constitutional considerations, interspersed with political observations, on the present state of Ireland* published in 1800 took up the legal issues surrounding the Union from the Irish perspective, its rhetoric explicitly echoing contemporary debates about parliamentary reform and human rights.[130] Weld quoted Richard Price, the champion of the American colonists. As 'the trustees of the nation', he averred that members of parliament who abandoned their duties would 'betray their constituents'.[131] To buttress his argument, Weld invoked several prominent English legal commentators including Blackstone who asserted that the Parliament, English or Irish, 'maintained a perpetual succession, and enjoyed a kind of legal immortality'.[132] With references to Chief Justice John Holt (1642–1710), Locke, and Price, Weld resolved 'From these authorities I am justified in positively denying the power of Parliament. Should they enact a Union, it would be, *ab initio*, nugatory (i.e. self negating) – to speak legally, *it would not be law*; there are bounds beyond which the Parliament cannot pass.'[133] In his rationale Weld fused American and French ideas about inalienable and inherent rights to the British legal and constitutional tradition. Citing these venerable English legal authorities, he appealed to their reputations as the most credible and authoritative sources on the subject. His rhetorical strategy credited Irish critics of union with true apprehension of the real spirit and meaning of the English legal and constitutional tradition, anointing himself and them the guardians of British rights and liberties.

According to Weld 'Parliament alone ... has so long preserved the English, and Irish from slavery.'[134] The Act constituted erratic legislation on Britain's part, a harbinger of tyranny because the annihilation of the Irish Parliament by its own hand could create a precedent that might lead to a similar end for the British legislature. Weld reminded the English of their own history and of the 'stigma' of 'arbitrary princes', 'capricious and evanescent' who defined 'the will of the prince [as] equivalent to law'.[135] Labeling union a Trojan horse, he professed that the English people 'well know that the annihilation of English liberty, must necessarily succeed the destruction of it in Ireland, and they must be convinced, that the Union will prove the curfew of freedom'.[136]

This discussion made unveiled allusions to the issues of constitutional reform and the question of representation that related to consent. Weld queried why Britain did not 'collect the general sense of the people' before moving ahead with this plan. Answering his own question, Weld declared 'they dare not meet the population of Ireland on the dispossession, I pledge myself they dare not'. Instead 'they shrink back, conscious of the abhorrence and loathing of the nation'.[137] His words could caption the images of union when he attributed to Pitt the following lines: 'What you contemptible Colony ... you barbarous, uncivilized state dare you refuse? – it is a measure I desire, no party cabal, no temporary clamour, no loss of popularity, nothing short of the last extremity shall prevent me to accomplish it.'[138]

At the service of his argument were the historical examples of Sweden, the United Provinces, and ancient Rome whose attempts to usurp borderlands by force failed to consolidate power, instead wreaking havoc and heralding the disruption or downfall of conglomerate kingdoms and empires.[139] He cited as positive examples, colonial situations from Greece and Rome, to Spain, Denmark, Sweden, Norway, and Lithuania where imperial powers tolerated the constitutions of their colonial acquisitions.[140] To counter England's justification of the Act as a means 'to restore harmony to the country, put down rebellion and close up the inlet to the enemies of empire', he described the violence, warfare, and rebellion in Wales, Scotland, and Ireland and speculated that union would 'unavoidably create jealousy', 'suspicion', 'discord and distrust'.[141] Weld held up the case of the American colonies 'deprived of a resident legislature' that 'availed themselves of foreign assistance and for ever have shaken off a yoke tyrannical and oppressive'.[142]

Weld wondered at the British legal understandings of the composition of the government: 'how ignorant too must they be of that constitution they are so studious to overturn'. He warned that the advocates of union, 'the champions of unity of power and consolidation of empire' would 'equally argue for the demolition of the constitution of England' if the English Houses of Lords and Commons disagreed on an issue'. He predicted a slippery slope from union to the abolition of the Parliament of Westminster to despotism when 'the will of the prince' would replace rule of law.[143] How ironic to have the Irish colonial subject writing back to the metropole warning of tyranny and despotism, those very forms of government against which Protestant Britain defined itself and by which it justified colonial expansion and colonial government, especially in Catholic Ireland.

Weld lambasted the British initiative for union, its Empire, and its claim to a civilizing mission. At the heart of his critique were the legal means Britain used to materialize its imperial aspirations. Speaking in satire he voiced the pro-Union argument:

> Come, or I will force your assistance to the empire, behold the Welsh have united to England – Scotland has been forced to do the same, why then you Hottentot Nation should you be so prone to Barbarity, so averse to *civilization*, as not to throw your constitution into the common mass, thus consolidating one great empire, unrivalled in home and glory, the deliverer of mankind!!! The safety of nations!! Thus adding wealth, peace, security, stability and permanence to the British Empire.[144]

With this invective Weld spelled out Britain's true imperial intentions: union served the empire's grandiose ambitions while the threats to safety, stability, and security were the real reasons for the pursuit of union. This jurisprudence of emergency gave cover to Britain's unconstitutional amendment.

Weld's reference to the Irish as a 'Hottentot Nation' recalls the image at the start of chapter 1 in which Britannia, the ever-generous mother, shelters and provides for 'vast Swarms of every sort', 'these, of ev'ry Realm the Scum' who beseech her for 'Relief of all their Wants'[145] as well as the depictions of 'wild Irish' in the broadsides discussed above.[146] The resentment of foreigners who consume resources contrasts with their compelled integration by union. Weld presented the pro-Union prejudice about British economic, political, constitutional, and cultural superiority as racialized. His sarcastic tone expressed Britain's surprise about Ireland's reservations: in the speaker's voice, the Irish have nothing to lose with union and everything to gain by it. Given their inferiority, the speaker conveyed his opinion that the Irish should feel lucky that they have this opportunity. Weld's authentic voice then entered the conversation disputing Ireland's need for civilization. He remarked that complicated laws were considered a sign of civility. Ireland's sacrifice of the capacity to make laws through union and the abolition of its legislative body would trigger degeneration.[147]

The power of Weld's argument crests when he raises the question of British hypocrisy and by implication the negation of rule of law and equality before the law: 'For it is saying to that people, some of whom are now bribed, and others influenced, and forced to unite to England, "there is one law for you, and another for England".'[148] He reiterated the double standard asking 'Why then should we be unjustly deprived of our constitution – the people of England well know the advantage of their constitution, they are well aware of the value of the checks on arbitrary power.'[149] Weld signaled the central role played by coercion and the threat of violence in the discussions of union. Ventriloquizing Pitt, he declaimed: 'Martial law shall compel Ireland to call for Union as terms of capitulation and mercy!!! There shall be one system of government for Ireland and another for us, until I frighten and force that kingdom to a Union!!!'[150] The expectation of uniformity of legal regimes and technologies resonates with similar calls for consistency in the treatment of Catholics across the Empire that we saw in chapter 3.

As for the advantages of union articulated in the propaganda campaign, Weld has only contempt calling them 'specious and frivolous' 'pretences for Union' 'thin and transparent that cloak, that can scarcely obscure the proffered degradation'. He took aim at the 'pitiful subterfuges that are resorted to' and the 'despicable sophisms held forth to cajole and betray the Irish people'.[151] He excoriated the Irish who complied with Britain to make the Union: 'ye placemen, ye pensioners, and ye sycophants, who now implicitly bend your neck to slavery, and support the degradation of that country, to which many of you, nay the majority, owe your birth', warning that if union passes, 'you shall sink to the level of original obscurity', 'those situations, places, pensions, employments' 'will on that event, be greedily given away to those that are Non-residents, the British satraps, and long the needy expectants of the Union oligarchy'.[152] It is 'ye servile tribe', those Irishmen and women who have allied with the British, who Weld condemned, calling them the 'self-instruments of your destruction' urging them away from the 'wages of your prostitution' to allow 'a spark of public virtue [to] animate' them.[153] The repeated references to slavery, servility, and subjugation remind us insistently that the Atlantic slave trade was always already the larger context for the conversation about freedom, rights, and constitution.[154]

Only civic duty, 'public spirit', and 'Hibernian virtue' could defend against 'this daring attack', 'on Irish freedom' made 'under pretext of Union'.[155] He credited those among the Irish Protestant elite who resisted union with knowing, understanding, and enacting British legal traditions and values better than the English, their purported source. He advised Ireland, threatened with oppression and enslavement at the hands of a tyrannical British government, to reclaim its freedom, defined as quintessentially English. This resistance would protect Ireland's interests as well as the freedom and fair governance that had once been described as a gift from the metropole. Weld did not propose the reimposition of an unmediated British tradition of constitutional monarchy: instead he advocated a new ideology of representative government, parliamentary reform, and human rights.

Weld's pamphlet explicitly calls our attention to the Union as a defensive position taken by Britain that marks it as a failure rather than a triumph. He trumpeted this conclusion when he dismissed the list of advantages of Union promulgated by its promoters as 'a pretence, the disinterested Union advocates now hold forth as a masque for their anxiety for that deep laid project'.[156] As the offspring of British imperialism, these Irish pamphleteers – settler colonists and 'internal others' – cited English law to demand and claim English rights. Their arguments delegitimized union and destabilized empire. These radical critiques seem to treat the idea of union as ridiculous and preposterous, similar to a marriage between two men.

The Empire strikes back

Of course many Irish Protestants defended the Union. They emphasized its necessity in the name of empire and argued that strengthening the Anglo-Irish connection would facilitate Ireland's participation in global trade networks while providing 'imperial opportunities' to ordinary Irishmen and women who would reap the benefits of imperial membership. Theobald McKenna (1765–1808) opined that: 'to be a member of the British Empire is indispensable to the good of Ireland'.[157] McKenna rejected the constitutionalist arguments against union pronouncing in their place that 'the public law of Europe recognizes no such state as independent Ireland' because the king represents the state.[158] As 'an undiscriminated portion of that [British] monarchy', McKenna argued that Ireland's government is 'inseparably annexed to the British Crown'. McKenna declared the Irish and the English 'blended in races by the intercommunity of that space of time; assimilated in manners, in customs, and in language'.[159] It was precisely the intermingling that worried Irish anti-unionists afraid that they would lose the local privileges and hierarchies that a Parliament allowed them in Ireland.

McKenna truncated Ireland's parliamentary powers, defining the Irish Parliament as a subsidiary of Britain's, its power completely derivative and restricted to municipal regulation. He traced Ireland's diminished status to 1171 when Henry II invaded and claimed the title of Lord Leinster and opined that in the process Ireland had 'forfeited', 'resigned', and 'surrendered' the right to an independent and sovereign parliamentary assembly. The influence and power of Ireland's legislative assembly continued to shrink under Henry VII with Poynings' Law. Blaming Irish resistance, 'deeds' which 'bar our claim to imperial splendor', McKenna asserted 'we never looked upon the scepter, but to declare our incompetence to wield it'.[160] As for the repeal of Poynings' Law in 1782, McKenna's interpretation rendered its removal of 'concurrent jurisdiction' as having made 'no alteration in the rights of the British Crown, to the obedience of the Irish people'.[161] He conceded that 'to each other, Great Britain and Ireland are distinct provinces' but averred that 'in the contemplation of mankind, they already form an incorporated state, under a single head, with all the external appearance of an united people'.[162] McKenna summarized his position: 'our Third Estate is, by fundamental provision, which we cannot alter, placed beyond our control, and entirely within that of the sister nation'.[163] For McKenna the Parliament of Ireland was endowed with only a 'qualified sovereignty' derived 'from the law and usage of the empire'. Its sole purpose: 'to bind the subjects of this land'. By virtue of the boundaries of its jurisdiction, its power was 'municipal' 'not imperial'.[164]

As in the discourse surrounding the Gordon Riots, the language of empire claimed a more cosmopolitan and open minded position, progressive and worldly, while portraying those who would deny Ireland this reach as provincial and under informed. As one dividend of this broader perspective, McKenna promised that Union would improve the status of Catholics contending that their treatment by the metropole would be far less harsh.[165] Ireland's unlawful nature necessitated Britain's imperial hand to guide, to restrain, and to civilize. McKenna predicted that Ireland would lose standing in the world if detached from Great Britain 'our co-estate, our equal and co-member'.[166]

Empire loomed large throughout McKenna's narrative. He emphasized that Ireland's tie to Britain bestowed Ireland legitimacy in the world and spoke of Ireland's place in the 'undivided empire'.[167] He compared Ireland's position without a union to an isolated and passive entity, 'a constituent part of the supreme authority', 'a subordinate state' promising that the Union would make Ireland 'the participating people'.[168] Union, according to McKenna, bestowed agency. By expressing consent for union McKenna acknowledged the power of law in making empire.

Both sides understood this. The history of the Act of Union between Britain and Ireland reveals a British government ready to use the law to try (again) to cement its relationship with Ireland, Britain's first colony. Pitt and his administration were determined to close off threatening and undesirable contingencies that could result from Ireland's parliamentary independence. To avoid another situation in which a colonial legislative body sanctioned by London resisted economic and political control or moved for a permanent separation, Britain acted to abolish the source of seemingly legitimate but always destabilizing consultation, negotiation, and resistance. To be sure Britain's determination to accomplish this goal was made more intense by the Irish Revolution of 1798, the persistent discussion of constitutional reform in both domestic and imperial settings, and the war with France.[169]

The solution was proclaimed in an article in *The Times* published on January 26, 1799. The author warning against Irish resistance, promising it would 'ruin the freedom, the constitution, and the people', and considering the current situation an 'awful crisis', the worst 'in the History of the Universe', pronounced that 'unity of action can alone save us'. The article advised against establishing 'deliberative assemblies ... in every county and city throughout the kingdom' because the debates they would host would distract Britain from the war and the 'ferocious Vandalism [that] is marching over Europe, and marking its progress by the destruction of every thing which bears the stamp of religion and morality'. Speaking directly to Charles Stanhope and other leaders among the Protestant elite, those 'patriots of Property' and 'patriots of less property', the author cautioned about activating the 'momentum of the physical power of the multitude'. The article concluded that 'society cannot exist without subordination ... take away subordination, and anarchy ensues'.[170] This argument defined Ireland as a lawless, uncivilized legal zone justifying extreme, unlawful legislation. Resorting to these large claims allowed the defenders of Union's legitimacy to avoid engaging with the legal, constitutional arguments against it. The irony was that the Act of Union brought this lawlessness straight to the heart of the metropole, to the heart of the British Empire, to its highest court – London's Parliament at Westminster.

Conclusion

As Britain renewed its efforts to seek Union, the pamphlet campaign heated up in the first months of 1800 as did the production of images. Speaking back to the unionist pamphleteers and their proposals of marriage between Britain and Ireland came the cautionary image entitled *Marriage against inclination, A step to separation* published in the *Hibernian Magazine* in April 1800. Set in a rotunda representing the Irish House of Commons, grotesque characters, crudely drawn, people the print. John Bull, fat and lecherous, holds out a hand to Erin, pictured as a tall, statuesque woman wearing a helmet and flanked on either side by Castlereagh and John FitzGibbon, First Earl of Clare (1748–1802) who served as Lord Chancellor of Ireland and championed the preservation of the Protestant Ascendancy through the Act of Union. In a reference to the corruption and patronage that made the Union, Castlereagh boasts 'I give her away by distributing the loaves and fishes'. When John Bull says 'Stop Dame Erin foolish prude Prithee be not quite so rude. Be quick – consent – Indipendence fling or else more troops – there hungry sing', he threatens military invasion if Ireland withholds consent to his proposal of union. The presiding cleric begins the marriage ceremony with 'If any know just cause ... [etc] let them hold their tongue.' In response Erin asks 'is this the return merited for the constant loyalty of my children – by thus forcing my hand, you forfeit all claim to my heart'.[171] Unlike the *Grand Battle* published in the immediate aftermath of the first attempt at union with Ireland's resistance prominently featured in a struggle whose outcome remained unknown, here Ireland's resignation to a union with Great Britain took center stage. The threat of English violence made Ireland's unfettered consent impossible.

Using queer theory allows us to see why the critique of union took the shape it did. The surprising event took place when Irish Protestant male elites voted in January 1799 to block the Union. Many of them had much to gain from union and more to lose if they remained independent of Britain, especially given the rebellion of 1798 and its nationalist rhetoric and threat of land redistribution. The queering moment came when the campaign for the Act of Union explicitly compared the Act to a marriage – a legal, contractually binding hierarchy. This queer turn mapped its imagined opposite, homosexual union. This claim to the norm, always already unstable, called for vigorous and vigilant enforcement further subverting the comparison.

The question of consent defined the controversy. The Act aimed to rearrange the legal and constitutional place of Ireland in the composite monarchy by eliminating Ireland's parliament, but the Act's legitimacy rested on securing the uncompelled consent of that representative body. The stakes of the Act were very much shaped by the discourse of rights and representativeness that had developed throughout the 1790s, which found traction in the discussion of union. The analogy to marriage simplified the terms of the debate and made apparent the extreme contradictions and inconsistencies within British definitions of rule of law. The metaphor of marriage unraveled in the face of these extreme contradictions calling attention to the inconsistencies of English ideology of rule of law.

James Kelley has reconstructed the opposition's defeat attributing the final outcome to a lack of momentum that set in almost from the moment of victory in January 1799.[172] How does the eventual failure of the opposition in June 1800 relate to the critique of union as discussed and analyzed here? I would suggest that at the end of the long campaign for union the question of proximity to the metropole, to power, whiteness, and the norm decided the outcome at least as much as patronage, borough compensation, and secret service funds. In the age of individual human rights the anachronistic constitutional issues raised in the pamphlets rang hollow. And the vision of a male Ireland who resisted union whether as a simpleton like Pat in 'Horrors of the Irish Union' or one who seemed drunk and not entirely in control in 'Party's Not Agreed' appealed far less than a more traditionally gendered Ireland as

Figure 5.11 'A Flight Across the Herring Pool'

a reluctant bride. As a woman, Ireland could both comply with the contract and register her resistance with forbearance. From this position, the Protestant elite aligned themselves with the metropole, garnering whatever benefits and privileges they could. The sacrifice of their own representative body seemed like a small price to pay.

An image that suggests this realization among Irish Protestant elites is 'A Flight Across the Herring Pool' (Figure 5.11) published on June 20, 1800 ten days before the passage of the Act of Union. Pitt stands on the shore holding an 'Imperial Pouch' containing ribbons, stars, and little men dressed for court, including orders. Pitt welcomes those who arrive assuring them 'Come on my little Fellows – there's plenty of room for you all.' Dundas, ever Pitt's loyal lieutenant, sits on a tall pile of what look like stacking crates, each one an office he held that translated into tremendous wealth and influence. Dundas beckons to the flying MPs, 'If you've only Conscience at a' here's enugh to satisfy ye a'.'[173] On the most superficial level the print speaks explicitly to the corruption and bribery that bought the union, but I wish to suggest a deeper significance. The image captures Irish Protestant elites taking their place in a new political and legal hierarchy: while they lost their local, colonial ascendance, they accepted the promise of a reconstituted metropolitan hierarchy that preserved their wealth, privilege, opportunity, and access to power.

MAKING THE UNION WITH IRELAND, 1800

Using contract and the analogy to marriage the Act of Union summarized the British perspective perfectly. With consent from each party, the union would be accomplished and Ireland's subordination assured. Starting with the word union, the Act expressed Britain's hope (and was the mechanism by which) the separate subordinated kingdom would become a settler colony that would generate a profitable, successful polity acquiescing to Britain's guidance and mimicking its metropolitan parent. The failure of union in 1799 served as yet another reminder of the anxiety that surrounded law; the ideology of rule of law promised stability and resolution while the contingencies of Ireland's parliamentary session in January 1799 insistently underscored law's inability to deliver the order, process, regularity, and predictability so desired by Britain. The prints and the pamphlets that argued against the constitutionality of the Act capture Britain's impotence and the endeavor's failure to produce a mimetic, obedient, successful, and disciplined colonial offspring. The constitutionalists speaking back to the metropole shifted from a question about uncoerced consent to pose a much more profound and fundamental question. Rejecting the metaphor of marriage for Union, they claimed a superior understanding of the spirit of British law and its constitutional traditions calling the merger unnatural, outrageous, and unthinkable. Both the pamphlets and the images announce that the measure's very success in July 1800 testified to its unlawful character and destined the Union to be unproductive and unconstitutional: sparking further resistance rather than extinguishing it.

Notes

1 The English Parliament at Westminster passed the Union with Ireland Act (39 & 40 Geo. III c. 67) which received royal assent on August 1, 1800. For the full text, see Raithby and Edlyne, *Statutes at Large*, vol. 20, pp. 395–424.
2 For more on the French Revolution and Ireland, see *Britain and the French Revolution*, ed. H. T. Dickinson (New York: St. Martin's Press, 1989), esp. Dickinson, 'Introduction: the Impact on Britain of the French Revolution and the French Wars, 1789–1815', pp. 1–20 and Marianne Elliott, 'Ireland and the French Revolution', pp. 83–102.
3 For plans for union, see Patrick Geoghegan, 'The Making of the Union', in *Acts of Union, The Causes, Contexts and Consequences of the Act of Union*, ed. Dáire Keogh and Kevin Whelan (Dublin: Four Courts Press, 2001), pp. 34–45. For more detailed accounts of the events referred to in this paragraph, see Patrick Geoghegan, *The Irish Act of Union: A Study in High Politics 1798–1801* (New York: St. Martin's Press, 1999); and James Kelly, *Prelude to Union: Anglo-Irish Politics in the 1780s* (Cork: Cork University Press, 1992).
4 William Blackstone stated unequivocally: 'Our law considers marriage in no other light than as a civil contract', Blackstone, *Commentaries*, vol. 1, p. 421. My focus on the Union as marriage found inspiration in Jane Elizabeth Dougherty, 'Mr. and Mrs. England: the Act of Union as national marriage', in *Acts of Union*, pp. 202–215; and Claire Connolly, 'Writing the Union', in *Acts of Union*, esp. pp. 180–181.

5 Support for the king's address passed with only the narrow margin of 107–105. James Kelly, 'The Failure of Opposition', in *The Irish Act of Union, 1800: Bicentennial Essays*, ed. Michael Brown, Patrick Geoghegan, and James Kelly (Dublin: Irish Academic Press, 2003), pp. 114–116; Geoghegan, 'The Making of the Union', in *Acts of Union*, ed. Keogh and Whelan, pp. 36–40; and Geoghegan, *Irish Act of Union*. A bill to create union was not presented to the Irish Parliament in 1799. Geoghegan explains that the British government wanted to avoid borough compensation out of concern about allegations of corruption and in the hope of keeping down the cost of passing the Irish Union.

6 James Kelly, 'The Failure of Opposition', in *Irish Act of Union, 1800*, pp. 108–128; and Geoghegan, 'The Making of the Union', in *Acts of Union*, ed. Keogh and Whelan, pp. 40–45. For a list of pamphlet titles, see W. J. McCormack, *The Pamphlet Debate on the Union between Great Britain and Ireland, 1797–1800* (Dublin: Irish Academic Press, 1996).

7 The Protestant Ascendancy gave Ireland's wealthy, Protestant landlords uncontested social, cultural, economic, and political power. The Penal Laws imposed by William III in 1695 after the Battle of the Boyne had barred Catholics, who in 1831 were 80.3 percent of the population, from holding state office, running for elected office, joining the armed forces, and practicing law. The rest of the population included 10.7 percent who belonged to the Church of Ireland and 8.1 percent who identified as Presbyterian. There were also small communities of Baptists, Congregationalists, Plymouth Brethren, Quakers, and Methodists. The laws restricted Catholics from sitting in the Irish Parliament, holding office, keeping a school, and owning a horse appraised at more than £5. The statistics on landownership demonstrate the severe disparity of wealth between Catholics and Protestant that became even more drastic over the course of the century: Catholics suffered confiscation of land that reduced their ownership from a very small 22 percent (down from 59 percent in 1641) to 14 percent. To ensure that this trend continued, the Act to Prevent the Further Growth of Popery passed in 1704 (2 Ann c. 6) prevented Catholics from acquiring any more land and required Catholics to practice partible inheritance, willing equitable portions to each son rather than the practice of primogeniture. The result was the division of large estates into smaller and smaller parcels of land. Ireland's population was 3 million in 1700 and rose to 4 million by the end of the eighteenth century. J. G. Simms, 'The Establishment of Protestant Ascendancy, 1691–1714', in *A New History of Ireland: Volume IV: Eighteenth-Century Ireland, 1691–1800*, ed. T. W. Moody and W. E. Vaughan (Oxford: Clarendon, 1986), pp. 1–30; and J. L. McCracken, 'Protestant Ascendancy and the Rise of Colonial Nationalism, 1714–1760', in *A New History of Ireland: Vol. IV*, ed. Mody and Vaughan, pp. 105–122.

8 When George III quashed Catholic Emancipation, William Pitt resigned as prime minister. Historians are still debating whether this was the real reason for Pitt's resignation. For more on the subject and a summary of the two sides, see Charles John Fedorak, 'Catholic Emancipation and the Resignation of William Pitt in 1801', *Albion* 24 (1992), pp. 49–64.

9 Isaac Cruikshank, 'An Irish Union!' (1799). Trinity Research Archive: http://www.tara.tcd.ie/handle/2262/9838. See also Stephens and George, *Catalogue of Prints and Drawings*, vol. 7, #9344.

10 Queer theory seeks to analyze and disturb 'relationships of power and knowledge that shape desires, behaviors, social institutions and social relations'. Sullivan, *A Critical Introduction*, p. 51. See also Ahmed, *Queer Phenomenology*; Butler, *Gender Trouble*; Sue-Ellen Case, 'Tracking the Vampire'; Cohen, 'Punks, Bulldaggers, and Welfare Queens'; Giffney, 'Introduction: The "q" word'; Moran, Monk, and Beresford, *Legal Queeries*; and Warner, *Fear of a Queer Planet*.

11 Brooks and Leckey, *Queer Theory*.

12 Elliott, 'Ireland and the French Revolution', in *Britain and the French Revolution*, ed. Dickinson, pp. 100–101.

13 There are three collections of essays based on conferences that celebrated the 200th anniversary of the Act. Brown, Geoghegan, and Kelly, *Irish Act of Union, 1800*;

Keogh and Whelan, *Acts of Union*; and *Transactions of the Royal Historical Society*, series 6, vol. 10 (2000), pp. 167–408.
14 Kelly, 'The Historiography of the Act of Union', in *Irish Act of Union*, ed., Brown, Geoghegan, and Kelly, p. 36.
15 One of the best known narratives from this perspective was Jonah Barrington, *Historic records and secret memoirs of the legislative union between Great Britain and Ireland* (Dublin: H. Colburn, 1844).
16 Kelly, 'Historiography', in *Irish Act of Union*, ed., Brown, Geoghegan, and Kelly.
17 Kelly, 'Historiography', in *Irish Act of Union*, ed., Brown, Geoghegan, and Kelly.
18 G. C. Bolton, *The Passing of the Irish Act of Union: A Study in Parliamentary Politics* (Oxford: Oxford University Press, 1966).
19 David Wilkinson, '"How Did They Pass the Union?" Secret Service Expenditure in Ireland, 1799–1804', *History* 82 (1997), pp. 223–251.
20 For republicanism in Ireland, see James Livesey, 'From the Ancient Constitution to Democracy: Transformations in Republicanism in the Eighteenth Century', in *1798: A Bicentenary Perspective*, ed. Bartlett, Dickson, Keogh, and Whelan, pp. 14–27; Geraldine Sheridan, 'Irish Periodicals and the Dissemination of French Enlightenment Writings in the Eighteenth Century', in *1798: A Bicentenary Perspective*, ed. Bartlett, Dickson, Keogh, and Whelan, pp. 28–51; Luke Gibbons, '"The Return of the Native:" The United Irishmen, culture and colonialism', in *1798: A Bicentenary Perspective*, ed. Bartlett, Dickson, Keogh, and Whelan, pp. 52–74; and Breandán Ó Buachalla, 'From Jacobite to Jacobin', in *1798: A Bicentenary Perspective*, ed. Bartlett, Dickson, Keogh, and Whelan pp. 75–97.
21 The full name of the Act passed in 1782 was the Repeal of Act for Securing Dependence of Ireland Act, 22. Geo. III c. 53. Poyning's Law, 'An Act that no parliament be holden in this land until the acts be certified into England', restricted the authority of both the Irish executive and its legislature to make law. Despite the law's design to limit the initiative of the Irish Parliament, starting with the Restoration of Charles II in 1660 the Irish Parliament met regularly and insisted on its power to initiate legislation. James Kelly, *Poynings' Law and the Making of Law in Ireland, 1660–1800* (Dublin: Four Courts Press, 2007).
22 The Declaratory Act (6 Geo. I c. 5) passed in 1719 had reaffirmed the authority of the British Parliament over Ireland. Kelly, *Poynings' Law*.
23 In 1784–85 William Pitt proposed an economic union between Britain and Ireland. For more on Pitt's commercial proposals, see James Kelly, 'The Origins of the Irish Act of Union: An Examination of Unionist Opinion in Britain and Ireland, 1650–1800', *Irish Historical Studies* 25 (1987), pp. 236–263.
24 For more on the Regency Crisis, see Neil Herman, 'Henry Grattan, The Regency Crisis and the Emergence of a Whig Party in Ireland, 1788–9', *Irish Historical Studies* 32 (2001), pp. 478–497. George III's mental incapacity is the subject of Ida Macalpine and Richard Hunter, *George III and the Mad-Business* (New York: Pantheon, 1970).
25 For more on the European context, see William Doyle, 'The Union in a European Context', in *Transactions of the Royal Historical Society*, series 6, 10 (2000), pp. 167–180.
26 James Liversey, 'Act of Union and Disunion: Ireland in Atlantic and European Contexts', in *Acts of Union*, ed. Keogh and Whelan, p. 100.
27 News of developments in France traveled quickly and was widely covered in newspapers in London and Dublin. Key events were also staged in the theaters in both capitals. For more on these re-enactments and the change of attitudes about the Revolution see John Hall Stewart, 'The Fall of the Bastille on the Dublin Stage', *The Journal of the Royal Society of Antiquaries of Ireland* 84 (1954), pp. 78–91 and 'The French Revolution on the Dublin Stage', *The Journal of the Royal Society of Antiquaries of Ireland* 91 (1961), pp. 183–192.
28 Patrick Geoghegan, 'The Making of the Union', in *Acts of Union*, ed. Keogh and Whelan, pp. 34–45.
29 The bicentennial anniversary of the rebellion coincided with the publication of new scholarship on the topic including Jim Smyth, *The Men of No Property: Irish Radicals*

and *Popular Politics in the Late Eighteenth Century* (New York: St. Martins, 1992); A. T. Q Stewart, *The Summer Soldiers: the 1798 Rebellion in Antrim and Down* (Belfast: Blackstaff Press, 1995); Daire Keogh and Nicholas Furlong, eds., *The Mighty Wave: the 1798 Rebellion in Wexford* (Dublin, Four Courts Press, 1996); Ruan O'Donnell, *The Rebellion in Wicklow, 1798* (Dublin, Irish Academic Press, 1998); Jim Smyth, ed. *Revolution, Counter-Revolution and Union: Ireland in the 1790s* (Cambridge: Cambridge University Press, 2000); and Bartlett, Dickson, Keogh, and Whelan, *1798: A Bicentenary Perspective.*

30 Ian McBride, 'The Irish Rebellion of 1798', *Historian* 59 (1998), pp. 25–29.
31 Marianne Elliott, *Partners in Revolution: The United Irishmen and France* (New Haven, CT: Yale University Press, 1982); and D. Dickson, Daire Keogh, and Kevin Whelan, eds., *The United Irishmen: Radicalism, Republicanism, Reaction* (Dublin: Lilliput Press, 1993).
32 Smyth, 'Introduction: the 1798 Rebellion and its Eighteenth-Century Contexts', in *Revolution, Counter-Revolution and Union*, ed. Smyth, p. 14.
33 Smyth, 'Introduction', in *Revolution, Counter-Revolution and Union*, ed. Smyth, p. 19.
34 Geoghegan, 'The Making of the Union', in *Acts of Union*, ed. Keogh and Whelan, pp. 36–40.
35 For more on the propaganda campaign, see Wilkinson, '"How Did They Pass the Union?"' For public opinion more generally, see Daniel Mansergh, 'The Union and the Importance of Public Opinion', in *Acts of Union*, ed. Keogh and Whelan, pp. 126–139.
36 Linebaugh and Rediker, *The Many-Headed Hydra.*
37 Act of Union, 39 & 40 Geo. III c. 67, Raithby and Edlyne, *Statutes at Large*, vol. 42, part 2, p. 648.
38 Most recently, Alvin Jackson's book *The Two Unions: Ireland, Scotland, and the Survival of the United Kingdom, 1707–2007* (Oxford: Oxford University Press, 2012). Allan I. Macinnes integrates a discussion of Ireland and the comparison with Scotland's union throughout his book *Union and Empire: The Making of the United Kingdom in 1707* (Cambridge: Cambridge University Press, 2007).
39 For more on the Union with Scotland in 1707, see Macinnes, *Union and Empire*; T. I. Rae, ed., *The Union of 1707: Its Impact on Scotland* (Glasgow: Blackie & Son Limited, 1974); John Robertson, ed., *A Union for Empire: Political Thought and the British Union of 1707* (Cambridge: Cambridge University Press, 1995); and Christopher Whatley with Derek T. Patrick, *The Scots and the Union* (Edinburgh: Edinburgh University Press, 2006).
40 For more on the Rising of 1715, see Daniel Szechi, *1715: The Great Jacobite Rebellion* (New Haven, CT: Yale University Press, 2006); and on the rebellion in 1745, Bruce Lenman, *The Jacobite Risings in Britain, 1689–1746* (Aberdeen: Scottish Cultural Press, 1980). On the Jacobites, see Paul Monod, *Jacobitism and the English People, 1688–1788* (Cambridge: Cambridge University Press, 1989). A recent evaluation of the Jacobite movement argues that it was not truly defeated (nor was it believed to be defeated) until the Bay of Quiberon in 1759. Zimmerman, *The Jacobite Movement in Scotland and in Exile, 1746–1759.*
41 Henry Dundas, *Substance of the speech of the Right Hon. Henry Dundas, in the House of Commons, Thursday, Feb. 7, 1799, on the subject of the legislative union with Ireland* (London: J. Wright, 1799), p. 44.
42 Dundas fails to mention too that England and Scotland excluded Ireland from the talks about Scottish union in 1706–1707 or that Britain rebuffed the Irish suggestion of a union with Britain in the aftermath of the passage of the Act of Union with Scotland.
43 For more on Dundas and his career, see Michael Fry, *The Dundas Despotism* (Edinburgh: Edinburgh University Press, 1992).
44 Theophilus Swift, *Hear him! Hear him! In a letter to the Right Honourable John Foster* (Dublin: J. Stockdale, 1799), p. 40.

45 Lynn Hunt, *The Family Romance of the French Revolution* (Berkeley, CA: University of California Press, 1992); and Joan Landes, *Women and the Public Sphere in the Age of the French Revolution* (Ithaca, NY: Cornell University Press, 1988) and *Visualizing the Nation: Gender, Representation, and Revolution in Eighteenth-century France* (Ithaca, NY: Cornell University Press, 2001).

46 According to Blackstone, 'By marriage, the husband and wife are one person in law: that is, the very being or legal existence of the woman is suspended during the marriage, or at least is incorporated and consolidated into that of the husband: under whose wing, protection, and cover, she performs every thing; and is therefore called in our law-French a *feme-covert*'. Blackstone, *Commentaries*, vol. 1, p. 430. The status of *feme covert* or coverture is described in *The Lawes Resolution of womens rights: or the laws provision for women. A methodicall collection of such statues and customes, with the cases, opinions and points of learning in the law, as doe properly concern women* (London: John More, 1632). Amy Erickson, *Women and Property in Early Modern England* (London: Routledge, 1993); Susan Staves, *Married Women's Separate Property in England, 1660–1833* (Cambridge, MA: Harvard University Press, 1990); and Walker, *Crime, Gender, and Social Order in Early Modern England* have shown that the status of *feme covert* was largely a legal fiction; women skirted these restrictions acting as legal agents with and without the help of their male kin in both criminal and civil courts in the early modern period.

47 John Ayliffe, *Parergon juris canonici anglicani: or, a commentary, by way of supplement to the canons and constitutions of the Church of England. Not only from* ... (London: D. Leach, 1726), p. 246.

48 Ayliffe, *Parergon*, p. 249.

49 Blackstone, *Commentaries*, vol. 1, pp. 422–428. The question of contract and states of *non compos mentis* is discussed in Joel Eigen, *Witnessing Insanity: Madness and Mad-Doctors in the English Court* (New Haven, CT: Yale University Press, 1995); Dana Rabin, *Identity, Crime, and Legal Responsibility in Eighteenth-Century England* (Houndmills: Palgrave Macmillan, 2004); and Nigel Walker, *Crime and Insanity in England*, Volume 1: *The Historical Perspective* (Edinburgh: Edinburgh University Press, 1968).

50 Most famously, Mary Wollstonecraft articulated women's rights in *A Vindication of the Rights of Woman* (1792), but the counter-revolutionary movement also generated anti-feminist writing. For consent in the Irish Union especially from a literary perspective, see Jane Dougherty, 'The Last of the Milesians: The 1801 Anglo-Irish Marriage Contract and the *Wild Irish Girl*', *Journal for Eighteenth Century Studies* 35 (2012), pp. 391–405; Willa Murphy, 'A Queen of Hearts or an Old Maid? Maria Edgeworth's Fictions of Union', in *Acts of Union*, ed. Keogh and Whelan, pp. 189–190; and Norman Vance, 'Irish Literary Traditions and the Act of Union', *Canadian Journal of Irish Studies* 12 (1986), pp. 29–47. For more on marriage and consent, see Rebecca Probert, *Marriage Law and Practice in the Long Eighteenth Century: A Reassessment* (Cambridge: Cambridge University Press, 2009). For more on affective marriage, see David Blewett, 'Changing Attitudes toward Marriage in the Time of Defoe: The Case of Moll Flanders', *Huntington Library Quarterly* 44 (1981), pp. 77–88; and Ingrid Tague, 'Love, Honor, and Obedience: Fashionable Women and the Discourse of Marriage in the Early Eighteenth Century', *Journal of British Studies* 40 (2001), pp. 76–106.

51 *Times of London*, March 1, 1799, issues 4422, p. 3, column B.

52 *Times of London*, March 1, 1799, issues 4422, p. 3, column B.

53 T. Canning, *The Wedding and Bedding: or, John Bull and his bride fast asleep. A satirical poem. Containing, an history of the happy pair. From their Infancy to the present Period. With Reasons for, and Means used to accomplish their Union. Also, the matchmakers matched; with their rueful lamentation for the loss of the bride cake* (London: Sidney and Evans, 1800), p. 7.

54 Canning, *Wedding and Bedding*, p. 9.

55 Canning, *Wedding and Bedding*, p. 8.

56 Canning, *Wedding and Bedding*, pp. 10, 11.
57 Canning, *Wedding and Bedding*, p. 35.
58 Canning, *Wedding and Bedding*, pp. 13–29.
59 Canning, *Wedding and Bedding*, p. 12.
60 Canning, *Wedding and Bedding*, p. 12.
61 Canning, *Wedding and Bedding*, p. 36.
62 Canning, *Wedding and Bedding*, p. 41.
63 Canning, *Wedding and Bedding*, p. 30.
64 Canning, *Wedding and Bedding*, p. 29.
65 Canning, *Wedding and Bedding*, p. 42.
66 Canning, *Wedding and Bedding*, p. 43.
67 Canning, *Wedding and Bedding*, p. 47.
68 Canning, *Wedding and Bedding*, p. 47.
69 Canning, *Wedding and Bedding*, p. 49.
70 Canning, *Wedding and Bedding*, p. 49.
71 Canning, *Wedding and Bedding*, p. 50.
72 Canning, *Wedding and Bedding*, p. 52.
73 Canning, *Wedding and Bedding*, p. 55.
74 *At the royal circus, near College-Green. For the benefit of Mrs. Ireland. On Wednesday, January 15, will be performed a grand pantomimical, serio-comic olio* (Dublin: Apollo Circulating Library, 1800). Olio refers to 'any mixture of many heterogeneous elements; a hotchpotch, medley, jumble', OED.
75 *An entirely new change of amusements, with several new performers. At the royal circus, near College-Green. For the benefit of the great Mrs. Britain ... On Wednesday February 5 ...* (Dublin: Apollo Circulating Library, 1800).
76 *An entirely new change of amusements ... For the benefit of the great Mrs. Britain ... February 5.*
77 *The great Mrs. Britain's second benefit, amphitheatre, near the College Square, on Wednesday, February 12, will be performed an entirely new politico-dramatic olio, called Self Immolation, or, The Wise-Men of Gotham, ...* (Dublin: Apollo Circulating Library, 1800). Note the 'little American Devil, from the classic theatre, will exhibit some extraordinary feats in political juggling, especially the famous protean feat in which he will exhibit himself in various changes of shape, colour, and principle'. This may reference the consensus of opinion in American papers supporting the Act of Union as a logical British response to the Irish Rebellion of 1798. Considering Irish support for the American Revolution a quarter century earlier, the 'little American Devil' and his change of 'shape, colour, and principle' might express Irish feelings of betrayal.
78 Canning, *Wedding and Bedding*, p. 43.
79 *At the royal circus, near College-Green ... On Wednesday, January 15.*
80 I have surveyed over 50 prints produced in response to the discussion and passage of Union between 1798 and 1800. They are found in the British Museum's collection of prints and drawings and in Irish libraries. For an overview of the prints and images created in response to the Act of Union, see Nicholas Robinson, 'Marriage against Inclination: The Union and Caricature', in *Acts of Union*, ed. Keogh and Whelan, pp. 140–158.
81 Stephens and George, *Catalogue of Prints and Drawings*, vol. 8, #9697.
82 *Miss Hibernia at John Bull's Family Dinner* (March 18, 1799), Trinity Research Archive: http://www.tara.tcd.ie/handle/2262/2338.
83 *Hibernian Magazine*, April 1800.
84 Stephens and George, *Catalogue of Prints and Drawings*, vol. 7, #9529.
85 John Cawse, 'John Bull Shewing his intended bride the Parliament House' (April 30, 1800), Trinity Research Archive, http://www.tara.tcd.ie/handle/2262/10136. See also, British Museum satires, BM Satires undescribed, AN69769001.
86 James Gillray, 'Horrors of the Irish-Union; botheration of poor Pat – or – a whisper across the Channel' (1798), Trinity Research Archive: http://www.tara.tcd.ie/handle/2262/10129. See also Stephens and George, *Catalogue of Prints and Drawings*,

vol. 7, #9284 and 'Union between England and Ireland!!', Trinity Research Archive: http://www.tara.tcd.ie/handle/2262/10131. See also Stephens and George, *Catalogue of Prints and Drawings*, vol. 7, #9462.
87 'Party's Not Agreed' (1800), Trinity Research Archive: http://www.tara.tcd.ie/handle/2262/10140. See also Stephens and George, *Catalogue of Prints and Drawings*, vol. 7, #9535, and 'An English Twig and an Irish Shillelee!!' Trinity Research Archive: http://www.tara.tcd.ie/handle/2262/9798. See also British Museum satires, undescribed, item #AN69761001.
88 *The Times of London*, January 31, 1799 Issues 4397, p. 3.
89 For more on idiocy and responsibility, see Rabin, *Identity*; Eigen, *Witnessing Insanity*, and Walker, *Crime and Insanity*.
90 'Union between England and Ireland!!' published February 20, 1799 by William Holland. Trinity Research Archive: http://www.tara.tcd.ie/handle/2262/10131.
91 Stephens and George, *Catalogue of Prints and Drawings*, vol. 7, p. 608.
92 Dickinson, *Caricatures and the Constitution*, pp. 23–29.
93 Dickinson, *Caricatures and the Constitution*, pp. 12–14.
94 Donald, *The Age of Caricature*, pp. 1–21.
95 'Caricature Shop' (P. Roberts, Middle Row, Holborn: London, 1801). Lewis Walpole Library, Yale University.
96 Donald, *Age of Caricature*, pp. 7, 21.
97 Andrew, *Aristocratic Vice*, pp. 9–10, 37–41.
98 Karl W. Schweizer, 'Newspapers, Politics and Public Opinion in the Later Hanoverian Era', *Parliamentary History* 25 (2006), p. 33.
99 Donald, *Age of Caricature*, pp. 1–21.
100 Donald, *Age of Caricature*, p. 19. Brian Cowan, 'What Was Masculine about the Public Sphere? Gender and the Coffeehouse Milieu in Post-Restoration England', *History Workshop Journal* 51 (2001), pp. 127–158 and Cowan, *The Social Life of Coffee* (New Haven, CT: Yale University Press, 2005); Ayton Ellis, *The Penny Universities: A History of the Coffee-Houses* (London: Secker and Warburg, 1956); and Markman Ellis, *The Coffee House: A Cultural History* (London: Phoenix, 2004). For more on communal reading practices, see J. Raven, Helen Small, and Naomi Tadmor, eds., *The Practice and Representation of Reading in England* (Cambridge: Cambridge University Press, 1995).
101 'Paddy's Escape from the Union Net' (1799), Trinity Research Archive: http://www.tara.tcd.ie/handle/2262/10134.
102 Cruikshank, 'An Irish Union!' (1799), Stephens and George, *Catalogue of Prints and Drawings*, vol. 7, #9344.
103 William Shakespeare, *The Merry Wives of Windsor*, Act 1, Scene 1.
104 Stephens and George, *Catalogue of Prints and Drawings*, vol. 7, #9344.
105 'Party's Not Agreed', British Museum satires #9535.
106 William Drennan, *Fugitive Pieces in Verse and Prose* (Belfast: F. D. Finlay, 1815), p. 13.
107 William Drennan, *A Letter to the Honourable William Pitt* (Dublin: James Moore, 1799), p. 33.
108 Ayliffe points out that 'Tho' the Parties betrothed should protest before the Act done, that they did not thereby intend, that the Espousals should become Matrimony; yet this Protestation is defeated by the ensuing Act: for by lying together they are presum'd to have swerved from their dishonest Protestation; and so the former Espousals are now presum'd to be honest matrimony. *Parergon Juris*, p. 250.
109 Burke, *Reflections*, p. 34.
110 Burke, *Reflections*, p. 56.
111 Burke, *Reflections*, p. 33.
112 Burke, *Reflections*, pp. 206–207.
113 Paine, *Rights of Man*, p. 122.
114 Paine, *Rights of Man*, p. 91. For more on the struggle over constitutionalism, see David Eastwood, 'John Reeves and the Contested Idea of the Constitution', *British Journal for Eighteenth-Century Studies* 16 (1993), pp. 197–212.

115 Dickinson, *Caricatures and the Constitution*, pp. 23–40 and the prints that follow. David Duff, analyzes the images depicting reading Burke and Paine 'Burke and Paine: Contrasts', in *British Literature of the French Revolution*, ed. Clemit, pp, 50–55.
116 *The Times* comments on the prominent position played by lawyers in Ireland and their loud condemnation of union. In an article published on January 26, 1799 the author expressed 'no great wonder' at this fact because 'union is their greatest enemy'. In fact, all of the pamphlets we will examine were written by lawyers.
117 Charles Stanhope, *An address to the nations of Great Britain and Ireland, on the projected union* (Dublin: J. Moore, 1799), p. 1.
118 Henry Maddock, *The power of parliaments considered, in a letter to a Member of Parliament* (London: J. Debrett, 1799), p. 10.
119 Maddock, *Power of parliaments considered*, pp. 18–19.
120 Maddock, *Power of parliaments considered*, p. 31.
121 Maddock, *Power of parliaments considered*, p. 19–20.
122 Maddock, *Power of parliaments considered*, p. 20.
123 Maddock, *Power of parliaments considered*, p. 25.
124 Maddock, *Power of parliaments considered*, p. 26.
125 Maddock, *Power of parliaments considered*, p 31.
126 Maddock, *Power of parliaments considered*, p. 53.
127 Maddock, *Power of parliaments considered*, p. 54.
128 Maddock, *Power of parliaments considered*, pp. 34–35.
129 Dickinson, *Caricatures and the Constitution*.
130 Weld, an Irish barrister, was the author of one other pamphlet titled *No union! being an appeal to Irishmen* published in Dublin in December 1798. Writing in the aftermath of the Irish Rebellion he warned his Irish audience that union would have a negative impact on Ireland's population and commerce. He argued that Scottish union had been detrimental to Scotland and that union would create Irish grievances similar to those that caused the American war of independence. Finally he warned that France would take advantage of the instability of union to invade and annex Ireland.
131 Weld, *Constitutional considerations*, p. 11.
132 Blackstone, *Commentaries*, vol. 1, p. 494.
133 Weld, *Constitutional considerations*, p. 14.
134 Weld, *Constitutional considerations*, p. 20.
135 Weld, *Constitutional considerations*, p. 17.
136 Weld, *Constitutional considerations*, p. 28.
137 Weld, *Constitutional considerations*, p. 30.
138 Weld, *Constitutional considerations*, pp. 44–45.
139 Weld, *Constitutional considerations*, pp. 39–41.
140 Weld, *Constitutional considerations*, p. 67.
141 Weld, *Constitutional considerations*, pp. 42–43.
142 Weld, *Constitutional considerations*, p. 67.
143 Weld, *Constitutional considerations*, p. 51.
144 Weld, *Constitutional considerations*, pp. 22–23, emphasis original.
145 'The Dreadful Consequences of a General Naturalization, to the Natives of Great-Britain and Ireland' (1751), Stephens and George, *Catalogue of Prints and Drawings*, volume 3, part 2, #3124, pp. 813–814.
146 *An entirely new change of amusements ... For the benefit of the great Mrs. Britain.. on Wednesday February 5*.
147 Weld, *Constitutional considerations*, p. 55.
148 Weld, *Constitutional considerations*, p. 55.
149 Weld, *Constitutional considerations*, p. 54.
150 Weld, *Constitutional considerations*, p. 55.
151 Weld, *Constitutional considerations*, p. 62
152 Weld, *Constitutional considerations*, p. 68.
153 Weld, *Constitutional considerations*, p. 69.

154 Gibbons, '"The Return of the Native"', and Buachalla, 'From Jacobite to Jacobin', in *1798*, ed. Bartlett, Dickson, Keogh, and Whelan.
155 Weld, *Constitutional considerations*, p. 69.
156 Weld, *Constitutional considerations*, p. 71.
157 Theobald McKenna, *Constitutional objections to the government of Ireland by a separate legislature, in a letter to John Hamilton, esq. Occasioned by his remarks on a Memoire on the projected union* (Ireland: s.n., 1799), p. iii. For more on this theme, see Thomas Bartlett, '"An Union for Empire": The Anglo-Irish Union as an Imperial Project', in *Irish Act of Union*, ed. Brown, Geoghegan, Kelly, pp. 50–57.
158 McKenna, *Constitutional objections*, p. 22.
159 McKenna, *Constitutional objections*, p. 24.
160 McKenna, *Constitutional objections*, p. 26.
161 McKenna, *Constitutional objections*, p. 27.
162 McKenna, *Constitutional objections*, p. 23.
163 McKenna, *Constitutional objections*, pp. 25–26.
164 McKenna, *Constitutional objections*, p. 25. A similar argument was made in the James Somerset case (1771–1772). See chapter 2.
165 McKenna, *Constitutional objections*, pp. 37–38.
166 McKenna, *Constitutional objections*, p. 18.
167 McKenna, *Constitutional objections*, p. 29
168 McKenna, *Constitutional objections*, p. 33.
169 The elimination of representative assemblies was repeated throughout Britain's colonial holdings. When Trinidad became a British colony, seized from Spain in 1797 and formally granted to Britain in the Peace of Amiens in 1802, no assembly was constituted. For more on Trinidad, see Epstein, *Scandal of Colonial Rule*.
170 *The Times of London*, January 26, 1799, issue 4393, page 3.
171 *Marriage against inclination, Hibernian Magazine,* April 1800.
172 Kelly, 'The Failure of Opposition', in *Irish Act of Union,* ed. Brown, Geoghegan, and Kelly.
173 'If you've any Conscience at all here's enough to satisfy you all'. Isaac Cruikshank, *Flight Across the Herring Pool* (June 20, 1800). Trinity Research Archive: http://www.tara.tcd.ie/handle/2262/579. See also, Stephens and George, *Catalogue of Prints and Drawings*, vol. 7, #9543.

CONCLUSION

In his 1775 argument for parliamentary reform, Granville Sharp declared that 'as all British subjects, whether in Great Britain, Ireland, or the Colonies, are *equally free* by the law of *Nature*, they certainly are *equally* entitled to the same *Natural* Rights that are *essential* for their own preservation'. According to Sharp, 'this privilege of *'having a share in the legislation'* is not merely a *British Right*, peculiar to *this island*, but it is also a *Natural Right*, which cannot, without the most flagrant and stimulating injustice, be withdrawn from any part of the British Empire'.[1] In addition to the liberty and 'natural equality' that Sharp pronounced as part and parcel of Britain and its Empire, the rule of law accorded with a 'maxim of the English Constitution, that Law, to bind all, must be assented to by all'.[2] As a negative example, Sharpe presented the legislative relationship between Ireland and Britain and attributed the inconsistent and unsuccessful results as a consequence of the limited consent solicited. He insisted that in order to implement 'the fundamental principles of the English Constitution' in the Empire and to avoid 'injustice and iniquity', each colony must establish a 'Legislature for *each province respectively*'.[3]

In his condemnation of slavery and the slave trade Sharp explicitly assigned to the British state responsibility for the practice of human bondage. 'The horrible Guilt therefore, which is incurred by Slave-dealing and Slave-holding, is no longer confined to the few hardened Individuals, that are immediately concerned in those baneful Practices, but alas! the WHOLE BRITISH EMPIRE is involved.'[4] Despite his support for the establishment of these legislative bodies in the colonies, he adamantly asserted the need for these 'provincial' assemblies 'to observe, most strictly, the fundamental principles of that constitution'.[5] He clarified the legal dimensions of this stipulation: 'for wheresoever the bounds of the British Empire are extended, there the Common Law of England must of course take place, and cannot safely be set aside by any private

CONCLUSION

law whatsoever'. The consistency in the rule of law was not for Sharp a matter of choice or abstraction: the stakes were high because 'the introduction of an unnatural tyranny must necessarily endanger the King's dominions'. Sharp cited the 'many alarming insurrections of Slaves in the several colonies' as proof of the 'horrid iniquity, injustice, and dangerous tendency' of the plantation laws establishing and enforcing slavery. For this reason he insisted that the Common Law of England must be 'established in every province' across the Empire.[6]

For a society claiming to be governed by rule of law in the name of liberty and freedom, chattel slavery and the transatlantic slave trade lay bare the contradictions and hypocrisies of eighteenth-century Britain. Most of the discourse about rule of law implied or demanded that all law be the same everywhere. Instead colonial elites all over the world established elected bodies creating a patchwork of legal regimes that each passed legislation to arbitrate and protect their local and global interests. But these colonial jurisdictions were not distinct or separate from metropolitan laws. The law created a web of empire that connected London, the Empire's metropolitan center, with these disparate places, their racial regimes, commercial ties, and cultural mores. And the flow was by no means unidirectional or predictable. People, ideas, newspapers, and commodities came through London and brought with it those internal others who settled in what Daniel Statt has called 'the foreigners' mecca'.[7]

The internal others who settled in London, calling it home, found themselves pulled in to the ideology of rights, rule of law, and equality before the law. Jews, Catholics, African slaves, and sailors who people this book fought to increase their rights and achieve the status of free born English men and women. It was in this multicultural and multiracial space that categories of difference based on gender, race, ethnicity, and religion were made and remade. Through the legal collisions recounted in this study whiteness emerged as an ascendant legal category of privilege and exclusion. The lines defining who was included and who was excluded were not inflexible and there was a sense that internal others might earn the rights of Englishmen (as Scots were seen to have done after 1707). The lines of inclusion and exclusion were relational and situational, often their placement dictated by the demands of the Empire as in the case of Catholic relief in the 1770s cannot be understood apart from Britain's desperate need for Irish and Catholic men to staff the military.

In the second half of the eighteenth century then, lines formed around the issue of foreigners and the legal treatment of Britain's internal others. Expectations of rule of the law and equality before the law collided with preconceptions about the normative legal subject: a white, male Protestant member of the Church of England. As opinions aired in pamphlets, coffeehouses, courtrooms, and parliamentary debates, positions coalesced around the issue of empire. Those who believed in a more expansive empire, those we have called cosmopolitans, tended to advocate a more capacious mindset that allowed for a circumscribed, hierarchized inclusion while those who imagined a traditional Englishman and his rights defended their cultural and legal borders because they could not envision a citizenry expanded by Jewish naturalization, African freedom, Catholic emancipation, or Irish autonomy.

In the interests of their position on empire eighteenth-century contemporaries on both sides of the issue of imperial expansion desperately desired the separation of colony from metropole in order to persuade their audience of public opinion that empire was possible and that it would not interfere or disturb metropolitan sensibilities. This fictional disentanglement of home and away has influenced some historians whose scholarship reflects this division as real. Despite two decades of research since the 'imperial turn', and the general acceptance by most historians that colony and metropole were co-constituted, that mixing is still generally located 'out there' in colonial spaces. The recent turn back to social history occludes both race and empire flattening the details of the story and the contradictions and complications of what really happened and how.[8] The cases analyzed here allow for the disclosure of the particularities that contradicted the ideology of rule of law; some of these contradictions met both resistance from 'the people' who insisted on equal treatment in different parts of legal system and support from a 'public opinion' that did not wish to extend rights to a given group whether they were working-class sailors or self emancipated slaves.

Government authorities reacted to the fray of public opinion. In 1753 MPs responded to popular dissent over the recently passed Jewish Naturalization Act and repealed it almost immediately. But over the course of the second half of the eighteenth century examined here, we can see a hardening of lines as law was used more often to construct racial, sexual, and ethnic categories. Even after five days of rioting in 1780, Parliament did not repeal the Catholic Relief Act 1778, instead imposing martial law to quiet the city. Nor did the pamphlet war and the constitutional arguments made by the Irish Protestants in 1800 result in a reconsideration of Union. Instead governing authorities employed legal mechanisms to strengthen rule from the center and advance imperial priorities defining difference and sameness in the name of Britain and its expanding empire.[9]

For Granville Sharp 'every inhabitant of the British colonies, black as well as white, bond as well as free, are undoubtedly the *King's*

CONCLUSION

subjects, during their residence within the limits of the *King's dominions*'. From this axiomatic position, they derived the privilege of 'personal protection, howsoever bound in service to their respective masters'.[10] This statement was perfectly consistent with the ideology of rule of law and equality before the law. London and its racial hierarchies were somewhat removed from slave societies that depended on the category of whiteness to compel black labor and pacify poor whites and had developed the complicated laws to enforce raced and chattel slavery. With a completely different economy and demographic profile, London the metropole was peripheral to the racial dynamics of the Caribbean or North American colonies. Yet from this marginal position we can get a perspective that has eluded scholars, especially about the ideology of rule of law and its operation. It was in the metropole that categories of difference collided and in the metropole that they were processed. The legal ramifications of difference as worked out in the cases analyzed in this book were felt at home and abroad, intimately connected and relevant to the many colonial nodes that made up the Empire. Because they were on the periphery of an already existing center, the contingent and opportunistic results exposed the inconsistencies and contradictions of empire and law.

Notes

1 Granville Sharp, *A declaration of the people's natural right to a share in the legislature; which is the fundamental principle of the British constitution of state* (London: B. White, 1775), pp. 2–3, emphases in the original.
2 Sharp, *Declaration*, p. 4. He quotes *Principia Leg. Et Aequit.*, p. 56.
3 Sharp, *Declaration*, pp. 26–27, emphasis in original.
4 Granville Sharp, *The law of liberty, or, royal law, by which all mankind will certainly be judged! Earnestly Recommended To The Serious Consideration Of All Slaveholders And Slavedealers* (London: B. White and E. and C. Dilly, 1776), p. 49.
5 Granville Sharp, *A representation of the injustice and dangerous tendency of tolerating slavery; Or of admitting the least claim of private property in the persons of men, in England* (London: B. White and Robert Horsfield, 1769), p. 71.
6 Sharp, *Representation*, p. 72.
7 Statt, *Foreigners and Englishmen*, p. 31.
8 James Vernon, *Distant Strangers: How Britain Became Modern* (Berkeley, CA: University of California Press, 2014).
9 Historians of the British Atlantic in the eighteenth century see a similar trend toward a more authoritarian rule from the metropole. For more, see Elizabeth Mancke, 'Chartered Enterprises and the Evolution of the British Atlantic World', in *The Creation of the British Atlantic World*, ed. Elizabeth Mancke and Carole Shammas (Baltimore, MD: Johns Hopkins University Press, 2005), pp. 237–262 and Elizabeth Mancke, 'Negotiating an Empire: Britain and its Overseas Peripheries, c. 1550–1780', in *Negotiated Empires: Centers and Peripheries in the New World, 1500–1820* ed. Christine Daniels and Michael V. Kennedy (New York: Routledge, 2002), pp. 235–265.
10 Sharp, *Representation*, p. 72, emphasis in original.

SELECT BIBLIOGRAPHY

AHR Forum: Unanswered Questions'. *American Historical Review* 113 (2008), pp. 1422–1430.
Ahmed, Sara. 'A Phenomenology of Whiteness'. *Feminist Theory* 8 (2007), pp. 149–168.
Ahmed, Sara. *Queer Phenomenology: Orientations, Objects, Others* (Durham, NC: Duke University Press, 2006).
Andrew, Donna T. *Aristocratic Vice: The Attack on Duelling, Suicide, Adultery, and Gambling in Eighteenth-Century England* (New Haven, CT: Yale University Press, 2013).
Aravamudan, Srinivas. *Tropicopolitans: Colonialism and Agency, 1688–1804* (Chapel Hill, NC: University of North Carolina Press, 1999).
Archer, John. *Social Unrest and Popular Protest in England, 1780–1840* (Cambridge: Cambridge University Press, 2000).
Baker, John H. *Introduction to English Legal History* (London: Butterworths, 1990).
Barrell, John. *Imagining the King's Death: Figurative Treason, Fantasies of Regicide, 1793–1796* (Oxford: Oxford University Press, 2000).
Barrell, John. *The Spirit of Despotism: Invasions of Privacy in the 1790s* (Oxford: Oxford University Press, 2006).
Bartlett, Thomas, David Dickson, Dáire Keogh, and Kevin Whelan, eds. *1798: A Bicentenary Perspective* (Dublin: Four Courts, 2003).
Baucom, Ian. *Specters of the Atlantic: Finance Capital, Slavery, and the Philosophy of History* (Durham, NC: Duke University Press, 2005).
Beattie, J. M. *Crime and the Courts in England, 1660–1800* (Princeton, NJ: Princeton University Press, 1986).
Beier, Lee. *Masterless Men: the Vagrancy Problem in England, 1560–1640* (London: Methuen, 1985).
Benton, Lauren. *A Search for Sovereignty: Law and Geography in European Empires, 1400–1900* (Cambridge: Cambridge University Press, 2010).
Benton, Lauren. *Law and Colonial Cultures: Legal Regimes in World History, 1400–1900* (Cambridge: Cambridge University Press, 2002).
Bhabha, Homi. 'The White Stuff'. *Artforum International* 36 (1998), pp. 21–24.
Bilder, Mary Sarah. *The Transatlantic Constitution: Colonial Legal Culture and the Empire* (Cambridge, MA: Harvard University Press, 2004).
Bolton, G. C. *The Passing of the Irish Act of Union: A Study in Parliamentary Politics* (Oxford: Oxford University Press, 1966).
Braddick, Michael and John Walter. 'Introduction: Grids of Power: Order, Hierarchy and Subordination in Early Modern Society'. In *Negotiating Power in Early Modern Society: Order, Hierarchy and Subordination in Britain and Ireland*, ed. Michael Braddick and John Walter (Cambridge: Cambridge University Press, 2001), pp. 1–42.
Brewer, John. *The Sinews of Power: War, Money and the English State, 1688–1783* (Cambridge: Cambridge University Press, 1990).

SELECT BIBLIOGRAPHY

Brewer, John and John Styles, eds. *An Ungovernable People? The English and Their Law in the Seventeenth and Eighteenth Centuries* (London: Hutchinson, 1980).
Brooks, Kim and Robert Leckey, eds. *Queer Theory: Law, Culture, Empire* (London: Routledge, 2010).
Brown, Christopher Leslie. *Moral Capital: Foundations of British Abolitionism* (Chapel Hill, NC: University of North Carolina Press, 2006).
Brown, Laura. *Ends of Empire: Women and Ideology in Early Eighteenth-Century English Literature* (Ithaca, NY: Cornell University Press, 1993).
Brown, Michael, Patrick Geoghegan, and James Kelly, eds. *The Irish Act of Union, 1800: Bicentennial Essays* (Dublin: Irish Academic Press, 2003).
Brunsman, Denver Alexander. *The Evil Necessity: British Naval Impressment in the Eighteenth-Century Atlantic World* (Charlottesville, VA: University of Virginia Press, 2013).
Burroughs, Robert. 'Sailors and Slaves: The "Poor Enslaved Tar" in Naval Reform and Nautical Melodrama'. *Journal of Victorian Culture* 16 (2011), pp. 305–322.
Butler, Judith. *Gender Trouble: Feminism and the Subversion of Identity* (New York: Routledge, 1999).
Butler, Judith. 'Merely Cultural'. *New Left Review* 227 (1998), pp. 33–44.
Carey, Jane, Leigh Boucher, and Katherine Ellinghaus, eds. *Re-Orienting Whiteness* (New York: Palgrave Macmillan, 2009).
Case, Sue-Ellen. 'Tracking the Vampire'. *Differences: A Journal of Feminist Cultural Studies* 3 (1991), pp. 1–20.
Coats, Ann Veronica and Philip MacDougall, eds. *The Naval Mutinies of 1797: Unity and Perseverance* (Woodbridge: Boydell Press, 2011).
Cohen, Cathy. 'Punks, Bulldaggers, and Welfare Queens: The Radical Potential of Queer Politics?'. *GLQ* 3.4 (1997), pp. 437–465.
Coleman, Deirdre. 'Janet Schaw and the Complexions of Empire'. *Eighteenth-Century Studies* 36 (2003), pp. 169–193.
Colley, Linda. *Britons: Forging the Nation, 1707–1837* (New Haven, CT: Yale University Press, 1992).
Colley, Linda. *Captives* (New York: Pantheon Books, 2002).
Cotter, W. R. 'The Somerset Case and the Abolition of Slavery in England'. *History* 79 (1994), pp. 31–56.
Cowan, Brian. *The Social Life of Coffee* (New Haven, CT: Yale University Press, 2005).
Cowan, Brian. 'What Was Masculine about the Public Sphere? Gender and the Coffeehouse Milieu in Post-Restoration England'. *History Workshop Journal* 51 (2001), pp. 127–158.
Dabydeen, David. *Hogarth's Blacks: Images of Blacks in Eighteenth Century English Art* (Athens, GA: University of Georgia Press, 1987).
Davis, David Brion. *The Problem of Slavery in the Age of Revolution, 1770–1823* (Ithaca, NY: Cornell University Press, 1975).
Davis, Kathleen. *Periodization and Sovereignty: How Ideas of Feudalism and Secularization Govern the Politics of Time* (Philadelphia, PA: University of Pennsylvania Press, 2008).
Deane, Seamus. *The French Revolution and Enlightenment in England, 1789–1832* (Cambridge, MA: Harvard University Press, 1988).
Dickinson, H. T., ed. *Britain and the French Revolution, 1789–1815* (New York: St. Martin's Press, 1989).
Dickinson, H. T. *British Radicalism and the French Revolution* (Oxford: Blackwell, 1985).
Dickinson, H. T. *Caricatures and the Constitution, 1760–1832* (Cambridge: Chadwyck-Healey, 1986).
Dickson, D., Daire Keogh, and Kevin Whelan, eds. *The United Irishmen: Republicanism, Radicalism, and Reaction* (Dublin: Lilliput Press, 1993).
Dickson, P. G. M. *The Financial Revolution in England: A Study in the Development of Public Credit, 1688–1756* (New York: Macmillan, 1967).
Donald, Diana. *The Age of Caricature: Satirical Prints in the Reign of George III* (New Haven, CT: Yale University Press, 1996).

SELECT BIBLIOGRAPHY

Donoghue, John. *Fire under the Ashes: An Atlantic History of the English Revolution* (Chicago, IL: University of Chicago Press, 2013).

Dorsett, Shaunnagh and John McLaren, eds. *Legal Histories of the British Empire: Laws, Engagements and Legacies* (New York: Routledge, 2014).

Doyle, William. 'The Union in a European Context'. *Transactions of the Royal Historical Society*, series 6, 10 (2000), pp. 167–180.

Drescher, Seymour. *Capitalism and Antislavery* (Oxford: Oxford University Press, 1987)

Drescher, Seymour. 'From Consensus to Consensus: Slavery in International Law'. In *The Legal Understanding of Slavery: From the Historical to the Contemporary*, ed. Jean Allain (Oxford: Oxford University Press 2012), pp. 85–104.

Drescher, Seymour. 'Manumission in a Society without Slave Law: Eighteenth-Century England'. *Slavery and Abolition* 10 (1989), pp. 85–101.

Drescher, Seymour. *The Mighty Experiment: Free Labor versus Slavery in British Emancipation* (Oxford: Oxford University Press, 2002).

Dugan, James. *The Great Mutiny* (New York: Putnam, 1965).

Elliott, Marianne. *Partners in Revolution: The United Irishmen and France* (New Haven, CT: Yale University Press, 1982).

Ellis, Markman. *The Coffee House: A Cultural History* (London: Phoenix, 2004).

Emsley, Clive. '"An Aspect of Pitt's Terror": Prosecutions for Sedition during the 1790s'. *Social History* 6 (1981), pp. 155–184.

Emsley, Clive. 'Repression, "Terror" and the Rule of Law in England during the Decade of the French Revolution'. *The English Historical Review* 100 (1985), pp. 801–825.

Endelman, Todd. *The Jews of Britain, 1656–2000* (Berkeley, CA: University of California Press, 2001).

Endelman, Todd. *The Jews of Georgian England, 1714–1830* (Ann Arbor, MI: University of Michigan Press, 1999).

Endelman, Todd. 'Writing English Jewish History'. *Albion* 27 (1995), pp. 623–36.

Epstein, James. *Scandal of Colonial Rule: Power and Subversion in the British Atlantic during the Age of Revolution* (Cambridge: Cambridge University Press, 2012).

Feldman, David. 'Conceiving Difference: Religion, Race and the Jews in Britain, c. 1750–1900'. *History Workshop Journal* 76 (2013), pp. 160–186.

Felsenstein, Frank. *Anti-Semitic Stereotypes: A Paradigm of Otherness in English Popular Culture, 1660–1830* (Baltimore, MD: Johns Hopkins University Press, 1995).

Ferguson, Moira. *Subject to Others: British Women Writers and Colonial Slavery, 1670–1834* (New York: Routledge, 1992).

Fiddes, Edward. 'Lord Mansfield and the Sommersett Case'. *Law Quarterly Review* 50 (1934), pp. 499–511.

Fisher, Michael. *Counterflows to Colonialism: Indian Travelers and Settlers in Britain, 1600–1857* (Delhi: Permanent Black, 2004).

Flynn, Carol Houlihan. 'Whatever Happened to the Gordon Riots'. In *A Companion to the Eighteenth-Century English Novel and Culture*, ed. Paula Backscheider and Catherine Ingrassia (Malden, MA: Blackwell Publishers, 2005), pp. 459–480.

Fortune, Stephen. *Merchants and Jews: The Struggle for British West Indian Commerce, 1650–1750* (Gainsville, FL: University Press of Florida, 1984).

Frankenberg, Ruth. *White Women, Race Matters: The Social Construction of Whiteness* (Minneapolis, MN: University of Minnesota Press, 1993).

Fry, Michael. *The Dundas Despotism* (Edinburgh: Edinburgh University Press, 1992).

Frykman, Niklas. 'Connections between Mutinies in European Navies'. *International Review of Social History* 58 (2013), pp. 87–107.

Fumerton, Patricia. *Unsettled: The Culture of Mobility and the Working Poor in Early Modern England* (Chicago, IL: University of Chicago: 2009).

Games, Allison. *The Web of Empire English Cosmopolitans in an Age of Expansion, 1560–1660* (Oxford: Oxford University Press, 2008).

Geoghegan, Patrick. *The Irish Act of Union: A Study in High Politics 1798–1801* (New York: St. Martin's Press, 1999).

George, Mary Dorothy. 'The Cartoon in the Eighteenth Century'. *History Today* 9 (1954), pp. 591–597.

SELECT BIBLIOGRAPHY

Gerzina, Gretchen Holbrook. *Black London: Life Before Emancipation* (New Brunswick, NJ: Rutgers University Press, 1995).
Giffney, Noreen. 'Introduction: The "q" word.' In *Ashgate Research Companion to Queer Theory*, ed Noreen Giffney and Michael O'Rourke (Farnham: Ashgate, 2009), pp. 1–13.
Gill, Conrad. *The Naval Mutinies of 1797* (Manchester: Manchester University Press, 1913).
Giuseppi, J. A. 'Early Jewish Holders of Bank of England Stock (1694–1725)'. *Miscellanies of the Jewish Historical Society of England* 6 (1962), pp. 143–174.
Glasco, Jeffrey. 'The Seaman Feels Him-self a Man'. *International Labor and Working-Class History* 66 (2004), pp. 40–56.
Gould, Eliga. 'Zones of Law, Zones of Violence: The Legal Geography of the British Atlantic, circa 1772'. *William and Mary Quarterly* 60 (2003), pp. 471–510.
Green, Jack P. *Peripheries and Center: Constitutional Development in the Extended Polities of the British Empire and the United States, 1607–1788* (Athens, GA: University of Georgia Press, 1986).
Hall, Catherine. *Civilising Subjects: Colony and Metropole in the English Imagination, 1830–1867* (Chicago, IL: University of Chicago Press, 2002).
Hall, Catherine. *Macaulay and Son: Architects of Imperial Britain* (New Haven, CT: Yale University Press, 2012).
Hall, Catherine and Sonya Rose, eds. *At Home with the Empire: Metropolitan Culture and the Imperial World* (Cambridge: Cambridge University Press, 2006).
Hall, Kim. *Things of Darkness: Economies of Race and Gender in Early Modern England* (Ithaca, NY: Cornell University Press, 1995).
Hall, Stuart. *Race: The Floating Signifier*, DVD, prod. and dir. Sut Jhally (Northampton, MA: Media Education Foundation, 1996).
Halliday, Paul. *Habeas Corpus: From England to Empire* (Cambridge, MA: Harvard University Press, 2010).
Harris, Michael. *London Newspapers in the Age of Walpole: A Study of the Origins of the Modern English Press* (Cranbury, NJ: Associated University Presses, 1987).
Hay, Douglas, Peter Linebaugh, John G. Rule, E. P. Thompson, and Cal Winslow, eds. *Albion's Fatal Tree: Crime and Society in Eighteenth-Century England* (New York: Pantheon, 1975).
Haydon, Colin. *Anti-Catholicism in Eighteenth-Century England, c. 1714–1780: A Political and Social Study* (Manchester: Manchester University Press, 1993).
Haydon, Colin. 'The Gordon Riots in the English Provinces'. *Historical Research* 16 (1990), pp. 354–359.
Haywood, Ian and John Seed, eds. *The Gordon Riots: Politics, Cultures and Insurrection in Late Eighteenth-Century Britain* (Cambridge: Cambridge University Press, 2012).
Hecht, J. J. *Continental and Colonial Servants in Eighteenth Century England* (Northampton, MA: Department of History Smith College, 1954).
Hecht, J. J. *The Domestic Servant Class in the Eighteenth Century* (London: Routledge, 1955).
Henriques, H. S. Q. *The Jews and the English Law* (London, J. Jacobs, 1908).
Hill, Bridget. *Women Alone: Spinsters in England, 1660–1850* (New Haven, CT: Yale University Press, 2001).
Holdsworth, W. S. *A History of English Law*, 7 vols. (London: Methuen, 1923).
Hunt, Lynn. *The Family Romance of the French Revolution* (Berkeley, CA: University of California Press, 1992).
Hussain, Nassar. *The Jurisprudence of Emergency: Colonialism and the Rule of Law* (Ann Arbor, MI: University of Michigan Press, 2003).
Hyams, Paul. *King, Lords and Peasants in Medieval England: The Common Law of Villeinage in the Twelfth and Thirteenth Centuries* (Oxford: Clarendon, 1980).
Hyamson, Albert M. 'The Jew Bill of 1753'. *Transactions of the Jewish Historical Society of England* 6 (1912), pp. 156–188.
Jacobs, Jane. *Edge of Empire: Postcolonialism and the City* (London: Routledge, 1996).

SELECT BIBLIOGRAPHY

Jacobson, M. Frye. *Whiteness of a Different Color: European Immigrants and the Alchemy of Race* (Cambridge, MA: Harvard University Press, 1998).

Jones, Cecily. *Engendering Whiteness: White Women and Colonialism in Barbados and North Carolina, 1627–1865* (Manchester: Manchester University Press, 2007).

Kaiser, Matthew. *The World in Play: Portraits of a Victorian Concept* (Palo Alto, CA: Stanford University Press, 2012).

Katz, David. *The Jews in the History of England, 1485–1850* (Oxford: Clarendon, 1994).

Kelly, James. *Prelude to Union: Anglo-Irish Politics in the 1780s* (Cork: Cork University Press, 1992).

Kelly, James. 'The Origins of the Irish Act of Union: An Examination of Unionist Opinion in Britain and Ireland, 1650–1800'. *Irish Historical Studies* 25 (1987), pp. 236–263.

Kent, D. A. 'Ubiquitous But Invisible: Female Domestic Servants in Mid-Eighteenth-Century London'. *History Workshop Journal* 28 (1989), pp. 111–128.

Keogh, Dáire and Kevin Whelan, eds. *Acts of Union, The Causes, Contexts and Consequences of the Act of Union* (Dublin: Four Courts Press, 2001).

King, Peter. *Crime, Justice, and Discretion in England, 1740–1820* (Oxford: Oxford University Press, 2000).

King, Peter. 'Ethnicity, Prejudice, and Justice: The Treatment of the Irish at the Old Bailey, 1750–1825'. *The Journal of British Studies* 52 (2013), pp. 390–414.

Kolsky, Elizabeth. *Colonial Justice in British India* (Cambridge: Cambridge University Press, 2010).

Krikler, Jeremy. 'The Zong and the Lord Chief Justice'. *History Workshop Journal* 64 (2008), pp. 29–47.

Kriz, Kay Dian. 'Marketing Mulàtresses in the Paintings and Prints of Agostino Brunias'. In *The Global Eighteenth Century*, ed. Felicity Nussbaum (Baltimore, MD: Johns Hopkins University Press, 2003), pp. 195–210.

Lambert, David. *White Creole Culture, Politics and Identity during the Age of Abolition* (Cambridge: Cambridge University Press, 2005).

Land, Isaac. 'Bread and Arsenic: Citizenship from the Bottom Up in Georgian England'. *Journal of Social History* 39 (2005), pp. 89–110.

Land, Isaac. *War, Nationalism and the British Sailor, 1750–1850* (New York: Palgrave Macmillan, 2009).

Landes, Joan. *Visualizing the Nation: Gender, Representation, and Revolution in Eighteenth-century France* (Ithaca, NY: Cornell University Press, 2001).

Landes, Joan. *Women and the Public Sphere in the Age of the French Revolution* (Ithaca, NY: Cornell University Press, 1988).

Langbein, John. *Origins of Adversary Criminal Trial* (Oxford: Oxford University Press, 2005).

Lawson, Philip. *The Imperial Challenge: Quebec and Britain in the Age of the American Revolution* (Montreal: McGill-Queen's University Press, 1990).

Lemmings, David. *Law and Government in England during the Long Eighteenth Century: From Consent to Command* (Houndmills: Palgrave Macmillan, 2011).

Lenman, Bruce. *The Jacobite Risings in Britain, 1689–1746* (Aberdeen: Scottish Cultural Press, 1980).

Liberles, Robert. 'The Jews and their Bill: Jewish Motivation in the Controversy of 1753'. *Jewish History* 2 (1987), pp. 29–36.

Lincoln, Margarette. *Representing the Royal Navy: British Sea Power, 1750–1815* (Aldershot: Ashgate, 2002).

Linebaugh, Peter and Marcus Rediker. *The Many Headed Hydra: Sailors, Slaves, Commoners, and the Hidden Story of the Revolutionary Atlantic* (Boston, MA: Beacon Press, 2000).

Lobban, Michael. 'Treason, Sedition and the Radical Movement in the Age of the French Revolution'. *Liverpool Law Review* 22 (2000), pp. 205–234.

Loomba, Ania. 'Periodization, Race, and Global Contact'. *Journal of Medieval and Early Modern Studies* 37 (2007), pp. 595–620.

Lorimer, Douglas. 'Black Slaves and English Liberty: a Re-examination of Racial Slavery in England'. *Immigrants and Minorities* 3 (1984), pp. 121–150.

SELECT BIBLIOGRAPHY

MacDonald, Janet. *The British Navy's Victualling Board, 1793–1815: Management and Competence and Incompetence* (Woodbridge: Boydell, 2010).

Macfarlane, Karen. ' "Does He Know the Danger of an Oath?": Oaths, Religion, Ethnicity and the Advent of the Adversarial Criminal Trial in the Eighteenth Century'. *Immigrants & Minorities* 31 (2013), pp. 317–345.

Macfarlane, Karen. 'Understanding Justice: Criminal Courtroom Interpretation in Eighteenth-Century London and Twenty-First Century Toronto'. *Traduction, Terminologie, Rédaction* 20 (2007), pp. 271–299.

Macinnes, Allan I. *Union and Empire: The Making of the United Kingdom in 1707* (Cambridge: Cambridge University Press, 2007).

Magra, Christopher. 'Anti-Impressment Riots and the Origins of the Age of Revolution'. *International Review of Social History* 58 (2013), pp. 131–151.

Makdisi, Saree. *Making England Western: Occidentalism, Race and Imperial Culture* (Chicago, IL: University of Chicago Press, 2014).

Mancke, Elizabeth. 'Negotiating an Empire: Britain and its Overseas Peripheries, c. 1550–1780'. In *Negotiated Empires: Centers and Peripheries in the New World, 1500–1820*, ed. Christine Daniels and Michael V. Kennedy (New York: Routledge, 2002), pp. 235–265.

Manwaring, G.E. and Bonamy Dobrée. *Mutiny: The Floating Republic* (London: G Bles, 1935).

Marshall, P. J. 'Britain and the World in the Eighteenth Century: IV, The Turning Outwards of Britain'. *Transactions of the Royal Historical Society* (sixth series) 11 (2001), pp. 1–15.

Marshall, P. J. 'Empire and Authority in the Later Eighteenth-Century'. *Journal of Imperial and Commonwealth History* 15 (1987), pp. 105–122.

Marshall, P. J. 'A Nation Defined by Empire, 1755–1776'. In *Uniting the Kingdom: The Making of British History*, ed. Alexander Grand and Keith Stringer (London: Routledge, 1995), pp. 208–222.

Massey, Doreen. *For Space* (London: SAGE Publications, 2005).

Matera, Marc. *Black London: the Imperial Metropolis and Decolonization in the Twentieth Century* (Oakland, CA: University of California Press, 2015).

Mayall, David. *Gypsy Identities 1500–2000: From Egipcyans and Moon-men to the Ethnic Romany* (London: Routledge, 2004).

McCormack, Matthew. 'Supporting the Civil Power: Citizen Soldiers and the Gordon Riots'. *London Journal* 37 (2012), pp. 27–41.

McCormack, W. J. *The Pamphlet Debate on the Union between Great Britain and Ireland, 1797–1800* (Dublin: Irish Academic Press, 1996).

McKenzie, Andrea. *Tyburn's Martyrs: Execution in England, 1675–1775* (London: Hambledon Continuum, 2007).

McLaren, John. *Dewigged, Bothered, and Bewildered: British Colonial Judges on Trial, 1800–1900* (Toronto: University of Toronto Press, 2011).

Measell, James. 'William Pitt and Suspension of *Habeas Corpus*'. *Quarterly Journal of Speech* 60 (1974), pp. 468–476.

Mercer, Keith. 'Northern Exposure: Resistance to Naval Impressment in British North America, 1775–1815'. *The Canadian Historical Review* 91 (2010), pp. 199–232.

Midgley, Claire. *Feminism and Empire: Women Activists in Imperial Britain, 1790–1865* (London: Routledge, 2007).

Mohanram, Radhika. *Imperial White: Race, Diaspora, and the British Empire* (Minneapolis, MN: University of Minnesota Press, 2007).

Molineux, Catherine. *Faces of Perfect Ebony: Encountering Atlantic Slavery in Imperial Britain* (Cambridge, MA, Harvard University Press: 2012).

Monahan, Michael. *The Creolizing Subject: Race, Reason, and the Politics of Purity* (New York: Fordham University Press, 2011).

Monod, Paul. *Jacobitism and the English People, 1688–1788* (Cambridge: Cambridge University Press, 1989).

Moran, Leslie, Daniel Monk, and Sara Beresford, eds., *Legal Queeries: Lesbian, Gay and Transgender Legal Studies* (London: Cassell, 1998).

SELECT BIBLIOGRAPHY

Morgan, Gwenda and Peter Rushton. *Banishment in the Early Atlantic World: Convicts, Rebels and Slaves* (London: Bloomsbury, 2013).

Morgan, Kenneth. *Slavery and the British Empire: From Africa to America* (Oxford: Oxford University Press, 2007).

Morgan, Philip. 'British Encounters with African and African Americans, 1600–1780'. In *Strangers within the Realm: Cultural Margins of the First British Empire*, ed. Bernard Bailyn and Philip Morgan (Chapel Hill, NC: University of North Carolina Press, 1991), pp. 157–219.

Mori, Jennifer. *Britain in the Age of the French Revolution* (Harlow: Longman, 2000).

Mori, Jennifer. *William Pitt and the French Revolution, 1785–1795* (Edinburgh: Keele University Press, 1997).

Myers, Norma. *Reconstructing the Black Past: Blacks in Britain, 1780–1830*. (London: F. Cass, 1996).

Newman, Brooke. *A Dark Inheritance: Race, Sex, and Subjecthood in the British Atlantic* (New Haven, CT: Yale University Press, forthcoming).

Nora, Pierre. 'The Return of the Event'. In *Histories: French Constructions of the Past*, ed. Jacques Revel and Lynn Hunt (New York: New Press, 1995), pp. 421–436.

Nussbaum, Felicity. *Torrid Zones: Maternity, Sexuality, and Empire in Eighteenth-century English Narratives* (Baltimore, MD: Johns Hopkins University Press, 1995).

O'Shaughnessy, Andrew Jackson. *An Empire Divided: the American Revolution and the British Caribbean* (Philadelphia, PA: University of Pennsylvania Press, 2000).

Oldham, James. *English Common Law in the Age of Mansfield* (Chapel Hill, NC: University of North Carolina Press, 2004).

Oldham, James. 'New Light on Mansfield and Slavery'. *Journal of British Studies* 27 (1988), pp. 45–68.

Paley, Ruth. 'After Somerset: Mansfield, Slavery and the Law in England, 1772–1830'. In *Law, Crime and English Society 1660–1830*, ed. Norma Landau (Cambridge: Cambridge University Press, 2002), pp. 165–184.

Paley, Ruth. 'Imperial Politics and English Law: the Many Contexts of Somerset'. *Law and History Review* 24 (2006), pp. 662–664.

Pamela Clemit. *The Cambridge Companion to British Literature of the French Revolution in the 1790s* (Cambridge: Cambridge University Press, 2012).

Perry, Thomas. *Public Opinion, Propaganda, and Politics in Eighteenth-Century England: A Study of the Jew Bill of 1753* (Cambridge, MA: Harvard University Press, 1962).

Petrie, Charles. 'The Elibank Plot'. *Transactions of the Royal Historical Society* 14 (1931), pp. 175–196.

Philip, Mark, ed. *The French Revolution and British Popular Politics* (Cambridge: Cambridge University Press, 1991).

Pincus, Steven. *1688: The First Modern Revolution* (New Haven, CT: Yale University Press, 2009).

Pollins, Harold. *Economic History of the Jews in England* (Rutherford, NJ: Fairleigh Dickinson University Press, 1982).

Poole, Robert. 'The March to Peterloo: Politics and Festivity in Late Georgian England'. *Past and Present* 192 (2006), pp. 109–153.

Quennell, Peter. *Hogarth's Progress* (New York: Viking Press, 1955).

Rabin, Dana. 'Seeing Jews and Gypsies in 1753'. *Cultural and Social History* 7 (2010), pp. 35–58.

Radzinowicz, Leon. *A History of English Criminal Law and its Administration from 1750*. 4 vols. Volume 1: *The Movement for Reform* (London: Macmillan, 1948).

Rae, T. I., ed., *The Union of 1707: Its Impact on Scotland* (Glasgow: Blackie & Son Limited, 1974).

Ragussis, Michael. *Theatrical Nation: Jews and Other 'Outlandish Englishmen' in Georgian Britain* (Philadelphia, PA: University of Pennsylvania Press, 2010).

Randall, Adrian. *Riotous Assemblies: Popular Protest in Hanoverian England* (Oxford: Oxford University Press, 2006).

Rauser, Amelia. *Caricature Unmasked: Irony, Authenticity, and Individualism in Eighteenth-Century English Prints* (Newark, DE: University of Delaware Press, 2008).

SELECT BIBLIOGRAPHY

Rediker, Marcus. *The Slave Ship: A Human History* (New York: Viking, 2007).
Robertson, John, ed. *A Union for Empire: Political Thought and the British Union of 1707* (Cambridge: Cambridge University Press, 1995).
Rodger, N. A. M. *The Command of the Ocean: A Naval History of Britain, 1649–1815* (New York: Norton, 2004).
Rodger, N. A. M. *The Wooden World: An Anatomy of the Georgian Navy* (London: Collins, 1986).
Roediger, David. *The Wages of Whiteness: Race and the Making of the American Working Class* (New York: Verson, 1999).
Rogers, Nicholas. 'Crowd and people in the Gordon Riots'. In *The Transformation of Political Culture: England and Germany in the late Eighteenth Century*, ed. E. Hellmuth (London: German Historical Institute, 1990), pp. 39–55.
Rogers, Nicholas. *Crowds, Culture and Politics in Georgian Britain* (Oxford: Clarendon, 1998).
Rogers, Nicholas. *Mayhem: Post-War Crime and Violence in Britain 1748–1753* (New Haven, CT: Yale University Press, 2012).
Rogers, Nicholas. 'The Gordon Riots Revisited'. *Historical Papers* 23 (1988), pp. 16–34.
Rogers, Nicholas. *The Press Gang: Naval Impressment and its Opponents in Georgian Britain* (London: Continuum, 2007).
Rogers, Nicholas. 'Vagrancy, Impressment and the Regulation of Labour in Eighteenth-Century Britain'. *Slavery and Abolition* 15 (1994), pp. 102–113.
Rogers, Pat. 'North and South'. *Eighteenth-Century Life* 12 (1988), pp. 101–111.
Rudé, George. *The Crowd in History: A Study of Popular Disturbances in France and England 1730–1848* (New York: Wiley, 1964).
Rudé, George. 'The Gordon Riots: A Study of the Rioters and their Victims: The Alexander Prize Essay'. *Transactions of the Royal Historical Society*, 5th series, 6 (1956), pp. 93–114.
Rupprecht, Anita. 'Excessive Memories: Slavery, Insurance and Resistance'. *History Workshop Journal* 64 (2008), pp. 6–28.
Russell, Gillian. *The Theatres of War: Performance, Politics, and Society, 1793–1815* (Oxford: Clarendon, 1995).
Schweizer, Karl W. 'Newspapers, Politics and Public Opinion in the Later Hanoverian Era'. *Parliamentary History* 25 (2006), pp. 32–48.
Scott, Joan. 'Gender as a Category of Analysis'. *American Historical Review* 91 (1986), pp. 1053–1075.
Selwood, Jacob. *Diversity and Difference in Early Modern London* (Burlington, VT: Ashgate, 2010).
Sen, Sudipta. 'Imperial Subjects on Trial: On the Legal Identity of Britons in Late Eighteenth-Century India'. *Journal of British Studies* 45 (2006), pp. 532–555.
Sewell, William. 'Historical Events as Transformations of Structures: Inventing Revolution at the Bastille'. *Theory and Society* 25 (1996), pp. 841–881.
Shapiro, James. *Shakespeare and the Jews* (New York: Columbia University Press, 1996).
Sharpe, J. A. '"Last Dying Speeches": Religion, Ideology and Public Execution in Seventeenth-Century England'. *Past and Present* 107 (1985), pp. 144–167.
Shaw, Jenny. *Everyday Life in the Early English Caribbean: Irish, Africans, and the Construction of Difference* (Athens, GA: University of Georgia Press, 2013).
Sherwood, Marika. 'Blacks in the Gordon Riots'. *History Today* 47 (1997), pp. 24–28.
Shiells, Georgia. 'Immigration History and Whiteness Studies: American and Australian Approaches Compared'. *History Compass* 8 (2010), pp. 790–804.
Shoemaker, Robert. *The London Mob: Violence and Disorder in Eighteenth Century England* (London: Hambledon, 2004).
Shyllon, Folarin. *Black People in Britain, 1555–1833* (Oxford: Oxford University Press, 1977).
Shyllon, Folarin. *Black Slaves in Britain* (Oxford: Oxford University Press, 1974).
Simpson, Alfred W. B. *An Introduction to the History of the Land Law* (Oxford: Oxford University Press, 1961).

SELECT BIBLIOGRAPHY

Singer, Alan. 'Aliens and Citizens: Jewish and Protestant Naturalization in the Making of the Modern British Nation' (PhD dissertation, University of Missouri, Columbia, 1999).

Singer, Alan. 'Great Britain or Judea Nova? National Identity, Property, and the Jewish Naturalization Controversy of 1753'. In *British Romanticism and the Jews: History, Culture, Literature*, ed. Sheila A. Spector (New York: Palgrave Macmillan, 2008), pp. 19–36.

Smyth, Jim ed. *Revolution, Counter-Revolution and Union: Ireland in the 1790s* (Cambridge: Cambridge University Press, 2000).

Smyth, Jim. *The Men of No Property: Irish Radicals and Popular Politics in the Late Eighteenth Century* (New York: St. Martin's Press, 1992).

Stanbridge, Karen. 'Quebec and the Irish Catholic Relief Act of 1778: An Institutional Approach'. *Journal of Historical Sociology* 16 (2003), pp. 375–404.

Statt, Daniel. *Foreigners and Englishmen: The Controversy over Immigration and Population, 1660–1760* (Newark, DE: University of Delaware Press, 1995).

Stoler, Ann. *Carnal Knowledge and Imperial Power: Race and the Intimate in Colonial Rule* (Berkeley, CA: University of California Press, 1995).

Stone, Christopher and Bencie Woll. '"Dumb O Jemmy and Others": Deaf People, Interpreters, and the London Courts in the Eighteenth and Nineteenth Centuries'. *Sign Language Studies* 8 (2008), pp. 226–240.

Straub, Kristina. *Domestic Affairs: Intimacy, Eroticism, and Violence between Servants and Masters in Eighteenth-Century Britain* (Baltimore, MD: Johns Hopkins University Press, 2009).

Straub, Kristina. 'Heteroanxiety and the Case of Elizabeth Canning'. *Eighteenth-Century Studies* 30 (1997), pp. 296–303.

Sullivan, Nikki. *A Critical Introduction to Queer Theory* (Edinburgh: Edinburgh University Press, 2003).

Sweet, Julie Anne. 'The British Sailors' Advocate: James Oglethorpe's First Philanthropic Venture'. *Georgia Historical Quarterly* 91 (2007), pp. 1–27.

Thompson, E. P. *Customs in Common* (London: Merlin Press, 1991).

Thompson, E. P. *The Making of the English Working Class* (New York: Pantheon, 1964).

Thompson, E. P. *Whigs and Hunters: The Origins of the Black Act* (New York: Pantheon, 1975).

Traub, Valerie. 'Mapping the Global Body'. In *Early Modern Visual Culture: Representation, Race, and Empire in Renaissance England*, ed. Peter Erickson and Clark Hulse (Philadelphia, PA: University of Pennsylvania Press, 2000), pp. 44–97.

Trumbach, Randolph. *Sex and the Gender Revolution. Volume 1: Heterosexuality and the Third Gender in Enlightenment London* (Chicago, IL: University of Chicago Press, 1998).

Ulrich, Nicole. 'International Radicalism, Local Solidarities: The 1797 British Naval Mutinies in Southern African Waters'. *International Review of Social History* 58 (2013), pp. 51–85.

Van Cleve, George. 'Somerset's Case and Its Antecedents in Imperial Perspective'. *Law and History Review* 24 (2006), pp. 601–645.

Vance, Norman. 'Irish Literary Traditions and the Act of Union'. *Canadian Journal of Irish Studies* 12 (1986), pp. 29–47.

Vernon, James. *Distant Strangers: How Britain Became Modern* (Berkeley, CA: University of California Press, 2014).

Vinogradoff, Paul. *Villainage in England: Essays in English Mediaeval History* (Oxford: Clarendon, 1892).

Walvin, James. *Black and White: the Negro and English Society, 1555–1945* (London: Penguin, 1973).

Walvin, James. *England, Slaves, and Freedom, 1776–1838* (Jackson, MS: University Press of Mississippi, 1986).

Walvin, James. *Making the Black Atlantic: Britain and the African Diaspora* (London: Cassell, 2000).

SELECT BIBLIOGRAPHY

War, Vron and Les Back. *Out of Whiteness: Color, Politics, and Culture* (Chicago, IL: University of Chicago Press, 2002).

Warner, Michael. *Fear of a Queer Planet: Queer Politics and Social Theory* (Minneapolis, MN: University of Minnesota Press, 1993).

Washburn, E. 'Somerset's Case and the Extension of Villeinage and Slavery in England'. *Proceedings of the Massachusetts Historical Society* 7 (1864), pp. 308–326.

Weiss Muller, Hannah. 'Bonds of Belonging: Subjecthood and the British Empire'. *Journal of British Studies* 53 (2014), pp. 29–58.

Whatley, Christopher with Derek T. Patrick. *The Scots and the Union* (Edinburgh: Edinburgh University Press, 2006).

Wheeler, Roxann. *The Complexion of Race: Categories of Difference in Eighteenth-Century British Culture* (Philadelphia, PA: University of Pennsylvania Press, 2000).

Wiecek, William. 'Somerset: Lord Mansfield and the Legitimacy of Slavery in the Anglo-American World'. *University of Chicago Law Review* 42 (1974), pp. 86–146.

Wiegman, Robyn. 'Whiteness Studies and the Paradox of Particularity'. *Boundary 2* 26 (1998), pp. 115–150.

Wilkinson, David. '"How Did They Pass the Union?" Secret Service Expenditure in Ireland, 1799–1804'. *History* 82 (1997), pp. 223–251.

Wilson, Kathleen, ed., *A New Imperial History: Culture, Identity, and Modernity in Britain and the Empire, 1660–1840* (Cambridge: Cambridge University Press, 2004).

Wilson, Kathleen. *A Sense of the People: Politics, Culture and Imperialism in England, 1715–1785* (Cambridge: Cambridge University Press 1995).

Wilson, Kathleen. 'Rowe's "Fair Penitent" as Global History: Or, a Diversionary Voyage to New South Wales'. *Eighteenth Century Studies* 41 (2008), pp. 231–251.

Wilson, Kathleen. *The Island Race: Englishness, Empire and Gender in the Eighteenth Century* (New York: Routledge, 2003).

Wolper, Roy. 'Circumcision as Polemic in the Jew Bill of 1753: The Cutter Cut?' *Eighteenth Century Life* 7 (1982), pp. 28–36.

INDEX

f denotes figure

abolitionists 14, 73, 74, 88, 98, 106, 171, 173
absentee planters, impact of 79
'Act for more effectually restraining Intercourse with the Crews of certain of His Majesty's Ships now in a State of Mutiny and Rebellion' 167
'Act for the better Prevention and Punishment of Attempts to seduce Persons serving in his Majesty's Forces, by Sea or Land, from their Duty and Allegiance to His Majesty, or to incite them to Mutiny or Disobedience' 167
Act in Restraint of Appeals (1533) 115
Act of 1709 24–25
Act of Parliament 22, 45, 47, 48, 92, 161
Act of Settlement (1701) 59, 116, 200
Act of Union with Ireland (1800) 1, 181, 191, 195, 199–202, 215, 227, 228, 229, 231
Acts for Catholic Relief 118
  see also Catholic Relief Act (1778); Catholic Relief Act in Ireland (1778)
Acts of Union with Scotland 55, 59, 192

Addison, Joseph 52–53
Address to the Nation, by the Seamen at St. Helen's, The 160, 161, 162
Address to the Nations of Great Britain and Ireland on the Projected Union, An (Stanhope) 220
'Advise to the Freeholders' 54
Africans 63, 128–129, 172, 173
  see also Somerset, James
Akerman, Richard 125, 126
American War of Independence 166, 196
Anglicanism 57, 130
Answer to a Pamphlet, An (Romaine) 58
anti-Catholicism 14, 111, 116, 117, 120, 123, 124–125, 129, 130, 134
anti-feminist writing 235n50
anti-Irish 113, 196
'Argus' 122–123, 123*f*
authority, ordinary people's envisioning of 17n24
Ayliffe, John 203

ballads 8, 13, 30, 110, 177
  see also songs
Ballard, Reeve 23, 24
Bank of England 23, 47, 109, 112, 131, 132

[254]

INDEX

Barnaby Rudge (Dickens) 112
Barnard, Sir John 62
Bate, James 23
Bell, Maria 79
Belle, Dido Elizabeth 79–80
Bell's Weekly 181
Belsham, William 108, 111
benefit of clergy 35, 167, 188n107
Benton, Lauren 7, 11, 95
Berry, Mary 155
Bill of Rights (1689) 59, 166
blackness
  as colonial attribute 98
  legal codification of 100n7
  as not equated with property 75
  occlusion of 98, 127
  as playing little or no role in legal decisions concerning status of black slaves in England 86
  relationship of with whiteness 102n28
blacks
  appearance of in media and arts 101–102n17
  influx of from colonies 78
  population of in England 76–77
Blackstone, William 3, 4, 5, 12, 81, 82, 97, 155, 165–166, 170, 171, 219, 222, 231n4
'Bloody Code' 115, 169
Bolton, G. C. 195
Bonds of Union 58
Bowsey, Benjamin 125, 126, 127, 136
Brewer, John 22
Bridport, Lord 157, 159
Britain, feminization of through Union and Empire 218
British
  fragility and divisiveness of in mid-eighteenth century 55
  intersection of imperial aspiration with law 31
  as white Christians 46
  as world leaders in slave trade 74

British Evening Post 135
Britishness
  anxious assertion of at margins of empire 113
  definition of 60
  future of 55
  rights to 146
  versions of 44
  see also Englishness
Buckner, Charles 163–164, 176
Bull, John 203–206, 207, 209f, 216, 228
Burke, Edmund 147, 152–155, 156, 178, 179, 219
Butts v. Penny (1677) 83, 86

Calvert, Sir William 28
Cameron, Archibald 22, 28, 114
Canning, Elizabeth 6, 10, 22, 29–45, 33f, 38f, 62, 76, 110
Canning, T. 204
Captives (Colley) 106n133
caricatures 8, 214
'Caricature Shop' 214, 215f
Carlyle, Alexander 175
'Carrying the Union' 207, 209f
cartoons/cartoonists 22, 79, 178, 199
Cartwright's Case (1569) 80
case studies
  expectation of consistency and universality in 5
  Gordon Riots 108–138, 166, 227
  Ireland's union with Great Britain 193–231
  James Somerset 6, 10, 73–76, 79, 80, 86, 89–99, 110, 114
  Jew Bill (Jewish Naturalization Act 1793) 1, 6, 22, 24, 29, 45–61, 62, 114, 137, 242
  Mary Squires and Elizabeth Canning 5, 6, 10, 22, 28, 29–45, 33f, 38f, 62, 76, 110, 114

[255]

INDEX

case studies (cont.)
  mutinies of 1797 145–173, 179–180
    see also Nore, mutinies at; Spithead, mutinies at
  purpose of 10, 12, 13
  as witnessing inconsistencies inherent in discussions about how to apply rule of law to internal others 29
Castlereagh 228
Catholic Church
  England as empire created in explicit opposition to 115
  as target of English fear and hatred 110
  see also Roman Catholic Church
Catholic civil rights 113
Catholicism, according to Britons 115–116
Catholic Relief Act (1778) 7, 110, 113, 114, 117
Catholic Relief Act in Ireland (1778) 110, 119
Catholics
  antipathy to in 1770s 110
  French Catholics 10, 139n15
  as fundamental to British imperial project 132
  Irish Catholics 9, 192
  legal restrictions on in England 116
Catholic toleration 15, 109, 114, 116–117, 118, 120, 134, 135, 136, 137
Cavendish, William Henry 167
Challoner, Richard 109, 119
Chamberline v. Harvey (1697) 83–84, 86
Charles I (king) 162
Charles II (king) 165, 166
chattel slavery 81, 82, 83, 84, 85, 87, 90, 95, 98, 151, 194, 241, 243
Child, Josiah 24
circumcision 28, 54, 55, 58, 60
'City Up and Down, or the Candidates Poiz'd, The' (Barnard) 62, 63f

Civil Government (Locke) 220
Clark, William 36
Coats, Ann 149
Coke, Edward 166, 221
Coleman, Richard 41
Colley, Linda 106n133, 116
Collingwood, Cuthbert 175–176
Colonial Justice in British India (Kolsky) 106n128
color, conception of in early modern period 102n28
Colpoys, John 161
Commentaries on the Laws of England (Blackstone) 4, 81, 165
common law (unwritten law) 4
Connor, Christopher 126
Considerations on the bill to permit persons professing the Jewish religion to be naturalized by Parliament (Salvador) 53, 59
constitution
  according to Burke 219
  according to Paine 219
  of England 4
Constitutional considerations, interspersed with political observations, on the present state of Ireland (Weld) 222–225
Constitutional Crisis of 1782 197
Cornwallis, Charles 204
Corporation Act 116
cosmopolitans 115, 135, 242
counterflow 61, 96
Cowper, William 138
Cox, Daniel 34
Cries of Blood, or Juryman's Monitor, The 5
Cromwell, Oliver 156
Cromwell, Thomas 115
Cruikshank, Isaac 176, 177, 178, 217f

Dalrymple, Sir John 118
Davis, Kathleen 81

[256]

INDEX

Davy, William 74, 89–90, 91–93
de Castro, John Paul 111
Declaratory Act 196
Defenders 198
'Delegates in Council or Beggars on Horseback, The' 176–177, 177f
denization 48, 49
de Vattel, Emmerich 221
Dickens, Charles 112
Dickinson, H. T. 212, 214
difference
  categories of 28
  categories of as colliding and processed in metropole 243
  creation or reinvention of 44
  definition of 4
  England's imperial policies as necessitating the integration and assimilation of 114
  organizing of hostility to 62
  problem of 2, 3
  system of 9
  theme of 18n28
  unfixed, contingent, and constantly changing meanings attached to 101n14
Dinah (biblical) 54–55, 57
Dissenters 48, 57, 59, 136, 140n28, 198
Dobree, Bonamy 150
Dodd, James 34
Dodd, William 6
Donald, Diana 110, 214
Donovan, Robert 117
do Porto, Domingo 49
'Dreadful Consequences of a General Naturalization, to the Natives of Great-Britain and Ireland, The' 25–26, 26f, 224
Drennan, William 218
Drescher, Seymour 93
Duane, Matthew 119
Duncan, Adam 163, 164
Dundas, Henry 160, 166–167, 201–202, 216, 230

Dunk, George Montagu 45
Dunning, John 88

East India Company 49, 50, 51
'Ecclesiastical and Political state of the Nation' 123, 124f
Election Entertainment, An (Hogarth) 61–62
Elibank Plot 59, 65n23
Elizabeth (queen) 116
emergency
  as co-constituted with rule of law 12, 148
  definition of 20n53
  see also jurisprudence of emergency
empire
  anxious assertion of Britishness at margins of 113
  configuration of 10
  consequences of expansion of 28, 30
  cultural, physical, and legal entanglements of Britain and its colonial holdings 76–80
  discomfort with and ambivalence about 65–66n28
  Gordon Riots as means of debating and resisting (as well as justifying and defending) imperial policies 110
  intersection of with law 20n49
  place of Jews in Britain's imperial expansion 47–50
  realities of 76, 96
  task of as necessitating change in older perceptions of those defined as others 61
Endelman, Todd 47
England
  as defined by Protestantism 111
  during the French Revolution 149, 183n18
  on eve of Union 196–199
  J. Fielding on bringing slaves to 78

England (cont.)
  legal restrictions on Catholics in 116
  as a Protestant and anti-papal empire 115
  racial diversity of in eighteenth century 76
  union with Ireland 193–231
  see also Britain
Englishness
  definition of 30, 43
  relational nature of 34
  see also Britishness
'English Twig and an Irish Shillelee!!, An' 210, 213f
Enlightenment 11, 96, 117, 141n49, 198
Enlightenment universalism 11, 12, 29
Epstein, James 7
equality before the law 1, 2, 3, 4, 5, 6, 8, 10–16, 17n25, 23, 28, 29, 39, 41, 44, 50, 62, 76, 97, 113, 121, 131, 136, 224, 241, 243
Erin 205, 206, 207, 216, 228–229
Estwick, Samuel 128
Eucharist, link to civil polity of 58
'exact representation of the Burning, Plundering and Destruction of Newgate, An' 125, 125f

family, as metaphor/analogy for Act of Union 193, 202
feudalism 81
Fielding, Henry 31, 35, 40, 41, 43, 44
Fielding, John 77–78, 87, 92, 93, 109
financial revolution, described 22–23
Fisher, Michael 61
FitzGibbon, John 228
'Flight Across the Herring Pool, A' 230, 230f
'Floating Republic, The' (song) 163
Flynn, Carol Houlihan 112
foreignness 44, 61
Foreign Protestants Naturalization Act 1709 24

Foster, John 202
Fox, Charles 159–160, 178
Frankenberg, Ruth 9
Franklin, Benjamin 97–98
free denizens, option of for Jews born abroad 48, 49
freedom
  as metropolitan attribute 98
  and whiteness 170–173
French Catholics 10, 139n15
French Revolution
  as exacerbating political and sectarian divisions in Ireland 191
  as first garnering British sympathy for cause of rights and liberties English believed they already enjoyed 148
  global wars between Britain and France in aftermath of 147
  as historical context for Act of Union with Ireland 196, 197
  impact of on Gordon Riots 112
  impact of on petitioning in mutinies 150, 155
  as intensifying conflict between Ireland and Britain 197
  and Ireland 231n2
  as jolting British Isles in 1790s 15, 166
  and language of sovereignty, nation, and will of the people 193
  meaning of for Britons 152
  republican ideas and Jacobin discourse as fueling 219
  as threatening regimes across Europe 197
Friends of the People at Southwark 178
Frykman, Nicholas 148
Further considerations on the act to permit persons professing the Jewish religion, to be naturalized by Parliament (Salvador) 53

[258]

INDEX

Gardiner, Charlotte 126, 127, 129, 130, 136
Garrick, David 165
Gascoyne, Sir Crisp 5, 28, 30, 41, 44
gender, race and the rule of law 3–7
General Naturalization Bill 50
Genesis 34 54
Gentleman's Magazine, The 77, 78, 92, 119
George, Dorothy 212
George II (king) 201
George III (king) 117, 191–192, 197
Giben, John 36, 37
Gideon, Esther 49
Gideon, Rowland 49
Gideon, Samson 28, 48–50, 51, 55
Gillray, James 207
Glorious Revolution 58–59
Glover, John 125, 126, 127, 136
Gordon, Lord George 109
Gordon Riots 108–138, 166, 227
Gould, Eliga 7, 12
Grand Battle 229
Green, Richard 23
Green, Sarah 41
Grenville, William Wyndham 199
Grevil, Thomas 37
Gypsy/Gypsies
  arrival in England of 35
  characterization of 37, 40
  laws against 35
  use of term 16n2
  see also case studies, Mary Squires and Elizabeth Canning
'Gypsy's instantanious Flight, The' 39f
'Gypsy's Triumph, The' 41, 42f

habeas corpus 12, 15, 94, 98, 99n1, 106n132, 160, 162, 166, 187n103
  see also writ of habeas corpus
Habeas Corpus Act of 1697 105–106n111, 119
Hale, Mathew 94

half-foreign juries 10
Hall, Catherine 7
Hall, Richard 171
Hall, Virtue 29, 30, 31, 39–41, 43
Halliday, Paul 7, 94
Hamor (biblical) 54, 55
Hanway, Jonas 58, 60
Hargrave, Francis 89, 94
Hastings, Warren 118
Hay, Douglas 7, 23
Hay, George 118
Haycock, Thomas 129–130
Haydon, Colin 116
Haywood, Ian 112
'Hearts of Oak' (song) 165, 177
Henley, Robert 85
Henry II (king) 226
Henry VII (king) 226
Hibbert, Christopher 111
Hibernian Magazine 210, 212, 228
Hill, John 41
Hill, Serjeant 106n112
historiography
  of Act of Union 194–195
  of Gordon Riots 111–114
  of Jew Bill (Jewish Naturalization Act 1793) 46
HMS *Grampus* 179
HMS *London* 161, 162
HMS *Sandwich* 163, 164
Hoare, Prince 98–99
Hogarth, William 61
Holcroft, Thomas 108, 127, 131–132
Holdsworth, William 81
Holt, John 83, 84, 90, 222
'Horrors of the Irish-Union' 207, 210f, 229
Howe, Richard 151, 152, 158, 176
humanity, laws of 145, 146, 181
human rights 99, 147, 155, 196, 197, 200, 220, 222, 225
humble Petition of the Sea-men, belonging to the Ships of the Commonwealth of England, The (Cromwell) 156

[259]

INDEX

Hume, David 146
Hussain, Nassar 12
Hutchinson, Thomas 79
Hyams, Paul 81, 82

immigration, debates about 22, 24, 27
'Imperial Politics and English Law' (Paley) 106n133
impressment, slavery and 146, 147, 151, 170–173
'Impromptu on the Irish Union' 210
Inister, John 37
insiders, permeable line between insiders and outsiders 136
integration, in nineteenth- and twentieth-century London 18n30
internal others
   accommodation of 10
   as both agents and subjects 1–2
   as comprised of 1, 3
   rationale for focus on 2
Ireland
   on eve of Union 196–199
   French Revolution and 231n2
   republicanism in 233n20
   union with Great Britain 193–231
Irish Catholics 9, 192
Irish Protestants 7, 10, 12, 15, 192, 226, 242
Irish Rebellion of 1798 191, 198, 205, 227
'Irish Union!, An' 193f, 216, 217

Jack Tar 146
Jacob (biblical) 54, 55
Jacobins 183n19
Jacobite Rebellion of 1745 49, 59
Jacobs, Jane 113
Jacobson, Matthew Frye 9
James (king) 58, 116
James II (king) 57, 58, 162, 166
Jenkinson, Charles 51
Jennings, Rose 127

Jew Bill (Jewish Naturalization Act 1793) 1, 6, 22, 24, 28, 29, 45–61, 62, 114, 137, 242
Jews
   assumption about as cohesive group that did not have the attributes of the rest of British society and never could 60
   gentile discussions of 69n104
   naturalization of 137
   place of in Britain's imperial expansion 47–50
   population of in British empire 70n111
   population of in England 55, 126
   profile of wants of and how they saw themselves fitting into Britain's national and imperial scene 51
'John Bull Shewing his Intended Bride the Parliament House' 207, 209f
Johnson, John 6
Johnson, Joseph 127
Johnson, Samuel 6, 137
Jolliffe, William 168
Jones, Cecily 9
Jones, Thomas 41
jurisprudence of emergency 7, 147, 148, 165, 166, 168, 179, 224

Kelly, James 194, 229
King Mob (Hibbert) 111
Knowles, John 73, 89
Kolsky, Elizabeth 106n128

Land, Isaac 126
law
   conceptions of in mutinies of 1797 145–173
   equality before the *see* equality before the law
   inconsistent ways of spreading of 7

INDEX

intersection of with British imperial aspiration 20n49, 31
ordinary people's envisioning of 17n24
and revolution 152–155
role of 9, 28
as site of struggle 6
as system 13
zones of 7, 11–12
laws of humanity 145, 146, 181
LCS (London Corresponding Society) 150, 152, 174, 178, 184n25
Lebarty, John 126, 129, 130
legal categories
consolidation of 11
whiteness as 1, 2, 3, 4, 9, 11, 96, 241
legal hierarchies, clashes of/competition between 11, 12
legal pluralism 7, 11
legal process, as maintaining and sustaining distinctions of class, gender, ethnicity, and religion 29
Lemmings, David 24
Lennox, Charles 120
Letter to the Right Honourable William Pitt, A (Drennan) 218
Levi, Jonas 45
Lewis, Thomas 88
liberties, restriction of 189n149
Lillburne, John 80
Lindsay, Elizabeth Dido 79–80
Lindsay, Sir John 79
Littleton, Thomas 82
Liversey, James 197
Locke, John 12, 51, 220, 221
London
as destabilized metropole 2
diversity of population of 113, 126, 128
as of eighteenth century 4
as important symbol 137
racial discrimination in 129
London Corresponding Society (LCS) 150, 152, 174, 178, 184n25
London Magazine, The 119

McBride, Ian 198
Macfarlane, Karen 10
McKenna, Theobald 226–227
McKenzie, Andrea 181
Madan, Martin 23
Maddock, Henry 220–222
'Mad Music Master, The' 207, 208f
Maitland, James 178
Mansfield, Chief Justice 75, 79, 88, 89, 93–95, 96, 97, 98, 105n81, 131
Manwaring, G. E. 150
marginalization 28
marriage, as metaphor/analogy for Act of Union 193, 194, 199–207, 216, 218, 220, 228, 229, 231
Marriage Against Inclination: A Step to Separation 207, 212, 216, 228
Marshall, P. J. 63, 111
martial law 14, 110, 132, 133, 135, 146, 164, 165, 166, 170, 224, 242
masculinity
circumcision and 54
of England 217–218
of Ireland 218
Jewish 54, 71n149
sailors and 146, 148, 159, 163, 179
Wilkes on 5
Mason, William 123
Mawhood, William 143–144n115
Mayhem: Post-War Crime and Violence in Britain 1748–1753 (Rogers) 19n43
Memoirs of Granville Sharp (Hoare) 98
Memoirs of Richard Parker, The 145, 179
Mervin, Henry 156
metropole
boundaries between colony and metropole 113
and colony, binary of 8, 97, 100n6

[261]

INDEX

'Miss Hibernia at John Bull's Family Dinner' 207
Montesquieu 12
More, Hannah 138
Murray, James 89
Murray, Michael 80
Murray, William, first earl of Mansfield 5, 73, 79, 109, 123f
mutinies of 1797 145–173, 191
  see also Nore, mutinies at; Spithead, mutinies at
Myers, Norma 76–77

Namier, Sir Lewis 25
Napean, Evan 172
naturalization
  debates about 22, 24–26, 50
  initiatives to facilitate 24
  issue of as applying to Jewish men born abroad 48
  of Jews 25, 137
Naturalization Act 1709 57
Naturalization Bill of 1751 26
naval crews, characterization of 148
Navigation Acts 155
Newman, Brooke 78–79
'New Song Called True Blue, A' (song) 165
newspaper circulation 214
Nicholls, James 41
non-white defendants, treatment of 20n48
Nora, Pierre 2
Nore, mutinies at 5, 15, 138, 145, 146, 147, 148, 149, 150, 151, 163–173, 174, 175, 176, 178, 179–180
North, Frederick 118
Nugent, Robert 27, 50
Nussbaum, Felicity 43

Oaths of Allegiance and Supremacy 116
Oglethrope, James 157
Oldham, James 93, 106n112
Orange Order 198

outsiders
  legal treatment of 7
  permeable line between insiders and outsiders 136

Paddy 210, 216, 218
'Paddy's Escape from the Union Net' 216, 217f
Paine, Thomas 146, 147, 152–155, 158, 161, 178, 179, 180, 197, 219
Paley, Ruth 106n133
pamphlets 8, 13, 15, 24, 25, 30, 32, 37, 38, 45, 46, 47, 51, 53, 54, 55, 57, 58, 61, 62, 110, 111, 112, 114, 115, 120–121, 134–135, 137, 145, 152, 153, 155, 160, 161, 180, 192, 199, 202, 215, 222, 225, 226, 228, 229, 231, 242
  see also specific pamphlets
Parker, Richard 145–146, 163, 164, 177, 178, 179, 180, 181
parliamentary reform 111, 113, 153, 166, 174, 179, 205, 218, 222, 225, 240
Party's Not Agreed 210, 212f, 217, 229–230
Pasley, Thomas 171
passing of the Irish Act of Union: a study in parliamentary politics, The (Bolton) 195
Pearne v. Lisle (1749) 85, 90
Pensive (anonymous author) 135
Periodization and Sovereignty (Davis) 81
petitioning/petitions 140n18, 150, 155, 156–157
Pigg. v. Caley (1618) 81
Piozzi, Hester 128
Pitt, William 146, 148, 152, 159, 160, 162, 164, 167, 168, 169–170, 179, 187n104, 191, 192, 195, 197, 198, 199, 217, 230, 232n8, 233n23
Plantation Act (1740) 27, 48

[262]

INDEX

playbills 206–207
political activity, repression of 187n104
populationists 24, 27, 50
Powell, John 86
power, ordinary people's envisioning of 17n24
Poynings' Law 196, 226, 233n21
Pratt, John 198
prerogative 20–21n54
press, role of during eighteenth century 8
Price, Richard 153, 222
print culture 8, 110, 158
prints 8, 13, 30, 39, 45, 46, 47, 55, 61, 62, 110, 115, 121, 123, 153, 178, 201, 207, 210, 212, 215, 219, 231, 236n80
see also specific prints
private lives, intrusion on 189n149
'Prospect of the New Jerusalem, A' 55, 56f
Protestant Ascendancy 192, 193, 228, 232n7
Protestant Association 109, 111, 112, 113, 114, 119, 121, 130, 132, 134, 137
Protestantism, Britons belief about 115
Pyle, Thomas 55

Quebec Act (1774) 109, 110, 117–118, 119
queer theory 19n41, 19n42, 194, 229, 232n10
Quota Acts 150

race
  as category with very real, physical, social, and economic consequences 76
  conception of in early modern period 102n28
  as defining power 4
  and nation 66n34
  in nineteenth- and twentieth-century London 18n30

race, gender, and rule of law 3–7
  and Somerset case 75
racial formation 16n9
racial hierarchies 9, 106–107n135, 243
Ramsay, Allan 37, 38
Rediker, Marcus 185n52
Reeves, John 219
Reflections on the Revolution in France (Burke) 147, 152, 153, 154
Regency Crisis (1788–1789) 197, 199, 233n24
religious affiliation, and slavery 102–103n31
religious factionalism, danger of rebellion born of 58–59
Rennell, Thomas 173–175
Renunciation Act 196
Repeal of Act for Securing Dependence of Ireland Act 233n21
Representation of the Injustice and Dangerous Tendency of Tolerating Slavery, A (Sharp) 86, 89
Rex v. Knowles, ex parte Somersett (1722) 73
Rex v. Stapylton (1771) 88
Richardson, William 171
Rights of Man (Paine) 147, 152, 154, 155, 158, 172, 180, 196
Rising of 1715 234n40
Roberts, Mary 126, 136
Robinson, Nicholas 216
Rodger, N. A. M. 150, 157
Rogers, Nicholas (Nick) 19n43, 25, 109, 171
Romaine, William 58, 60
Roman Catholic Church, British Empire as equated with 14, 110
Roman Catholic Relief Act 1778 5, 14, 109, 110, 113, 114, 117, 119, 120, 121, 137, 242
Royal Africa Company 47
Rudé, George 111, 112

INDEX

'Rule Britannia' (song) 146, 163
rule of law
  application of to internal others 10, 29, 62
  as co-constituted with emergency 12, 148
  contradictions and inconsistencies within British definitions of 229
  discourse about 241
  elements of 4
  emergence of 1, 3
  fear of imperial implications of at home 42
  financial revolution, rule of law, and naturalization 22–27
  foundations of 11
  guarantee of 116
  interrupted and inconsistent application of 4
  and jurisprudence of emergency 165–170
  overturning of 15
  race, gender, and 3–7
  reality of 2
  as responsibility 5
  as sitting uncomfortably beside jurisprudence of emergency 147
  suspension of 12

Sailors Advocate, The (Oglethorpe) 157
Salt, Mr. 40
Salvador, Francis 50
Salvador, Jacob 50
Salvador, Joseph 50–51, 53, 55, 58, 59–60
Sancho, Ignatius 114, 128, 129, 130–131, 134, 135–136
satirical poems 204–206, 207
satirical prints 110, 153, 214, 215, 219
Savile, George 109
'Scene of Scenes for the Years 1853, A' 27–28, 27f

Scotland, political union with 200, 201, 202, 234n39
Scots Journal 128
Scottish Catholic Relief Bill 110, 119, 120, 134
Second Treatise (Locke) 12
Seed, John 112
Selden, John 81
Seven Years' War 10, 25, 49, 114, 118
sexuality 3, 5, 8, 9, 13, 30, 31, 34, 36, 43, 45, 55, 207
Shanley v. Harvey (1762) 85, 104n62
Sharp, Granville 13, 73, 74, 75, 86–88, 89, 93, 95, 171, 240–241, 242
Sharpe, J. A. 180
Shaw, Jenny 9
Sheridan, Richard Brinsley 159, 160, 169, 170, 178
Shirley, Laurence 6
Singer, Alan 47
slave codes 74
slavery
  as colonial attribute 98
  comparison of villeinage to 90, 93
  distinction between slavery and villeinage 81, 82, 83
  earliest mention of in English courts 80–81
  and impressment 170–173
  legality of 73, 74, 81, 83, 88
  much of Britain's wealth as built on slave trade and slave labor 95
  Sharp's condemnation of 240
  white slavery 106n133
  see also chattel slavery
'Slavery, a Poem' (More) 138
Smith, Joseph 216–217
Smith, Robert 198
Smith, Samuel 55
Smith v. Brown and Cooper (1701) 84, 90
Smith v. Gould (1705/6) 84–85

INDEX

Society for Constitutional Information 150, 152, 178, 184n25
Society for the Promotion of Christian Knowledge 138
Society of the Friends of the Liberty of the Press 178
Society of United Irishmen 150, 198, 218
Solomons, Samuel 126, 127–128, 136
Somerset, James 6, 10, 73–76, 79, 80, 86, 89–99, 110, 114
Some Thoughts upon a Bill for General Naturalization (anonymous) 51–52
songs
  'Floating Republic, The' 163
  'Hearts of Oak' 165, 177
  'New Song Called True Blue, A' 165
  from Nore mutinies 171–172
  'Rule Britannia' 146, 163
  'True Blue an Old Song' 177
  see also ballads
South Sea Company 47
Spelman, Henry 81
Spencer, Earl George 152, 163, 172
Spirit of the Laws, The (Montesquieu) 12
Spithead, mutinies at 5, 15, 138, 145, 146, 147, 148, 149, 150, 151–152, 157, 158, 159, 160, 161, 162, 163, 164, 167, 173, 176, 179–180
Squires, George 40
Squires, Mary 5, 10, 22, 28, 29–45, 38f, 114
Stanbridge, Karen 117
Stanhope, Charles 178, 220, 228
Stapylton, Robert 88
Statt, Daniel 4, 241
statutory law 106n123
Sterne, Laurence 129
Stewart, Charles 73, 80, 89
St James Chronicle 135

Straub, Kristina 34
Stuart, Charles Edward 201
Stuart, James Francis Edward 201
Stuart, John 122, 123f

'Table Talk' (Cowper) 138
Talbot, Charles 85
Tenures in England (Littleton) 82
Test Act 116
'The Children of Erin Seeking Protection from their Foster Father' 210
Thelwall, John 178
'The Union Olio' 210
Thompson, E. P. 7, 23, 111–112, 149–150
Thomson, James 146
'Times, The' 121, 122f
Times, The 157, 162, 203, 210, 220, 227
Toland, John 24, 25, 53
toleration
  Catholic toleration *see* Catholic toleration
  Locke's views on 70n125
Toleration Act of 1689 51
Tone, Theobald Wolfe 198
Tooke, John Horne 178
Treason and Sedition Bills of 1795 169
treason trials 187n103
trial by jury 5
trover 83, 84
Tucker, Josiah 24, 52, 60

unfree labor, impact of Mansfield's judgment on 98
Union
  defense of by many Irish Protestants 226
  Ireland and Great Britain 193
  see also Act of Union with Ireland (1800)
  Irish resistance to 220
'Union between England and Ireland' 207, 210, 211f

INDEX

Union with Ireland Act *see* Act of Union with Ireland (1800)
universalism 29
universality, expectation of 13
universal manhood suffrage 178, 179
unwritten law (common law) 4

Van Cleve, George 75, 106n112
Villains of All Nations: Atlantic Pirates in the Golden Age (Rediker) 185n52
villeinage 73–74, 81, 82–84, 86–87, 89–90, 92, 93, 95, 96, 98

Walpole, Horace 52, 59, 119–120, 124–126, 129, 155
War of Austrian Succession 10, 25, 49, 146
Ways and Means or Vox Populi!! 210
Wedding and Bedding 204–206, 207
Welch, James 41
Weld, Matthew 222–225, 238n130
Wells, Susannah 29, 30, 31, 32, 34, 35, 36, 39, 40, 43
Whitehall Evening Post 131
whiteness
   association of villeinage with 74, 86
   Britain's legal apparatus as defining and privileging 13
   as constituted as race 75
   creation of 76
   critics of 19n35
   as cultural concept 4
   discourses of 44–45
   freedom and 170–173
   as legal category 1, 2, 3, 4, 9, 11, 96, 241
   as metropolitan attribute 98
   racialization of 104n68
   relationship of with blackness 102n28
   scholarship on 8–9
   third aspect of 19n37, 68n95
   use of term 8
Whiteness of a Different Color (Jacobson) 9
Wilkes, John 5, 111
Wilkinson, David 195
William, James 147
Wilson, Kathleen 7, 25, 112
Wollstonecraft, Mary 235n50
women
   in case of Mary Squires and Elizabeth Canning 29–45
   legal status of in England 3, 43
   rights of 235n50
Wooddeson, Richard 221
writ of habeas corpus 73, 75, 85, 93, 94
   see also habeas corpus
written law 4

xenophobia 25

Yorke, Philip 85, 90
Yorke-Talbot decision of 1729 85

EU authorised representative for GPSR:
Easy Access System Europe, Mustamäe tee 50,
10621 Tallinn, Estonia
gpsr.requests@easproject.com

www.ingramcontent.com/pod-product-compliance
Lightning Source LLC
Chambersburg PA
CBHW051606230426
43668CB00013B/1996